Vacation I

Thomas Hughes

Alpha Editions

This edition published in 2024

ISBN : 9789362092144

Design and Setting By
Alpha Editions
www.alphaedis.com
Email - info@alphaedis.com

Contents

PREFACE

Dear C——— So you want me to hunt up and edit all the "Vacuus Viator" letters which my good old friends the editors of *The Spectator* have been kind enough to print during their long and beneficent ownership of that famous journal! But one who has passed the Psalmist's "Age of Man," and is by no means enamoured of his own early lucubrations (so far as he recollects them), must have more diligence and assurance than your father to undertake such a task. But this I can do with pleasure-give them to you to do whatever you like with them, so far as I have any property in, or control over them.

How did they come to be written? Well, in those days we were young married folk with a growing family, and income enough to keep a modest house and pay our way, but none to spare for *menus plaisirs*, of which "globe trotting" (as it is now called) in our holidays was our favourite. So, casting about for the wherewithal to indulge our taste, the "happy thought" came to send letters by the way to my friends at 1 Wellington Street, if they could see their way to take them at the usual tariff for articles. They agreed, and so helped us to indulge in our favourite pastime, and the habit once contracted has lasted all these years.

How about the name? Well, I took it from the well-known line of Juvenal, "Cantabit vacuus coram latrone viator," which may be freely rendered, "The hard-up globe trotter will whistle at the highwayman"; and, I fancy, selected it to remind ourselves cheerfully upon what slender help from the Banking world we managed to trot cheerfully all across Europe.

I will add a family story connected with the name which greatly delighted us at the time. One of the letters reached your grandmother when a small boy-cousin of yours (since developed into a distinguished "dark blue" athlete and M.A. Oxon.) was staying with her for his holidays. He had just begun Latin, and was rather proud of his new lore, so your grandmother asked him how he should construe "Vacuus Viator." After serious thought for a minute, and not without a modest blush, he replied, "I think, granny, it means a wandering cow"! You must make my peace with the "M.A. Oxon." if he should ever discover that I have betrayed this early essay of his in classical translation.

Your loving Father,

THOS. HUGHES.

October 1895.

EUROPE—1862 to 1866

Foreign parts, 14th August 1862.

Dear Mr. Editor-There are few sweeter moments in the year than those in which one is engaged in choosing the vacation hat. No other garment implies so much. A vista of coming idleness floats through the brain as you stop before the hatter's at different points in your daily walk, and consider the last new thing in wideawakes. Then there rises before the mind's eye the imminent bliss of emancipation from the regulation chimney-pot of Cockney England. Two-thirds of all pleasure reside in anticipation and retrospect; and the anticipation of the yearly exodus in a soft felt is amongst the least alloyed of all lookings forward to the jaded man of business. By the way, did it ever occur to you, sir, that herein lies the true answer to that Sphinx riddle so often asked in vain, even of *Notes and Queries*. What is the origin of the proverb "As mad as a hatter"? The inventor of the present hat of civilisation was the typical hatter. There, I will not charge you anything for the solution; but we are not to be for ever oppressed by the results of this great insanity. Better times are in store for us, or I mistake the signs of the times in the streets and shop windows. Beards and chimney-pots cannot long co-exist.

I was very nearly beguiled this year by a fancy article which I saw in several windows. The purchase would have been contrary to all my principles, for the hat in question is a stiff one, with a low, round crown. But its fascination consists in the system of ventilation—all round the inside runs a row of open cells, which, in fact, keep the hat away from the head, and let in so many currents of fresh air. You might fill half the cells with cigars, and so save carrying a case and add to the tastefulness of your hat at the same time, while you would get plenty of air to keep your head cool through the remaining cells.

My principles, however, rallied in time, and I came away with a genuine soft felt after all, with nothing but a small hole on each side for ventilation. The soft felt is the only really catholic cover, equal to all occasions, in which you can do anything; for instance, lie flat on your back on sand or turf, and look straight up into the heavens—the first thing the released Cockney rushes to do. Only once a year may it be always all our lots to get a real taste of the true holiday feeling; to drop down into some handy place, where no letter can find us; to look up into the great sky, and over the laughing sea, and think about nothing; to unstring the bow, and fairly say: "There shall no fight be got out of us just now; so, old world, if you mean to go wrong, you may go and be hanged!" To feel all the time that blessed assurance which does come home to one at such times, and scarcely ever at any other, that our falling out of the fight is not of the least consequence; that, whatever we may do, the old world will not go wrong but right, and ever righter—not our way, nor any other man's way, but God's way. A good deal of sneering and snubbing has been wasted of late, sir (as you have had more occasion than one to remark), on us poor folks, who will insist on holding what we find in our Bibles; what has been so gloriously put in other language by the great poet of our time:—

That nothing walks with aimless feet;

That not one life shall be destroy'd,

Or cast as rubbish to the void,

When God hath made the pile complete.

I suppose people who feel put out because we won't believe that the greatest part of creation is going to the bad can never in the nature of things get hold of the true holiday feeling, so one is wasting time in wishing it for them. However, I am getting into quite another line from the one I meant to travel in; so shall leave speculating and push across the Channel. There are several questions which might be suggested with advantage to the Civil Service Examiner, to be put to the next Belgium attachés who come before them. Why are Belgian hop-poles, on an average, five or six feet longer than English? How does this extra length affect the crops? The Belgians plant cabbages too, and other vegetables (even potatoes I saw) between the rows of hops. Does it answer? All the English hop-growers, I believe, scout the idea. I failed to discover what wood their hop-poles are? One of my fellow-travellers, by way of being up to everything, Informed me that they were grown in Belgium on purpose; a fact which did not help me much. He couldn't say exactly what wood it was. Then a very large proportion of the female population of Belgium spends many hours of the day, at this time of year, on its knees in the fields; and this not only for weeding purposes, for I saw women and girls cutting the aftermath and other light crops in this position. Certainly, they are thus nearer their work, and save themselves stooping; but one has a sort of prejudice against women going about the country on all fours, like Nebuchadnezzar. Is it better for their health? Don't they get housemaid's knees? But, above all, is it we or the Belgians who don't, know in this nineteenth century, how to make corn shocks? In every part of England I have ever been in in harvest time, we just make up the sheaves and then simply stand six or eight of them together, the ears upwards, and so make our shock. But the Belgian makes his shock of four sheaves, ears upwards, and then on the top of these places another sheaf upside down. This crowning sheaf, which is tied near the bottom, is spread out over the shock, to which it thus forms a sort of makeshift thatch. One of the two methods must be radically wrong. Does this really keep the rain out, and so prevent the ears from growing in damp weather? I should have thought it would only have helped to hold the wet and increase the heat. If so, don't you think it is really almost a *casus belli?* Quin said to the elderly gentleman in the coffee-house (after he had handed him the mustard for the third time in vain), dashing his hand down on the table, "D——— you, sir, you shall eat mustard with your ham!" and so we might say to the Belgians if they are wrong, "You shall make your shocks properly." Fancy two highly civilised nations having gone on these thousand years side by side, growing corn and eating bread without finding out which is the right way to make corn shocks.

Bonn, 22nd August 1862.

I am sitting at a table some forty feet long, from which most of the guests have retired. The few left are smoking and talking gesticulatingly. I am drinking during the intervals of writing to you, sir, a beverage composed of a half flask of white wine, a bottle of seltzer water, and a lump of sugar (if you can get one of ice to add it will improve the mixture). I take it for granted that you despise the Rhine, like most Englishmen, but, sir, I submit that a land where one can get the above potation for a fraction over what one would pay for a pot of beer in England, and can, moreover, get the weather which makes such a drink deliciously refreshing, is not to be lightly thought of. But I am not going into a rhapsody on the Rhine, though I can strongly recommend my drink to all economically disposed travellers.

All I hope to do, is, to gossip with you, as I move along; and as my road lay up the Rhine, you must take that with the rest.

Our first halt on the river was at Bonn. A university town is always interesting, and this one more than most other foreign ones, as the place where Prince Albert's education was begun, and where Bunsen ended his life. I made an effort to get to his grave, which I was told was in a cemetery near the town, but could not find it. I hope it will long remain an object of interest to Englishmen after the generation who knew him has passed away. There is no one to whom we have done more scanty justice, and that unlucky and most unfair essay of W————'s is the crowning injustice of all. I am not going into his merits as a statesman, theologian, or antiquary, which, indeed, I am wholly incompetent to criticise. The only book of his I ever seriously tried to master, his *Church of the Future*, entirely floored me. But the wonderful depth of his sympathy and insight!—how he would listen to and counsel any man, whether he were bent on discovering the exact shape of the buckle worn by some tribe which disappeared before the Deluge, or upon regenerating the world after the newest nineteenth century pattern, or anything between the two—we may wait a long time before we see anything like it again in a man of his position and learning. And what a place he filled in English society! I believe fine ladies grumbled about "the sort of people" they met at those great gatherings at Carlton Terrace, but they all went, and, what was more to the purpose, all the foremost men and women of the day went, and were seen and heard of hundreds of young men of all nations and callings; and their wives, if they had any, were asked by Bunsen on the most thoroughly catholic principles. And if any man or woman seemed ill at ease, they would find him by their side in a minute, leading them into the balcony, if the night were fine, and pointing out, as he specially loved to do, the contrast of the views up Waterloo Place on the one hand, and across the Green Park to the Abbey and the Houses, on the other, or in some other way setting them at their ease again with a tact as wise and subtle as his learning. But I am getting far from the Rhine, I see, and the University of Bonn. Of course I studied the titles of the books exposed for sale in the windows of the booksellers, and the result, as regards English literature, was far from satisfactory. We were represented in the shop of the Parker and Son of Bonn, by one vol. of Scott's *Poems*; the puff card of the London Society, with a Millais drawing of a young man and woman thereupon, and nothing more; but, by way of compensation I suppose, a book with a gaudy cover was put in a prominent place, and titled *Tag und Nacht in London*, by Julius Rodenburg. There was a double picture on the cover: above, a street scene, comprising an elaborate equipage with two flunkeys behind, a hansom, figures of Highlanders, girls, blind beggars, etc., and men carrying advertisements of "Samuel Brothers," and "Cremorne Gardens"; while in the lower compartment was an underground scene of a policeman flashing his bull's eye on groups of crouching folks; altogether a loathsome kind of book for one to find doing duty as the representative book of one's country with young Germany. I was a little consoled by seeing a randan named *The Lorelei* lying by the bank, which, though not an outrigger, would not have disgraced any building yard at Lambeth or at Oxford. Very likely it came out of one of them, by the way. But let us hope it is the first step towards the introduction of rowing at Bonn, and that in a few years Oxford and Cambridge may make up crews to go and beat Bonn, and all the other German Universities, and a New England crew from Cambridge, Massachusetts. What a course that reach of the Rhine at Bonn would make! No boat's length to be gained by the toss for choice of sides, as at Henley or Putney; no Berkshire or Middlesex shore to be paid for. A good eight-oar race would teach young Germany more of young England than any amount of perusal of *Tag und Nacht*, I take it. I confess myself to a strong sentimental feeling about Rolandseck. The story of Roland the Brave is, after all, one of the most touching of all human stories, though tourists who drop their H's may be hurrying under his tower every day in cheap steamers; and it is one of a group of the most characteristic stories of the age of chivalry, all having a connecting link at Roncesvalles. What other battle carries one into three such groups of romance as this of Roland, the grim tragedy of Bernard del Carpio and his dear father, and that of the peerless Durandarté? When I was a boy there were ballads on all these subjects which were very popular, but are nearly forgotten by this time. I used to have great trouble to preserve a serene front, I know, whenever I heard one of them well sung, especially that of "Durandarté" (by Monk Lewis), I believe. Ay, and after the lapse of many years I scarcely know where to go for the beau ideal of knighthood summed up in a few words better than to that same ballad:

Kind in manners, fair in favour,

Mild in temper, fierce in fight,—

Warrior purer, gentler, braver,

Never shall behold the light.

But much as I prize Rolandseck for its memories of chivalric constancy and tenderness, Mayence is my favourite place on the Rhine, as the birthplace of Gutenburg, the adopted home, and centre of the work of our great countryman, St. Boniface, and the most fully peopled and stirring town of modern Rhineland. We had only an hour to spend there, so I sallied at once into the town to search for Gutenburg's house—the third time I have started on the same errand, and with the same result. I didn't find it. But there it is; at least the guide-books say so. In vain did I beseechingly appeal to German after German, man, woman, and maid, "Wo ist das Haus von Gutenburg— das Haus wo Gutenburg wohnte?" I got either a blank stare, convincing me of the annoying fact that not a word I said was understood, or directions to the statue, which I knew as well as any of them. At last I fell upon a young priest, and, accosting him in French, got some light out of him. He offered to take me part of the way, and as we walked side by side, suddenly turned to me with an air of pleased astonishment, and said, "You admire Gutenburg, then?" To which I replied, "Father!" Why, sir, how in the world should you and I, and thousands more indifferent modern Englishmen, not to mention those of all other nations, get our bread but for him and his pupil Caxton? However, the young priest could only take me to within two streets, and then went on his way, leaving me with express directions, in trying to follow which I fell speedily upon a German fair. I am inclined to think that there are no boys in Germany, and that, if there were, there would be nothing for them to do; but for children there is no such place. This fair at Mayence was a perfect little paradise for children. Think of our wretched merry-go-rounds, sir, with nothing but some six or eight stupid hobby-horses revolving on bare poles, and then imagine such merry-go-rounds as those of Mayence fair. They look like large umbrella tents ornamented with gay flags and facetious paintings outside, and hung within, round the central post which supports the whole, with mirrors, flags, bells, pictures, and bright coloured drapery. Half concealed by the red or blue drapery, is the proprietor of the establishment, who grinds famous tunes on a first-rate barrel organ when the merry-go-round is set going, and keeps an eye on his juvenile fares. The whole is turned by a pony or by machinery. Then, for mounts, the children have choice of some thirty hobby-horses, or can ride on swans or dragons, richly caparisoned, or in easy *vis-à-vis* seats. When the complement of youthful riders is obtained, on a signal off goes the barrel organ and the pony and the whole concern—pictures, looking-glasses, bells, drapery, and all begin to revolve, with a fascinating jingling and emphasis! and at twice the pace of any British merry—go-round I ever saw. It is very comical to watch the gravity of the little *Deutsch* riders. They are of all classes, from the highly dressed little *madchen*, down to the ragged carter-boy, with a coil of rope over his shoulder, and no shoes, riding a gilded swan, but all impressed with the solemnity of the occasion. But here I am running on about fun of the fair, and missing Gutenburg's house, as I did in reality, finding in the midst of my staring and grinning that I had only time to get to the boat; so with one look at Gutenburg's statue I went off.

The crops through all these glorious Rhine valleys right away up to Heidelberg look splendid, particularly the herb pantagruelion, which is more largely grown than when I was last here. Rope enough will be made this year from hemp grown between Darmstadt and Heidelberg to hang all the scoundrels in the world, and the honest men to boot; and the tobacco looks magnificent. They were gathering the leaves as we passed. A half-picked tobacco field, with the bare stumps at one end, and the rich-leaved plants at the other, has a comically forlorn look.

Heidelberg I thought more beautiful than ever; and since I had been there a very fine hotel, one of the best I have ever been in, has been built close to the station, with a glass gallery 100 feet long, and more, adjoining the "Speisesaal," in which you may gastronomise to your heart's content, at the most moderate figure. Here we bid adieu to the Rhineland.

Munich, 29th August 1862.

A bird's-eye view of any country must always be unsatisfactory. Still it is better than nothing, and in the absence of a human view, one may be thankful for it. My view of Wurtemberg was of the most bird's-eye kind. The first thing that strikes one is the absence of all fences except in the immediate neighbourhood of towns. Even the railway has no fence, except for a few yards where a road crosses the line, and here and there a hedge of acacia, or barberry bushes (the berries were hanging red ripe on the latter), which are very pretty, but would not in any place keep out a seriously-minded cow or pig.

Wurtemberg is addicted to the cultivation of crops which minister to man's luxuries rather than to his necessities. The proportion of land under fruit, poppies, tobacco, and hops, to that under corn, was very striking. There was a splendid hemp crop here also. They were gathering the poppy-heads, as we passed, into sacks. The women and girls both here and in Bavaria seem to do three-fourths of the agricultural work; the harder, such as reaping and mowing, as well as the lighter. The beds of peat are magnificent, and very neatly managed. At first I thought we had entered enormous black brick-fields, for the peat is cut into small brick-shaped pieces, and stacked in rows, just as one sees in the best managed of our brick-fields. As one nears Stuttgart the village churches begin to show signs of the difference in longitude. Gothic spires and arches give place to Eastern clock-towers, with tops like the cupolas of mosques, tinned over, and glittering in the hot sun. I hear that it was a fancy of the late Emperor Joseph to copy the old enemies of his country in architecture; but that would not account for the prevalence of the habit in his neighbour's territory. I fancy one begins to feel the old neighbourhood of the Turks in these parts. The houses are all roomy, and there is no sign of poverty amongst the people. They have a fancy for wearing no shoes and scant petticoats in many districts; but it is evidently a matter of choice. Altogether, the whole fine, open, well-wooded country, from Bruchsal to Munich, gives one the feeling that an easy-going, well-to-do people inhabit and enjoy it.

As for Munich itself, it is a city which surprised me more pleasantly than almost any one I ever remember to have entered. One had a sort of vague notion that the late king had a taste for the fine arts, and spent a good deal of his own and his subjects' money in indulging the taste aforesaid in his capital. But one also knew that he had been tyrannised over by Lola Montes, and had made a countess of her—and had not succeeded in weathering 1848; so that, on the whole, one had no great belief in any good work from such a ruler.

Munich gives one a higher notion of the ex-king; as long as the city stands, he will have left his mark on it. On every side there are magnificent new streets, and public buildings and statues; the railway terminus is the finest I have ever seen; every church, from the Cathedral downwards, is in beautiful order, and highly decorated; and it is not only in the public buildings that one meets with the evidences of care and taste. The hotel in which we stayed, for instance, is built of brick, covered with some sort of cement, which gives it the appearance of terra-cotta, and is for colour the most fascinating building material. The ceilings and cornices of the rooms are all carefully and tastefully painted, and all about the town one sees frescoes and ornamentation of all kinds, which show that the people delight in seeing their city look bright and gay; and every one admits that all this is due to the ex-king Lewis. But he has another claim on the gratitude of the good folk of Munich. The Bavarians were given to beer above all other people, and the people of Munich above all other Bavarians, long before he came to the throne; and former kings, availing themselves of the national taste, had established a "Hof-Breihaus," where the monarch sold the national beverage to his people. King Lewis found the character of the royal beer not what it should be, and the rest of the metropolitan brewers were also falling away into evil ways of adulterating and drugging. He reformed the "Hof-Breihaus," so that for many years nothing but the soundest possible beer was brewed there, which is sold to the buyers and yet cheaper than in any other house in Munich. The public taste has been thus so highly educated that there is no selling unwholesome beer now. A young artist took me to this celebrated tap. Unluckily it was a wet evening, so we had to sit at one of the tables, under a long line of sheds, instead of in an adjacent garden. There was a great crowd, some 300 or 400 imbibers jammed together, of all ranks. At our table the company were the artist and myself, a Middlesex magistrate, two privates, and a non-commissioned officer, and a man whom I set down as a small farmer. My back rubbed against a vociferous student, who was hobnobbing with all comers. There were Tyrolese and other costumes about, one or two officers, and a motley crowd of work people and other folk. The royal brew-house is in such good repute that no trouble whatever is taken about anything but having enough beer and a store of stone drinking-mugs, with tops to them forthcoming. Cask after cask is brought out and tapped in the vaulted entrance to the cellars, and a queue of expectant thirsty souls wait for their turn. I only know as I drank it how heartily I wished that my poor overworked brethren at home could see and taste the like. But it would not pay any of our great brewers to devote themselves to the task of selling really wholesome drink to the poor; and I fear the Prince of Wales is not likely to come to the rescue. He might find easier jobs no doubt, but none that would benefit the bodily health of his people more. The beer is so light that it is scarcely possible to get drunk on it. Many of the frequenters of the place sit there boosing for four or five hours daily, and the chance visitors certainly do not spare the liquor; but I saw no approach to drunkenness, except a good deal of loud talk.

The picture collections, which form, I believe, the great attraction of Munich, disappointed me, especially the modern ones in the new Pinacothek, collected by the ex-king, and to which he is constantly adding now that he is living at his ease as a private gentleman. I daresay that they may be very fine, but scarcely any of them bite; I like a picture with a tooth in it—something which goes into you, and which you can never forget, like the great picture of Nero walking over the burning ruins of Rome, or the execution picture in the Spanish department, or the Christian slave sleeping before the opening of the amphitheatre, or Judas coming on the men making the cross, in the International Exhibition. I have read no art criticism for years, so that I do not know whether I am not talking great heresy. But, heresy or not, I am for the right of every man to his own opinion in matters of art, and if an inferior painting gives me real pleasure on account of its subject, I mean to enjoy it and praise it, all the fine art critics in Christendom notwithstanding. The pictures of the most famous places in Greece, made since the election of the Bavarian Prince Otho to the throne of Greece, have a special interest of their own; but apart from these and some half dozen others, I would far sooner spend a day in our yearly exhibition than in the new Pinacothek. The colossal bronze statue of Bavaria is the finest thing of the kind I have ever seen; but the most interesting sight in Munich to an Englishman must be the Church of St. Boniface, not the exquisite colouring proportions, or the magnificent monolithic columns of gray marble, but the frescoes, which tell the story of the saint from the time when he knelt and prayed by his sick father's bed to the bringing back of his martyred body to Mayence Cathedral. The departure of St. Boniface from Netley Abbey for Rome, to be consecrated Apostle to the Germans, struck me as the best of them; but, altogether, they tell very vividly the whole history of the Englishman who has trodden most nearly in St. Paul's footsteps. We have reared plenty of great statesmen, poets, philosophers, soldiers, but only this one great missionary. Yet no nation in the world has more need of St. Bonifaces than we just now. The field is ever widening, in India, China, Africa. We can conquer and rule, and teach the heathen to make railways and trade, nut don't seem to be able to get at their hearts and consciences. One fears almost that were a St. Boniface to come, we should only measure him by our common tests, and probably pronounce him worthless, or a dangerous enthusiast. But one day, when men's work shall be tested by altogether different tests from ours of the enlightened nineteenth century kind, it will considerably surprise some of us to see how the order of merit will come out. We shall be likely to have to ask concerning St. Boniface—whose name is scarcely known to one Englishman in a hundred—and of others like him in spirit, of whom none of us have ever heard, Who are these countrymen of ours, and whence come they? And we shall hear the answer which St. John heard: "Isti sunt qui venerunt ex magna tribulatione et laverunt stolas suas in sanguine Agni." I felt very grateful to Munich for having appreciated the great Apostle to the Germans.

The one building in Munich which is quite unworthy of the use to which it is put, is the English Church. The service is performed in a sort of dry cellar, under the Odeon. We had a very small congregation, but it was very pleasant to hear how they all joined in the responses. What a pity it is that we are always ready to do it abroad, and shut up again as soon as we get home. Even the singing prospered greatly, though we had no organ. But, alas! sir, the Colonial Church Society have done their best to spoil this part of our service abroad. They seem to have accepted from the editor as a gift, the stereotyped plates of a hymn-book, copies of which were placed about in the Munich church, and, I daresay, may be found all over the Continent. The editor has thought it desirable to improve our classical hymns. Conceive the following substitution for Bishop Ken's "Let all thy converse be sincere"—

In conversation be sincere;

Make conscience as the noon-day clear:

Think how th' all-seeing God thy ways

And all thy secret thoughts surveys.

This is only a fair specimen of the book. Surely the Colonial Church Society had better hastily return the stereotype plates with thanks.

The Tyrol, 2nd September 1862.

Next to meeting an old friend by accident, there is nothing more pleasant than coming in long vacation on some flower or shrub which reminds one of former holiday ramblings. In the Tyrol the other day we came suddenly on a bank in the mountains gemmed over with the creamy white star of the daisy of Parnassus, and it accompanied us, to our great delight, for 200 miles or more, till we got fairly down into the plains again. The last time I had seen it was on Snowdon years ago. When we got a little higher I pounced on a beautiful little gentian, which I had never seen before except on the Alps above Lenk, in Switzerland (the Hauen Moos the pass was called, or some such name—how spelt, goodness knows), which I once crossed with two dear friends on the most beautiful day I ever remember.

The flora of the Tyrol, at least that part of it which lies by the roadside, seems to be much the same as ours. With the above exceptions, I scarcely saw a flower which does not grow on half the hills in England; but their size and colouring was often curiously different. The Michaelmas daisy and ladies' fingers, for instance, were much brighter and more beautiful; on the other hand, there was the most tender tiny heartsease in the world, and forget-me-nots, which were very plentiful here and there, were quite unlike ours—delicate little creatures, of the palest blue in the world, all the fleshiness and comfortable look, reminding one of marriage settlements and suitable establishments, gone clean out of them. In moving eastward with the happy earth you may easily get from Munich to Strasburg in one day; but, if you do, you will miss one of the greatest treats in the world, and that is a run through the Tyrol, which you may do from Munich with comfort in a week. There is a little rail which runs you down south or so to Homburg, on the edge of the mountain country, from whence you may choose your conveyance, from post carriage down to Shanks' nag. If you follow my advice, whatever else you do you will take care to see the Finstermunz Pass, than which nothing in the whole world can be more beautiful. I rather wonder myself that the Tyrol has not drawn more of our holiday folk, Alpine Club and all, from Switzerland. The Orteler Spitz and the glaciers of his range are as fine, and I should think as dangerous, as anything in the Swiss Alps—the lower Alps in the Tyrol are quite equal to their western sisters; and there is a soft Italian charm and richness about the look and climate of the southern valleys, that about Botzen especially, which Switzerland has nothing to match. The luxuriance of the maize crops (the common corn of the country) and of the vines trained over trellis work in the Italian fashion, and of the great gourds and vegetable marrows which roll their glorious leaves and flowers and heavy fruit over the spare corners and slips of the platforms on which the vineyards rest—the innumerable fruit-trees, pears, apples, plums, peaches, and pomegranates all set in a framework of beautiful wooded mountains, from which the course of the streams may be traced down through all the richness of the valley by their torrent beds of tumbled rock—. remind us vividly of the descriptions of the Promised Land in the Old Testament. Then the contrast of the people to the Bavarians is as great as that of the countries. The latter seem to live the easiest, laziest life of all nations, in their rich low flats, which the women are quite aide to cultivate, while the men drink beer and otherwise disport themselves. But in the part of the Tyrol next Bavaria it is all grim earnest: "Ernst is das Leben" must be their motto if they are to get in their crops at all, and keep their little patches of valley and hanging fields cultivated—and it does seem to be their motto. After passing through the country one can quite understand how the peasantry came to beat the regular troops of France and Bavaria time after time half a century ago, and the memoirs of that holy war hang almost about every rock. There is no mistake here about battle-fields, and no difficulty in realising the scene: the march of columns along the gorges, the piles of rock and tree above, with Tyrolean marksmen behind, the voices calling across over the heads of the invaders "Shall we begin?"

"In the name of the Holy Trinity, cut all loose"; and then the crash and confusion, the panic and despair, and the swoop of the mountaineers on the remnant of their foes. A great part of the country must be exceedingly poor, and yet only in the neighbourhood of two or three villages were we asked for alms, and then only by small children, who had apparently been demoralised by the passage of carriages. Except from one of these children, a small boy who flirted his cap in my face, and made a villainous grimace, when he got tired of running, and from the dogs, we had no uncourteous look or word. The dogs, however, are abominable mongrels, and there was scarcely one in the country which did not run barking and snapping after us. The people seem to me very much pleasanter to travel amongst than the Swiss.

I had expected to find them a people much given to the outward forms and ceremonies of religion at any rate—every guide-book tells one thus much; but I was not at all prepared for the extraordinary hold which their Christianity had laid upon the whole external life of the country. You can't travel a mile in the Tyrol along any road without coming upon a shrine—in general by the wayside, often in the middle of the fields. I examined several hundreds of these; many of them little rough penthouses of plank, some well-built tiny chapels. I wish I had kept an exact account of the contents, but I am quite sure I am within the mark in saying that nine out of ten contain simply a crucifix; of the rest, the great majority contain figures or paintings of the Virgin or Child, and a few those of some patron saint. All bore marks of watchful care; in many, garlands of flowers or berries, or an ear or two of ripe maize, were hung round the Figure on the cross. Then in every village in which we slept, bells began ringing for matins at five or six, and in every ease the congregation seemed to be very large in proportion to the population. I was told, and believe, that in all the houses, even in the inns of most of these villages, there is family worship every evening at a specified hour, generally at seven. We met peasants walking along the road bare-headed, and chanting mass. I came suddenly upon parish priests and poor women praying before the crucifix by the wayside. The ostlers and stable-men have the same habit as our own, of pasting or nailing up rude prints on the stable-doors, and of all those which I examined while we were changing horses, or where we stopped for food or rest, there was only one which was not on a sacred subject. In short, to an Englishman accustomed to the reserve of his own country on such subjects, the contrast is very startling. If a Hindoo or any other intelligent heathen were dropped down in any English country, he might travel for days without knowing whether we have any religion at all; but, most assuredly, he could not do so in the Tyrol. Now which is the best state of things? I believe Her Majesty has no stauncher Protestant than I amongst her subjects, but I own that a week in the Tyrol has made me reconsider a thing or two. Outwardly, in short, the Tyroleans are the most religious people in Europe. Of course I am no judge after a week's tour whether their faith has gone as deep as it has spread wide. You can only speak of the bridge as it carries you. Our bills were the most reasonable I have ever met with, and I could not detect a single attempt at imposition in the smallest particular. I went into the fruit market at Meran, and, after buying some grapes, went on to an old woman who was selling figs. She was wholly unable to understand my speech, so, being in a hurry, I put a note for the magnificent sum of ten kreutzer (or 3d. sterling) into her hand, making signs to her to put the equivalent in figs into a small basket I was carrying. This she proceeded to do, and when she had piled eight or ten figs on the grapes I turned to go, but by vehement signs she detained me, till she had given me the full tale, some three or four more. She was only a fair specimen of what I found on all sides. The poor old soul had not mastered our legal axiom of *caveat emptor*, but her trading morality had something attractive about it. They may be educated in time into buying cheap and selling dear, but as yet that great principle does not seem to have dawned on them.

There may be some danger of superstition in this setting up of crucifixes and sacred prints by the wayside and on stable-doors, but, on the other hand, the Figure on the cross, meeting one at every corner, is not unlikely, I should think, to keep a poor man from the commonest vices to which he is tempted in his daily life, if it does no more. He would scarcely like to stagger by it drunk from the nearest pot-house. If stable-boys are to have rough woodcuts on their doors, one of the Crucifixion or of the *Mater Dolorosa* is likely to do them more good than the winner of the Derby or Tom Sayers.

But my letter is getting too long for your columns, so I can only beg all your readers to seize the first chance of visiting the Tyrol. I shall be surprised if they do not come away with much the same impressions as I have. It is a glad land, above all that I have ever seen—a land in which a psalm of joy and thankfulness seems to be rising to heaven from every mountain top and valley, and, mingled with and beneath it, the solemn low note of a people "breathing thoughtful breath"—an accompaniment without which there is no true joy possible in our world, without which all attempt at it rings in the startled ear like the laugh of a madman. Those words of the old middle-age hymn seemed to be singing in my ears all through the Tyrol:—

Fac me vere tecum flere,

Crucitixo condolere,

Donee ego vixcro.

I shall never find a country in which it will do one more good to travel.

———————————————————

Vienna, 10th September 1862.

The stage Englishman in foreign countries must be always an object of interest to his countrymen. He is a decidedly popular institution in Germany, not the least like the Dundreary type, or the sort of top-booted half fool, half miscreant, one sees at a minor theatre in Paris. The latest Englishmen on the boards of the summer theatres here are a Lord Mixpickl, and his man Jack, but the most popular, and those which appear to be regarded in fatherland as the real thing, are the Englishmen in a piece called "The Four Sailors." It opens with a yawning chorus. Four young Englishmen are discovered sitting at a German watering-place, reading copies of the *Times* and *Post*, and yawning fearfully. The chorus done, one says, "The funds are at 84."

"I bet you they are at 86," says another, and on this point they become lively. It appears by the talk which ensues, that they have come abroad resolved on finding some romantic adventure before marrying, which they are all desirous of doing. This they found impossible at home; hitherto have not succeeded here; have only succeeded in trampling on the police arrangements, and getting bored. They all imitate one another in speech and action, saying "Yaas" in succession very slowly, and always looking at one another deliberately before acting. Now the four sailors appear, who are three romantic young women and their maid, disguised as sailors, under the care of their aunt, a stout easy-going old lady, dressed as a boatswain, and of lax habits In the matters of tobacco and drink. After hornpipe dancing and other diversions, the young ladies settle to go and bathe, and cross the stage where the Englishmen are carrying their bathing-dresses. A cry is raised that their boat is upset; whereupon the Englishmen look at one another. At last one gets up, takes off his coat, folds it up, and puts it carefully on his chair, ditto with waistcoat and hat, the others doing the same. They walk off in Indian file, and return each with a half-drowned damsel across his shoulders. Having deposited their burthens, they return to the front of the stage to dress, when one suggests that they have never been introduced, upon which, after a pause, and looking solemnly at each other and the audience, they ejaculate all together, "Got dam!" They then take refuge in beer, silence, and pipes. At last one says, "This is curious!" Three yaas', and a pause. Another, "This is an adventure!" Three yaas', and a longer pause. At last, "Dat ist romantisch!" propounds another. Tumultuous yaas' break forth at this discovery. The object of their journey is accomplished, they marry the four sailors, and return to love and Britain.

The summer theatres are charming institutions, but somewhat casual. For instance, while we were at Ischl, there were no performances because the weather was too fine. Ischl itself is wonderfully attractive, and as he has not the chance of getting a seaside watering-place, the Kaiser Konig has shown much taste in the selection of Ischl. The Traun and Ischl, which meet here, are both celebrated for beauty and trout (a young Englishman was wading about and having capital sport while we were there). You get fine views of glaciers from the hills which rise on all sides close to the town, and the five valleys at the junction of which it lies are all finely wooded and well worth exploring. The town is furnished with a drinking-hall (but no gambling), baths, a casino, pretty promenades, and Herzogs and other grand folk, with Hussar and other officers in plenty to enliven them. You can dance every evening almost if you like, and gloves are fabulously good, and only a florin a pair for men, or with two buttons, for ladies, a florin and ten kreutzers; so, having regard to the number which are now found necessary in London, it would almost pay young persons to visit Ischl once a year to make their purchases. There is also a specialty in the way of pretty old fashioned looking jewellery made and sold here cheap, but the Passau pearls found in the great cockle-shells of these parts are dear, though certainly very handsome. I must not forget the rifle-range amongst the attractions of the place. I fell in with two members of the Inns of Court, and we heard the well-known crack, and soon hunted out the scene of operations. We found some Austrian gentlemen practising at 100 yards at a target with a small black centre, within which was a scarcely distinguishable bull's-eye. When a centre is made the marker comes out, bows, waves his arms twice, and utters two howls called "yodels." When the bull's-eye is struck a shell explodes behind, the Austrian eagle springs up above the target, and a Tyrolean, the size of life, from each side—which performance so fascinated one of my companions that he made interest with the shooters, who allowed him to use one of their rifles. I rejoice to say that he did not disgrace the distinguished corps to which he belongs. At his first shot he obtained the bow and two howls from the marker, and at his fourth the explosion and appearances above described followed, whereupon he wisely retired on his laurels.

You proceed eastwards from Ischl, down the beautiful valley of the Traun to Eben; see the great store-place for the salt and wood of the district. The logs accompany you, in the river, all the way down; and it is amusing to watch their different ways of floating. Such of them as are not stopped in transit by the hooks of the inhabitants are collected by a boom stretched across the head of the Gmünden Lake, on which you take boat at Eben See. The skipper of the steamer is an Englishman, who has been there for thirty years—a quiet matter-of-fact man, who collects his own tickets, wears no uniform, and has a profound disbelief in the accuracy of the information furnished to tourists in these parts by the natives. Long absence from home has somewhat depressed him, but he lights up for a few moments when he gets on his paddle-box and orders the steam to be put on to charge the boom. But travellers should consult him if they want correct information, and should not trust in "Bradshaw." The lion of the neighbourhood is the Traun Falls;

and a station has been opened on the railway to Lintz to facilitate the seeing of the falls, which station is not even mentioned in the "Bradshaw" for August 1862. This is too bad.

I had considerable opportunities of seeing the state of the country in Austria. The people are prosperous and independent to a degree which much astonished me. They are almost all what we should call yeomanry, owning from twenty to two hundred acres of land. Even the labourers, who work for the great proprietors, own their own cottages and an acre or so of land round; in fact, the Teutonic passion for owning land is so strong that, unless a man can acquire some, he manages to emigrate. Since 1848 the communes have stepped into the position of lords of the manors, and own most of the woods and the game. The great proprietors pay them for the right of sporting over their own lands. In faet, whatever may be the case with the higher classes, the people here seem to have it much their own way since 1848. We spent a Sunday afternoon in the palace gardens at Schonbrunn, into which half the populace of Vienna, smoking vile-smelling cigars, seemed to have poured in omnibuses and cabs, which stood before the palace, and on foot. We (the people) occupied the whole of the gardens, and a splendid military band played for our behoof. You reach the gardens by passing under the palace, so that King People was everywhere, and the Kaiser Konig, if he wants retirement, must stay in his private rooms. A report spread that the Emperor and Empress were coming out, whereupon King People, and we amongst them, swept into the lower part of the palace, and right up to a private staircase, at the foot of which an open carriage was standing. A few burly and well-behaved guardsmen remonstrated good-humouredly, but with no effect. There we remained in block, men, women, and children, the pipes and cigars were not extinguished, and the smell was anything but imperial. Presently the Emperor and Empress came down, and the carriage passed at a foot's pace through the saluting and pleased crowd. The Empress is the most charming-looking royal personage I have ever seen, and seemed to think it quite right that the people should occupy her house and grounds. Fancy omnibuses driving into the Court-yard of Buckingham Palace, and John Bull proceeding to occupy the private gardens! John himself would decidedly think that the end of the world was come. The Constitution, too, seems to work well from all I heard. The Court party has ceased almost to struggle for power. It revenges itself, however, in social life. Society (so called) is more exclusive in Vienna than anywhere else, and consists of some 400 or 500 persons all told. Even the most distinguished soldiers and statesmen have not the *entrée*. Benedek's family is not in society, nor Schmerling's, though I hear his daughter is one of the prettiest and most ladylike girls in Austria. All which is very silly, doubtless, but the chief sufferers are the 400 inhabitants who drive in the Prater, and go to the Leichtenstein and Schwartzenburg parties, and after all, if aristocracies in the foolish sense are inevitable, an aristocracy of birth is preferable to one of money, or, *me judice*, of intellect, seeing that the latter gives itself at least as absurd airs, and is likely to be much more mischievous. On the other hand, my Hungarian sympathies have been somewhat shaken since visiting the country. I suppose the national dress has something to say to it. An Englishman cannot swallow braided coats, and tight coloured pants, and boots all at once, and the carriage and airs of the men are offensive. I say this more on the judgment of several of my country-women on this point than on my own, but from my own observation I can say that Pesth, to a mere passer-by, has all the appearances of the most immoral capital in the world. In the best shops, in the best streets, there are photographs and engravings exhibited which, with us, would speedily call Lord Campbell's Act into operation. And the Haymarket is in many respects moral in comparison with many parts of Pesth. It is the only place in Europe where I have seen men going about drunk before midday. In short, you will perceive that my inspection inclines me to suspect that there may he more than one has been wont to believe in the assertion, that the Constitution we hear so much of is aristocratic and one which will give back old feudal privileges to a conquering race and enable them to oppress Slaves, Croats, etc., as they did before 1848. There is, everybody admits, a large discontented class in Hungary, composed chiefly of the poor nobility (who have long ago spent their compensation money), and professional men, especially advocates, but it is strenuously maintained that the great mass of the people have been far better off in all ways and more contented since 1849. I don't pretend to give you anything except the most apparently truthful evidence I can pick up by the wayside, and the observations of my own eyes, and certainly the latter have not been favourable to Hungary in any way, though they look certainly very like a fighting race, these Magyars. The railroad from Pesth to Basiash, where one embarks on the Danube, passes through enormous flats, heavy for miles and miles with maize and other crops, and very thinly peopled. It is a constant wonder where the people can come from to reap and garner it all. The great fault of the country is the dust, which is an abominable nuisance. Certainly the facilities for travelling are getting to be all that can be wished in our time. A little more than forty-eight hours will bring a man, who can stand night journeys, to Vienna; after resting a night, eighteen hours more will bring him to Basiash, where he will at once plunge into the old world of turbans and veiled women, minarets and mosques; man and beast and bird, houses and habits, all strange and new to him; and if the Danube fares were not atrociously high, there are few things I would more earnestly recommend to my holiday-making countrymen than a trip down that noblest, of European rivers. Considering the present state of political matters, too, in the world, he can hardly select a more interesting country. Certainly the Eastern question gains wonderfully in interest when one has seen ever so little of the lands and people about which the wisest heads of all the wisest statesmen of our day are speculating and scheming—not very wisely, I fear, at present.

The Danube, 13th September 1862.

The Rhine may, perhaps, fairly be compared with the Upper Danube, between Lintz and Vienna, even between Vienna and Pesth. There is no great disparity so far, either in the size of themselves or of the hills and plains through which they run. The traveller's tastes, artistic and historical, decide his preference. The constant succession of ruined holds of the old oppressors of the earth which he meets on the Rhine, are wanting on the Danube. It is certainly a satisfaction to see such places thoroughly ruined—to triumph over departed scoundrelism wherever one comes on its relics. As a compensation, however, he will find on the Danube a huge building or two, such as that of the Benedictine Monastery at Molk, or the Cathedral and Palace of the Primate of Hungary at Gran, of living interest, and with work still to do in the world. There is not much to choose between the banks of the two streams in the matter of general historical interest, though to me the long struggle between the Christian and the Moslem, the footprints of which meet one on all sides, gives the Danube slightly the advantage even in this respect. There are longer gaps of flat uninteresting country on the eastern stream, no doubt, which may be set off against the sameness and neatness of the perpetual vineyard on the western; and on the Danube you get, now and then, a piece of real forest, which you never see, so far as I remember, on the Rhine.

Below Belgrade, however, all comparison ceases. The Rhine is half the size of its rival, and flows westward through the highest cultivation and civilisation to the German Ocean, while the huge Danube rushes through the Carpathians into a new world—an eastern people, living amidst strange beasts and birds, in a country which is pretty much as Trajan left it. You might as well compare Killiecrankie to the Brenner Pass, as any thing on the Rhine to the Kazan, the defile by which the Danube struggles through the western Carpathians. Here the river contracts in breadth from more than a mile to between 200 and 300 yards; the depth is 170 feet. The limestone rocks on both sides rise to near 2000 feet, coming sheer down to the water in many places, clothed with forest wherever there is hold for roots. Along the Servian side, on the face of the precipice, a few feet above the stream, run the long line of sockets in which the beams were fastened for the support of his covered road by Trajan's legions. A tablet and an inscription 1740 years old still bear, I believe, the great Roman's name, and a memorial of his Dacian campaign, though I cannot vouch for the fact, as we shot by it at twenty miles an hour; but I could distinctly see Roman letters. On the left bank the Austrians have carried a road by blasting and masonry; and a cavern which was held for weeks by 400 men against a Turkish army in 1692 commands the whole pass.

We had scarcely entered the defile when some eight or ten eagles appeared sweeping slowly round over a spot in the hanging wood, where probably a deer or goat was dying. I counted upwards of thirty before we left the Kazan; several were so near the boat that you could plainly mark the glossy barred plumage, and every turn of the body and tail as they steered about upon those marvellous, motionless wings. One swooped to the water almost within shot, but missed the fish, or whatever his intended prey might be. A water ouzel or two were the only other living creatures which appeared to draw our attention for a moment from the sway of the mighty stream and the succession of the dizzy heights. Below the pass the stream widens again. You lose something of the feeling of power in the mass of water below you, though the superficial excitement of whirl, and rush, and eddy, is much increased. Here, at Orsova, a small military town on the frontier line between Hungary and Wallachia, we turned out into a flat-bottomed steamer, with four tiny paddle-wheels, drawing only some three feet of water, which was to carry us over the Iron Gates, as the rapids are called; and beautifully the little duck fulfilled her task. The English on board, three ladies and five men, had already fraternised; we occupied the places in the bows. The deck was scarcely a yard above water, and there were no bulwarks, only a strong rail to lean against. The rush of the stream here beat any mill-race I have ever seen, and the little steamer bounded along over the leaping, boiling water at the rate of a fast train. Twice only she plunged a little, shipping just enough water to cause some discomposure amongst the ladies' dresses, and to wet our feet. We shot past the wreck of a Turkish iron Steamer in the wildest part, which had grounded on its way up to Belgrade with munitions of war. The Servians had boarded and burnt her, and there she lay, and will lie, till the race washes her to pieces, for there is nothing to be got out of her now except the iron of her hull. Below the Iron Gate, a fine Austrian steamer received us, and we moved statelily out into the stream on our remaining thirty hours' voyage. We had left the mountains, but were still amongst respectable hills covered with forest, full of game, an engineer officer who was on board told us, and plenty of wolves to be had in the winter—too many, indeed, occasionally. A friend of his had knocked up a little wooden shooting-box in these Wallachian forests—a rough affair, with a living-room below, a bedroom above. He had found the wolves so shy that he scarcely believed in them; however, to give the matter a fair trial, he asked three or four friends to his box, bought a dead horse, and roasted him outside. The speedy consequence was such a crowd of wolves that he and his friends had to take refuge in the bedroom and fight for their lives; as it was, the wolves were very near starving them out. And now the river had widened again, and water-fowl could rest and feed on the surface.

The hot evening, for hot enough it was, though cool in comparison of the day, brought them out in flocks round the islands and over the shallows. I was just feasting my eyes with the sight of wild swans, quite at their ease in our neighbourhood, when three huge white birds came sailing past with a flight almost as steady as the eagles we had seen in the Kazan. "What are they?" I said eagerly to my companion, the engineer. "Pelicans," he answered, as coolly as if they had been water-hens. In another moment they lighted on the water, and I saw their long bills and pouches. Fancy the new sensation, sir! But on this part of the Danube there is no want of new sensations. Our first stop at a Bulgarian village—or town, perhaps, I should call it, for it boasted a tumble-down fort, with some rude earthworks, and half a dozen minarets shot up from amongst its houses and vineyards—may be reckoned amongst the chief of these. What can be more utterly new to an Englishman than to come upon a crowd of poor men, who have their daily bread to earn, half of whom are quietly asleep, and the rest squatting or standing about, without offering, or thinking of offering, to help when there is work to be done under their noses? One was painfully reminded of the eager, timid anxiety to be allowed to carry luggage for a penny or two which one meets with at home. Here one had clearly got into the blissful realms where time is absolutely of no account, and if you want a thing done, you can do it yourself. Our arrival was evidently an event looked forward to in some sort, for there were goods on the wharf waiting for us, and several of the natives had managed to bring down great baskets full of grapes, by which they had seated themselves. We were all consumed with desire for grapes, and headed by the steward of the vessel, who supplies his table here, rushed ashore and fell upon the baskets. It seemed to be a matter of perfect indifference to the owners whether we took them or let them alone, or how many we took, or whether we paid or not. The only distinct idea they had, was that they would not take Austrian money. Our English emissary returned with six or seven huge bunches for which he had given promise to pay two piastres to somebody. The piastre was then (ten days ago) worth one penny, it is now worth twopence—a strange country is Turkey. There were some buffaloes lying in the water, with their great ears flopping, to move the air a little, and keep off flies. A half-grown Turkish lad was squatted near the head of one of them, over which he was scooping up the water with his hands, the only human being in voluntary activity. His work was thoroughly appreciated; I never saw a more perfect picture of enjoyment than the buffalo who was getting this shower-bath. The costumes, of course, are curious and striking to a stranger, but turbans and fezzes, camel's hair jackets, and loose cotton drawers,—even the absence of these in many instances, and the substitute of copper-coloured flesh as a common garb of the country—are after all only superficial differences. It is the quiet immobility of the men which makes one feel at once that they are a different race, and the complete absence of women in the crowds. The cottages, in general, look like great mole-hills. They look miserable enough, but I believe are well suited to the climate, being sunk three or four feet in the ground, which keeps them cool in summer and warm in winter. Our Crimean experience bears this out. The mud huts sunk in the ground and thatched roughly were far more comfortable all weathers than those sent out from England. The campaign between the Russians and Turks at the beginning of the late war became much clearer to me as we passed down the river. It must be a very difficult operation to invade Bulgaria from the Principalities, for the southern bank commands the dead flat of the Wallachian banks almost all the way down. The serious check which the Russians got at Oltenitza was a great puzzle in England. We could not make out how it happened. Omar Pasha seemed to have made a monstrous blunder in throwing a single division across the river, and we wondered at his luck in getting so well out of it. The fact is that it was a real stroke of generalship. The Russian corps were about to cross at points above and below. Omar's cannon posted on the Bulgarian heights completely commanded the opposite plain, where a considerable stream runs into the Danube. This stream protected the left flank of the division which crossed, and they threw up earth-works along their front and right. The Russians recalled the corps which were about to cross, thinking to annihilate them, and attacked under a plunging fire from the Turkish artillery on the opposite bank, which, combined with that from the earth-works, was unendurable, and they were repulsed with enormous loss. It is by no means so easy, however, to understand why they did not take Silistria. Here they had crossed, were in great force, and had no strong position to attack. The famous work of Arab Tabia, the key of the position which was so gallantly held by Butler and Nasmyth with a few hundred Turkish soldiers under them, is nothing but a low mound, which you can scarcely make out from the steamer. Why they should not have marched right over it and into the town is a mystery.

The village of Tchernavoda where the steamer lands passengers for Constantinople, consists of a very poor inn, some great warehouses for corn, and some half-dozen Turkish cottages. An English company has made the railroad across to Kustandjie, on the Black Sea, so that you escape the long round by the mouths of the Danube. I fear it must be a very poor speculation, but it is very convenient. The line runs through a chain of lakes, by which it is often flooded. Once last winter the water came nearly into the carriages. The train was, of course, stopped, and had to remain in the water, which froze hard in the night. I believe the passengers had to proceed over the ice. If any young Englishman who combines the tastes of a sportsman and naturalist wants a field for his energies, I can't fancy a better one than these lakes. The birds swarm; every sort of duck and sea-bird one had ever heard of, besides pelicans, wild swans, bitterns, (the first I ever saw out of a museum) and herons, and I know not what other fowl were there, especially a beautiful white bird exactly like our heron, but snowy white. I saw two of these. I don't believe they were storks, at least not the common kind which I have seen.

We had been journeying past the scene of the late conferences, and of the excitement which was so nearly breaking out into war a month or two back, and had plenty of Servians and other interested persons on board; but, so far as I could learn, everything is quieting down into its ordinary state—an unsatisfactory one, no doubt, but not unlikely to drag on for some time yet. Should the Servians and other discontented nationalities, however, break out and come to be in need of a king, or other person of that kind, just now, they may have the chance of getting two countrymen of ours to fill such posts. We left them preparing to invade Servia on a shooting and exploring expedition, armed with admirable guns, revolvers, and a powder for the annihilation of insects. They were quite aware of the present unsettled state of affairs, and prepared to avail themselves of anything good which might turn up on their travels.

Constantinople, 34th September 1862.

The Eastern question! It is very easy indeed to have distinct notions on the Eastern question. I had once, not very long ago neither. Of course, like every Englishman, I was for fighting, sooner than the Russians, or any other European Power, should come to the Bosphorus without the leave of England, and that as often as might be necessary, and quite apart from any consideration as to the internal state of the country. But as for the Turks, I as much thought that their time was about over in Europe as the Czar Nicholas when he talked of the sick man to Sir Hamilton Seymour. They were a worn-out horde, the degenerate remnant of a conquering race, who were keeping down with the help of some of the Christian Powers, ourselves notably amongst the number, Christian subjects—Bulgarians, Servians, Greeks, and others—more numerous and better men than themselves. I could never see why these same Christian subjects should not be allowed to kick the Turks out of Europe if they could, or why we should take any trouble to bolster them up. Perhaps I do not see yet why they should not be allowed, if they can do it by themselves; but I am free to acknowledge that the Eastern question, the nearer you get to it, and the more you look into it, like many other political questions, gets more and more puzzling and complicated and turns up quite a new side to you. A week or two on the Bosphorus spent in looking about one, and sucking the brains of men of all nations who have had any experience of this remarkable country, make one see that there is a good deal to be said for wishing well to the Turks, notwithstanding their false creed and bad practices. I hear here the most wonderfully contradictory evidence about these Turks. They have one quality of a ruling nation assuredly in perfection—the power of getting themselves heartily hated. But so far as I could test them, the common statements as to their dishonesty and corruption are vague and general if you try to sift them, and I find that even those who abuse them are apt in practice to prefer them to Creeks, Armenians, or any other of the subject people in these parts. On the other hand, you certainly do hear much of the honesty of the lower classes of the Turks. For instance, it seems that contracts are scarcely ever made here in writing, and in actions of debt if a Turk will appear and swear that he was never indebted, the case is at an end, and he walks out of court a free man. Admiral Slade, amongst his other functions, is judge of a court which is a sort of mixture of an Admiralty and County Court, in which he tries very many actions of debt in the year. After an experience of nearly three years he told my informant that he had had only two cases in which a defendant had adopted this summary method of getting out of his difficulties. Again in the huge maze of bazaars in Stamboul there is a quarter, some sixty yards square, at least, I should say, which is *par excellence* the Turkish bazaar. The Jews, Armenians, and Greeks, who far out-number the Turks in the other quarters of the bazaars, have no place here; or if an Armenian or two creep in, it is only on sufferance. The Turks are a very early nation, and not given to overwork themselves, and this bazaar of theirs is shut at twelve o'clock every day, or soon afterwards, and left in charge of one man. I passed through it one day when many of the shops were closing. The process consisted of just sweeping the smaller articles into a sort of closet which each merchant has at the back of the divan on which he sits, and leaving the heavier articles (such as old inlaid firelocks, swords, large china vases, and the like) where they were, hanging or standing outside. Most of the merchandise, I quite admit, is old rubbish; still there are many articles of considerable value and very portable, and certainly every possible temptation to robbery is given both to those who shut up latest and to the man who is left in charge of all this property, and yet a theft of the smallest article is unheard of. In this very bazaar I saw an instance of honesty which struck me much. The custom of trade here is, as every one knows, that the vendor asks twice or three times as much as he will take, and you have to beat him down to a fair price. I accompanied a lady who had to make some purchases. After a hard struggle, she succeeded in getting what she wanted at her own price; but her adversary evidently felt aggrieved, and declared that he should be a loser by the transaction. She cast up the total in her head, paid the money; her *cavass* (as they call the substitutes for footmen here, who accompany ladies about the streets with scimitars by their sides, and sticks in their hands, to belabour the Jews and Greeks with who get in the way) had taken up the things, and we had left the shop, when the aggrieved merchant came out, called us back, explained to her that she had made a wrong calculation by ten francs or so, and refunded the difference. I was much surprised. The whole process was so like an attempt to cheat that it seemed very odd that the man who habitually practised it should yet scruple to take advantage of such a slip as this. But my companion, who knows the bazaars well, assured me that it was always the case. A Turk does not care what he asks you, often loses impatient customers by asking fabulously absurd prices, but the moment he has made his bargain is scrupulously exact in keeping to it, and will not take advantage of a farthing in changing your foreign money, or of your ignorance of the value of his currency. This was her experience. I might multiply instances of Turkish honesty if it were of any use, but have been unable to collect a single instance of the like virtue on the part of Greeks or Armenians. Every man's word seems against them, though their sharpness in trade and cleverness and activity in other ways are admitted on all hands. I found that every one whose judgment I could at all depend on, however much he might dislike the Turks, preferred them to any other of the people of the country whenever there was any question of trust. So, on the whole, notwithstanding their idleness, their hatred of novelties and love of backsheesh, their false worship and bigotry, and the evils which this false worship brings in its train, I must say that the immense preponderance of oral evidence is in their favour, as decidedly the most upright and respectable of the races who inhabit Turkey in Europe. One does not put much faith in one's own eyes in a question of this kind, but, taking them for what they are worth, mine certainly led me to the same conclusion. The Turkish boatmen, porters, shopmen, contrast very favourably with their Greek and other rivals.

In short, they look particularly like honest self-respecting men, which the others emphatically do not.

If this be true, and so long as it continues to be true, I for one am for keeping the Turks where they are. And this does not involve any intervention on our parts. They are quite able to hold their own if no foreign power interferes with them, and all we have to do is to see that they are fairly let alone, which is not the case at present. For the present Government of Fuad Pasha is the best and strongest Turkey has seen for many a year. Fuad's doings in Syria led one to expect considerable things of him, for few living statesmen have successfully solved such a problem as putting down the disturbances there, avenging the Damascus massacre, quieting the religious excitement, and getting the French out of the country. All this, however, he managed with great firmness and skill, and since he has been Prime Minister he has given proofs of ability in another direction equally important for the future of his country. Turkish finance was in a deplorable state when he came into power. I don't suppose that it is in a very sound condition now, but at any rate the first, and a very important, step has been successfully made. Until within the last few months the paper currency here, called *caimé*, has been the curse of the country. There were somewhere about five million sterling's worth of small notes, for sums from ten piastres (2s.) to fifty piastres in circulation. The value of these notes was constantly fluctuating, often varying thirty or forty per cent in a few days. The whole of these notes have been called in by the present Government and exchanged for small silver coin within the last two months, so that now the value of the piastre in Turkey is fixed. A greater blessing to the country can scarcely be conceived, and the manner in which the conversion has been effected has been most masterly. The English loan, no doubt, has enabled Fuad to do this, and he has had Lord Hobart at his elbow to advise and assist him in the operation. But, making all proper drawbacks, a very large balance of credit is due to the Turkish Government, as will appear when the English Commissioner's Report appears in due course, the contents of which I have neither the knowledge nor the wish to anticipate. The settlement, for the present, at least, of the Servian and Montenegrin difficulties are further proofs, it seems to me, of the vigour and ability of the present Government. But still, giving the Turkish statesmen now in power full credit for all they have done, one cannot help feeling that this Eastern question is full of the most enormous difficulties, is, in short, about the most complicated of all the restless, importunate, ill-mannered questions that are crying out "Come, solve me," in this troublesome old continent of ours.

For it hardly needs a voyage to the East to convince any man who cares about such matters that this Turkish Empire is in a state of solution. If one did want convincing on the point, a few days here would be enough to do it. Let him spend a few hours as I did last week at the Sweet Waters of Asia on a Turkish Sunday (Friday), and he will scarcely want further proof. The Sweet Waters of Asia are those of a muddy little rivulet, which flow into the sparkling Bosphorus some four miles above Constantinople. Along the side of this stream, at its junction with the Bosphorus, is a small level plain, which has been for I know not how long the resort of the Turkish women. Here they come once a week on their Sundays, to look at the hills and the Bosphorus without the interference of blinds and jalousies, and at some other human beings besides the slaves and other inmates of their own harems. You arrive there in a caique, and find yourself at a jump plump in the middle of the Arabian Nights' Entertainments. The Sultan has built a superb kiosk (summer-house) here, with a façade and balustrade of beautiful white marble, one hundred yards long, fronting the Bosphorus. (They tell me, by the way, that the whole kiosk is of the same white marble, and so it may be, but, at any rate, if it be, it is most superfluously covered with yellow stucco.) Outside the enclosure of his kiosk, at the Bosphorus end of the little plain, and some fifty yards from the shore, is a fine square marble fountain, with texts from the Koran in green and gold upon it, and steps all round. A few plane-trees give a little shade round it. On all the steps of the fountain, along the kiosk garden wall, under the plane-trees, and out on the turf of the valley, are seated Turkish women of every rank, from the Grand Vizier's wife and family, on superbly embroidered cushions and carpets, and cloaked in the most fascinating purple and pink silks, down to poor men's wives, in faded stuffs, on old scraps of drugget which a rag-collector would scarcely pick out of the gutter. Others of the veiled women are driving slowly round the little plain in the strangest carriages, just like Cinderella's coach in the children's books, or in arabas drawn by two oxen, and ornamented with silk or cotton hangings. Here the poor women sit, or drive, or walk for an hour or two, and smoke cigarettes, and eat fruit and sweetmeats, and drink coffee, which viands are brought with them or supplied by itinerant dealers on the ground. So far, the scene is just what it might have been in the days of Haroun Alraschid, and the black eunuchs standing about or walking by the carriages seem to warn off all contact with the outer world. But what is the fact? There were English and French ladies sitting on the carpets of the Grand Vizier's wife and talking with her. There were men and women of all nations walking about or sitting close by the veiled groups, and plenty of Turkish men looking on, or themselves talking to unbelievers, and seeming to think that it was all quite natural. It is impossible in a few words to convey the impression of utter incongruity which this and other scenes of the same kind give one. Islamism and Frankism—Western civilisation, or whatever you like to call it,—I dare not call it Christianity,—are no longer at arm's length. They are fairly being stirred up together. What will come of it? At a splendid garden *fête*, given by a great Pasha in the spring, amongst other novelties dancing was perpetrated. The Pasha is a Turk of advanced ideas. His wife (he has only one) and the other women of his household were allowed to look on from the harem windows. "In two years they will be down here, in five they will be dancing, and in ten they will wear crinolines," said an Englishman to one of the French Embassy with whom he was walking. "Et alors l'empire serait sauvé," replied the Frenchman. Not exactly so, perhaps, but still the speakers were touching the heart of the Eastern question. The harem or the Turks will have to go down in Europe in the next few years. But as this letter is already too long, I hope you will let me say what I have to say on the subject in my next.

Constantinople, 30th September 1862.

Amongst the many awkward facts which the Turks in Europe have to look in the face and deal with speedily, there is one which seems specially threatening. They have no class of educated men. "Some remedy *must* be found for this," say their friends; "things cannot go on as they are. The body of your people may be, we believe they are, sound and honest as times go, superior indeed in all essentials to the other races who are mixed up with them, but this will not avail you much longer." Steamboats, telegraphs, railways, have invaded Turkey already. The great tide of modern material civilisation is flooding in upon the East, with its restless, unmanageable eddies and waves, which have sapped, and are sapping, the foundations, and overwhelming the roof trees, of stronger political edifices than that of the Sublime Porte. If you Turks cannot control and manage the tide, it will very soon drown you. Now where are your men to do this? You have just now Fuad Pasha, and three or four other able men, and reasonably honest, who understand their time, and are guiding your affairs well. Besides them you have a few dozen men—we can count them on our fingers—who have educated themselves decently, and who may possibly prove fit for the highest places. But that is doubtful, and for all minor offices, executive, administrative, judicial, you have no competent men at all. The places are abominably filled, and for one Turk who is able to fill them even thus badly you have to employ ten foreigners, generally renegades. This is what Turkish patriots have to look to. You *must* find a class of men capable of dealing with this modern deluge, or you will have to move out of Europe, all we can say or do to the contrary notwithstanding.

All very true, say the enemies of the Turks. The facts are patent enough, but the remedy! That is all moonshine. You *cannot* have an educated class of Turks, and you cannot stop the deluge; so you had better stand back and let it sweep over them as soon as may be, and look out for something to follow.

I believe that this dispute does touch the very heart of the Eastern question, for it goes to the root of their social life; and the answer to it must depend, in great part, upon the future of their "peculiar institution"—the harem. For, alas the day! the harem is the place of education for Turkish boys of the upper classes. And how can it be helped? The boys must be with the women for the first years of their lives, and the women must be in the harems. We need not believe all the stories which are current about the abominations of these places. It is quite likely that the number of child-murders and other atrocities, which one hears of on all sides, may be exaggerated. But where there is a part of every rich man's house into which the police cannot enter, which is to all intents beyond the reach of the law—in which the inmates, all of one sex, are confined, with no connection with the outer world, and no occupations or interests whatever except food and dress (they are not even allowed to attend mosque)—one can hardly be startled by anything which one may be told of what is done in them; and it is impossible to conceive a more utterly enervating and demoralising place for a boy to be brought up in. There is nothing in Turkey answering to the great schools, colleges, and universities of Western Europe. There is no healthy home life to substitute for them. The harem is the place of education, and, with very rare exception, the boys come out of its atmosphere utterly unfitted for any useful active life.

This is the great difficulty of the Turks in Europe. If they could break the neck of it the others need not frighten them; and so the best of them feel, and are doing something towards meeting the difficulty. Many Turks are setting the example of taking only one wife, and of living with her in their own houses as the men of Christian nations do. A few have done away with the separate system, so far as they themselves are concerned, and their harems are so only in name. They encourage foreign ladies to call on their wives, and would gladly go further. Some of them have even tried taking their wives with them into public; but this has been premature. The nation will not stand it yet. The women themselves object. The few who feel the degradation of their present lives, and are anxious to help their husbands in getting rid of it, are looked upon with so much suspicion that they dare not move on so fast. Honest female conservatism has taken fright, and combines with vice, sloth, and jealousy, to keep things as they are. However, the women will come round fast enough if the men are only in earnest. They get all their outer-world notions from the men, and as soon as the men will say, "We wish you to live with us as the Giaours' wives live with them," the thing will be done.

I may say, then, from what I have myself seen and heard, that a serious attempt is being made by the Turks—few in number, certainly, at present, but strong in position and character—to break the chain of their old customs, especially this of the harem, and to conform outwardly to Western habits and manners. This is being done mainly for political reasons, and if nothing more enters into the movement will probably fail; for, in spite of the great changes which have taken place in Turkey in Europe of late years, there is a tremendous power of passive resistance and hatred of all change amongst the people, which no motives of expediency will be able to break through. It will take something deeper than political expediency to do that. Is there the sign of any such power above the horizon?

Well, sir, of course my opinion is worth very little. A fortnight's residence in a country, whatever opportunities one may have had, and however one may have tried and desired to use them, cannot be of much use in judging questions of this kind. Take my impressions, then, for what they are worth, at any rate they are honest, and the result of the best observation of a deeply interested spectator. Islamism as a religious faith is all but gone in Turkey in

Europe. Up to 1856 the Turks were still a dominant and persecuting race, and Islamism a persecuting creed. Since the Hatti humayoun, which was, perhaps, the most important result of the Crimean war, there has been nominally absolute religious toleration—actually something very nearly approaching to it—in Turkey in Europe. Islamism was spread by the sword, and the consequence of this method of propagation was that large layers of the population were only nominally converted. These have never since been either Moslem or Christians but a bad mixture of the two. Since 1856 this has become more and more apparent. I will only mention one fact bearing on the point, though I heard many. An American missionary traveller in a part of Roumelia not very far from Constantinople found the people, though nominally Turks, yet with many Christian practices and traditions, to which they were much attached, but which they had till lately kept secret. They did not seem inclined to make any further profession of Christianity, or to give up their Moslem profession, but were anxious that he should read the Bible to them. They had not heard it for generations, but had preserved the tradition of it. He did so; and afterwards parties of them would come to the Bosphorus to his house to hear him read, and, I believe, do so still. It is a curious story to hear of bodies of men sitting to hear the old Book read, and weeping and going away. It takes one back to the finding of the Book of the Law in Josiah's day. Amongst the Turks proper there is only one article of Islamism which is held with any strength, and that is the hatred of any approach to image worship. In this they are fanatics still. Thirty years ago the then Sultan nearly caused a revolution by having his likeness put on coin. The issue was called in, and to this day there is nothing but a cipher on the piastres and other Turkish coin. The rest of their faith sits very lightly on them, and is much more of a political than a religious garment. There is a strong feeling of patriotism amongst the people (though it, and all else that is noble, seems to have died out amongst the insignificant upper class, if one may speak of such a thing here)—a patriotism of race more than of country; and it is this, and not their faith, which is holding the present state of things together.

Now, I am not going to tell you, sir, that the Turks in Europe are about to be converted to Christianity. I only say that Islamism is all but dead on our continent; that the most able and far-seeing of the Turks see and feel this more and more every day themselves; that they are themselves adopting, and are trying to introduce, practices and habits which are utterly inconsistent with their old creed; that they have, in fact, already virtually abandoned it. "We must have a civilisation," the best men amongst them say; "but what we want is a Turkish civilisation, and not a French, or Russian, or English civilisation." Yes; but on what terms is such a civilisation possible for you? Well, sir, I am old-fashioned enough to believe myself that the Christian faith is the only possible civiliser of mankind. The only civilisation which has reached the East—the outside civilisation of steam, gas, and the like—will do nothing but destroy, unless you have something stronger to graft it upon. What is the good of sending messages half round the world in a few seconds, if the messages are lies; of carrying cowards and scoundrels about at the rate of fifty-miles an hour; of forging instruments of fearful power for the hands of the oppressors of the earth? Not much will come of this kind of civilisation alone for any nation; and, as for these poor Turks, it is powerful enough to blow them up altogether, and that is all it will do for them.

When one stands in Great Sophia, and sees the defaced crosses, and the names of Mahomet and his successors, on huge ugly green sign-boards, hanging in the most prominent places of the noblest church of the East, it is difficult not to feel something of the Crusading spirit. But, if the Turks were swept out of Europe to-morrow, I doubt whether it would not be a misfortune for the world. We should not only be expelling the best race of the country, but they would retire into Asia sullen and resentful, hating the West and its faith more than ever. Islamism would gain new life from the reaction which would take place; for the Turks will not go without making a strong fight, and Turkey in Europe would be left to a riff-raff of nominal Christians, with more than all the vices and none of the redeeming virtues of their late masters. It would be a far higher and nobler triumph for Christendom to see the Turks restoring the crosses and taking down the sign-boards. That sooner or later they will become Christians I have no sort of doubt whatever, after seeing them; for they are too strong a race to disappear. No nation can go on long without a faith, and there is none other for them to turn to. Modern Greeks may regret their old Paganism—here they say seriously that many of them openly avow it; but for a Turk who finds Islamism crumble away beneath him, it must be Christianity or nothing. The greatest obstacle to the conversion of Turkey will be the degradation of the subject Christian races. It is, no doubt, a tremendous obstacle, but there have been tremendous obstacles before now which have been cleared by weaker people.

I daresay I shall seem lunatic to you, sir, though I know it will not be because you think the Christian faith is itself pretty well used up, and ought to be thinking of getting itself carried out and buried decently, instead of making new conquests. But if you had been living for a fortnight on the Bosphorus, you could not help wishing well to the old Turks any more than I, and I don't believe you, any more than I, could by any ingenuity find out what good to wish them, except speedy conversion. With that all reforms will follow rapidly enough.

If you are not thoroughly outraged by these later productions of mine I will promise to avoid the Eastern question proper, and will try to give you something more amusing next week. Meanwhile, believe me ever faithfully yours.

Athens, 1st October 1862.

I am afraid, to judge by my own café, it is quite impossible to give anything like a true idea of Constantinople to those who have never been there; at any rate it would require a volume and not two columns to do it, but I can't help trying to impart some of my own impressions to your readers. Miles away in the Sea of Marmora you first catch sight of the domes and minarets (like huge wax candles with graceful black extinguishers on them) of the capital of the East. As you near the mouth of the Bosphorus, on the European side lies the Seraglio Point with its palaces, Sublime Porte, and public offices and gardens full of noble cypresses. On the Asiatic side lies Scutari, the great hospital, with the English cemetery and Marochetti's monument in front of it, occupying the highest and most conspicuous point. Midway between the two shores is a rock called Leander's rock, on which is a picturesque little lighthouse. Passing this you turn short to the left round Seraglio Point, and open at once the view of the whole city. The Golden Horn runs right away in front of you, and on the promontory between it and the Sea of Marmora lies the old town of Stamboul, crowned with the mosques of St. Sophia and Sultan Achmet. A curious old wooden bridge, some five hundred yards in length, crosses the Golden Horn and connects it with Galata, a mass of custom-houses, barracks and offices, broken by a handsome open square, at one end of which is the Sultan's mosque. Behind these the houses are piled up the steep hill side, and at the top stands the striking old tower of Galata, from which you get the finest view of Constantinople. Beyond comes Pera, the European quarter, where are the Embassies and Missouri's Hotel. Of course a vast city lining such a harbour and strait as the Golden Horn and the Bosphorus must be beautiful, but there is something very peculiar in the beauty of Constantinople, which the splendid site alone will not account for. I tried hard to satisfy myself what it was, and believe that it lies in the wonderful colouring of the place. The mosques are splendid, but not so fine as many Gothic churches, and the houses in general are far inferior to those of most other capitals; and yet, seen in the mass, they are strikingly beautiful, for those which are not of wood are almost all covered with boarding, which is stained or painted in many different colours. Many of them are a deep russet brown, others slate gray, or blue, or deep yellow, some pale green with the windows picked out in red. The colours are not fresh, but toned down. Then very many of the houses have court-yards, or small gardens, and you get the fresh foliage of orange-trees, and figs, and cypresses, as a further contrast, and for flooring and ceiling the blue of the Bosphorus water and of the cloudless Eastern sky. The moment you get into the wretched, narrow, unpaved streets, the charm goes; but while you keep to the great high street of the Bosphorus, I don't believe there is any such treat in the world for the lover of colour. And the shape of the houses, too, is picturesque: as a rule they have flat roofs and deep overhanging eaves, and rows of many windows with open Venetian shutters. As we have no time to spare, we will not attempt the town, but stick to the high street.

There are three accepted ways of passing up and down the Bosphorus. There is the common market-boat of the country—a huge, lumbering, flat-bottomed affair, about the size of a Thames lighter, but with high bows and stern. It is propelled by six or eight boatmen, each pulling a huge oar some eighteen feet long. They pull a long, steady stroke, each man stepping up on to the thwart in front of him at the beginning of his stroke, and throwing himself back till his weight has dragged his oar through, and he finds himself back on his own seat, from which he at once springs up and steps forward again for a fresh stroke. It must be splendid training exercise, and they make a steady four miles an hour against the stream;—no bad pace, for the boats are loaded with fruit-baskets and packages and passengers—the veiled women sitting in a group apart in the stern. Then there are the steamers, which ply every hour up and down, the express boats touching at one or two principal piers, and doing the twelve miles from the bridge at Stamboul to Bajukdere in an hour and a quarter, the others stopping at every pier, and taking two hours or more. They are Government boats, for passengers only, and the fares are somewhat higher than those of our Thames steamers. They have a long glazed cabin on the after-deck for the first-class male passengers, and a small portion screened off further aft, where the veiled women are crowded together. Until lately, all women were accustomed to travel behind this screen, but the unveiled are beginning to break the rule, and to intrude into the cabin of the lords of creation. You see the Turks lift their eyebrows slightly as women in crinoline squeeze by them and take their seats, but it is too late for any further demonstration. An awning is spread over the whole deck, cabin and all, and under it the passengers, who are too late to get seats in the cabin, sit about on small low stools. Such a *colluvies gentium* and Babel of tongues no man can see or hear anywhere else I should think. By your side, perhaps, sits a scrupulously clean old Turk, with his legs tucked up under him and his slippers on the floor beneath. He has the vacant hopeless look of an opium-eater, and you see him take out his little box from his belt, and feel with nervous fingers how large a pellet he may venture on in consideration of the bad company he is in. On the other side an English sailor boy, delighted to be able to talk broad Durham to somebody, is telling you how he has been down to the bazaars and has bought a "hooble booble," and a bottle of attar of roses for the folk at home, and speculating how they would give £5, he knows, at Sunderland, to see one of those women who look as if they were done up in grave-clothes. Opposite you have a couple of silky-haired Persians, with their long soft eyes and clear olive skins, high head-dresses and sombre robes, and all about a motley crowd of Turks, Circassians, and Greeks, Europeans with muslin round their wideawakes,

Maltese, English, and French skippers, soldiers in coarse zouave and other uniforms, most of them smoking, and the waiters (Italians generally), edging about amongst them all with little brazen coffee-trays. An artist wishing to draw the heads of all nations could find no richer field, and in the pursuit of his art would not of course object to the crush and heat and odour; but as we are more bent on comfort, we will go up the Bosphorus in the third conveyance indicated above, a caique—and a more fascinating one can scarcely be conceived. You may have your caique of any size, from one pair of sculls up to the splendid twelve-oared state affairs of ambassadors and pashas; but that with three caiquejees or rowers seems to be the most in use amongst the rich folk, so we can scarcely do wrong in selecting it.

Our three-manned caique shall belong to an English merchant, the happy owner of a summer villa at Therapia or Bajukdere. He shall be waiting for us, and shall board the steamer as it drops anchor opposite Seraglio Point. While our portmanteau is being fished up from the hold, we have time to examine critically his turn-out. The caique is about the size of an old-fashioned four-oar, but more strongly built, with a high sharp bow and a capital flat floor, and lies on the water as lightly as a wild duck. The caiquejees' seats are well forward. The stern is decked for some eight feet, and in this deck is a hole, so that you can stow your luggage away underneath. When the ladies use the caique, their *cavass*, with his red fez, blue braided coat and scimitar, sits grimly with his legs in the hole and gives their orders to the caiquejees. Comfortable cushions lying on a small Turkey carpet, between the little deck and the stretcher of the stroke oar, in the roomiest part of the boat, await you. You will lounge on them with your shoulders against the deck, a white umbrella over your head, and a cigarette in your mouth. In the climate of the Bosphorus, cigarettes of Turkish tobacco supersede all other forms of the weed. The caiquejees are wiry, bronzed Turks; their costume, the red fez, a loose coloured jacket, generally blue, which they strip off for work, and appear in Broussa shirts of camels' hair fitting to the body, with loose sleeves reaching only to the elbow, and baggy white cotton drawers tied at the knee. The stroke wears stockings, which the others dispense with; each of them keeps his slippers under his own seat. They each pull a pair of straight sculls fastened to a single thole pin by a greased thong. You follow your friend and portmanteau down the gangway and start, and are at once delighted at the skill with which your crew steer through the crowds of Maltese boats and caiques, and under great steamers and merchant ships, and fall into their regular stroke, twenty-eight to the minute, which they never vary for the whole twelve miles. Their form, too, is all that can be desired, and would not discredit a London waterman. Turning up the Bosphorus you soon lose sight of the Golden Horn, and the old rickety bridge which spans it from Stamboul to Galata. You pull away at first under the European shore, past the magnificent palace of the present Sultan, gleaming white in the sun; and then come other huge piles, some tumbling to pieces, some used as barracks, and private houses of all sizes and colours, in their little gardens, and warehouses, coffee-shops, cemeteries, fruit-markets and mosques. Not a yard of the bank but is occupied with buildings, and the houses are piled far up the hillside behind. It is the same on the Asiatic side, except that there the houses next to the water are chiefly those of the rich Turks, as you may guess from the carefully barred and jalousied windows of the harems, and that the line of houses is not so deep. And so on for five miles you glide up the strait, half a mile or more wide, alive with small boats moving about, and men-of-war steamers riding at anchor, through one continuous street. Then comes the narrowest part, where the current runs like a mill-tail against you. On the European side stand the three towers, connected with battlemented walls, built by Mahomed's orders in the winter before the taking of Stamboul and the extinction of the Western Empire. Roumelie Hissa the point is called now, and behind it rises the highest hill on the Bosphorus. If it is not too hot, your friend will land and walk up with you, and when you have reached the top you will see Olympus and the distant Nicomedian mountains over the Sea of Marmora to the south, and the whole line of the Bosphorus below you, and the Giants' Mountain and the Black Sea away to the north. Behind you lie wild moorlands, covered with heather and gum cistus, and arbutus bushes, and a small oak shrub. Here and there in the hollows are small patches of vines and other culture, with occasional clumps of stone pine and Scotch fir, and chestnut and beech, amongst which scanty herds of buffaloes and goats wander, watched by melancholy, truculent-looking herdsmen, in great yellow capotes and belts, from which a brace of long, old-fashioned pistols and the hilt of a long straight dagger stick out. But, desolate as the European side is, it is a garden compared to the Asiatic. You look across there, and behind the little bright belt of life along the Bosphorus, there is nothing between you and the horizon but desert heathery hills, running away as far as the eye can reach, without a house, a tree, a beast, or the slightest sign of life upon them. I scarcely ever saw so lovely a view, and it is thrown out into the most vivid contrast by the life at your feet. You descend to your caique again, and now are aware of a towing-path which runs at intervals along in front of the houses. A lot of somewhat wretched-looking Turks here wait with ropes to tow the caiques and other boats up the rapids. Your stroke catches the end of the rope, and fastens it, exclaiming, "*Haidee babai*" (so it sounds), "Push on, my fathers; push on, my lambs"; and two little Turks, passing the rope over their shoulders, toil away for some hundred yards, when they are dismissed with a minute backsheesh. And now the Bosphorus widens out: on the Asiatic side comes the valley of the Sweet Waters of Asia, and the new kiosk of the Sultan, which I spoke of before, and afterwards only occasional villages and the palaces of one or two great pashas. On the European side the houses are still in continuous line, but begin to get more elbow-room, and only in the little creeks, where the villages lie, are the hillsides much built on. Now you begin to see the summer villas of the Europeans, and accordingly an esplanade faced with stone, and broad enough for carriages to pass, begins. This upper part of the Bosphorus has its own charm. The water is rougher, as there is generally a breeze from the Black Sea; and porpoises roll about, and flocks of sea-swallows (âmes damnées) flit for ever over the little restless waves. The banks between the houses and the wild common land of the hill tops are now often taken into the gardens and cultivated in terraces; and where this is not so they are clothed with fine Scotch fir and stone pine, and avenues of cypress of the height of forest trees, with magnificent old gray trunks, marking where paths run up the hillside or standing up alone like sombre sentinels. It is not until you get almost to Therapia that there is any break in the row of houses. Therapia, where Medea is said to have prepared her potions, is a Greek village, built round a little bay, the busiest and almost the prettiest place on the Bosphorus. There are always half a dozen merchantmen lying there, and a sprinkling of European sailors appear amongst the fezzes frequenting the quays formed by the esplanade, and there is a café restaurant, and a grog shop, where the British sailor can be refreshed with the strong liquors of his country. Behind the village is the little cemetery of the Naval Brigade, sadly neglected and overshadowed with beech and chestnut trees, where Captain Lyons and many another fine fellow lie, to whom their countrywomen have raised a large, simple white marble cross, which stands up mournfully amongst the tangled grass which creeps over the rows of nameless graves. One grieves that it is shoved away out of sight of the Bosphorus, up which the brave fellows all went with such stout hearts.

You pass more handsome villas and the summer residences of the English and French ambassadors just above Therapia, and then comes the Bay of Bajukdere, the broadest part of the Bosphorus, with the village of the same name on its north shore, the last and handsomest of the suburbs of Constantinople, where are the other embassies and the palaces of the richest merchants. It was the place where Godfrey of Bouillon encamped with his Crusaders. Beyond, the strait narrows again, and runs between steep cliffs with a sharp turn into the Black Sea, and close to the mouth are the storm-lashed Symplegades.

You must fill up the picture with ships of all sorts under the flags of all the nations of the earth passing up and down, and people the banks with figures in all the quaint and picturesque costumes of the East; but no effort of imagination, I fear, can realise the frame in which the whole is set, the water of the Bosphorus, and the unfathomable Eastern sky. I never had an idea of real depth before. I doubt if it be possible to imagine it. I am sure it is impossible to forget it.

Athens, 4th October 1862.

We left Constantinople for the Piraeus in a French packet. The sun set behind Pera just before we started, and at the same moment a priest came out into the little balcony which runs round each dizzy minaret some three parts of the way up, and called the faithful to prayer. The poor faithful! summoned there still at sunrise and sunset to turn towards Mecca, and fall down before Him who gave that great city, and the fair European countries behind it, to their fathers:—they must pray and work hard too if they mean to stay there much longer. We steamed slowly out from the Golden Horn, round Seraglio Point, and into night on the Sea of Marmora. I was up early the next morning, and saw the sun rise over the islands just as we were entering the Dardanelles. We stopped between Lesbos and Abydos to take in cargo, time enough to charter one of the fruit boats and pull off for a good swim in that romantic water. By ten o'clock we were opening the Ægean Sea, with the road close under our larboard bow and Tenedos in front of us. We saw the mounds on the shore, known as the tombs of Achilles and Ajax, and so passed on wondering. There were half a dozen young Englishmen on board, carrying amongst them a Homer, a *Childe Harold*, and other classics. We had much debate as we passed point after point as to the possible localities, but I am not sure that we came to any conclusions which are worth repeating. About noon, after we had become familiar with island after island, well remembered as names from school and college days, but now living realities, a faint peak was discovered in the far north-west. What could it be? We applied to an officer, and found it was Athos. You may fancy what the atmosphere was, sir, for Athos must have been at least sixty miles from us at the time.

Night came on before any of us were tired of the Ægean. Next morning at daybreak we were off the southern point of Euboea, with the coast of Attica in sight over the bows. By breakfast-time we were rounding Sunium, with the fair columns of a temple crowning the height, the bay of Salamis before us, and "Morea's Hills" for a background; and presently the cliffs on the Attic coast gave way to low ground, and one of our company, who had been in these parts before, startled us with "There is the Acropolis!" "Where?" Operaglasses were handed about, and eager looks cast over the plain, till we were aware of a little rocky hill rising up some three miles from the shore, and a town lying round the foot of it. The buildings of the town gleamed white enough in the sun, but the ruins on the Acropolis we could scarcely make out. They were of a deep yellow, not easily distinguishable on this side, and at this distance from the rock below. The first sensation was one of disappointment—we were all candid enough to admit it. We had seen barren coasts enough, but none so bare as this of Attica. Hymettus lay on the right, and Pentelicus further away on the north, behind Athens and the Acropolis;

and from their feet right down to the Piraeus, no tree or shrub or sign of cultivation was visible, except a strip of sombre green, a mile or so broad, which ran along the middle of the plain marking the course of the Ilyssus. In the early spring and summer they do get crops off portions of the plain, but by the end of September it is as dry, dusty, and bare as the road to Epsom Downs on a Derby Day.

The little arid amphitheatre, not larger than a moderatesized English county, with its capital and Acropolis, looked so insignificant, and but for the bright sunshine would have been so dreary, that to keep from turning away and not taking a second look at it, one was obliged to keep mentally repeating, "It is Attica, after all!" Matters improved a little as we got nearer, and before the Acropolis was hidden from our view by the steep little hill crowned with windmills which rises up between the Piraeus and Munychia, we could clearly make out the shape of the Parthenon, and confessed that the rock on which it stood was for its size a remarkable one, and in a commanding position.

You see nothing of the Piraeus till you round this hill and open the mouth of the harbour, narrowed to this day by the old Athenian moles, so that there is scarcely room for two large vessels to pass in it. It is a lively little harbour enough. Three men-of-war, English, French, and Greek, were lying there when we entered, and an Austrian Lloyd steamer and a dozen or two merchantmen. We were surrounded by dozens of boats, the boatmen dressed in the white cotton petticoats and long red fezzes, not mere scull-caps like those of the Turks—a picturesque dress enough, but not to be named for convenience or beauty with that of the Bosphorus boatmen.

Most of our party started at once for Athens, but I and a companion, resolved on enjoying the Mediterranean as long as we could, crossed the hill, and descended to the Munychia for a bath, which we achieved in the saltest and most buoyant water I have ever been in. The rocks (volcanic, apparently), on which we dressed and were nearly grilled, were all covered with incrustations of salt, looking as if there had been a tremendous frost the night before. After our bath we strolled through the little port town, hugely amused with the Greek inscriptions over the shop-doors, and with the lively, somewhat rowdy look and ways of the place; and, resisting the solicitations of many of the dustiest kind of cab-drivers, who were hanging about with their vehicles on the look-out for a fare to Athens, struck across the low marsh land, where the Ilissus must run when he can find any water to bring down from the hills, and were soon in amongst the olive groves. Here we were delivered from the dust at any rate, and in a few minutes met a Greek with a basket of grapes on his head, from whom, for half a franc, we purchased six or seven magnificent bunches, and went on our way mightily refreshed. We had made up our minds to be disappointed with the place, and so were not sorry to be out of sight of it, and the olive groves were quite new to us. Some of the old trees were very striking. They were quite hollow, but bearing crops of fruit still quite merrily, as if it were all right, and what was left of the trunk was all divided into grisly old fretwork, as if each root had just run up independently into a branch, and had never really formed part of the tree. They looked as if they might be any age—could Plato have sat or walked under some of them?

Vines grow under the olives, just as currant and gooseberry bushes under the fruit-trees in our market gardens. They were loaded with fine grapes, and the vintage was going lazily on here and there. There were pomegranates too scattered about, the fruit splitting with ripeness. It was tremendously hot, but the air so light and fresh that walking was very pleasant. Presently we came to an open space, and caught a glimpse of the Acropolis; and now that we were getting round to the front of it, and could catch the outline of the Parthenon against the sky, it began to occur to us that we had been somewhat too hasty.

In among the olive groves again, and then out on another and another opening, till at last, when we came upon the *Via sacra*, we could stand it no longer. The ruins had become so beautiful, and had such an attraction, that giving up the grove of the Academy and Colonus, which were not half a mile ahead of us, and which we had meant to visit, we turned short to the right, and walked straight for the town at a pace which excited the laughter of merry groups dawdling round the little sheds where the winepresses were working. The town through which we had to pass is ugly, dusty, and glaring. There are one or two broad streets, with locust-trees planted along the sides of them, but not old enough yet to give shade; and in the place before the palace, on which our hotel looked, there are a few shrubs and plenty of prickly pears, which seem to be popular with the Athenians, and are the most misshapen hot-looking affairs which I have yet met with in the vegetable world. But shade, shade—one longs for it, and there is none; and the glare and heat are almost too much, even at the beginning of October—in summer it must be unendurable. If the Athenians would only take one leaf out of the book of their old enemies, and stain and paint their houses as the Turks of the Bosphorus do! But though the houses are as ugly as those of a London suburb, and there are no tolerable public buildings except one church, the modern town is a very remarkable one, when one comes to remember that thirty years ago there were only ten or twelve hovels here. But you may suppose that one scarcely looks at or thinks of the modern town; but pushing straight through it, makes for the Acropolis. A fine broad carriage-road runs round the back of the hill, and so up with a long sweep to the bottom of the western face, the one which we had seen from the olive groves. You can manage to pass the stadium and the columns of Jupiter on your left, as you ascend, without diverging, but even to reach the Parthenon you cannot go by the theatre of Dionysus, lying on your right against the northern face of the Acropolis, without stopping. They are excavating and clearing away the rubbish every day from new lines of seats; you can trace tier above tier now, right up the face of the hill, till you get to precipitous cliff; and down below, in the dress circle, the * marble seats are almost as fresh as the day they were made; and most comfortable stalls they are, though uncushioned, with the rank of their old occupants still fresh on them. You could take your choice and sit in the stall of a [Greek phrase] as you fancied. Below was the actual stage on which the tragedies of Sophocles and Æschylus were played to audiences who understood even the toughest chorus; and, for a background, Hymettus across the plain, and the sea and islands! We passed yet another theatre as we went up the hill, but nothing now could turn us from the Parthenon, and certainly it very far exceeded anything I had ever dreamt of. Every one is familiar with the shape and position and colour of the ruins from photographs and paintings. We look at them and admire, and suppose they grew there, or at any rate scarcely give a thought to how they did get there.

But I'll defy any man to walk up the Propylæa and about the Parthenon without being struck with wonder at the simple question, how it all got there. Can the stories we have all been taught be true? Leaving beauty altogether out of the question, here you are in the midst of the wreck of one of the largest buildings you ever were in. You see that it was built of blocks of white marble; that the columns are formed of these blocks, each some four feet high, and so beautifully fitted together that at the distance of two thousand years you very often cannot find the joints, except where the marble is chipped. You see that the whole of this building was originally surrounded by most elaborate sculpture; you see that the whole side of the hill up which you approach the great temple was converted into a magnificent broad staircase of white marble—in short, you see probably the greatest architectural feat that has ever been done in the world, and are told that it was done by a small tribe—not more numerous than the population of a big English town—who lived in that little barren corner of earth which you can overlook from end to end from your standing-place, in the lifetime of one generation; that Pericles thought the idea out, and the Athenians quarried the marble, carried it up there, carved it, and built it up, in his lifetime. Well, it *is* hard to believe; but when one has sat down on one of the great blocks, and looked over Salamis and Ægina, and the Isthmus of Corinth, and then down at the groves of the Academy and the Pynx and the Areopagus, and remembered that at this very time the thoughts, and methods of thought, of that same small tribe are still living, and moulding the minds of all the most civilised and powerful nations of the earth, the physical wonder, as usual, dwarfs and gives way before the spiritual. We saw the sunset, of course, from the front of the Parthenon, and then descended to the Areopagus, and stood on, or at any rate within a few feet of, the place where the glorious old

Hebrew of the Hebrews stood, and looking up at those marvellous temples made by man, spoke a strange story in the ears of the crowd, whose only pleasure was to hear or tell some new thing. It is the only place where I have ever come in my journeyings right across the Scripture narrative, and certainly the story shines out with new light after one has stood on the very rock, and felt how the scene before Paul's eyes must have moved him.

We got to our inn after dark, and after dining went to a Greek play. Theatre and acting both decidedly second-rate, the audience consisting chiefly of officers—smart-looking young fellows enough. There were two murders in the first act, but I regret to say that we could none of us make out the story of the play. There were half a dozen young men, all with good brains, none of whom had left our Universities more than two years, at which the Greek language is all but the most prominent study, and yet they might as well have been hearing Arabic. As for myself—unluckily my ear is so bad that I can never catch words which are not familiar to me—on this occasion, indeed, I could almost have sworn the actors were using French words. But it really is a pity that we can't take to the modern Greek pronunciation in England. One goes into Athens, and can read all the notices and signs, and even spell through a column of newspaper with a little trouble, and yet, though one would give one's ears to be able to talk, cannot understand a word, or make oneself understood. We managed, however, to get a clear enough notion that something serious was going to happen; and from several persons, French, Italian, and Greek, learned positively that Prince Alfred was to be King of Greece shortly, which remarkable proposition has since spread widely over the world. We sailed from Athens, after a two days' stay, in an Austrian Lloyd boat. The sailors were all Italians, and there were certainly not much more than half the number which we found on the French boat from Constantinople. And yet the Austrian Lloyd Company has not lost a boat since it was a company, and the Messageries Impériales have done nothing but lose theirs. Happily, the French are not natural sailors, or there would be no peace on sea or land.

The Run Home, October 1862.

We ran from Athens to Syra through the islands, in a bright moonlight, and half a gale of wind, the most enjoyable combination of circumstances in the world for those who are not given to sea-sickness. The island is a rock almost as bare as Hymettus, and that is the most barren simile I can think of—any hill in the Highlands would look like a garden beside it. But it has a first-rate small harbour, which has become the central packet-station of the Levant; and the town which has sprung up round the harbour is the most stirring place in the East, and the commercial capital of Greece. A very quaint place to look at, too, is Syra, for at the back of the lower town, which lies round the harbour, rises a conical hill, very steep, right up to the top of which a second town is piled, with the Bishop's palace on the highest point. This second, or pyramidal, town is built on terraces, and is only accessible to foot passengers, who ascend by a broad stone staircase, running from the lower town up to the Bishop's palace, and so bisecting the pyramid. As restless a place as ever I was in, in which nothing seems to be produced, but everything in the world exchanged—a very temple of the Trade Goddess, of whom I should say there are few more devout or successful worshippers than the Greeks. Here we waited through a long broiling day for the steamer, which was to take us westward—homewards.

In travelling there is only one pleasure which can be named with the start— that luxurious moment when one unstrings the bow, and leaving one's common pursuits and everyday life, plunges into new scenes—and that is, the turning home. I had never been so far or so long away from England before, so that the sensation was proportionately keen as we settled into our places in the *Pluto*, one of the finest of the Austrian Lloyd boats, which was to take us to Trieste. And a glorious run we made of it. In the morning we were off the Lacedaemonian coast. Almost as bare, this home of the Spartans, as that of their old rivals in Attica; in fact, all the south of the Peloponnesus is barren rock. We might almost have thrown a stone on to Cape Matapan as we passed. Above, the western coast soon begins to change its character, and scanty pine forests on the mountains, and not unfrequent villages, with more or less of cultivated land round them, are visible. Towards evening we steam past the entrance of Navarino Bay, scarcely wider than that of Dartmouth harbour, but with room inside for four modern fleets to ride and fight; as likely a place for a corsair to haunt and swoop out of, in old days, as you could wish to see. Night fell, and we missed the entrance to the Gulf of Corinth; and Ithaca, alas! was also out of sight astern before we were on deck again. But we could not complain; the Albanian coast, under which we were running, was too beautiful to allow us a moment for regret— mountains as wild and barren, and twice as high, as those of Southern

Greece, streaked with rich valleys, and well-clothed lower hills. By midday we were ashore at Corfu, driving through the old Venetian streets, and on, over English macadamised roads, through olive groves finer than those of Attica, up to the one-gun battery—the finest view in the fairest island of the world. Bathing, and lunching, and all but letting the steamer go on without us! Steaming away northward again, leaving the shade of the union-jack under which we had revelled for a few hours, and the delightful sound of the vernacular in the mouth of the British soldiers, for a twenty-four hours' run up the Adriatic, and into Trieste harbour, just in time to baulk a fierce little storm which came tearing down from the Alps to meet us.

Trieste is the best paved town I was ever in, and otherwise internally attractive, while in the immediate neighbourhood, on the spurs of the great mountains and along the Adriatic shore, are matchless sites for country houses, and many most fascinating houses on them. For choice, the situation, to my mind, even beats the celebrated hills round Turin, for the view of the Adriatic turns the scale in favour of the former. But neither city nor neighbourhood held us, and we hurried on to Venice by rail, with the sea on our left, and the great Alpine range on our right—now close over us, now retiring—the giant peaks looking dreamily down on us through a hot shadowy haze all the day long. Poor Venice! we lingered there a few days amidst pictures and frescoes and marbles; at night drinking our coffee in the Place of St. Mark, on the Italian side, watching the white and blue uniforms on the other, and hearing the Austrian military band play, or gliding in a gondola along the moonlit grand canal. English speculators are getting a finger in house property at Venice. There were placards up in English on a dozen of the palaces, "To be let or sold," with the direction of the vendors below. What does this portend? Let us hope not restoration on Camberwell or Pentonville principles of art.

Then we sped westward again, getting an hour in the Giotto chapel at Padua, a long day at Verona, amongst Roman ruins and Austrian fortifications, and the grand churches, houses, and tombs of the Scaligers. Over the frontier, then, into Italy. 'While the Austrian officials diligently searched baggage and spelt out passports, I consoled myself with getting to a point close to the station, pointed out by a railway guard, and taking a long look at the heights of Solferino and the high tower—the watch-tower of Italy, a mile or two away to the south. To Milan, through mulberries and vines—rich beyond all fancy; the country looked as we passed as if peace and plenty had set up their tent there. But little enough of either was there in the people's homes. The news of Garibaldi's capture and wound was stirring men's minds fearfully; and all the cotton mills, too, of which there are a good number scattered about, were just closing; wages, already fearfully low, were falling in other trades. I came across a Lancashire foreman, who had escaped the day before from the mill in which he had been employed for five years, and only just escaped with his life. Sixteen men had been stabbed and carried to the hospitals in the closing row. He was making the best of his way back. "What was the state of things in Lancashire to what he had just got out of," he answered, when I spoke of our distress. "He had been standing for three hours and more in a dark corner, with two men within a few feet of him waiting to stab him." I rejoice to say that in the streets of Milan we saw everywhere unmistakable signs that Italy is beginning to appreciate her faithful ally. Some of the best political caricatures were as good as could be— as Doyle's or Leech's—and bitter as distilled gall. At Turin we had time to see the monuments of the two Queens, the mother and wife of Victor Emmanuel, in a little out-of-the-way Church of Our Lady of Consolation, where they used constantly to worship in life; their statues are kneeling side by side in white marble—as touching a monument as I have ever seen. Murray does not mention it (his last edition was out before it was put up), so some stray reader of yours may perhaps thank me for the hint. Over the Mount Cenis, and down into Savoy, past the mouth of the tunnel which, in six years or so, is to take us under the Alps to the lovely little town of St. Michael, where the rail begins, we went, pitying the stout king from whom so beautiful a birthplace had been filched by the arch robber; and so day and night to Paris; and, after a day's breathing, a drive along the trim new promenades of the Bois de Boulogne, and a look round the ever-multiplying new streets of the capital of cookery and gilded mirrors, in ten hours to London.

Poor dear old London! groaning under the last days of the Great Exhibition. After those bright, brave, foreign towns, how dingy, how unkempt and uncared for thou didst look! From London Bridge station we passed through a mile and a half of the most hideous part of Southwark to the west. Even in the west, London was out at elbows, the roads used up, the horses used up; the omnibus coachmen and cads,—the cabbies, the police, the public, all in an unmistakable state of chronic seediness and general debility. In spic-and-span Paris yesterday, and here to-day! Well, one could take thee a thought cleaner and more cheerful, and be thankful, Old London; but after all, as we plunge into thy fog and reek and roar, and settle into our working clothes again, we are surer than ever of one thing, which must reconcile any man worth his salt to making thee his home,—thou art unmistakably the very heart of the old world.

Dieppe, Sunday, 13th September 1863.

I have just come away from hearing a very remarkable sermon at the Protestant church here, of which I should like to give you some idea before it goes out of my head. The preacher was a M. Bevel, a native of Dieppe, now a minister at Amsterdam, where he has a high reputation. He is here visiting his mother, which visit I should say is likely to be cut short if he goes on preaching such sermons as he gave us to-day, or else a liberty is allowed in the pulpit in France which is not to be had elsewhere. The service began with a hymn. Then a layman read out the Commandments at a desk. Then we sang part of Psalm xxv.; one of the verses ran:

Qui craint Dieu, qui veut bien,

Jamais ne s'égarera,

Car au chemin qu'il doit suivre

Dieu même le conduira—

À son aise et sans ennui

Il verra le plus long âge,

Et ses enfans après lui

Auront la terre en partage.

Good healthy doctrine this, and an apt introduction to the sermon. While we were singing, M. Revel mounted the pulpit. He is a man of thirty-five or thereabouts; middlesized, bald, dark; with a broad brow, large gray eyes, and sharp, well-cut features. After two short extempore prayers—almost the only ones I have ever heard in which there was nothing offensive—he began his sermon on a text in Ecclesiastes. As it had little bearing on the argument, and was never alluded to again, I do not repeat it.

"There is much talk," M. Revel began, "in our day about an order of nature. All acknowledge it; as science advances it is found more and more to be unchangeable. We ought to rejoice in this unchangeableness of the order of nature, for it is a proof of the existence of a God of order. Had we found the earth all in confusion it would have been a proof that there could be no such God. But this God has established a moral order for man as unchangeable as the order of nature. It was recognised by the heathen who worshipped Nemesis. The whole of history is one long witness to this moral order, but we need not go back far for examples. Look at Poland, partitioned by three great monarchs, and at what is happening and will happen there. Look at America, the land of equality, of freedom, of boundless plenty, and what has come on her for the one great sin of slavery. Look at home, at the story of the great man who ruled France at the beginning of our new era, the man of success—'*qui éblouissait lui-même en éblouissant les autres*,' who answered by victory upon victory those who maintained that principle had still something to say to the government of the world, and remember his end on the rock in mid-ocean.

"Be sure, then, that there is an unchangeable moral order, and this is the first law of it, '*Qui fait du mal fait du malheur.*' The most noticeable fact in connection with this moral order which our time is bringing out is the *solidarité* of the human race. The *solidarité* of the family and the nation was recognised in old times. Now, commerce and intercourse are breaking down the barriers of nations. A rebellion in China, a war in America, is felt at once in France, and the full truth is dawning upon us that nothing but a universal brotherhood will satisfy men. But you may say that punishment follows misdoing so slowly that the moral order is virtually set aside. Do not believe it. '*Qui fait du mal fait du malheur.*' The law is certain; but if punishment followed at once, and fully, on misdoing, mankind would be degraded. On the other hand, '*Qui fait du bon fait du bonheur*,' and this law is equally fixed and unchangeable in the moral order of the world.

"You may wonder that I have scarcely used the name of Christ to you to-day; but what need? I have spoken of humanity; He is the Son of Man, of a universal brotherhood which has no existence without Him, of which He is the founder and the head."

As we came out of church it was amusing to hear the comments of the audience, at least of the English portion. Some called it rank Socialism, others paganism, others good sound Christian teaching; but all seemed to agree that it was very stirring stuff, and that this would be the last time that M. Bevel would be allowed to address his old fellow-townsmen from the pulpit. Indeed, his sketch of Napoleon I. was much too true to be acceptable to Napoleon III., and though his doctrine of universal brotherhood may be overlooked, I should scarcely think that his historical views can be. I was utterly astonished myself to hear such a sermon in a French pulpit. I had never heard M. Bevel before; but his reputation, which seems to be very great, is thoroughly deserved. The sermon of which I have tried to give you a skeleton lasted for fifty minutes, and never flagged for a moment. Sometimes he was familiar and colloquial, sometimes impassioned, sometimes argumentative, but always eloquent. He spoke with his whole body as well as with his voice, which last organ was managed with rare skill; and, indeed, every faculty of the man was thoroughly trained for his work, and so well trained, that notwithstanding my English dislike to action or oratory in a pulpit, I never felt that it was overdone or in bad taste. In short, I never heard such scientific preaching, and came away disabused of the notion that extempore sermons must be either flat, or vulgar, or insincere. I only wish our young parsons would take the same pains in cultivating their natural gifts as M. Revel has done, and hope that any of them who may chance to read this will take an opportunity the next time they are at Amsterdam of going to hear M. Revel, and taking a lesson. I have been trying to satisfy myself for the last three days what it is which makes this town so wonderfully different from any English provincial town of the same size. I do not mean the watering-place end of it next the sea, which is composed of the crystal palace known as the *établissement des bains*, great hotels, and expensive lodging-houses,—this quarter is inhabited by strangers of all nations, and should be compared to Brighton or Scarborough,—but the quiet old town behind, which has nothing in common with the watering-place, and is as hum-drum a place as Peterborough. As far as I can make out, the difference lies in the enjoyment which these Dieppois seem to take in their daily business. We are called a nation of shopkeepers now by all the world, so I suppose there must be some truth in the nickname. But certainly the Englishman does his shopkeeping with a very bad grace, and not the least as if he liked it. He sits or stands at his counter with grim, anxious face, and it requires an effort, after one has entered his trap and asked a question as to any article, to retire without buying. The moment his closing time comes, up go the shutters, and he clears out of the shop, and takes himself off out of sight and hearing of it as fast as he can. But here in Dieppe (and the rule holds good, I think, in all French towns) the people seem really to delight in their shops, and by preference to live in them, and in the slice of street in front of them, rather than in any other place. In fact, the shops seem to be convenient places opened to enable their owners to *causer* with the greatest possible number of their neighbours and other people, rather than places for the receipt of custom and serious making of money. I doubt if any man is a worse hand at shopping than I, and yet I can go boldly into any shop here, and turn over the articles, and chaffer over them, and then go out without buying, and yet feel that I have conferred a benefit rather than otherwise on the proprietor of the establishment. And as to closing time, there is no such thing. The only difference seems to be that after a certain hour, if you choose to walk into a shop, you will probably find yourself in a family party. No one turns off the gas until he goes to bed, so as you loiter along you have the advantage of seeing everything that is going on, and the inhabitants have what they clearly hold to be an equivalent, the opportunity of looking at and talking about you. The master of the shop sits at his ease, sometimes reading his journal, sometimes still working at his trade in an easygoing way, as if it were a pleasure to him, and chatting away as he works. His wife is either working with her needle or casting up the accounts of the day, but in either case is ready in a moment to look up and join in any talk that may be going on. The younger branches of the family disport themselves on the floor, or play dominoes on the counter, or flirt with some neighbour of the opposite sex who has dropped in, in the further corners. The pastrycooks' seem favourite social haunts, and often you will find two or three of the nearest shops deserted, and the inmates gathered in a knot round the sleek, neatly-shaved citizens who preside in spotless white caps, jackets, and aprons, over these temples of good things. In short, the life of the Dieppe burgher is not cut into sharp lengths as it would be with us, one of which is religiously set apart for trade and nothing else. Business and pleasure seem with him to be run together, and he surrounds the whole with a halo of small-talk which seems to make life run off wonderfully easily and happily to him. Whether his method of carrying on trade results in as good articles as with us I cannot say, for the Dieppois is by no means guileless enough to part with his wares cheap, so that I have had very little experience of them. But certainly the general aspect of his daily life, so much more easy, so much more social than that of his compeer in England, has a good deal of fascination about it. On better acquaintance very possibly the charm might disappear, but at first one is inclined strongly to wish that we could take a leaf out of his book, and learn to take things more easily. The wisdom which has learnt that there are vastly few things in this world worth worrying about will, I fear, be a long time in leavening the British nation.

The people of Dieppe are a remarkably well-conducted and discreet folk in every way—wonderfully so when one considers their close neighbourhood to the richest and most fashionable crowd which frequents any French watering-place. Of these, and their amusements, and habits, and wonderful costumes in and out of the sea, I have no room to speak in this letter. They are now gone, or fast going, and this is the time for people of moderate means and quiet tastes, who wish to enjoy the deliciously exciting air and pretty scenery of this very charming old sea town, which furnished most of the ships for the invasion of England eight hundred years ago, and will well repay the costs of a counter invasion. Only let the English invader take care when he sets his foot on the Norman shore, unless he thinks it worth while to be fleeced for the honour and glory of being under the same roof with French dukes, Russian princes, and English milords, to give a wide berth to the Hotel Royal. I am happy to say I do not speak from personal experience, but only give voice to the universal outcry against the extortion of this huge hotel, the most fashionable in Dieppe. The last story is that an English nobleman travelling with a courier, who arrived late one evening, did not dine, and left early the next morning, had to pay a bill of 75 francs for his entertainment. The bill must have been a work of high art.

I hope in another letter to give you some notions of the watering-place life, which is very quaint and amusing, and as unlike our seaside doings as the old town is unlike our ordinary towns.

Bathing at Dieppe, 17th September 1863.

That great work, the *Sartor Resartus*, should have contained a chapter on bathing-dresses, and I have no doubt would have done so had the author been a frequenter of French watering-places. Each of these—even such a little place as Treport—has its *établissement des bains*, its etiquettes and rules as to the dress and comportment of its bathing populations; and Dieppe is the largest, and not the least quaint, of them all. The *établissement* here is a long glass and iron building like the Crystal Palace, with a dome in the middle, under which there are daily concerts and nightly balls; and a transept at each end, one of which is a very good reading-room, while in the other a mild kind of gambling goes on, under the form of a lottery, for smelling bottles, clocks, and such like ware. I am told that the play here is by no means so innocent as it looks, and that persons in search of investments for spare cash can be accommodated to any amount, but to a stranger nothing of this discloses itself. Between this building and the sea there runs a handsome esplanade, the favourite promenade, and immediately underneath are the rows of little portable canvas huts which serve as bathing machines. The ladies bathe under one end of the esplanade, and the gentlemen under the other, while the fashionable crowd leans over, or sits by the low esplanade wall, inspecting the proceedings. This contiguity is, no doubt, the cause of the wonderful toilets, *spécialités des bains*, which fill the shops here, and are used by all the ladies and many of the men. They consist of large loose trousers and a jacket with skirts, made of fine flannel or serge, of all shades of colour according to taste, and of waterproof bathing caps, all of which garments are trimmed with blue, or pink, or red bows and streamers. Over all the *baigneurs comme il faut* throw a large cloak, also tastefully trimmed. Thus habited the lady walks out of her hut attended by a maid, to whom when she reaches the water's edge she hands her cloak, and, taking the hand of one of the male *baigneurs*, proceeds with such plunges and dancings as she has a fancy for, and then returns to the shore, is enveloped in her cloak by her maid, and re-enters her hut. These male *baigneurs* are a necessary accompaniment of the performance. I have only heard of one case of resistance to the custom, which ended comically enough. A young Englishman, well known in foreign society, was here with his wife, who insisted on bathing, but vowed she would go into the water with no man but her husband. He consented, and in due course appeared on the ladies' side with his pretty wife, in most discreet apparel, went through the office of *baigneur*, and returned to his own side. This raised a storm among the lady bathers, and the authorities interfered. The next day the lady went to the gentlemen's side; but this was even more scandalous, and was also forbidden. The persecuted couple then took; to bathing at six in the morning; but, alas! on the second morning the esplanade was lined even at that untimely hour by young Frenchmen, who, though by no means early risers, had made a point of being out to assist at the bath of their eccentric friends, and as these last did not appreciate the *éclat* of performing alone for the amusement of their friends, the lawless efforts of *ces Anglais* came to an end. In England, where dress for the water is not properly attended to by either sex, one quite understands the rule of absolute separation; but here, where every lady is accompanied by a man in any case, where she is more covered than she is in a ballroom, and where all her acquaintance are looking on, it does not occur to one why she should not be accompanied by her husband. For, as on the land, here people are much better known by their dress in the water than by anything else. A young gentleman asked one of his partners whether she had seen him doing some particular feat of swimming that morning; she answered that she had not recognised him, to which he replied, "Oh! you may always know me by my straw hat and red ribbon." The separation here is certainly a farce, for at sixty yards, as we know from our musketry instructors, you recognise the features of the party; and the distance between the men and women bathers is not so much. The rule is enforced, however, at any depth. A brother and sister, both good swimmers, used to swim out and meet one another at the boat which lies in the offing in case of accidents. But this was stopped, as they talked together in English, which excited doubts as to their relationship. I suppose it would be more improper for girls and boys of marriageable age to swim together than to walk; but I vow at this moment I cannot see why.

You may fancy, sir, that in such a state of things as I have described, good stories on the great bathing subject are rife. The last relates to a beauty of European celebrity, who is known to be here and to be bathing, but keeps herself in such strict privacy that scarcely a soul has been able to get a look at her, even behind two thick veils. Had she really wished to be unnoticed she could not have managed worse. The mystery set all the female world which frequents the *établissement* in a tremor. They were like a knot of sportsmen when a stag of ten tines has been seen in the next glen, or when a 30 lb. salmon has broken the tackle of some cunning fisherman, and is known to lie below a certain stone. Of course, they were sure that something dreadful must have happened to her looks, which she who should be happy enough to catch her bathing would detect. In spite of all, the beauty eluded them for some time, but at last she has been stalked, and I am proud to say, sir, by a sportswoman of our own country. By chance this lady was walking at eight in the morning, when the tide was so low that no one was bathing. She saw a figure dressed *en bourgeoise* approaching the bathing-place, apparently alone, but two women suspiciously like maids followed at a respectful distance. It flashed across our countrywoman that this must be the incognita; she followed. To her delight, the three turned to the bathing-ground, and disappeared in two huts which had been placed together apparently by accident. She took up a position a few yards from the huts.

After an agonising pause the door opened, and a head appeared, which was instantly withdrawn, but now too late. The mystery was solved. It was too late-to send maids to the *directeur* of the baths to warn off the spectator, and, moreover, useless, for she politely declined to move, though there was nothing more to discover. The whole establishment is ringing with the news that the beauty is *pale comme une morte*, and the inference, of course, follows that paint has been forbidden. You will also, sir, no doubt, be interested to know that she wears a red rose on the top of her bathing-cap, which, having regard to her present complexion, does not say much for her taste in the choice of colours.

But if the water toilets here are fabulous, what shall I say of those on the land? The colours, the textures, the infinite variety, and general loudness of these bewilder the sight and baffle the pen of ordinary mortals. The keenest rivalry is kept up amongst the fair frequenters of the establishment. They sit by hundreds there working and casing of afternoons, while the band plays from three to six, or sweeping about on the esplanade; and in the evening are there again in ever new and brighter colours. The *Dieppe Journal* comments on the most striking toilets. It noticed with commendation the purple velvet petticoats of the ladies of a millionaire house; it glowed in describing the "*toilette Écossaise*" of another rich Frenchwoman. An officer on reading the announcement laid down the paper, and addressed a lady, his neighbour, "Mais, madame, comment est que ça se fait?" He, worthy man, had but one idea of the toilet in question, which he had gained from the Highland regiments in the Crimea. I am happy to say, both for their own sakes and their husbands and fathers, that the Englishwomen are by far the most simply dressed. The men generally speaking are clad like rational beings, but with many exceptions. I hear of a celebrity in gray velvet knickerbockers and pink silk stockings, but have not seen him. A man in a black velvet suit, and a red beard reaching his waist, has just walked past, without apparently exciting wonder in any breast but that of your contributor.

Dieppe must be a paradise to the rising generation. The children share all the amusements of their elders, and have also special entertainments of their own, amongst which one notes specially two balls a week at the establishment. The whole building is brilliantly lighted every evening, and on these nights the space under the central dome is cleared of chairs, and makes a splendid ballroom. Here the little folk assemble, and go through the whole performance solemnly, just like their elders. The raised permanent seats are occupied by mammas, nurses, governesses, and the public. The girls sit round on the lowest seats, and the boys gather in groups talking to them, or walking about in the centre. They are of all nations, in all costumes—one boy in a red Garibaldian blouse and belt I noted as the most dangerous flirt. There were common English jackets and trousers, knickerbockers of many colours, and many little blue French uniforms. There was no dancer older than fifteen, and some certainly as young as seven. When the music began, the floor was at once covered with couples, who danced quadrilles, waltzes, and a pretty dance like the Schottische, to the tune of "When the green leaves come again." At the end of each dance the girls were handed to their chairs with bows worthy of Beau Brummel. There were at least 200 grown folk looking on, and a prettier sight I have seldom seen, for the children danced beautifully for the most part. Should I like my children to be amongst them? That is quite another affair. On the whole, I incline to agree with the ladies with whom I went, that it would, perhaps, do boys good, but must be utterly bad for the girls. I certainly never saw before so self-possessed a set of young gentlemen as those in question, and doubt if any one of them will ever feel shy in after-life.

Last Sunday afternoon: again, we had a *fete des vacances* for the children. The *Gazette des Bains* announced, "À deux heures, ascensions grotesques, l'enlèvement du phoque; à deux heures et demie, distribution de jouets et bonbons; à trois heures, course à ânes, montés par des jockeys grosse-tête,"—a most piquant programme. Not to mention the other attractions, what could the *enlèvement du phoque* be? In good time I went into the *établissement* grounds at the cost of a franc, and was at once guided by the crowd to the brink of a small pond, where sure enough a veritable live seal was swimming about, asking us all as plainly as mild brown eyes could speak what all the rout meant, and then diving smoothly under, to appear again on the other side of the pond. Were the cruel Frenchmen actually going to send the gentle beast up into the air? My speculations were cut short by the first comic ascent and the shouts of the juveniles. A figure very like Richard Doyle's Saracens in the illustrations to Rebecca and Rowena, with large head, bottle nose, and little straight arms and legs, mounted suddenly into the air, and went away, wobbling and bobbing, before the wind. Another and another followed, as fast as they could be filled with gas. The wind blew towards the town, and there was great excitement as to their destiny, for they rose only to about the height of the houses. I own I was surprised to find myself so deeply interested whether the absurd little Punchinellos would clear the chimneys. One only failed, a fellow in a three-cornered hat like a beadle's, and, refusing to mount, was soon torn in pieces by the boys. The last was a balloon of the figure of a seal, and I was much relieved when we all trooped away to the distribution of *bonbons*, leaving the real phoca still gliding about in his pond with wondering eyes. The *bonbons* were distributed in the most polite manner, the handfuls which were thrown amongst the crowd only calling forth a "Pardon Monsieur," "Pardon Mademoiselle," as they were picked up, instead of the hurly-burly and scramble we should have had at home. The donkey races might better be called processions, which went three times round the *établissement*. The winner was ridden by a jockey whose *grosse tête* was that of a cock, in compliment, I suppose, to the national bird; the lion jockey was nowhere, but he beat the cook's boy, who came in last. The figures were well got up, and some of the heads really funny. At night we had fireworks, and a grand pyrotechnic drama of the taking of the old castle, which stands on the chalk cliff right over the *établissement* and commanding the town. The garrison joined in the fun, and assaulted the walls twice amidst discharges of rockets and great guns. The third assault was successful, and the red-legged soldiers swarmed on the walls in a blaze of light and planted the tricolour. A brilliant scroll of "*Vive l'Empéreur*" came out on the dark castle walls above their heads, and so the show ended. The castle, by the way, is a most picturesque building. One of the towers has been favourably noticed by Mr. Ruskin. It is also to be reverenced as the stronghold of Henry IV. and the Protestants. It was here, just before the battle of Arques, that he made the celebrated answer to a faint-hearted ally, who spoke doubtfully as to the disparity of numbers, "You forget to count God and the good cause, who are on our side." It will never be of any use in modern warfare, but makes a good barrack and a most magnificent place for a pyrotechnic display for the delectation of young folk, in which definition for these purposes may be included the whole of the population of France.

As I am writing, a troop of acrobats pass along the green between this hotel and the sea, followed by a crowd of boys. There is the strong man in black velvet carrying the long balancing triangle, on which he is about to support the light fellow in yellow who walks by his side.

There is an athletic fellow in crimson breeches, carrying a table on his head, and a clown with two chairs accompanying. There they have pitched on the green, and are going to begin, and the English boys are leaving their cricket, and the French boys their kites and indiarubber handballs, and a goodly ring is forming, out of which, if they are decent tumblers, I hope they may turn an honest franc or two.

They are not only decent but capital tumblers, the best I have seen for many a day, especially the man in crimson. He has balanced three glasses full of water on his forehead, and then lain down on his back, and passed himself, tumblers and all, through two small hoops. He has placed one chair upon the table, and then has tilted the second chair on two legs upon the seat of the first, and on this fearfully precarious foundation has been balancing himself with his legs straight up in the air while I could count thirty! The strong man has just run up behind the man in yellow, who was standing with his legs apart, and, stooping, has put his head between the yellow man's legs and thrown him a backward somersault! I must positively go down and give them half a franc. It is a swindle to look on at such good tumbling for nothing.

P.S.—Imagine my delight, sir, when I got down on the green to find they were the tumblers of my native land. They joined a French circus for a tour some weeks back, but could get no money, and so broke off and are working their way home. They can speak no French, and find it very difficult to get leave to perform, as they have to do in all French towns. The crowd of English boys seemed to be doing their duty by them, so I hope they will speedily be able to raise their passage-money and return to the land of double stout and liberty.

Normandy, 20th September 1863.

To an Englishman with little available spare cash and time, and in want of a thorough change of scene and air, which category I take to include a very handsome percentage of our fellow-countrymen, I can recommend a run in Normandy without the slightest hesitation. I am come to the age when one learns to be what the boys call *cocksure* of nothing in this world, but am, nevertheless, prepared to take my stand on the above recommendation without fear or reservation. For in Normandy he will get an exquisitely light and bracing air, a sky at least twice as far off as our English one (which alone will raise his spirits to at least twice their usual altitude), a pleasant, lively, and well-to-do people, a picturesque country, delicious pears, and, to an Englishman, some of the most interesting old towns in the world out of his own island. All this he may well enjoy for ten days for a five-pound note, or thereabouts, in addition to his return fare to Dieppe or Havre. So let us throw up our insular vacation wide-awakes, and bless the men who invented steam, and pears, and Norman architecture, "and everything in the world beside," as the good old song of "the leathern bottèl" has it, and start for the fair land from which our last conquerors came before the days get shorter than the nights. Alas! how little of that blissful time now remains to us of the year of grace 1863.

It is some few years, I forget how many, since I was last in a Norman town, and must confess that in some respects they have changed for the better, externally at least, now that the Second Empire has had time to make itself felt in them. All manner of police arrangements, the sweeping, lighting, and paving, are marvellously improved, and there is an air of prosperity about them which does one good. Even in Rouen, the centre of their cotton district, there are scarcely any outward signs of distress, although, so far as I could see, not more than one in three of the mills is at work. I was told that there are still nearly 30,000 operatives out of work in the town and neighbourhood, who have no means of subsistence except any odd job they can pick up to earn a few sous about the quays and markets, but if it be so they kept out of sight during my wanderings about the town. But there is one characteristic sign of the empire to be noted in all these same Norman towns, for which strangers will not feel thankful, though the inhabitants may. The building and improving fever is on them all. In Rouen, amongst other improvements, a broad new street is being made right through some of the oldest parts of the town, from the quays straight up to the boulevards, which it joins close by the railway-station. This Grand Rue de l'Empereur will be a splendid street when finished, to judge by the few houses which are already built at the lower end. Meantime, the queer gables of the houses whose neighbours have been destroyed, and a chapel or two, and an old tower, standing out all by itself, which would make the architectural fortune of any other city, and which find themselves with breathing room now, for the first time, I should think, in the last five hundred years, look down ruefully on the cleared space, in anticipation of the hour rapidly approaching, when they will be again shut out from human ken by four-storied stone palaces, and this time, undoubtedly, for good and all. They can never hold up until another improving dynasty arrives.

At Havre the same process is going on. New houses are springing up all along the new boulevards. Between the town and Frescati's great hotel and bathing establishment, which faces the sea, there used to stand a curious old round tower of great size, which commanded the mouth of the harbour, and some elaborate fortifications of more modern date. All these have been levelled, old and new together, and the ground is now clear for building, and will, no doubt, be covered long before I shall see it again. Large seaports are always interesting towns, and Havre, besides the usual attractions of such places, has a sort of shop in greater perfection than any other port known to me. In these you can buy or inspect curiosities, alive and dead, from all parts of the world. Parrots of all colours of the rainbow scream at the door, long cages full of love-birds, and all manner of other delicate little feathered creatures one has never seen elsewhere, hang on the walls, or stand about amongst china monsters, and cases of amber, and inlaid stools from Stamboul, and marmoset monkeys, and goodness knows what other temptations to solvent persons with a taste for collections or pets. To neither of these weaknesses can I plead guilty, so after a short inspection I stroll to the harbour's mouth, and do wonder to think over the astounding audacity of our late countryman, Sir Sidney Smith, who ran his ship close in here, and proceeded in his boats to cut out a French frigate under the guns of the old fortifications. His ship got aground, and was taken; he also. But, after all, it was less of a forlorn hope than throwing himself with his handful of men into Acre, and facing Bonaparte there, which last moderately lunatic act made him a name in history. *Audace! et encore d'audace! et toujours d'audace!* was the rule which brought our sailors triumphantly through the great war. And there is another picture in that drama which Havre harbour calls up in the English mind, to put in the scale against Sir Sidney's failure—I mean Citizen Muskein and his gunboats skedaddling from Lieutenant Price in the *Badger*. Do you remember, sir, Citizen Muskein's—or rather Canning's—inimitable address to his gunboats in the *Anti-Jacobin?*—

Gunboats, unless you mean hereafter

To furnish food for British laughter,

Sweet gunboats, and your gallant crew,

Tempt not the rocks of St. Marcou,

Beware the *Badger's* bloody pennant

And that d——d invalid Lieutenant!

Enough of war memories, and for the future the very last thing one wishes to have to do with this simple, cheery, and, for all I can see, honest people, is to fight them.

There are packets twice a day from Havre across the mouth of the Seine, a seven miles' run, to Honfleur, described in guide-books as a dirty little town, utterly without interest. I can only say I have seldom been in a place of its size, not the site of any great historic event, which is better worth spending an afternoon in, and I should strongly advise my typical Englishman to follow this route. In the first place, the situation is beautiful. From the steep wooded heights above the town, where are a chapel, much frequented by sailors, and some villas, there are glorious views up the Seine, across to Havre, and out over the sea. Then, in the town, there is the long street, which runs down to the lighthouse, and which, I suppose, the guide-book people never visit, as it is out of the way. It is certainly as picturesque a street as can be found in Rouen, or any other French town I have ever seen—except Troyes, by the way. The houses are not large, but there is scarcely one of them which Prout would not be proud to ask to sit to him.

Then there is the church in the centre of the town by the market-place, with the most eccentric of little spires. It seems, at an early period of the Middle Ages, to have taken it into its clock—or whatever answers to a spire's head—that it would seer more of the world, and to have succeeded in getting about thirty yards away from its nave. Here, probably finding locomotion a tougher business than it reckoned on, it has fallen asleep, and, while it slept, several small houses crept up against its base and fell asleep also. And there it remains to this day, looking down over the houses in which people live, and many apples and pears are being sold, and crying, like the starling, "I can't get out." There is a splendid straight avenue, stretching a mile and a half up the Caen road, and a good little harbour full of English vessels, which ply the egg and fruit trade, and over every third door in the sailors' quarter you see "Cook-house" written up in large letters, for the benefit of the British sailor.

The railway to Lisieux passes through a richly wooded, hilly country, and then runs out into the great plain in which Caen lies. The city of William the Conqueror is quite worthy of him, which is saying a good deal. For, though one may not quite share Mr Carlyle's enthusiasm for "Wilhelmus Conquestor," it must be confessed that he is, at least, one of the three strongest men who have ruled in England, and that in the long run he has done a stroke of good work for our nation. The church of the Abbey *des Hommes*, which he began in 1066, and of which Lanfranc was the first abbot, stands just as he left it, except the tops of two towers at the west end, which were finished two centuries later. It is a pure Norman church, 320 feet long, and 98 feet high in the nave and transepts, and the simplest and grandest specimen of that noble style I have ever seen. William's grave is before the high altar, the spot marked by a dark stone, and no king ever lay in more appropriate sepulchre. The Huguenots rifled the grave and scattered his bones, but his strong stern spirit seems to rest over the place. There is an old building near the Abbey surmounted by a single solid pinnacle, under which is a room which tradition says he occupied. It is now filled with the wares of a joiner who lives below. Caen is increasing in a solid manner in its outskirts, but seems less disturbed and altered by the building mania than any of her sisters. There was an English population of 4000 and upwards living here before 1848, but the English Consul fairly frightened them away by assurances of his inability to protect them (against what does not seem to have been settled) in that wild time, and now there are not as many hundreds. One of the survivors is the Commissionaire of the Hôtel d'Angleterre, West by name, a really intelligent and serviceable man, well up to his work. It is scarcely ever worth while to spend a franc on a commissionaire, but West is an exception to the rule. His father was in the lace trade, which is active in Caen, but his premises were burnt down some years since, and an end put to his manufacture. West is now trying to revive the family business, and one of his first steps was to get over a new lace machine, and a man to work it, from England. It has not proved a good speculation as yet, for no one else can manage the machine, and the Englishman insists on being drunk half his time.

We left by one of the steamers which ply daily from Caen to Havre. The run down the river is chiefly interesting from the quarries on its banks. They are not the principal quarries, but are of very considerable extent; and from the quantities of tip, heaped into moderate-sized grass-covered hills by the river side, it is plain that they must have been in work here for centuries. You see the stone in many places lying like rich Cheddar cheese, and cut as regularly in flakes as a grocer would cut his favourite cheeses. The stone is very soft when it comes first from the quarries, but gains its great hardness and sharpness after a short exposure. After passing the quarries we got between salt marshes haunted by abundance of jack snipe, and so we passed out to sea.

Gleanings from Boulogne

There is one large portion of the French people which has improved marvellously in appearance in the last few years, and that is the army. The setting up of the French soldier of the line used to be much neglected, but now you never see a man, however small and slight, who does not carry himself and move as if every muscle in his body had been thoroughly and scientifically trained. And this is the actual fact. They have the finest system of military gymnastics which has ever been seen. In every garrison town there is a gymnasium, in which the men have to drill as regularly as on the parade-ground. The one close to the gate of the old town of Boulogne is an admirable specimen, and well worth a visit. Our authorities are, I believe, slowly following in the steps of the French, but little has as yet been done. There is no branch of army reform which may more safely be pressed on. We have undoubtedly the finer material. The English soldier is a bigger and more muscular man than the French soldier, but is far behind him in his physical education, and must remain so until we provide a proper system of gymnastic training, which, by the bye, will benefit the general health of the men, and develop their intelligence as well as their muscles.

During our stay at Boulogne there was some very heavy weather. A strong sou'-wester came on one night, and by two o'clock next day, when I went down, was hurling the angry green waves against the great beams of the southern pier in fearful fashion. The entrance to the harbour, as most of your readers will remember, is quite narrow, not one hundred yards across between the two pier heads. The ebb-tide was sweeping down from the north, and, meeting the gale right off the harbour's mouth, made a battling and raging sea which brought one's heart into one's mouth to look at. The weather was quite bright, and though the wind was so strong that I held my hat on with difficulty, the northern pier was crowded, as the whole force of the sea was spent against the southern pier, over which it was leaping every moment. We were in comparative shelter, and could watch, Without being drenched with spray, the approach of one of the fishing smacks of the port, which was coming home. I shall not easily forget the sight. We stood there, jammed together, rough sailors, fishwomen, Cockneys, weatherbound soldiers, well-dressed ladies, a crowd of all ranks, the wind singing through us so that we could scarcely make our nearest neighbours hear. Not that we wanted to talk. The sight of the small black hull and ruddy brown sail of the smack, now rising on the crest of a great wave, and the next moment all but disappearing behind it, took away the desire, almost the power, of speech. Two boats, manned with fishermen, pulled to the harbour's mouth, and lay rolling in the comparatively still water just within the shelter of the southern pier head. It was comforting to see them there, though if any catastrophe had happened they could never have lived in that sea. But the gallant little smack needed no help. She was magnificently steered, and came dancing through the wildest part of the race without shipping a single sea, seeming to catch each leaping wave just in the spot where it was easiest to ride over. As she slid out of the seething cauldron into the smooth water past the waiting boats the crowd drew a long breath, and many of us hurried back to get a close view of her as she ran into her place amongst the other fishing boats alongside the quay. I envied the grizzly old hero at the helm, as he left his place, threw off his dreadnought coat, and went to help the two men and two boys who were taking in the sail and coiling away the ropes. There was much shouting and congratulation from above; but they made little answer, and no fuss. Their faces struck me very much, especially the boys', which were full of that quiet self-contained look one sees in Hook's pictures. There was no other boat in the offing then, so I went home; but within a few hours heard that a smack had capsized in the harbour's mouth, with the loss of one man. I only marvel how the rest could have been saved.

On the 1st of October in every year there is a solemn festival of the seafaring people of Boulogne, and the sea is blessed by their pastors. I was anxious to wait for the ceremony, but was unable to do so. There seems to be a strange mixture of trust in God and superstition in all people who "occupy their business on the great waters." There is a little chapel looking down on Boulogne port full of thank-offerings of the sailors' wives, where the fishwomen go up to plead with God, and pour out the agony of their souls in rough weather. There are propitiatory gifts, too, by the side of the thank-offerings, and the shadow of a tyrannous power in nature, to be bought off with gifts, darkens the presence of the true Refuge from the storm. There are traces, too, of a more direct idolatry in the town. In the year 643 of our era the Madonna came to Boulogne in an open boat, so runs the story, and left an image with the faithful, which soon became the great religious lion of the neighbourhood, drawing largely, and performing a series of miracles all through the Middle Ages. When Henry VIII. took the town the English carried off the image, but it was restored in good condition when peace came, and as powerful as ever for wonder-working. The Huguenots got hold of it half a century later, and were supposed to have destroyed it; but an image, which at any rate did duty for it, was ultimately fished up out of a well. Doubts as to identity, however, having arisen, the matter was referred to the Sorbonne, and a jury of doctors declared in favour of the genuineness of the article which was forthcoming. And so it continued to practise with varying success until the Revolution, when the Jacobins laid hands on it, broke it up, and burnt it, thinking to make once for all an end of this and other idol-worships. But a citizen not so enlightened as his neighbours stayed by the fire, and succeeded at last in rescuing what he declared to be an arm of the original image, which remains an object of veneration still, and is said not to have lost all healing power. But it is far inferior in this respect to some drops of the holy blood, for the reception of which a countrywoman of ours has built a little chapel in the suburbs.

Boulogne has all the marks of rapidly increasing material prosperity which may be seen now in every French town, one of the many fruits of which is a wonderful improvement in the condition of the streets and thoroughfares. The fine new buildings, the look of the shops and of the people, all tell the same tale. In fact, one comes away from France now with a feeling that, so far as surface polish and civilisation are concerned, this is the country which is going to the front. Whether it goes any deeper is a matter upon which a traveller flitting about for a few weeks cannot venture an opinion.

I came back in one of the daily packets to London Bridge, which, besides carrying seventy passengers, was piled fore and aft with cargo. There were 400 cases of wine on deck, besides other packages, which sorely curtailed our walking privileges. But the boats are good boats, and the voyage past Dover, through the Downs, round the North Foreland, and up the Thames, is so full of life and interest that it is well worth making a long day of it, if one is a moderately good sailor. The advertisements call it eight and a half hours, which means eleven; but it is not a moment too long.

Blankenberghe

Yesterday (14th August) we were warned by meagre fare at the *table d'hôte* of our hotel that it was the vigil of some saint's day. Our gastronomic knowledge was enlarged by the opportunity of partaking of boiled mussels. A small and delicate species of this little fish—despised of Englishmen—is found in extraordinary quantities on this coast. The sand is dotted with the shells after every ebb. The wattles of the jetties are full of them. After the first shock of having a salad bowl full of small black shells presented to one, following immediately on a delicate *potage à l'oseille*, the British citizen may pursue his education in this direction fearlessly, with the certainty of becoming acquainted with a delicate and appetising morsel; and he will return to his native country with at least a toleration for "winks" and "pickled whelks," when he sees them vended at corner stalls in Clare Market or in the Old Kent Road, for the benefit of the dangerous classes of his fellow-citizens who take their meals in the street. In these Flemish parts they are eaten with bread and butter, and even as whitebait, and by all classes.

After the meal I consulted the calendar in my pocket-book as to the approaching festival, not wishing to thrust my heretical ignorance unnecessarily on the notice of the simple folk who inhabit the *Lion d'Or*. That obstinately Protestant document, however, informed me simply that the Rev. E. Irving was born on this day in 1792, probably not the saint I was in quest of. A *Churchman's Almanac*, with which the only English lady in the place was provided, was altogether silent as to the day. In the end, therefore, I was obliged to fall back upon the bright-eyed little *demoiselle de la maison*, who informed me that it was the vigil of the Assumption of the Virgin, and that the *fête* was one greatly honoured by the community of Blankenberghe.

Thus prepared, I was not surprised at being roused at five in the morning by the clumping of sabots and clinking of hammers in the street below—my room is a corner one, looking from two windows on the Rue d'Eglise, the principal street of the place, and from the other two on the Rue des Pecheurs, or "Visschurs' Straet," which runs across the northern end of the Rue d'Eglise. A flight of broad steps here runs up on to the Digue, or broad terrace fronting the sea, and at the foot of these steps they were erecting a temporary altar, and over it a large picture of fishermen hauling in nets full of monsters of the deep. They had brought it from the parish church, and, as such pictures go, it was by no means a bad one. Presently tricoloured flags began to appear from the windows of most of the houses in both streets, and here and there garlands of bright-coloured paper were hung across from one side to the other. As the morning advanced the bells from the church and convent called the simple folk to mass at short intervals, six, half-past seven, nine, and grand mass at ten. The call seemed to be answered by more people than we had fancied the town could have held. At eleven there was to be a procession, and now miniature altars with lighted candles appeared in many of the ground-floor windows, both of shops and private houses; and the streets were strewed with rushes and diamond-shaped pieces of coloured paper. Punctual to its time the head of the procession came round the corner of "Visschurs' Straet," half a dozen small boys ringing bells leading the way. Then came the beadledom of Blankenberghe, in the shape of several imposing persons in municipal uniform, then three little girls dressed in white, with bouquets, more boys, including a diligent but not very skilful drummer, six or seven other maidens in white, somewhat older than their predecessors, of whom the centre one carried some ornament of tinsel and flowers. Then came the heavy silk canopy, supported by four light poles carried by acolytes, and surrounded by choristers, of whom the leader bore a large silver censer, and under the canopy marched a shaven monk in cream-coloured brocade satin, carrying the pyx, and a less gorgeously attired brother with an open missal. Around the whole of the procession, to protect it from the accompanying crowd, were a belt of bronzed fishermen in their best clothes, some carrying staves, some hymn-books, and almost all joining in the chant which was rolled out by the priest, in a powerful bass with a kind of metallic ring in it, as they neared the altar at the foot of the steps. Here the whole procession paused, and the greater part knelt, while the priest put incense in the censer, and made his obeisances and prayed in an unknown tongue, and the censer boy swung his sweet-smelling smoke about, and the fishermen and their wives and children prayed too, in their own tongue, I suppose, and their own way, probably for fair weather and plenty of fish, and let us hope for brave and gentle hearts to meet whatever rough weather and short commons may be in store for them by land or water, Then the procession rose, and passed down the Rue d'Eglise, pausing at the corner of the little market-place opposite a rude figure of the Madonna in a niche over some pious doorway, [Greek phrase] and so out of sight. And the *bourgeois* blew out the candles and took away the chairs on which, while the halt lasted, they had been kneeling from their shop windows, putting back the bathing dresses, and the shell boxes, and other sea-side merchandise, while the whole non-shopkeeping population, and the neighbours from Bruges, and the strangers who fill the hotels and lodging-houses turned out upon the splendid sands and on the Digue to enjoy their *fête*-day. In the afternoon the *corps de musique* of the communal schools of Bruges gave a gratuitous concert to us all by the permission of the communal administration of that town, as we bathed, or promenaded, or sipped coffee or liqueurs in the broad verandahs of the *cafés* which line the Digue. Gaily dressed middle-class women (of upper classes, as we understand them, I see none), in many-coloured garments and immense structures of false back hair, such as these eyes have never before seen; a sprinkling of Belgian officers in uniform, Russians, Frenchmen,

Germans a few, and two Anglo-Saxons, Englishmen I cannot say, for one is an American citizen and the other your contributor, who compose the only English-speaking males, so far as I can judge; groups of Flemish women of the people in long black cloth cloaks, with large hoods lined with black satin, more expensive probably, but not nearly so picturesque as the old red cloak which thirty years ago was the almost universal Sunday dress of women in Wiltshire, Berkshire, and other Western counties; little old-fashioned girls in nice mob caps, and the fishermen in excellent blue broad-cloth jackets and trousers, and well-blacked shoes or boots, instead of the huge sabots of their daily life; in short, every soul, I suppose, in Blankenberghe, from the Bourgmestre who sits on his throne, to the donkey-boy who drives along his Neddy under a freight of children, at half a franc an hour, whenever he can entice the small fry from the superior attraction of engineering with the splendid sand, spends his or her three or four hours on the Digue, enjoying whatever of the music, gossip, coffee, beer, or other pastimes they are inclined to or can afford; and in that whole crowd of pleasant holiday-making folk there is not one single trace of poverty, not a starved face, not a naked foot, not a ragged garment. It is the same on the week-days. The people, notably the fishermen and *baigneurs*, dress roughly, but they have all comfortable thick worsted stockings in their sabots, and their jerseys and overalls are ample and satisfactory. Why is it that in nine places out of ten on the Continent this is so, and that in England you shall never be able to find a watering-place which is not deformed more or less by poverty and thriftlessness? Right across the sea, there, on the Norfolk coast, lie Cromer and Sherringham. More daring sailors never manned lifeboat, more patient fishermen never dragged net, than the seafaring folk of those charming villages. They are courteous, simple, outspoken folk, too, singularly attractive in their looks and ways. But, alas! for the rags, and the grinding poverty, declaring itself in a dozen ways, in the cottages, in the children's looks, in the women's premature old age. When will England wake up, and get rid of the curse of her wealth and the curse of her poverty? When will an Englishman be able again to look on at a fête-day in Belgium, or Switzerland, or Germany, or France, without a troubled conscience and a pain in his heart, as he thinks of the contrast at home, and the bitter satire in the old, worn-out name of "Merry England?" It is high time that we all were heartsick over it, for the canker grows on us. Those who know London best will tell you so; those who know the great provincial towns and country villages will tell you so, except perhaps that the latter are now getting depopulated, and so contain less altogether of joy or sorrow. However, sir, there are other than these holiday times in which to dwell on this dark subject. I ought to apologise for having fallen into it unawares, when I sat down merely to put on paper, if I could in a few lines, and impart to your readers the exceeding freshness of the feeling which the feast-day at this little Belgian watering-place leaves on one. But who knows when he sits down, at any rate in the holidays, what he is going to write? However good your intentions, at times you can't "get the hang of it," can't say the thing you meant to say.

You may wonder, too, at this sudden plunge into the *fête* of the Assumption at Blankenberghe, when I have never warned you even that I had flitted from my round on the great crank which grinds for us all so ruthlessly in the parts about the Strand and the Inns of Court. Well, sir, I plead in my defence the test that a very able friend of mine applies to novels. He opens the second volume and reads a chapter; if that tempts him, on he goes to the end of the book; if it is very good indeed, he then goes back, and fairly begins at the beginning. So I hope your readers will be inclined to peruse in future weeks some further gossip respecting this place, which should perhaps have preceded the *fête*-day. If they should get to take the least interest in Blankenberghians and their works and ways, it is more than these latter can be said to do about them, for in the two or three cheap sheets which I find on the table here, and which constitute the press of this corner of Belgium, there is seldom more than a couple of lines devoted to the whole British Empire. The fact that there is not another Englishman in the place, and that the American above mentioned, the only other representative of our English-speaking stock here, went once to see the Derby, and got so bored by two o'clock that he left the Downs and walked back to Epsom station, enduring the whole chaff of the road, and finding the doors locked and the clerks and porters all gone up to the race, ought to be enough to make them curious— curious enough at any rate for long-vacation purposes. There are plenty of odds and ends of life a little out of our ordinary track lying about here to make a small "harvest for a quiet eye," which I am inclined to try and garner for you, if you think well. And are not the new King and Queen coming next week to delight their subjects, and witness many kinds of fireworks, and a *"concours des joueurs de boule, dits pas baenbolders,"* whatever these may be?

Belgian Bathing

I should like to know how many grown Englishmen or Englishwomen, apart from those unfortunates who are preparing for competitive examinations, are aware of the existence of this place? No Englishman is bound to know of it by any law of polite education acknowledged amongst us, for is it not altogether ignored in Murray?

Even Bradshaw's *Continental Guide* is silent as to its whereabouts. This is somewhat hard upon Blankenberghe, sturdy and rapidly growing little watering-place that she is, already exciting the jealousy of her fashionable neighbour, Ostend. It must be owned, however, that she returns the compliment by taking the slightest possible interest in the contemporary history of the British Empire. Nevertheless, the place has certain recommendations to persons in search of a watering-place out of England. If you are content with an hotel of the country, of which there is a large choice, you may have three good meals a day and a bedroom for six and a half francs, with a considerable reduction for families. Even at the fashionable hotels on the Digue the price is only eight or nine francs; and when you have paid your hotel bill you are out of all danger of extravagance, for there is literally nothing to spend money upon. Your bathing machine costs you sixpence. There are no pleasure boats and no wheeled vehicles for hire in the place, and no excursions if there were; shops there are none; and the market is of the smallest and meagerest kind. There are no beggars and no amusements, except bathing and the Kursaal. These, however, suffice to keep the inhabitants and visitors in a state of much contentment.

But now for the geography. From Ostend harbour to the mouth of the Scheldt is a dead flat, highly cultivated, and dotted all over with villages and farmhouses, but somewhat lower than high-water mark. The sea is kept out by an ancient and dilapidated-looking dyke, some fifty feet high, on the slopes of which flourishes a strong, reedy sort of grass, planted in tufts at regular intervals, to hold the loose soil together. The fine sand drifts up the dyke and blows over it, lying just like snow, so that if you half-close your eyes and look at it from fifty yards' distance, you may fancy yourself on a glacier in the Oberland. Blankenberghe is an ancient fishing village, lying just under the dyke, between eight and nine miles from Ostend. When it came into the minds of the inhabitants to convert it into a watering-place they levelled the top of their dyke for some 600 yards until it is only about twenty-five feet above high-water mark. They paved the sea face with good stone, and the fine flat walk on the top, thirty yards broad, with brick, and called it the Digue, in imitation of Ostend. They built a Kursaal, three or four great hotels, and half a dozen first-class lodging-houses, opening on to the Digue, with deep verandahs in front, and they brought a single line branch of the Flanders railway from Bruges, and the deed was accomplished. There is no such a sea-walk anywhere that I can remember as Blankenberghe Digue, from which you look straight away with nothing but sea between you and the North Pole. From the Digue you descend by a flight of twenty-four steps on one side to the sands, on the other into the town, the chief of these latter flights being at the head of the Rue d'Eglise, the backbone, as it were, of the place, which runs from the railway station to the Digue. There may be 1500 inhabitants out of the season, when all the Digue hotels and lodging-houses are shut up; at present, perhaps, another 1000, coming and going, and attracted by the bathing.

Of this institution an Englishman is scarcely a fair judge, as it is conducted on a method so utterly unlike anything we have at home at present. My American friend assures me that we are 100 years behind all other nations in this matter, that the Belgians conduct it exactly as they do in the States, and that theirs is the only decent mode of bathing. It may be so. One sees such rapid changes in these days, and advanced opinions of all kinds are being caught up so quickly by even such Philistines as the English middle classes, that he is a bold man who will assert that we shall not see the notions of Brighton and Dover yield to the new ideas of Newport and Blankenberghe before long. In one respect, indeed, it is well that they should, for the machines here are convenient little rooms on wheels, with plenty of pegs, two chairs, a small tub, a looking-glass, and everything handsome about them. But the wheels are broad, and very-low; consequently you are only rolled down to the neighbourhood of the water, thinking yourself lucky if you get within five or six yards of it. Now, as the occupants of the machine on your left and right are probably sprightly and somewhat facetious young Belgian or French women, and as the beach shelves so gently that you have at least a run of fifty yards before you can get into deep enough water to swim with comfort, the root difference between Blankenberghian and English habits discloses itself to you from the first. Of course, as men, women, and children all bathe together, costumes are necessary, but those in which the men have to array themselves only make bathing a discomfort, without giving one the consciousness of being decently clad. You have handed to you with your towels a simple jersey, with arms and legs six or eight inches in length, reaching perhaps to the middle of the biceps and femoral muscles. Into this apology for a dress you insert and button yourself up (it is well for you, by the way, if one or two buttons be not missing), and then are expected to walk calmly out into the water through groups of laughing girls in jackets and loose trousers. Having threaded your way through these, and avoided a quadrille party on the one hand, and an excellent fat couple, reminding you of the picture of Mr. and Mrs. Bubb in the one-horse "chay," who are bathing their family on the other, you address yourself to swimming. As you descended from the Digue you read, "Bathers are expressly recommended to hold themselves at least fifteen yards from the breakers by buoys designed." You do not see any breakers, but there is a line of buoys about eighty yards out to which you contemptuously paddle, and after all find that you are scarcely out of your depth. When you have had enough you return, poor, dripping, forked mortal, to a last and severest trial. For the universal custom is to sit about on chairs amongst the machines; and on one side of your door are perhaps a couple of nursemaids chatting while their children build sand castles, on the other a matron or two working and gossiping. Now, sir, a man who has been taking the rough and the smooth of life for a good many years within half a mile of Temple Bar is not likely to be oversensitive, but I would appeal to any contributor on your staff, sir, or to yourself, whether you would be prepared to go through such an ordeal without wincing? On my return from my first swim I recognised my American cousin in his element. He was clad in a blue striped jersey,—would that I could have sprinkled it with a few stars,—and was sauntering about with the greatest coolness from group to group, enjoying the whole business, and no doubt looking forward complacently to the time when differences of sex shall be altogether ignored in the academies of the future. He threw a pitying glance at me as I skedaddled to my machine, secretly vowing to abstain from all such adventures hereafter. Since that time I have taken my dip too early for the Belgian public to be present at the ceremony, but, like the rest of the world, I daily look on, and, unlike them, wonder. As to the morality of it, I can't say that I think the custom of promiscuous bathing as practised here seems to me either moral or immoral. Occasionally when the waves are a little rough you see couples clinging together for mutual support more than the circumstances perhaps strictly require; but there is very little of this. The whole business seemed to me not immoral, but in our conventional sense vulgar, much like "kissing in the ring," which I have seen played by most exemplary sets of young men and women on excursions in Greenwich or Richmond Park, but which would not do in Hamilton Gardens or a May Fair drawing-room. Meanwhile, I hope that as long at least as I can enjoy the water we shall remain benighted bathers in the eyes of our American cousins and of the brave Belgians. To a man the first requisite of a really enjoyable bath is surely deep water, and the second, no clothes, for the loss of either of which no amount of damp flirtation can compensate, in the opinion at least of your contributor, who, nevertheless in these Belgian parts, while obliged to record his opinion, has perhaps a great consciousness that he may be something of an old fogey.

I suppose that a man or nation is to be congratulated about whom their neighbours have nothing to say. If so, the position of England at this time is peculiarly enviable out here. I read the *Indépendance Belge* diligently, but under the head "Nouvelles d'Angleterre," for which that journal retains, as it would seem, a special correspondent, I never learn anything whatever except the price of funds. We occupy an average of perhaps twelve lines in its columns, and none at all in those of the *La Vigie de la Côte*, the special production of Blankenberghe, or of the Bruges and Ostend journals.

Oh! wad some power the giftie gie us,

To see oursels as ithers see us!

Certainly a short residence at Blankenberghe should be taken in conjunction with the volume of essays on international policy by Mr. Congreve and his fellow Comtists, which I happen to have brought with me for deliberate perusal, if one wants to feel the shine taken out of one's native land. I don't.

Belgian Boats

Blankenberghe has one branch of native industry, and one only. From time immemorial it has been a fishing station. The local paper declares that there has been no change in the boats, the costumes, or the implements of this industry since the sixteenth century, with the exception noticed below. One can quite believe it, as far as the boats are concerned. They are very strongly built tubs, ranging from twenty to thirty tons, flat-bottomed, the same breadth of beam fore and aft, built I should think on the model of the first duck which was seen off this coast, and a most sensible model too. They have no bowsprit, but a short foremast in the bows, carrying one small sail, and a strong mainmast amidships, carrying one big sail. Each of these sails is run up by a single rope, rigged through a pulley in the top of the masts, and of other rigging there is none. The boats are all of a uniform russet-brown colour, the tint of old age, looking as if they had been once varnished, in the time, let us say, of William the Silent, and had never been touched since. There is not a scrap of paint on the whole fleet. In short, I am convinced that the local paper by no means exaggerates their antiquity. Instead of finding it hard to believe that sixteenth-century men went to sea in them, I should not be startled to hear that our first parents were the original proprietors, or at any rate that the present fleet was laid down by Japhet, when the Ark was broken up. The habits of the fleet are as quaint as their looks. There is no scrap of anchorage or shelter of any kind here, the sands lie perfectly open to the north and west, and the surf seems about as rough as it is elsewhere. But the Blankenberghe fishermen are perfectly indifferent, convinced no doubt that neither sea nor sand will do anything to hurt them or their boats, for old acquaintance' sake. To me, accustomed to the scrambling, and shouting, and hauling up above high-water mark, the running of naked-legged boys into the water, and the energetic doings of the crew when a fishing boat comes to land at home, there is something of the comically sublime in the contrast presented by these good Flemings. As one of the old brown tubs rolls towards the shore, looking as if she scarcely had made up her mind which end to send in first, you see a man quietly pitch a small anchor over the bows, and then down come the two sails. Sometimes the anchor begins to hold before the boat grounds, but just as often she touches before the anchor bites, but nobody cares. The only notice taken is to unship the rudder and haul it aboard; then comes a wave which swings her round, and leaves her broadside to the surf. Nobody moves. Bang comes the next breaker, lifting her for a moment, and bumping her down again on the sand, her bows perhaps a trifle more to sea, but the crew only smoke and hold on. And so it goes on, bang, bump, thump, till sooner or later she swings right round and settles into her place on the sand. When she has adjusted this to her own satisfaction one of the crew just drops over the stern with another anchor on his shoulder, which he fixes in the sand, and then he and the rest leave her and walk up to the Digue, and generally on to vespers at the church, which is often three parts filled with these jolly fellows. Getting off again is much the same happy-go-lucky business. The men shoulder the anchor which is out at the stern, or, as often as not, leave it on shore with their cable coiled, ready for their return. Then they clamber into their tub, which is bumping away, held only by the anchor out at the bows. They wait for the first wave that floats them, then up go the sails, on goes the rudder, they get a haul on the anchor, and after heading one or two different ways get fairly off.

Their costume is picturesque,—thick red flannel shirts, the collars of which fold over their tightly buttoned blue jackets, and give a tidy, uniform appearance to a group of them. The old stagers still wear huge loose red knickerbockers and pilot boots, but the younger generation are degenerating into the common blue trousers and sabots, the latter almost big enough to come ashore on in case of wreck. Altogether they are the most well-to-do set of fishermen to look at that I have ever seen, though where their money comes from I cannot guess, as they seem to take little but small flounders and skate. There used to be good cod-fishing in the winter, they say, but of late years it has fallen off. The elder fishermen attribute this to the disgust of the cod at an innovation in the good old ways of fishing. Formerly two boats worked together, dragging a net with large meshes between them, but this has been of late superseded by the English bag-net system, which brings up everything small and great, and disturbs the *pâture accoutumée* of the cod, whereupon he has emigrated.

Disastrous islanders that we are, who never touch anything, from Japan to Blankenberghe, without setting honest folk by the ears and bringing trouble! The "Corporation of Fishers," a close and privileged body, who hold their heads very high here, are looking into the matter, and it seems likely that this destructive *chalut, d'origine Anglaise*, may yet be superseded. It remains to be seen whether the cod will come back.

We have had abominable weather here, but nothing in the shape of a storm. I confess to have been looking out for a good north-wester with much interest. Assuming that the effect as to breakers and surf would be much the same as elsewhere, one is curious to ascertain whether these fishing boats are left to bump it out on the sands. If so, and no harm comes to them, the sooner our fishermen adopt the Blankenberghe model of boat the better. I fear, however, that with all their good looks and old traditions, the seafaring folk on this coast are wanting in the splendid daring of our own 'long-shore people. On Monday night the mail packet from Ostend to Dover went out in a stiffish breeze, but nothing which 'we should call a gale, at eight o'clock. By some curious mismanagement both her engines got out of order and came to a dead stop almost immediately. Strange to say, her anchors were down in the hold under the luggage (the boats are Belgian, not English manned), and she had a very narrow escape of drifting right on shore. Luckily the crew, managed to get up an anchor in time to prevent this catastrophe, and there she lay right off the harbour, perfectly helpless, throwing up rockets and burning blue lights for hours. Neither tug, nor lifeboat, nor pilot boat stirred, and she rode at anchor till morning, when the wind went down. I venture to think that such a case is unheard of on our coasts. It occurs to one to ask whether there is such an official as a harbourmaster at the port of Ostend, and if so, what his duties are. There were sailors enough in harbour to have manned fifty lifeboats, for the Ostend fishing fleet of 200 boats had come back from their three months' cruise on that very afternoon. The contingency of riding out a stormy night in a mail packet within a few hundred yards of a lee shore, in front of a great port full of seamen, is scarcely one of those on which we holiday folk reckon when we book ourselves for the Continent.

Coming out on the Digue one night, soon after my arrival, I was brought to a stand-still by the appearance of the sea. It was low water, so that I was about 200 yards off, and at first I could scarcely believe my eyes, which seemed to tell me that every breaker was a flood of pale fire. I went down close to the water to confirm or disenchant myself, and found it more beautiful the nearer I got. Of course one has seen the ordinary phosphorescence of the sea in a hundred places, but this was quite a different affair. The sand under one's feet even was molten silver. The scientific doctor says it is simply the effect of the constant presence on this coast of great numbers of an animalcule which can only be seen through a microscope, called the *Noctiluca miliaris*. It looked on that evening as if huge fiery serpents were constantly rising and dashing along. People here say that they have it always, but this is certainly not so. On several other evenings the breaking waves were slightly luminous, but scarcely enough to attract attention. If you could only make sure of seeing sea and shore ablaze as it was on that particular night, you ought at once, sir, to pack traps and off, notwithstanding these abominably high winds. I cannot help thinking that, besides a monster gathering—probably a Reform League meeting—of the Noctiluca miliaris, there must have been something very unusual in the atmosphere on that particular night. It was a kind of "eldritch" night, in which you felt as if you had got into the atmosphere of Tennyson's *Morte d'Arthur*, and a great hand might come up out of the water without giving you a start. There was light right up in the sky above one's head, a succession of half luminous rain clouds were drifting rapidly across at a very low elevation from the northwest, not fifty yards high, as it seemed, while the smoke of my cigar floated away slowly almost in the opposite direction. Luckily, sir, my American friend was with me on the night in question, to whom I can appeal as to the truth of my facts, and we had had nothing but one bottle of very moderately strong *vin ordinaire* at the *table d'hote*. If your scientific readers say that the thing is impossible, I can only answer that so it was.

Parson Wilbur, when he is considering the question whether the ability to express ourselves in articulate language has been productive of more good than evil, esteems his own ignorance of all tongues except Yankee and the dead languages as "a kind of martello tower, in which I am safe from the furious bombardments of foreign garrulity." There is something comforting and fascinating in this doctrine, but still on the whole it is decidedly disagreeable to be reduced to signs for purposes of intercourse, as is generally the case here. Not one soul in a hundred can speak French. Their talk sounds like a sewing machine, with an occasional word of English interspersed in the clicking. I am told that if you will only talk broad Durham or Yorkshire they will understand you, but I do not believe it, as the sounds are quite unlike. The names of these people are wonderful. For instance, those on the bathing machines just opposite my hotel are, Yan Yooren, Yan Yulpen, Siska Deneve, Sandelays, and Colette Claes, abbreviated into Clotty by two English schoolboys who have lately appeared, and are the worst dressed and the best bathers of all the young folk here. They are fast friends, I see, with a young Russian, whose father, an old officer, sits near me at the *table d'hôte*. Poor old boy! I never saw a man so bored, in fact he has disclosed to me that he can stand it no longer. Blankenberghe has been quite too much for him. Lest it should also prove so to your readers, I will end with his last words (though I by no means endorse his judgment of the little Flemish watering-place), *"Maintenant je n'y puis plus!"*

AMERICA

My father in 1870 went to America for the first time. His time was so much occupied there that he could write only home letters. My mother has allowed me to make extracts from these, thinking that they serve to introduce his later letters from America, which were addressed to the Spectator.

It was owing to the fact of my father's having publicly taken the side of the North in the Civil War that his reception in the United States in 1870 was so particularly warm and hearty.

Peruvian, 6.45 p.m.

Here I am, in my officer's cabin, a small separate hole in our little world on the water, all to myself. At this moment I look out of my porthole and see the Welsh mountains coming out against a bed of daffodil sky, for though it has been misty all day it is now a lovely clear evening. The sea is quite calm, and there is scarcely any motion in the ship. The tea-bell is ringing, so I must stop for a little, but I shall have plenty of time to tell you all that has happened as yet, as we shall be lying off Londonderry nearly all day to-morrow. The mail does not come off to us till about 5 P.M., and we shall be there about nine in the morning or thereabouts. I may perhaps run up to Derry to see the old town and the gate and walls, etc., sacred to the glorious, pious, and immortal memory of the great and good king William.

8.45 p.m.

Tea was excellent, and afterwards R———— and I went on deck, and saw the sun go down gloriously in the line of our ship's course; we were steaming right up a great road of fire. The sea gets calmer and calmer, and, in fact, there couldn't be less movement if we were in Greenwich reach. So now for the narrative of all my adventures since I left you at the window. The moment we got on board, there was the rush and scramble for places at the saloon table, which Harry I———— warned me about. We were on board amongst the first, but agreed not to join the scramble, taking any places that might happen to be going. There is something so ludicrously contemptible to me in seeing people eagerly and seriously struggling about such matters that I am quite unable to join in the worry. I doubt if I could even if the ship were going down, and we were all taking to the boats. It isn't the least from any virtuous or heroic feeling, but simply from the long dwelling in the frame of mind described in a chapter in *Past and Present*. When every one had taken the seats they liked, we settled down very comfortably into two which were vacant, and which, for all I can see, are as good as any of the rest.

8 a.m., Friday.

Off the north coast of Ireland, and a splendid coast it is. A stout party, on whom I do not the least rely, told me an hour or so ago, when I first went on deck, that we were passing the Giant's Causeway. The morning is deliciously fresh, and there is just a little roll in the vessel which is slightly discomforting some of the passengers, I see. I slept like a top without turning, for which, indeed, I haven't room in my tray on the top of the drawers. My only mishap has been that when they were sluicing the decks this morning, the water running down the ship's side naturally turned into my wide-open porthole to see if I was getting up. The device was quite successful, as I shot out of bed at once to close it up and save my things lying on the sofa below. No damage done fortunately.

9.30 a.m., Friday.

Here we are lying quietly at anchor in Lough Foyle after an excellent breakfast. We wait here for the mails, but as it is nineteen miles I find by road up to Derry, I shall not make the attempt. The plot thickens on board, and I am already deeply interested. There are 150 emigrants from the East End, who are being taken over by their parson and a philanthropist whose name I haven't caught yet. I have been forward amongst these poor folk, and have won several hearts or at least opened many mouths by distributing some few spare stamps I luckily had in my pocket. Lovely as the morning is, and delicious as the contrast between the exquisite air on deck, where they are all sitting, when contrasted with Whitechapel air, I can't help looking at them with very mingled feelings. They are a fine steady respectable class of poor. The women nursing and caring for their children with grave, serious, sweet faces, and the men really attentive. All of them anxious to send off scraps of letters to their friends in Great Babylon. There is one slip of the foredeck roped off entirely for nursing mothers and small children, and there are a lot of quaint little plumps rolling and tumbling about there, with some of whom I hope to make friends. A bird-fancier from the East End has several cages full of larks and sparrows, and a magpie and jay in state cabins by themselves, all of which he hopes to make great merchandise of in Canada, where English birds are longed for, but are very hard to keep. He had lost his hempseed in Liverpool, but luckily a boat has gone ashore, and I think there is good hope of getting him a fresh supply. There is a little gathering of the emigrants for service at eight in the evening forward. I didn't know of it last night, but shall attend henceforth. No thought of such a thing in the state saloon! "How hardly shall they that have riches"!

Here, as elsewhere, the truest and deepest life, because the simplest, lies amongst those who have little of the things of this world lying between them and their Father and this invisible world, with its realities.

On board the Peruvian.

We are well out on the broad Atlantic, which at present we are inclined to think a little of an imposture. There is certainly a swell of some kind, for the ship pitches more or less, but to the unpractised eye looking out on the waste of waters it is quite impossible to account for the swell, for, except for the better colour, the sea looks very much as it does off the Isle of Wight; great waves like the slope of a chalk down, following one another in solemn procession, up which the long ship climbs like a white road. However, it is early days to grumble about the want of swell, and when it comes I may not like it any more than another. After finishing my letter to you this morning, I went ashore to post it, and found that after all it wouldn't reach London till to-morrow night. So I sent you a telegram, which I hope you got before bed-time at any rate, and redirected my letter to Cromer. To pass the time I took a jaunting car with two other passengers, and we drove to an old castle looking over Lough Foyle, formerly a stronghold of the O'Doherty's till it was sacked and knocked about their ears by an expedition of Scotch Campbells, who did a good work for the district by destroying it. We found lots of shamrock in the ruins, and enjoyed the drive and still more a bathe afterwards. The country seems very prosperous. The people, strapping, light-haired, blue-eyed Celts, handsome and well-to-do; in fact, evidently much better fed and better educated than almost any English country district I know. The mails came down from Derry in a tender, which brought us the news of the first battle and the Prussian victory, which I for one always looked for, and we got away by seven, two hours later than we expected. However, the wind is fair and we are making famous way, and by the time I get up in the morning I expect we shall be 200 miles from the Irish coast.

9.30 p.m., Saturday.

A long calm day and we have made a splendid run—shall be in Quebec in good time to-morrow week if this weather holds; but knowing persons say it won't, and that we have seen the last of fine weather, and must look out for squalls—for why? the wind has gone round against the sun, and it has settled to rain hard with a barometer steadily going down. The Roman Catholic bishop (who is not very expert in weather that I know of, but is a very, jovial party, who enjoys his cigar and gossip, and was one of the first to go in for a game of shovel-board on deck this morning) declares that we shall have it fine all the way, as he has made the passage six times and has never had bad weather yet. In any case I hope it won't be rough to-morrow, for we are to have a real treat in the way of spiritual dissipation. First, the bishop is to have some kind of mass and preach a short sermon at nine (N.B. a time-table conscience clause is to run all day, so that only latitudinarians like me will go in for it all). Then the captain who is a rare good fellow, with a spice of sentiment about him, which sits so well on such a bulletheaded, broad-shouldered, resolute Jack-Tar, has his own service at eleven, in which he will do the priest himself, an excellent example, with a sermon by the emigrant parson, whose name is H————, afterwards. These in the saloon; then at 2.30 a service in the steerage by H————, or G————, the other parson, and a final wind up, also in the steerage at 7.30. G————is the clergyman of Shaftesbury, George Glyn's borough; was formerly in the Navy, and was in the Ragged School movement of '48, '49, when I used to go off twice a week in the evening to Ormond Yard, when poor old M———— had the gas turned out, and his hat knocked over his eyes by his boys. He knew Ludlow and Furnival, but I don't remember him. However, he is a right good fellow, and gave us a really good *extempore* prayer last night at the midships' service. The steerage is certainly most interesting. There are now nearly 500 emigrants on board there, and the captain says they are about the best lot he has ever had. Going round this morning I was struck by a dear little light-haired girl, who was standing with her arm round the neck of a poor woman very sick and ill, and such tenderness and love in her poor little face as she turned it up to us as almost brought tears into one's eyes. Of course I thought the woman was her mother. No such thing; she was no relation at all. The little dear had never seen her till she met her on board, but was attracted by her misery, and had never left her side since she had been so ill. The poor woman had two strapping daughters on board who had never been near her. How strangely folk are fixed up in this queer world.

Monday.

We know what a good swell in mid-Atlantic means at last. We were pitching when I went to bed, finding it hard to get on with my penmanship. Off I went as fast as usual, and never woke except for one moment to grunt and turn round, or rather, try to turn round, in my tray on top of the drawers at something which sounded like a crash. In the morning we were swinging and bowing and jerking, so that I had to wait for a favourable moment to bolt out of bed for fear of coming a cropper if I didn't mind.

As soon as I was out I saw what the crash had been in the night. My big portmanteau, which had been set on its end the night before, had had a jumping match with my water-jug in the night. Both of them had thrown a somersault across the cabin against the door, but the jug being brittle (jugs shouldn't jump against portmanteaus), and coming down undermost, had gone all into little bits, and the water, all that wasn't in my shoes at least, had soaked my carpet at the door end. But it was a glorious bright morning and the dancing hills of water and the bounding ship sent me up dancing on the deck. My high spirits were a little subdued after breakfast, for I had scarcely got on deck when parson H———— came to me to say the emigrants wanted me to give them an address. Well, I couldn't refuse, as my heart is full of them, poor dear folk, so down I went to get my ideas straight, and put down the heads on paper. I thought I wouldn't miss the air, though, so set open my porthole window, which as I told you is about a foot across, and set to work—as I write, this blessed porthole is about a yard away from my right ear, and perhaps two feet above my head. Well, I was just getting into swing with my work, when suddenly a great pitch, and kerswash! in comes all of a wave that could squeeze through my porthole, right on to my ear and shoulder, over my desk, drenching all my papers, lucifer-match boxes, hair-brushes, wideawake, tobacco-pouch and other chattels, and flooding all of my floor which my water-jug had left dry. I bolted to the porthole and closed him up before another curious wave could come prying in, and soon rubbed everything dry again with the help of the Captain's cabin-boy, and no harm is done except that I have to sit with my feet up on my portmanteau while I write. This sheet was dowsed in my shower-bath this morning, but I laid it on my bed, and it seems all right now and doesn't even blot; I shall however envelope it now with another sheet for safety, as I'm not going to keep my porthole shut notwithstanding the warning, and I don't want my letters to you floated again.

Peruvian, 9th August 1870.

Since I put my last sheet into No. 1 envelope, everything in the good ship *Peruvian* has been dancing. The long tables in the saloon, at which we are always eating and drinking, have been covered with a small framework, over which the cloth is laid, and which has the effect of dividing them into three compartments; a sort of trough down each side in which are the dishes. Notwithstanding these precautions there are constant catastrophes in the shape of spoons, forks, tumblers, and sometimes plates, jumping the partitions suddenly as the ship heels over. The story of the Yankee skipper saying to the lady on his left, "I'll trouble you, marm, for that 'ere turkey—" the bird in question having fled from the table into her lap as he was beginning to serve it—becomes quite commonplace. How the steward's men get about with plates and dishes, goodness knows; but though there is a constant clatter and smash going on all over the ship I haven't seen them drop anything. I am almost the only passenger who hasn't even had a twinge of squeamishness, but we muster pretty well considering all things. The Captain is one of the cheeriest fellows alive, and keeps up the spirits of all the women. If he sees any one of them who is still about looking peeky, he whisks her off under his arm and walks her up and down the deck, where they stagger along together, and the fresh breeze soon revives the damsel. He is a sort of temporary father to all the girls, and constantly has, it seems, three or four entrusted to him to take over or bring back.

Of course there is a great deal of discomfort on board, but I have visited the steerage and am delighted with the arrangements for feeding, ventilation, etc. To poor seasick people, however, it must be very trying. This morning I carried off to my cabin a poor forlorn young married couple, whom I had noticed on shore at Moville, and afterwards on board. I am sure they hadn't been married a week, and they were evidently ready to eat one another. When I saw them settling down on a large bench in a covered place amidships where were twenty or thirty folk, mostly ill, and several men smoking, she with her poor head tied up tidily in a red handkerchief nestling on to his shoulder, I couldn't stand it, and took them off to my cabin, where they could nurse one another for a few hours' in peace. We have had a birth too on board, and mother and child, I am glad to say, are doing well. She is a very nice woman, I am told by one of the ladies who visits her, the wife of a school teacher. The baby is to have Peruvian for one of its names. I have really enjoyed the rough weather much; it has never been more than half a gale, I believe, though several men have been thrown from the sofas to the cabin floor, and more or less bruised. The cheery Captain has comforted us all by announcing that we shall be through the storm before midnight.

Up the St. Lawrence they say we shall want light summer clothing. If the weather settles down we are to have an amateur concert on board, which will be, I take it, very lame on the musical side, but amusing in other ways.

R—— was entrusted by the Captain with the task of getting it up, and before we got into rough weather had booked some six or seven volunteers. I daresay he will be well enough to-morrow morning to go on with it. My address is of course postponed for the present.

Wednesday.

The Captain was quite right—we sailed clear out of the storm before midnight yesterday, and though to-day some swell is left, it is so calm that the saloon tables have quite filled up again at meal-times. I was of course nailed by the parson for my address in the afternoon, and placed on one of the flat skylights amidships, as no other equally convenient and fixed stump could be found. As I know you would sooner get rubbish of mine than poetry of any one else, I give the outline. "I was there," I said, "at their parson's request, to talk, but it seemed to me that in the grand scene we were in, the great waves, the bright sky, the free breezes, could talk to them more eloquently than human lips. We were wont to use proverbs all our lives without realising their meaning. 'We're all in the same boat' had never impressed me till now. Our week's experience showed us before all things that the first duty of those in the same boat was to help, comfort, and amuse the rest. If I could do either I should be glad. What were we to talk about? (Shouts of 'Canada.') Well we would come to Canada, but first a word or two of the old country they were leaving. Love of our birthplace, otherwise called patriotism, is one of the strongest and noblest passions God has planted in man's heart. You have a great birthright as Englishmen, are members, however humble, of the nation which has spread free speech and free thought round the world, which was the first to declare that her flag never should fly over a slave. Fellow-countrymen of Wycliffe, Shakespeare, Milton. Wherever you go cherish these memories, be loyal to the old country, keep a soft place in your heart for the land of your birth. You are now making the passage from the old world to the new, enjoying one of those rare resting-places which God gives us in our lives. It is time for bracing up the whole man for new effort, for casting off old, bad habits. One strong resolution made at such times often is the turning-point in men's lives. As to the land you are going to, Remember you are getting a fresh start in life and all will depend on yourselves. In the old land there is often not enough work for strong and willing hands; in the new there are a hundred openings, and in all more work than hands. One thing wanted is honest, hard work. Whatever your hands find to do, do it with all your might, and you are sure of comfort and independence. Your new home is England's eldest child and has a great destiny to work out. Be loyal therefore and true to your birthplace, keeping old memories alive and giving her a share of your love; be loyal to your new home, giving her your best work; above all, be loyal and true to yourselves and you shall not be false to any man or any land." This, spread over half an hour, was my talk.

When I had finished I called on the Captain, who warned them against drink in a straightforward sailor's speech. Then a grizzled old boy, who had been calling out "That's true" whenever I spoke of hard work, scrambled up on the skylight and told them that he had come out thirty years ago from England with nine shillings in his pocket and seven children. He had given each of his daughters fifteen hundred dollars on their marriage, and helped each of his sons into a farm, and had a farm of his own, which he was going back to after visiting his old home in Cornwall. All this he had done by hard work. He was a blacksmith, but would turn his hand to anything. Times were just as good now as then, and every one of them might do the same. This was a splendid clencher to the nail I had tried to drive in. The parson wound up with more advice as to liquor, and an account of how well the sixteen hundred he had already sent out had done. The whole was a great success, and we all went off to dinner in the cabin in high spirits. If the fair weather lasts we shall see land to-morrow afternoon. To-morrow night we are to have our concert. My young couple have turned up trumps: he plays the old piano in the saloon famously, being an excellent musician, and she sings, they say, nicely when not sea-sick. The Canadians on board assure him he will be caught up as an organist directly to help out his other means of livelihood. Then for Friday we are to have "Box and Cox" in the cabin, played by the Captain and R———, who knows the part of

Cox perfectly already, having played it at Cambridge. Mrs. Bouncer has not yet been fixed on, but a nice little Canadian girl will, I think, play it.

Tuesday evening.

We had a fog this morning which lost us a couple of hours, seeing however, as compensation, a fog rainbow—a colourless arch, which as you looked over the side seemed to spring from the two ends of the ship. As the fog cleared away and we went ahead we saw an iceberg to the north, which soon looked like a great white lion lying on the horizon. During the day, which has been wonderfully bright and cold, we have seen several more icebergs and a lot of whales, one of which came quite close to the ship. We sighted land about seven, and in six miles more we should have passed into the Bay of St. Lawrence, when a rascally fog came on and forced us to lay-to. The Captain can't leave the deck, so we didn't have our concert, and we are all going to bed anxious to hear the screw at work again.

Friday.

We lay-to all last night, the jolly Captain up on the bridge, to watch for any lifting of the fog, so that he might go ahead at once; but the fog wouldn't lift, and so we lay until eight this morning. Just before breakfast it cleared, and away we went, and soon entered the strait between Newfoundland and Labrador. By the time we had done breakfast we were running close by a huge iceberg, like a great irregular wedding cake, except near the water, where the colour changed from sugary white into the most delicious green. There were nine other icebergs in sight to the north, and a number of others round us, just showing above the water, one like a great ichthyosaurus creeping along the waves, or a white bear with a very long neck. Had we gone on last night it would have been a perilous adventure. Soon afterwards we sighted the *North American*, a companion ship belonging to the same Company, running some miles in front of us to the north. We had a most exciting race, coming abreast of her about twelve, and communicating by signals. Then we drew ahead, and shall be in Quebec nearly a day before her. Then we played shovel-board on deck, the air getting more balmy every minute as we drew out of the ice region. We had a grand gathering of emigrants amidships, and sung hymns, "Jesus, lover of my soul," and others, with a few words from G———, the busy parson, who has recovered from his long sea-sickness at last, and is a famous fellow. The concert of the Peruvians came off with a great *eclat* after dinner. They put me in the chair, and I introduced the performers with a slight discourse about the Smith family (the Captain's name is Smith), and at the end they voted thanks to me, imparting the great success of the voyage to my remarkable talent for making folk agree and pull together—very flattering, but scarcely accurate. Then somebody discovered that it was a glorious moonlight, so up we all went, and very soon there was a fiddler and a dance on deck, which is only just over. We are well in the Gulf of St. Lawrence, and all going as well as possible.

Mouth of the St. Lawrence.

I am much pleased with the specimens of Canadians whom we have on board. There are some twenty of them, with their wives, daughters, and small boys. They are a quiet, well-informed, pleasant set of men, and ready and pleased to talk of their country and her prospects. My conversation runs to a great extent, as you may suppose, on the chances of farming in Canada West, which is the part of the colony with the greatest future, and I am much pleased with what I hear. Any man with a capital of from £2000 to £3000 may do very well, and make money quite as fast as is good for him, if he will only keep steady and work; and the life is exceedingly fascinating for youngsters.

There is a very nice fellow on board, a gentleman in the conventional sense, who is returning from a run to Gloucestershire to see his friends. He has been out for seven years only, two of which he spent as an apprentice with a farmer, learning his trade. He is quite independent now, and I would not wish to meet a better specimen of a man.

I doubt whether you, being so orderly a party, would quite appreciate what appears to be the favourite form of pleasuring amongst the up-country farmers, but I own that it would have suited my natural man down to the ground. Half a dozen of them, in the bright, still wintertime, will agree that they haven't seen Jones for some weeks, so will give him "a surprise." Accordingly they all start from their own houses so as to meet at his farm about 9.30 or 10 o'clock—the time he would be going to bed.

They drive over in sledges, each taking his wife, sister, or sweetheart, a good hamper of provisions and plenty of buffalo robes. Jones finds his yard full of neighing horses and sledges as he is going to bed. If he has already gone they knock him up. They then take possession of his house and premises. The men litter down their horses, the women light his fire and lay the supper, the only absolute rule being, that Jones and his family and servants do nothing at all.

They all sit down to supper and then dance till they are tired, and then the women go to bed; and the men, if there are no beds for them, as generally happens, roll themselves in their buffalo robes and go to sleep. In the morning they breakfast, and then start away home again over the snow in their sledges, after the men have cut up firewood enough to keep Jones warm for a week.

There is magnificent trout and salmon fishing, and deer, wolf, and bear shooting, for those who like to seek it in the backwoods, and plenty of time for sport when the farm work is over, or in the winter. At the big towns, such as Montreal and Toronto, there is plenty of society, and evidently cultivated society, though young Guardsmen may speak shudderingly of colonists.

Box and Cox, by the way, went off very well considering that the Captain, who played Box, had been up on the bridge almost the whole of the two previous nights, and consequently did not quite know his part.

Sunday 14th.

Last night we danced on deck till nearly eleven under the most lovely soft moon I have ever seen. This morning we are running up the St. Lawrence along the southern bank, the northern being dim in the extreme distance. There is a long continuous range of hills covered entirely with forest, except just along the water's edge, where it has been cleared by the French-Canadian settlers. They live along the shore, too close, I should say, to the water line for comfort; but as their chief occupation is fishing, I have no doubt they have good reasons for their selection. There is scarcely a quarter of a mile for the last twenty or thirty miles, I should say, in which there is not a cottage, but the villages are far between. The people are a simple, quiet folk, living just as their fathers lived, happy, clean, contented, and stationary. This last quality provokes the English of Upper Canada dreadfully, who complain that the French make everything they require at home, and buy nothing whatever which contributes to the revenue of the Dominion except a little cheap tea. However, there is much to be said for the Frenchmen, and I am very glad that our English people have constantly before them the example of such a self-sufficing and unambitious life. In two or three hours, probably before our morning service is over, the pilot will be on board with papers, and we shall know what has been doing in the great outside world. I was thinking of telegraphing to you, but as the Company telegraph, and publish our arrival "all well" in the English papers, it seems scarcely worth while.

The pilot has just come on board and brought us Canadian papers with copies of telegrams, and general vague rumours of terrible reverses for France. I always looked for them, as you know. This frightful reign of eighteen years, begun in perjury and bloodshed, and continued by constant pandering to the worst tendencies of France, must have taken the power and heart out of any nation. I pity the poor Canadians who still hold themselves more French than anything else, as indeed they are. They gather on deck and tell one another that the news is German, that it is all mere rumour. They will find it too true in another day or two. I am very glad to hear that the Orleans princes are now to go back. They are a family of very gallant and able gentlemen, and ought to be with France at this moment. Wrong as I think her, I hope she may soon be able to rally, shake off the charlatans whom she has allowed to misrule her, and conclude an honourable peace. The pilot-boat went back at once, and when she lands our safe arrival will be telegraphed at once, so that I hope you may see it before to-morrow evening—if you only know where to look in the newspaper. I often think how very different those short announcements at the head of the Shipping news will seem to me in the future.

"Allan Line. The *Peruvian* arrived off Father Point yesterday. All well."

Wednesday.

Events have been crowding us during the last thirty-six hours—bless me, I mean the last sixty hours—I had positively written Tuesday instead of Wednesday at the top of this. I let my watch run down on the *Peruvian*, as it was too provoking to have to put it back thirty-five minutes every morning. Since then time has gone all whiz! however, I shall pick up the time now and get to my bearings, at least I shall try. Well, all Sunday afternoon we ran up the glorious St. Lawrence, past the mouths of what we should call big rivers, past the Canadian watering-places, past one long straggling village except where the hills are too steep or the soil absolutely barren. The view is not unlike many Scotch ones, substituting scrub or stunted forest for heather. This of course is a great disadvantage in a picturesque point of view, but it is more than compensated by the great river. I am very glad I came to the new world up the St. Lawrence. Nothing could have brought the startling contrast of the old and new world so vividly home to me as this steaming literally day after day up the stream, and finding it still at 700 miles from the mouth two miles broad, with anchorage for the largest ships that float. We went the round of the ship with the Captain after dinner, to see the wonderful detail of the storerooms, and the huge fire-system which goes glowing on through all the voyage. The sight of the twenty-five great furnaces glowing, and consuming fifty-two tons of coal a day, quite scared several of the ladies, who seemed to think that the Peruvian was flying, I should say sailing, presumptuously in the face of Providence not to have caught fire during the voyage. Luckily we were within a few hours of port, so their anxiety was not of long duration. I went to bed for the last time in my crib on the top of the drawers, leaving word for the quartermaster to call me when we were getting near Quebec. Accordingly I was roused at about three from one of the sleeps without a turn even (by reason that there is no room to turn) which one gets on board ship, and scuffled up on deck in my trousers and fur coat to find myself in the most perfect moonlight rounding the last point below Quebec. Then up went three rockets, and as we slacked our speed at the side of the wharf right opposite the citadel, two guns were fired and the voyage of the Peruvian was over. My packing was all done, so while the vessel was being unladen I went quietly to bed again and slept for another two or three hours amid all the din. Between six and seven I turned out again and had a good breakfast on board, after which came leave-takings, and then those of us who were not going on by train and were ready to start, went on board a little tug ferry-boat and were paddled across to Quebec. I have sent a small map to show you how the land lies. Our ferry-boat took us over from Port Levi to the quay just under the Citadel along the line I have dotted, and we at once chartered two carriages to visit the falls of Montmorency, to which you will see a line drawn on the map and which is about six miles from Quebec. Oh, the air! You know what it is when we land at Dieppe, or at Brussels, or Aix. Well, all that air is fog, depressing wet blanket compared to this Canadian nectar. I really doubt whether it would not be almost worth while to emigrate merely for the exquisite pleasure of the act of living in this country.

Montreal, 19th August 1870.

I must get on with my journal or shall fall altogether astern—you have no idea how hard it is even to find time to write a few lines home; however if I can only make up the time to-day I hope to keep down the arrears more regularly hereafter. We had a long day of sightseeing in and about Quebec. First we drove down to the Montmorency Falls, 220 feet high and very beautiful, then back to the Citadel, which rises some 600 or 700 feet right above the river—a regular little Gibraltar; then we went off to the Heights of Abraham, at the back of the Citadel, where Wolfe fought his battle and was killed after scaling the cliffs in the early morning. Then we drove down into the town, and had lunch at a restaurant, and walked about to see the place. Well worth seeing it is; a quaint, old, thoroughly French town of the last century dropped down into the middle of the new world. In the evening we went on board the great river steamer, and came away all night up the St. Lawrence to Montreal. There were 1000 passengers on board, every one of whom had an excellent berth—mine was broader and lighter than that on the *Peruvian*. We were not the least crowded in the splendid saloon (some 150 feet long), and the open galleries running all round the ship in two tiers. I preferred the latter, though there was music, Yankee and Canadian, in the saloon, and spent my evening till bedtime out in the stern gallery looking at the most superb moonlight on the smooth water you can conceive. We had a small English party there, and there were half a dozen constantly changing groups round us. The girls have evidently much more freedom than at home, at least more than they had in our day—two or three would come out with as many young men, and sit round in a ring. The men lighted cigars, and then they would all set to work singing glees, songs, or what not, and chaffing and laughing away for half an hour perhaps, after which they would disappear into the saloon. There was a regular bar on board at which all manner of cool drinks were sold. We tried several, which I thought, I must say, very nasty, especially brandy-smash. After a most comfortable night I awoke between five and six as we were nearing Montreal. The city is very fine, the river still two miles broad, and ocean steamer drawing twenty feet and more of water able to lie right up against the quay. S———, a friend of Sir J. Rose's, a great manufacturer here, whom I had taken to the "Cosmopolitan," was in waiting on the landing-place, and took us at once up to his charming house on the hill (the mountain they call it) at the back of the city. He is a man of forty-three or forty-four; his wife, a very pleasant woman a little younger, and adopted daughter, Alice (a very sweet girl of nineteen, just home from an English school), form the whole family. I can't tell you how kind they are and how perfectly at home they have made us. After breakfast we went down to see the city, got photographed with the rest of the above-named Peruvians, had a delicious lunch of fried oysters at a luncheon shop kept by a Yankee, washed it down with a drink called John Collins, a pleasant, cold, weak, scented kind of gin and water. Sir Geo. Carter and Sir Fras. Hinks, two of the present Government, both of whom I had met in England, came to dinner, also Holton the leading senator of the Opposition, and the two young Roses, one bringing his pretty young wife, and we had a long and very interesting political talk afterwards. Nothing could have suited me better, as there are many points of Canadian politics I am very anxious to get views on. We didn't get to bed till 12.30, so I had no time to write. On Wednesday we saw more of the city which I shan't attempt to describe till I can sit by you with photographs and explain, lunched at the Club, of which we have been made honorary members, with a large party of merchants and other big folk, and then at three were picked up by Mrs. S.——, who drove us up the river to a place called Lachine, past the rapids (see Canadian boat-song), "The rapids are near and the daylight's past." Lachine gets its queer name from the first French Missionaries who started up the St. Lawrence to get to China, and for some unaccountable reason thought they had reached the flowery land when they got to this place, so settled down and called it China. The air was still charming, but the sky was beginning to get less bright, and Mrs. S—— and A————agreed that there must be a forest burning somewhere. And so it proved, for in a few hours the whole sky was covered with a smoke-cloud, light but not depressing, like our fogs, but still so dense that we could scarcely see across the river. We got back in time for dinner, to which came Colonel Buller, now commanding the Rifles here; Hugh Allan, the head of the great firm of ship-owners to whom the *Peruvian* and all the rest of the Allan line packets belong; and several young Canadians. It was very pleasant again, and again I got a heap of information on Canadian subjects from Allan, who is a longheaded able old Scotchman, the founder of the immense prosperity of himself and all his family. He has his private steam yacht and a great place on a lake near here, wherein is a private telegraph, so that he can wire all over the world from his own hall. Prince Arthur went to stay with him when he was out here in the late autumn and spring, and the Queen wired him every day while he was there. Early next morning S————,

Miss A————, I, and R———— were off by rail to a station ten or twelve miles up the river, where we waited till the Montreal market-boat came down and picked us up to shoot the rapids. We had a very pleasant run to Quebec, and the shooting the rapids is very interesting, but neither dangerous nor even exciting. The river widens out perhaps to two and a half miles in width, and for some mile or mile and a half breaks into these rapids, which boil and rush along at a great pace, and in quite a little boat would no doubt keep the steerer and oarsmen on the stretch. The approach to Montreal under the great Victoria Bridge, two miles long, is very noble. We got back to breakfast at ten, and afterwards went up the mountain at the back of the town, but the haze from the burning forest quite spoiled the view. The carriage is announced, so I must close.

Montreal, 20th August 1870.

I hurried up my letters yesterday, so as to bring my journal down to the day I was writing on, fearing lest otherwise I should never catch the thread again. I doubt whether I told you anything about this very fine city, in the suburbs of which we are stopping, and which we leave to-day. Well, I scarcely know how to begin to give you an idea of it. It isn't the least like an English or indeed any European town, the reason being, I take it, that it has been built with the necessity of meeting extremes of heat and cold, which we never get. Except in the heart of the city, where the great business streets are, there are trees along the sides of all the thoroughfares—maples, which give real shade, and are in many places indeed too thick, and too near the houses for comfort I should say—as near as the plane-tree was to our drawing-room window at 33. This arrangement makes walking about very pleasant to me, even when the thermometer stands at 90° in the shade as it did yesterday. Then instead of a stone foot-pavement you have almost everywhere boards, timber being the most plentiful production of the country. Walking along the boards in the morning you see at every door a great lump of ice, twenty pounds weight or so, lying there for the maid to take in when she comes out to clean. This is supplied by the ice merchants for a few shillings a year. The houses are square, built generally of a fine limestone found all over the island (Montreal is an island thirty-six miles long by nine wide), and have all green open shutter-blinds, which they keep constantly shut all day, as in Greece, to keep out the heat, and double windows to keep out the cold. The roofs are generally covered with tin instead of tiles or slates, and all the church steeples, of which there are a very large number, are tinned, as you remember we saw them in parts of Austria and Hungary. There are magnificent stores of dry goods, groceries, etc., but scarcely any shops in our sense. No butcher, milkman, greengrocer, etc., calls at the door, and the ladies have all to go down to the market or send there. Nothing can be better than the living, but Mrs. S——— complains that it is very hard work for *hausfraus*, and I have heard Lady K——— say the same thing. This house is in one of the shaded avenues on the slopes of the mountain, two miles I should say from the market. Mrs. S——— drives down every marketday and buys provisions, market-days being twice a week, but the stalls are open on other days also, so that if a flood of company comes in on the intermediate days, the anxious housewife need not be absolutely done for. The living is as good as can be, not aspiring to first-rate French cookery, but equal to anything you find in good English houses. Prices are very reasonable except for fancy articles of clothing, etc. Furs, which you would expect to find cheap, are at least as high as in London, and R———made an investment in gloves for which he paid six shillings a pair. The city is the quietest and best-behaved I ever was in. We dined at the mess of the 60th Rifles last night, and walked home through the heart of the city at 10.30. Every one had gone to bed, apparently, for there wasn't a light in fifty houses and we literally met no one—not half a dozen people certainly in the whole distance. Altogether I am very much impressed with the healthiness of the life, morally and physically, and can scarcely imagine any country I would sooner start in were I beginning life again.

Tuesday morning, 23rd August 1870.

Well, to continue, on Saturday we broke up from Montreal, having I think seen very thoroughly all the persons and things best worth seeing in the place. Our host had arranged that we should go and spend Sunday with Mr. Hugh Allan, the head of the family which has established the line of mail steamers to Liverpool and Glasgow. He has been forty years out here, and when he came Montreal had only 17,000 inhabitants, now it has 150,000; there was scarcely water for a 200 ton ship to lie at the wharf, now you can see steamers of 2000 tons and upwards always there. Hugh Allan is evidently a very rich man now. He has a big house on the mountain behind Montreal, and this place where I am now writing from, on Memphremagog Lake, which if you have a good map, you will find half in Canada and half in the New England state of Vermont. It is a lovely inland sea, about thirty-five miles long and varying from one to three miles broad. Mr. Allan's house, where he entertained Prince Arthur in the spring, stands on the top of a high well-wooded promontory, about half-way up. It is a good, commodious, gentleman's house, with deep verandahs, thoroughly comfortable, but without pretence or show of any kind. There is a large wooden out-building called the Hermitage, about one hundred yards off, divided entirely into bedrooms, so that there is room for lots of guests besides the family, seven or eight of whom are here. In another building there is an American bowling-alley, and an excellent croquet ground before the house. Mr. Allan keeps a nice steam yacht, which runs about the lake daily with any one who likes to go, and there are half a dozen rowing boats, so time need not hang heavily on the most restless hands. I accepted the invitation, as a few days at Memphremagog is evidently considered the thing to do by all Canadians, and the last twenty miles or so of the railway to Newport (Vermont), the place at the foot of the lake at which you embark, has only just been finished, right through the forest, so that it was a good chance of seeing the beginnings of colonial life in the bush. And I am very glad that I did come, for certainly if the journey (120 miles altogether) had been planned for the purpose, it couldn't have been more interesting. After leaving Montreal we travelled I should say for from thirty to forty miles through reclaimed country, dotted with French villages and the homesteads of well-to-do farmers. Then we gradually slipped into half-cleared woods, and then into virgin forest. Presently we came across a great block of the forest on fire, but in broad daylight the sight is not the least grand, though unpleasant from the smoke, and melancholy from the waste and mischief which the fires do. I think I told you in my last that the forests about Ottawa, the capital of the Dominion, were on fire last week. The fire became so serious that great fears were entertained for the town, the militia and volunteers were called out, and a special train with fire-engines was sent up from Montreal. Scores of poor settlers were in the streets, having with difficulty escaped with their lives, and last of all several wretched bears trotted out of the burning woods into the town. The fire we passed through was not at all on this scale, and didn't seem likely to get ahead. There were the marks of fires of former years on all sides in these forests. Tall stems by hundreds, standing up charred and gaunt out of the middle of the bright green maple underwood, which is fast growing up round them, and in a very short time makes the tangle as thick as ever. Before long we came to small clearings of from three to four acres, on each of which was a rough wooden shanty, with half a dozen wild, brown, healthy-looking children rolling and scrambling about it, and standing up in their single garments to cheer the train. On these plots the trees had all been felled about two feet from the ground, and the brushwood cleared away, and there were crops of Indian corn, oats, or buckwheat growing all round the stumps. Then we came to plots which had been occupied longer, where the shanty had grown into a nice-sized cottage, with a good-sized outhouse near. Here all the stumps had been cleared, and the plot divided by fences, and three or four cows would be poking about. Then we came to a fine river and ran along the bank, passing here and there sawmills of huge size, and stopping at one or two large primitive villages, gathered round a manufactory. In short, in the day's run we saw Canadian life in all its phases, ending with a delicious twelve miles' run up the lake in Mr. Allan's steam yacht, with the whole sky flickering with Northern lights, which shot and played about for our special delight. Our railway party were Mr.

Allan; Mr. and Mrs. S———, and Miss B———, their adopted daughter; General Lindsay, whom I knew well in England and like very much; Colonel Eyre, his military secretary, and ourselves. Then there are eight children here. "We had a most luxurious car, with a little sitting-room in which we each had an easy chair, and there were two most enticing-looking little bedrooms, everything as clean and neat as you could have it, and we could walk out on to a platform at either end to look at the view. There was a boy also in attendance in a little sort of spare room where the luggage went, who ministered any amount of iced water to any one who called. This is decidedly the most luxurious travelling I ever had, but then the car was the private one of the manager of the Grand Trunk Railway; and the democratic cars in which every one else went, and in which indeed we had to travel for the last few miles, were very different affairs. Fancy my intense delight on Sunday morning, as I walked from the Hermitage up to the house to breakfast through some flower-beds, to see two humming-birds, poising themselves before flower after flower while probing and trying the blooms with their long bills, and then springing back with a stroke of their lovely little tails, and whisking off to the next bloom. They were green and brown, not so lovely in colour as many you have seen in collections, but exquisite as eye need ask to look at. The humming-birds have been certainly my greatest natural history treat as yet, not excepting the whales. I had seen a whale before, a small one, in the Hebrides, and I had never seen a hummingbird except stuffed; moreover I expected to see whales, but not humming-birds. We saw a fine great bald-headed eagle to-day, too, sailing over the lake, but his flight was not anything like so fine as those we saw soaring over the Iron Gates as we went spinning down the Danube nine years ago. We have a very charming visit here steaming about the lake, driving along the banks, playing croquet and bowls and billiards, and laughing, chaffing, and loafing to any extent. The family are very nice, and I hope he will soon be made a baronet and one of the first grandees of the Dominion. To-morrow morning at five we start for Boston in the steam yacht, which takes us down to Newport at the end of the lake. So by the evening I shall perhaps get a letter from you. How I do thirst for home news after three weeks' absence.

Elmwood, Cambridge, Massachusetts, 25th August 1870.

I forget just where I left off, whether I had brought my journal up to our leaving Memphremagog or not. The last day there was as pleasant as the rest. The young folks played croquet and American bowls all the morning, while I lay on the grass watching for humming-birds and talking occasional politics to any one who would join me. At about twelve a retired judge, Day by name, who lives four or five miles off, drove over with a member of the Government (I forget his name) who was to start from the pier below the house in the lake steamer. Mr. Allan owns this steamer, which stops at his pier whenever he runs up a flag; so you see the privileged classes are not extinct by any means in the British dominion in the new world. Now the Judge, having a seat in his light sort of phaeton, proposed to drive me over to the post-office, about four miles off, where he was going, and to bring me back to luncheon. So I embarked behind his two strong little trotting nags and had a most interesting drive. The roads were not worse than many Devonshire lanes, and where the pitches were steepest, the stout little nags made nothing of them.

The views of the lake were exquisite, and the Judge one of the pleasantest of men. He had been employed in 1865 on a mission to Washington, and gave me very graphic accounts of his interviews with Lincoln and the other leading men there, and confirmed many of my own views as to the comparative chances of the two great sections of our race in the new world in the future. He is less apprehensive of Canada joining the United States than most men of his standing, and I think has good reason for his confidence. Material interest will perhaps for a time (or rather, after a time, for at present it is very doubtful on which side they weigh) sway in the direction of annexation to the United States, but the ablest and most energetic of the younger men of the cultivated classes are so strongly bent on developing a distinct national life, that I expect to see them carry their country for independence rather than annexation, when the time comes, if it ever should, of a final cutting of the ropes which bind them to us. After luncheon we went off in the steam yacht to a bay in the lake, and then in row boats four or five miles up the bay into the heart of the hills, where we saw bald-headed eagles, and black and white king-fishers five times the size of ours, and after a very interesting and pleasant excursion got back to dinner, finishing the evening with dancing. At five next morning we heard the steamer's whistle calling us. The young ladies were up to give us a cup of coffee and parting good words, and then we-steamed down for Newport, where we were to take the rail through the Connecticut valley to Boston. On the Newport wharf which joins the station we said good-bye to Allan and Stephen, and shall carry away most charming memories of our stay in Canada. General Lindsay and Eyre went with us, and their companionship made the journey very agreeable, though it was as hot as the Lower Danube, and the dust more uncomfortable and dirtying than any we have at home. Most part of the way the soil is as light and sandy as that about Dorking, and the trains seem to raise greater clouds of it.

The greater part of the journey was along the banks of the Merrimac, a fine river with as much water as the Thames at Richmond, I should say, but spread over a bed generally twice as broad. We saw the White Mountains at a distance on our left, and passed through a number of flourishing towns. The thing that struck me most was the apparent fusion into one class of the whole community. As you know, every one goes into the same long carriages, holding from sixty to eighty people. Of these there were four or often five on our train, and I often passed through them (as you may do, up the middle, without disturbing the passengers, who sit in pairs with their faces to the engine on each side of the passage), as there was a great deal of local traffic, seventy people often getting out at a station, I thus saw really a very considerable number of people on this first day in the States, and certainly should have been exceedingly puzzled to sort them in the broadest way, either into rich and poor, gentlemen or ladies (in the conventional sense) and common people, or any other radical division. I certainly saw at some stations children running about without shoes, and workmen in as dirty blouses as those of Europe; but in the trains they were all well dressed, quiet, self-respecting people, without any pretence to polish, or any approach to vulgarity. The bad taste in women's dress, which I am told to expect elsewhere, does not certainly prevail in New England. All the women wore neat short dresses, with moderate trimmings according to taste; but I did not see an extravagant garment or, I am bound to add, a really pretty one along the whole line. On the whole I thought the women as good looking as any I have ever travelled amongst, but paler and sadder, or at any rate quieter, than a like number of Englishwomen. Once or twice men in stove-pipe hats (the ordinary tile of so-called civilisation), and wearing perhaps better cloth and whiter linen than the average, got in, but not one whom you would have picked out as a person bred and brought up in a different way, and occupying a station above or apart from the rest, as you see in every train in England. It may have been chance, but certainly it was startling. Then another surprise. They are certainly the least demonstrative people so far as strangers are concerned that I have ever been amongst. I had the prevailing idea that a Yankee was a note of interrogation walking about the world, and besides craving for all sorts of information about you, was always ready to impart to you the particulars of his own birth, parentage, and education, and his opinion on everything, "from Adam's fall to Huldy's bonnet." Well, I left our party purposely several times on the journey to try the experiment of sitting on one of the small seats carrying two only with a Yankee. In not one single case did either of those I sat by say a single word to me, and when I commenced they just answered my question very civilly and relapsed into total silence. I may add that this first experience has been confirmed since, both in street and railway cars.

We got to Boston at about seven, and then had our first experience of the price of things here. It is only four miles out to Lowell's, who lives on the other side of Cambridge, but we were obliged to pay five dollars for a carriage to get out there. We could get nothing but a great handsome family coach with two horses, and in that, accordingly, out we lumbered. Cambridge is a very pretty suburb of Boston, the centre point of it being Harvard College, consisting of four or five large blocks of red brick building and a stone chapel, standing in the midst of some fine trees. Elmwood Avenue in which Lowell lives is about half a mile beyond the College—a broad road shaded on both sides by tows of trees planted as in the Boulevards, as indeed is done along all the roads. The Professor's house is a good, roomy, wooden one standing in the midst of some thirty acres of his own land, on which stand many good trees, and especially some pre-revolutionary English elms of which he is very proud. He was sitting on the piazza of the house with his wife and Holmes' brother, taking a pipe and not the least expecting us. The Irish maid told us to "*sit right down*" while she went to fetch him. In a minute he and his wife came and put us at our ease, explaining that no letter had ever come since we had landed. Mabel was away at the sea for a few days.

Elmwood Avenue, Cambridge, 31st August 1870.

I managed with some difficulty and scramble to get off a letter to you by yesterday's post, which *ought* to go by steamer from New York to-day, bringing my narrative up to our arrival here. We found Lowell on his verandah with his wife and friend, and sat there talking till ten. I am not the least disappointed with him, Henry Cowper notwithstanding. I have never met a more agreeable talker, and his kindness to me is quite unbounded. Then he has not a grain of vanity in his composition, but is as simple and truthful as the best kind of boy. The house is a wooden one, as four-fifths of the houses in New England are. It is roomy, airy, and furnished with quaint old heavy pieces, bureaus like ours, and solid heavy little mahogany tables, all dating from the last century. The plate in the same way is all of the Queen Anne shape, like your little tea-service and my grandmother's milk jugs and tea-pots which George has. The plainness and simplicity of the living, too, is most attractive. We breakfast at 8.30, beginning with porridge, and following up with eggs, some hot dish, corn cakes, toast and fruit. Then there is no regular meal till six—a terribly late and fashionable dinner hour here, as the prevalent hour is two or three—and afterwards we have a cup of coffee and crackers (good plain biscuits) and a glass of toddy at ten. Miss Mabel and others have given us a desperate idea of the difficulties as to service, but they certainly do not exist in this establishment just now. The principal servant that we see is an Irish girl, Rose by name, who reminds me of one of Mrs. Cameron's servants except that she is far more diligent. The ingenious way in which she hid away all my wardrobe in the ample cupboards and recesses of the bureau in my room was a perfect caution, and she whisks away my things and gets them beautifully washed, wholly refusing to allow me to pay for them. The parlour-maid is a little, slight, ladylike girl, who certainly is not a first-rate waiter, but then there is no need of one. The dinner is confined to one thing at a time—soup, sometimes fish, a joint, or chickens, and a sweet. The Professor opens his own wine at the table and passes it round, and very good it is, but one scarcely needs it in this climate. A cook whose acquaintance I have also made, and an Irishman who has been thirty years on the place in a roomy cottage, and attends to the cows, garden, and farm of thirty acres, complete the establishment. Mrs. Lowell, who is a very nice, quiet, and clever woman, is very fond of flowers, and manages to keep a few beds going about the house, and there are a number of very fine trees, so that though there is no pretence to the neatness and finish of English grounds and garden, the place has a thoroughly homely, cultivated atmosphere and look which is very attractive, and the whole town of Cambridge seems to be made up of just such houses. We have lost no time in lionising men and places. On Thursday we took the car into Boston and ascended the monument on Bunker's Hill, 290 steps up a dark spiral staircase. Lowell had never been up it before, nor indeed has any native as far as I can find out. The view at the top repays you thoroughly for the grind with the thermometer at eighty in the shade. Boston Harbour, where the tea was thrown out of the English ships in 1775, and> the whole town and suburbs lie below you like a map, and are very striking. After descending we hunted up a number of people, including young Holmes, our Colonel, who was as charming as ever, absorbed in his law at which he is doing famously, and resolved in his first holiday to revisit England. He came out to dine, and fraternised immensely with R——, and with him a young Howells, the editor of the Atlantic Monthly, whom Conway had brought to our house years ago, and I had entirely forgotten. However he is a very nice fellow, and I don't think I betrayed my obliviousness. Next day, Friday, we had a long country drive in the morning through broad avenues lined with three fascinating wooden houses, each standing with plenty of elbow-room in its own grounds, up to a wooded hill from which we got a splendid view of the city. Then I went into Boston and called on the Autocrat of the Breakfast Table, who is one of the best talkers I ever met, and quite worthy to be the Colonel's father. He is one of Motley's oldest friends, and deeply grieved, as all good men here, at his recall. His chief talk was of his memories of his English visits, and the folk he met, and so I find it with all the best men and women here. Notwithstanding the bitterness which our press created during the war, I am convinced that with a very little tact and judicious handling on our side the international relations may be easily made all we can wish as far as New England is concerned. Afterwards I sauntered about the town, looking at some good statues in their park (Boston Common), and letting the place sink into me. The Common is about the size, I should say, of Green Park, but of a regular shape. It lies on the side of a hill at the top of which are the State House and other public buildings and private houses. It is well wooded with fine American and English elms (pre-revolutionary, they say, but I don't believe it. They are not used to our elms, and I doubt whether any of these are 100 years old) on the upper part and along the sides; the middle is a great playground for the boys, who are diligent there all day at base-ball, our rounders, which I should think must spoil the enjoyment of the place for ladies and children. However they can always take to the pretty gardens at the lower end, in which is a very fine equestrian statue of Washington, and one of Everett by Story, by no means fine in my opinion. How should it be, when he insisted on being taken with his arm right up in the air, his favourite attitude in speaking, and stands up in that attitude in ordinary buttoned frock coat and trousers? Everett has not been a trustworthy public man to my mind, and is simply nothing unless it is an orator, and I can't say I think it wise to put him up there on the palpable stump. But we have made so many mistakes in our public statues that I suppose it must run in the blood. The best houses in the town, really charming residences, line the two sides and top of the Common, and fine stores the bottom. I have never seen a place I would so soon live in out of England as in one of these houses looking on to Boston Common. The old business town is being rebuilt just as London—red brick two or three story houses giving way everywhere to five or six stories of granite or stone. The town has as old and settled a look and feeling about it as any I know; but they have few old buildings, and I am afraid are going to pull down the most characteristic, the old State House, because it has ceased to be used for public purposes, and its removal will make a fine broad place and relieve the traffic of several narrow streets in the heart of the town. It will be a sad pity, and so unnecessary here, for they might carry it off bodily to any other site. You know how we have often heard, and wondered, scarce believing, of the raising bodily of the great hotels, etc., at Chicago. Well, suddenly, in Boston I came across a great market, three stories high (the upper part being occupied as houses) and 150 or 200 feet long, as big, say, as three houses in Grosvenor Square, which they were moving bodily back on rollers so as to widen the street. There were the wooden ways and the rollers, and the great block with all its marketing and living inhabitants lying on them, and already some twelve feet on its journey. It did not look any the worse for its journey unless it were in the foundations, where there were a few places which had been filled up, I saw, with new brickwork. The long pit twelve feet deep which has been left between the market and the street will now be turned into cellars, over which the new pavement will pass. On the Saturday we dined with the Saturday Club at 2.30 P.M., where were all the New England notables now in town. I sat on the right of Sumner, the State Senator, who was in the chair, with Boutwell, the Secretary of the Treasury, on my right, and Emerson on the other side of Sumner. So you may fancy how I enjoyed the sitting. Emerson is perfectly delightful: simple, wise, and full of humour and sunshine. The number of good Yankee stories I shall bring back unless they burst me will be a caution. Forbes, a great Boston merchant who owns an island seventy-two miles long off the coast close to Nantucket and Cape Cod, which you will find in the map, came up and claimed to have seen me for five minutes when I had the small-pox in 1863.

He knows J——— well, and insisted on carrying us off to his island that night, that we might attend a huge campmeeting on a neighbouring island on Sunday. So he drove up here with us and we packed—the dear Professor agreeing that we ought to do it—went down sixty miles by rail, slept on his yacht, and found ourselves in the morning at his wharf on the island. Your second letter came to hand from Cromer when we returned here, and has as usual lighted up my life.

Cambridge, 2nd September 1870.

We are off this afternoon for Newport on our way to New York, and so south and west. The express man will be here directly for my luggage, which will be a little curtailed, as these dear kind people insist on our returning, and leaving all we don't want in our rooms. So I shall drop my beaver, leaving it with the most serious admonitions in the charge of Rose, the Irish girl, who is a character. I will now take up the thread of my story, merely remarking that what you seem to think a dull catalogue of small doings at a small watering-place is quite unspeakably delightful to me away here. On the wharf at Nashont Island we found the two young F————s, the elder a colonel in the war, and five months a prisoner in the South, the younger, Malcolm, just left college. I never saw two finer young men, both of them models of strength. They had come down to meet us and bathe, so we stopped and had a splendid header off the wharf and a swim in the bay, after careful inquiries by R———— as to sharks, to which young F———— replied with a twinkle in his eye, that they didn't lose *many* friends that way. We walked up to the house after our dip, a large wooden building, with deep verandahs and sun-blinds, furnished quite plainly, even roughly, but capable of holding nearly any number of people. We were about eighteen at breakfast: Mrs. F———— a handsome, clever, elderly lady, born a Quaker, and with their charm of manner, who made tea for the party, and on whose right I sat. Opposite her was her husband with Mrs. L————, the young widow of Lowell's nephew Charles, the famous soldier, on his left, and therefore opposite me. On my right, a young woman, a cousin of the F————s, a Mrs. P————, whose husband sat down towards the end of the table, the manager of a Western railway, who has given us free passes over his line. Colonel F————, the eldest son, was Lowell's major, and served with distinction in the war, in which he was taken prisoner, and spent five months in Southern prisons; his wife, a buxom young woman with very good eyes, is Emerson's daughter, and her brother, a bright boy of twenty-two or twenty-three, was near me. There were two daughters of the family, and two other girls and several boys, all pleasant and easy in hand; but the gem of the party was the young widow. She is not actually pretty, but with a face full of the nobleness of sorrow, which has done its work. I have seldom been more touched than in watching her gentle, cheerful ways, and her sympathy with all the bright life around her. Since the war, in which her husband and only brother R. S————(who commanded the first coloured regiment from Massachusetts, and was buried under his negroes at Fort Wagner) were killed, she has devoted herself to the Freedmen, and is Honorary Secretary to the Society for educating them. After breakfast we started in the yacht for the neighbouring island, on which the great Methodist camp-meeting was going on. This Sunday was the great day. They have occupied this island for some years, and have built there a whole town of pretty little wooden houses like big Chinese toys, dotted about amongst the trees. Most of them consist of only one long room, divided by curtains in the middle. The front half opens to the street, but raised one step above it is the sitting-room, and the inmates sleep in the back, behind the curtains. A few houses have a story above; but F———— bought a lot of photographs for us, which will show you the style of house better than a page of description. There were literally thousands of people on the island, upwards of two thousand collected in a huge circular tent in the middle of the houses, where a preacher was shouting to them. We sat on the skirts of the congregation and listened for some time, but as he was only talking wildly about Nebuddah, Positivism, Theodore Parker, and other heresies and heretics, I was not edified, and got no worship till he had done, when we all stood up and sang the doxology, which was very impressive. I was much disappointed at the gathering in a religious point of view. It was a rare chance for a man with a living word in him, those thousands of decent, sober, attentive New England men and women. They told me that in the evening it would be much more interesting, when there would be great singing of hymns, and many persons would tell how they came to experience religion as they call it; but we could not stay for this. The meeting lasts for weeks, and is in fact an excuse for the gathering at a pretty sea-place in the early autumn of a number of good folk who would think the ordinary watering-places ungodly, but have a longing for a break in their ordinary colourless lives. We sailed back in time for early dinner, meeting on the way huge steamers packed with passengers for the campmeeting, till they were top heavy. Next day we spent in, fishing off the rocks for blue-fish, and in a beautiful little lake of three-quarters of a mile long (one of several in the island) for bass. I caught a blue fish of nine lbs., the biggest and strongest I have ever caught, also the only bass which was taken; so I naturally crowed loudly. The island hours are: breakfast, eight o'clock or half past eight; dinner, two or three; tea, with cold meat, half-past six or seven. After tea on both evenings we got into full swing on the war. I found Mr. F———— and his wife deeply grieved and prejudiced as to our conduct, our feeling to them as a nation, etc., and set myself to work hard to remove all this as far as I could. As he is a very energetic and influential man it is worth taking any amount of trouble about, and I think I succeeded. In the evenings the young folk sang a number of the war songs, several composed by or for the negro soldiers, going to famous airs, and full of humour and pathos. The March through Georgia is very spirited, and a version of the "John Brown" March, which seems to have superseded "We'll hang Jef Davies," etc., exceedingly touching—at least I know it was so to me, as all the young folk sang—

He hath sounded forth the trumpet that shall never call retreat,

He is sifting out the souls of men before His judgment seat:

Be swift, my soul, to welcome Him! be jubilant, my feet.

In the beauty of the lilies, Christ was born across the sea,

With a glory in His bosom that transfigures you and me.

As he died to make men holy, let us die to make them free.

Our God is marching on.

To think of what that sweet young woman had gone through (the news of her husband's death at the head of his brigade, was read by her in a newspaper), and to see her sitting there calmly and trying to join in the chorus, was quite too much for me. However, nobody noticed my emotion. Our last morning, Tuesday, was spent in a famous wild ride over the island. After breakfast we found seven very excellent riding horses (three with sidesaddles) at the door. At home there would have been three grooms, here each horse has a leathern strap fixed to the bit, which you just buckle round his neck till you want to stop, and then fasten it to the nearest tree or lamp-post. The whole turn-out is of course rough, but I don't wish to see nicer ladies' hacks than the three which the two Miss F———s and Mrs. P——— rode. We sailed back in the yacht to another little port, a few miles north of New Bedford, F——— having provided us as a parting present with free passes over almost all the Western railways, which will save me at least £20 I should think. He is Chairman of several, and so can do it without any trouble. We found the dear Lowells expecting us, and my second letter also waiting, so you may think that I had a joyful evening. Next day, Wednesday, we drove to Concord to dine with Judge Hoar, the late Attorney-General of the United States, a very able, fine fellow. We passed over classic ground, the very road along which the English troops marched in April 1776 to destroy the stores, when the first collision of the War of Independence took place at Concord Bridge and in the village of Lexington. You may perhaps remember in the second series of the *Biglow Papers* "Sumthin' in the Pastoral Line," in which old Concord Bridge and the monument which has been put up to commemorate the fight, talk together over the *Trent* affair. The Judge's two sons, very nice young fellows, pulled us up Concord River, which runs at the bottom of their garden, to the spot, and on the way (which is very pretty) we saw lots of tortoises sitting and basking on the stones, and popping in when we approached, and heard a lot of capital Yankee stories from the Judge. Dinner at three; Emerson came, and there were two Miss H———s, and a Miss S———, a handsome girl, sister of the best oar in the Harvard boat of last year. I enjoyed the dinner and smoke afterwards immensely, and am at last quite sure that I am doing some good with some of these men, all of whom are influential, and most of them sadly prejudiced against us still as a nation. For myself it is quite impossible to express their kindness. They seem as if they can never do enough for me. When we got back to Cambridge, we found Miss M——— and Dr. Lowell, brother to James, an English clergyman, and quite charming too in his way.

New York.

I think I have told you already the sort of royal progress I am making. Some principal citizen always comes to the station to meet us in his carriage, books our luggage by the express (an admirable institution which saves you all the trouble with luggage), drives us up to his house, lodges us in the best rooms, has all the best folks in the neighbourhood to meet us at breakfast, dinner, tea, takes us to the sights of the neighbourhood, keeps all his servants out of sight when we are going, so that we can't give any one a penny or even pay our washing bills, and finally sends us and our luggage down to the next boat or steamer, when we are booked already probably by a new friend. Certainly I never saw, heard of, or could imagine anything like the hospitality. It is no doubt in some degree, and in individual cases, owing to the part I took during the war in England, but Democrats as well as Republicans have been amongst our warmest hosts; in fact, I am fairly puzzled, and allow the tide at last to carry me along, floating down it and enjoying everything as well as I can. I think in my last I got to our start from Boston. No! was it? At any rate, I wrote about our day at Concord, I know, as to which I shall have to tell you more when we meet. After we got home Miss Mabel rushed upstairs, got into her photographing dress, the quaintest turn-out you can conceive, and commenced a series of groups, etc., which you shall have specimens of when I get back. She is endless fun; has the most arch way of talking to her father as "sir" every now and then; is charming with her stepmother; and altogether as bright a bit of life about a house as you would meet on a summer's day. I parted from Lowell and his home feeling that the meeting had been more than successful. For these eighteen or nineteen years I have revelled in his books—indeed, have got so much from them and learned to love the parent of them so well, as I imagined him, that I almost feared the meeting, lest pleasant illusions should be broken. I found him much better than his books. We had a pleasant three hours' rail to Newport, finding Mr. Field, a Philadelphian banker, at the station with his carriage. We were friends at once, for he is a famous, frank, goodlooking, John Bullish man of the world, who has travelled all over Europe and retained his new world simplicity and heartiness. He drove us all round the fashionable watering-place, the description of which I must postpone or I never shall get through (as we say here). His cottage, as he calls it, in accordance with the fashion here, is a charming villa, on the most southern point of Newport, close to the rocks on which the grand Atlantic roll was beating magnificently as we drove up.

Saturday morning a lot of men came to breakfast, including Colonel H——
—, the officer who had been the first to volunteer to take command of negroes in Virginia, before the New England States even began mustering them. I was delighted to make his acquaintance, as I knew his name in my

anti-slavery standard as a real, advanced Radical, and I was anxious to realise that type of Yankee of which I had only seen Lloyd Garrison in England. He was very fascinating to my mind, and the most refined man in manners and look I have yet met, but I should say decidedly a cracked fellow in the good sense. We adjourned to the spouting rock, just at the point where the surf was beating gloriously, and as I continued talking with H————, of course I got a ducking by getting too near this rock, which is hollow underneath, so that it sends a spout of water up like a huge whale some second or two after the breaker hits it. The sight was superb, and well worth the payment of an unstarched waistcoat and shirt. We got home, and I changed at 11.30 or thereabouts, and when I came in to dress for dinner there was my waistcoat, washed and starched, on the bed. Mrs. Field had heard me say in joke that I should be out of white waistcoats. We went to the Episcopal Church on Sunday morning and had a good sermon of a quarter of an hour, sitting in the pew of an acquaintance of the previous day, a Mrs. H———— of New York, who drove us about in her handsome carriage, and insisted on giving me two books—one being extracts from Lincoln's *Speeches and Letters*, which I am very glad to have. In the evening we were sent down to the pier, where we were picked up by the most magnificent steamer ever seen in the world, I should think, and by six next morning were running along the north river, one of the many entrances by sea to New York harbour. The approaches to the city are superb, but the first view of it disappointed me, the buildings along the water-side being for the most part poor and almost mean. We found Hewitt's carriage waiting, he being out of town for his Sunday, and drove up through Broadway and Fourth Avenue to his house, which is a splendid roomy one, belonging to his father-inlaw, Mr. Cooper. The dear old gentleman, a hearty veteran of seventy-nine, is the founder of the Cooper's Institute, a working-man's college on a large scale. He has spent nearly a million dollars upon it, and it is certainly the best institution of the kind I have ever seen. He is one of the most guileless and sweetest of old men, and I shall have much to tell you of him. Mr. Hewitt, my friend, who is in partnership with him, and his wife and family live with the old gentleman. Here I found free admission to the four best clubs in New York—the Union League, the Century, and even the Manhattan, a democrat club of which Hewitt is a distinguished member. The nice brisk woman in the house gave us an excellent breakfast, and we started for the town about eleven. One of the first places I went to was Roebuck's store, where I found him very flourishing. But I can't go on to catalogue our doings or shan't get this off. As very few folk are in New York, we are off to-day to West Point up the Hudson, where we stay for a military ball to-morrow night; on Friday we get to Niagara, and then away west, certainly as far as Omaha, to see prairies, etc., and possibly to San Francisco. We must be back here or in New England on the 1st of October, on the 6th is the Harvard Memorial ceremony, laying the first stone of their memorial building, on the 11th I am in for an address, and after that shall set my face homewards. I have looked at myself in the glass at your request and believe I look fabulous.

Garrison's Landing, opposite West Point, Friday, 9th September 1870.

I already look wistfully along the pages of my pocket-book which intervene between this and the beginning of November, and feel very like bolting home instead of going west. The only moments I have for writing are early (it is now 6.30) or after I come up to bed, as the dear, good folk provide occupation for all the rest of the time. Well, we got to New York on Monday mornings by the East River, and left it on Wednesday afternoon by the Hudson, having, I think, seen it superficially, so that I should retain a clear idea of it if I never saw it again. We dined on Monday at the Union League Club, Tuesday at the Manhattan, going in afterwards to the Century—all three clubs as complete, I think, as ours and open to strangers in every corner. We left New York on Wednesday afternoon with Mr. O———, Chairman of the Illinois Central Railway, who has this delicious place on the slope of the mountain opposite West Point. As usual there were carriages at the pier, and all trouble, expense, etc., has been taken off our hands. Mrs. O——— is the nicest Yankee lady we have seen (except Mabel), like Mrs. Goschen in face and charmingly appreciative. Her husband, staunch American, about fifty. The more fanatic Americans they are the more they seem to like to do for me, and as I spend the greater part of my time in showing them how mistaken they must be in their views as to England, else how is it that we didn't interfere and get to war, I feel I am doing good work. They take to me, I can see, apart from my proclivities.

I am obliged to give up poor old Pam, the mercantile community of England, and the majority of the aristocracy; but when I have made a Jonah of these, I always succeed in bringing these good, simple, candid, impulsive fellows to admit that we did them no bad turn in their troubles. We leave to-day for Niagara, and during the next fortnight I hardly know how or when I can write.

Clifton Hotel, opposite Niagara Falls, 11th September 1870.

I am glad to find that I shall be able to get off this one more letter to you by regular post before we plunge away west for nearly a fortnight. I do so long for you every now and then when there is something to see which you would specially appreciate, not only then as you well know, but then specially, in the glorious reaches of the Hudson near West Point, for instance, where you have all the beauty of the Scotch Highlands, with a hundred well-kept rich men's houses, and a monster hotel or two crowning some high point,—an excellent substitute, in my view, for the ruined keeps of robber barons on the Rhine,—and endless steamers and sloops, with their white sails and great tows, as they call them, of a dozen large flats lashed together and bringing down lumber and corn from the west, passing up and down; but, above all, last night, when we went under the light of a glorious full moon and saw these mighty falls from above, and then went down some 200 steps, and along under the overhanging cliffs, till we actually got under the end of the horse-shoe fall on the Canadian side, and looked up and saw the moon through the falling water. Just as we descended, an American gentleman and his daughter and an English girl with them came up, to whom we gave our seats, and when we came back they were still there, so we told them what we had seen and offered to escort them down. They were delighted, and "papa" did not object, so down we all went, and so we had a second treat behind the cataract, and being with these ladies made me horribly wishful to get you there. The girl (Philadelphian) was very pretty and simple, so I handed her over to R———, and gave my arm to the English one. To-day we went across the ferry amid a great turbulence of waters, and looked up at the descending rivers, to the English Church on the opposite side. An American bishop preached, and afterwards we walked on Goat Island, above and between the two falls, and saw such effects of rainbows, and lilac and green and purple and pure white surges, as it is utterly impossible to describe, but I shall try to do it by the help of photographs when I get back. Then we had a bath in the rush just above the Falls; you have a little room through which a slice some four feet wide of the water is allowed to rush; you get in at the side, in the back water, and then take hold of a short rope fixed close above the rush, and let the waters seize and tear at you, which it does with a vengeance, tugging as if it would carry off your legs and pull you in two in the middle. You can get out of it in a moment by just slewing yourself round, and the sensation is marvellously delicious. I forget whether you had one of the baths at Geneva, where the blue Rhone rushes through at about a third of the pace. That is the only bath I ever remember the least to be compared to this above Niagara. But let me see, I hadn't got farther with you than our chateau on the Hudson. Well, we left it on Friday after breakfast at about nine o'clock, and travelled away steadily with only twenty minutes' stop at Albany, where we dined, and a quarter of an hour at Rochester. The greater part of the road was decidedly pretty, especially the earlier part which ran along the banks of the Hudson. We stopped at Rome, Syracuse, and Utica amongst other places, all busy, stirring places apparently, with their streets all converging on and open to the line of rail. Every one has to look out for themselves, and you get in and out of the trains at your own peril. I have heard of very few accidents, and I don't believe there are as many as with us; but I should think a good many people must often be left behind, as the train starts without any signal, leaving you to climb in as you can, an easy enough feat for an active man, but scarcely for any one else. This journey was our first really long one; we did not get to Suspension Bridge, where we slept, till past midnight, but I didn't find it very tiring. There was a drawing-room car on, but I would not go in it. The other cars are quite comfortable enough, and I like seeing and being with the people, though they continue to be the most silent and reserved of any race I have ever been amongst. Next day (Saturday) just glanced at the Falls; we ran round the west of Lake Ontario, by Hamilton, to Toronto, the capital of the province, and were exceedingly struck and pleased with the signs of vigour and prosperity both in the country and cities. The farming is certainly cleaner and better than on the American side of the lake, and the towns don't lose by comparison with those of the same size over the border. At Toronto I found Dymond, one of my best Lambeth supporters, in the Globe Office, and we called on one of our *Peruvian* acquaintances, who regaled us with champagne in his huge store; we went over the law courts and other public buildings, dined, and then on to the boat to cross back to Niagara. It is about two hours' sail and very pleasant. There were quite a number of young and pretty girls on board going across for the trip, as you might drive out in a carriage to any suburb. It seems the regular afternoon amusement and lounge, and the heads of families take season tickets which pass all their belongings. There were three Canadian M.P.'s also on board, with whom I got a good deal of useful and pleasant chat; one of them (M.P. for Niagara) induced me to "drink" twice in ginger-ale and brandy, and again in champagne, which was the first instance of that pressingly convivial habit supposed to be universal on this side that I have seen. I am uncommonly glad it doesn't really prevail, as nothing I detest more than this irregular kind of drinking. The pick-me-up is decidedly one of the most loathsome inventions of a decrepit civilisation. We got to our hotel here, right opposite the Falls, by about six, saw them first before tea and afterwards by moonlight, as I have already narrated. In an hour's time we start for Chicago. Our late host, Mr. O———, the President of the Illinois Central Rail, one of the greatest of the Western's system of railways, has followed us here, and is going round a tour of inspection of his line, and to open 150 miles of new way for traffic. So we shall go round in an express train with him, seeing everything in the most luxurious and easiest manner—a wonderful piece of luck. It was his nice wife who persuaded him to come off and do it now at once while he could have us with him. I am sitting at my open window, outside of which is a broad verandah with a magnificent view of the Falls. I am getting what I take to be my last look at them, and for the last time the sound of many waters, the finest to be heard in the world, I suppose, is in my ears. The mid-Atlantic when the waves were highest struck me more, but nothing else I have ever seen in Switzerland or elsewhere comes near this. It is the first great hotel we have been in, and not a bad specimen I imagine. We get heaps of meals, and though the cooking is not all one could wish, there is nothing to hinder your living very well. We are waited on by some fifteen or twenty real darkies—good, grinning, curly-pated Sambos and Pompeys—so, of course, I am happy so far as service goes. Seriously, though, they are much more obliging and quite as intelligent as their white compeers here and in the States.

Storm Lake, 13th. September 1870.

One line from this odd little station, right in the middle of the Iowa prairies, which slope away right out of sight in every direction. It is the highest point between Fort Dodge and Sioux City. Fifteen months ago there were not three settlers' cabins on the whole 140 miles; now they are dotted along every mile or so, sometimes turf huts, sometimes wooden, with generally a group of barefooted, healthy children tumbling about the doors. We are sitting in the little wooden post-office here, on the walls of which hang maps of the splendid town which is to be run up in the next three or four years, and notices of a meeting of the citizens of Storm Lake to hear the addresses of Captain Jackson Orr, the Republican candidate for Congress of the district, and of Governor G———, who comes to support him. The whole place at present consists of some ten or twelve wooden huts, with two more ambitious buildings running up, one an hotel and the other a big store. The settlers are a fine rough set of fellows, but full of intelligence, and determined to make their place the most important city in the State. It is a most exquisite climate, with a lake four miles by two, in which there are plenty of pickerel, and as we came along in our express train we have put up lots of coveys of prairie hens, like big tame grouse, most delicious eating too. *Express train*, you will look at with wondering eyes. Well, or rather wââl, as they pronounce it here, that is the explanation of the whole *city*, and accounts for all that is going to happen on this glorious prairie. A line of rail has been *built* right across it by some enterprising folk in New York, who want now to lease it to the Illinois Central Railway, with which it makes connections at Fort Dodge. We left Chicago yesterday morning, got to Dubuque on the Mississippi by night, travelled all through the night to Fort Dodge, and are on here now fifty-three miles farther inspecting. It is regal travelling. We have two carriages,—one a charming sleeping-car, in which I have a beautiful little state-room, another carriage for dining, etc., equally commodious, all our stores on board, so that we live splendidly, two negro boys to wait on us. O———, the present president, and the vice-president of the line, are our only fellow-passengers, each of whom is as well lodged as I am. We go along as we please, sometimes at forty, sometimes at ten miles an hour, talking to the people at each little log-house station, and enjoying the confines of civilisation in the most perfect luxury. While they are talking about the price of land round here I have just this ten minutes, and find I can fire off this note with some chance that it may get off by the New York boat of Saturday, so that I shan't lose a post or you a letter.

Fort Dodge, 13th September 1870.

Here we are! September 15, 2 p.m. You will see, if you have got my last from Sioux City, that the above heading is somewhat wild. The fact is, that just as I had written the three first words (in fact, while I was writing them, which accounts for their jerky look), our little train moved on from Fort Dodge and I couldn't write, even on our superb springs. Now we are at Council Bluffs, opposite Omaha. Why, hang it! here we go again moving on, and I must stop again.

3 p.m.—We only ran three miles and then stopped to lunch and let a Union-Pacific train pass. Now after a famous lunch in our second or commissariat car, I am getting a smoke and a few more lines to you before we are off eastward again. Thank Heaven! after all the wonderful new sights and sensations of the last three and a half days since we left Niagara, I confess to the utmost delight at feeling that we have made our farthest point, and that I am already some three miles plus the breadth of the Missouri River and Omaha City on my way back to you. It is still more than a month before we embark for home (if I can hold out as long); still, we are on our way! However, you must not think that I am not enjoying myself wonderfully. I am, and am also, I hope, good company, for when one is treated like the Grand Turk or the Emperor of Russia, the least one can do is to be pleasant. But if I go on with my sensations, I shall never pick up my narrative; as it is, I shall be obliged to leave thousands of things till we meet, when I do hope I shan't have forgotten anything. Well, didn't I leave off at Niagara? We left the hotel in front of the Falls there on Monday morning after breakfast with O——, who had no power except for himself till we got to Chicago; we had been furnished with free passes, and rode in the ordinary cars through Ontario province to Windsor, opposite Detroit. In Canada, again, the difference was at once visible between the two peoples; but I am not at all prepared to admit that the Canadians have the worst of it, certainly not in the roadside cookery, for we had the best joint of beef we have seen since we left home at dinner, and the best bread and butter at tea. At Windsor the train ran quietly on to the huge ferry-boat-steamer, and we had a moonlight passage to the railway station at Detroit. Here we secured berths in the Pullman sleeping car, for which you pay rather more than you would for a bed at a first-class hotel. However, they are an admirable institution, and enable one to get through really wonderful travelling feats. We were at Chicago early next morning, and transferred ourselves directly into our small express train, getting glimpses of the city of forty years, which within living men's memory was a small Indian station.

It is enormous, spreading over certainly three times the space which an English city of 250,000 inhabitants would occupy. We shall see the town on our return; meantime, as we ran out of the suburbs, we saw a house of considerable size waiting at the crossing for our train to pass before it went over, as coolly as a farmer's waggon of hay would wait in England. O——— —told us that all the old houses in Chicago are moved in this way. As building is very expensive, when one of the big folk wants to put up some splendid new structure—bank, store, or the like—there are always men ready to buy the old house as it stands. They then just cut away its foundation, put it on rollers, and tote it away to the site they have bought in the suburbs. We fell upon breakfast in a half-famished state as we steamed away westward, and through the whole day were kept on the stretch. Not that there was any great beauty in the scenery, but the interest of getting actually into half-settled country was exceedingly absorbing. The most notable town we passed was Galena, in Northern Illinois, from which Grant went to the war, leaving his leather yard for that purpose. The citizens of Galena have bought and presented him a good square house of red brick on the top of the hill there. Then we ran along a tributary of the Mississippi, and about 4.30 came out on the father of waters; where we struck the mighty stream it was not impressive. We came upon a mighty swamp, not a river, miles and miles of trees, some of them fine large ones, standing in the water and covered with creepers. The river was luckily high, so that we had this effect of a forest rising out of water to perfection. Then there were miles of swamp, half water, half land, dreary and horrible to look at, sometimes sound enough for cattle to pick about, and then only fit for alligators and wild-fowl; of the latter we saw a number, including a white heron. At last we came upon the river, some three-quarters of a mile wide-up there, 1600 miles from the sea, and crossed by a gossamer bridge, a real work of high art. On the opposite side we stopped for tea-dinner at Dubuque, one of the largest towns in Iowa, and the first border city we had seen,—very quaint to behold, with streets laid out as broad as Regent Street, here and there a huge block of stores full of dry goods or groceries, and then a lot of wooden hovels, a vacant plot perhaps, and then a big hotel, or another great store,—the streets all as soft as Rotten Row, and much deeper in dirt, side pavements of wood, every house placarded in huge letters with the name and business of the owner. Here, for the first time, we saw emigrants' waggons packed with their household goods and lumber (sawed planks) for their houses, bound for the prairies beyond, on which they settle under the homestead acts. In short, the pushing slipshod character of the great West was thoroughly mirrored in the place, and above all the other buildings was a fine common school open to every child in the place. This is the one universal characteristic of these towns and villages; almost the first thing they do is to build a famous big school. The member of Congress for the place and one or two other notables came down to see us after tea, and smoked a cigar with us in our saloon car before we started. The talk was, of course, on the wonders of the West, and the chances of Dubuque to be a big city in a year or two. Then we turned in and ran all night to Fort Dodge, from which the first line of this letter was written, a village with the same characteristics as the towns, except that the only building not of wood was the station, which, strange to say, was built of gypsum, found in great quantities here, and the only sort of stone they have. The president of the line—a shrewd, honest, Western man named Douglas, one of our party—guessed that in another five years they would have to pull the station down and manure the land with it. From this place we ran right up into the wild prairies, and at the highest point between the Mississippi and Missouri, at Storm Lake, I wrote you the hasty note which, I hope, you have received from those unknown parts. It is about the largest settlement in the 180 miles, consisting of perhaps twelve or fourteen wooden houses, one of which was a billiard saloon kept by an old Cornish man. He said that quite a number of Cornish miners are over in this district, some at lead and coal mines of a very primitive kind, others farming. On the whole, the people seemed a good, steady, independent lot, and the children looked wonderfully healthy, running about barefooted on the shore of the little lake or amongst the prairie grass. We made acquaintance with prairie chicken and the little earth squirrel, a jolly little dog, with a prettily marked back, who frisks into his hole instead of up a tree like ours. Then we dropped down, still through wild prairie, over which the single line of rail runs with no protection at all, till we came to Sioux City on the Missouri, and the biggest town on the river for 2000 miles from its source. There are 12,000 inhabitants, and precisely the same features as at Dubuque, except that it is a far more rowdy place, being still almost under the dominion of Judge Lynch. Only the day before we arrived, a border ruffian had been swaggering about the town, pistol in hand, and defying arrest. However, they did take him at last, and he was safe in prison. A fortnight earlier a rascal, who confessed to nine murders, had been taken and hung on the other side of the river. There are sixty-three saloons, at most of which gambling goes on regularly every night. The editor of the *Sioux Tribune*, an Irish Yankee of queer morals and extraordinary "go," took us into one, stood drinks round, and expounded the ingenious games by which the settlers and officers of the Indian fort up the stream are cleared of their money. A rowdy, loafing, vagabond city, but there they have three or four fine schools (one had just cost 45,000 dollars), for which they tax the saloons mercilessly. I have no doubt the place will be quite respectable in another five years. We slept quietly and dropped down south along the Missouri to Council Bluffs, from which the earlier part of this was written. The Missouri is a doleful stream, shallow, with huge sandbanks in the middle, and great swamps at the side, but striking green bluffs rising above on the east bank under which we went; and behind them I saw the sun rise in great beauty. We just crossed the river to Omaha to say we had been in Missouri and seen the terminus of the Union-Pacific Railway, and a fine go-ahead place it is, like

Dubuque, only twice as big and finely situate on hills above the Missouri River. We are now back at Chicago, having seen more frontier towns and prairies on our way here, and in five days, by the good fortune of this private train, have done more than we could have managed otherwise in nine.

Chicago, September 1870.

I am so afraid that I shan't get off a letter regularly twice a week from this run in the West, that I begin this in a spare three minutes between packing and a testimonial which is to be given me here by a lot of young graduates of the American Universities at the Club at four o'clock. This place is the wonder of the wonderful West, as you know already. A gentleman I met to-day tells me he came up to this place in 1830, when it consisted of a fort with two companies, a dozen little wooden huts, and an encampment of 3000 or 4000 Indians who had come in to get their allowances under treaty with the United States. Now it is one of the handsomest cities I ever saw, with 300,000 inhabitants, and progressing at the rate of 1500 a week or thereabouts. We have had our first experience of a first-rate American hotel, the Fremont House here. It is decidedly not cheap. At present rates about fifteen shillings or four dollars a day; but you can eat and drink anything but wine and spirits all day, with the exception of one hour in the afternoon between lunch and dinner. I ordered a peach just now for lunch, and they brought me a whole plateful, not so good as our hot-house ones, but very fine fruit. Yesterday I went twice to hear Robert Collyer, a famous Unitarian minister here. He was born in Yorkshire, where he worked as a blacksmith, preaching as a Methodist, and finally, twenty years ago, came out to the West and established himself here. He has great and deserved influence, and is altogether the finest man of the kind I have ever met. His text was out of Job: "Dost thou know the springs of the deep?" I forget the exact words, but you will find them in the splendid 38th chapter, where God is showing Job who is master (as the cabman put it). He had been for his holiday at the sea, and was full of thoughts which, as he said, he wanted to get off to his people. He began by a quotation from Ruskin as to the fantastic power and beauty of the sea, said that no trace of love for the sea could be found in the Bible, only fear of it. In the New Jerusalem, St. John dreamed "there shall be no more sea." Same with all great poets, even English, illustrated by Burns and Shakespere, and Dr. Johnson's saying, "That a ship was a prison with a chance of being drowned." Even sailors don't really look on sea as home, and fear it, and weave mystical notions of all kinds round it. Yet the sea has its sweet and gentle side too; it nourishes every plant and flower that grows by its exhalations, and keeps the rivers sweet and running; and look at one of the exquisite little shells which you may find after the fiercest storm, or the bit of sea-weed lying on the shore, or the limpet on the rock. The lashing of the storm has done them no harm, and there they lie as perfect as if it had never been raging. about them. So the great stormy sea of life has its gentle and loving side for every one of us so long as we trust in God and just obey His laws and do His will. I have given you the very barest outline of a very striking sermon. In the evening I went to tea with him, and there was a large bunch of grapes on my plate with the enclosed little paper, "To Mr. Hughes from the children," which touched me much. The children are very nice. Robert Lincoln, Abe's son, and a lot of his friends are our entertainers to-day, and in the evening we go by the night train to St. Louis. I laid aside the other sheet to go off to this club dinner with the young Chicago men, and I have never had a more hearty greeting or kinder words and looks than amongst these youngsters, all graduates of some university, most of them officers in the late war, who are settled down in the great money-making town, and are living brave and sterling and earnest lives there. I really can't tell you the sort of things they said (they drank your health, and the proposer made one of the prettiest little speeches in proposing it I ever heard); in short, I was positively ashamed, and scarcely knew how to meet it all or what to say to them; but it was less embarrassing than it would have been with any other young men, for this kind of young American (like Holmes) is so transparently sincere that you can come out quite square with him before you have known him an hour. Our good friends of the Illinois Central gave us free passage to St. Louis, to which we travelled all night. It is the biggest town in Missouri, was a great slave-holding place in 1860, and very "secesh" during the war. A fine city it is too, with its grand quay lined with huge steamers, and its miles of fine streets. Rowdy though, still, full of low saloons and gambling-houses. The most drunken town in the United States, the gentleman who met us, and drove us about and got us free papers here to Cincinnati, told us. The most characteristic thing that happened to me was that I was shaved by a negro (and better shaved than I ever was in my life before). He had been body servant to his master, a rich Southern planter, through the first three years of the war. His master was at last shot and he managed to get taken, and so "I'se no slave now," as he said, with all his ivories shining. His education has not been much improved, however, for he thought England was at war, as being somehow part either of France or Germany, he couldn't just say which, and would scarcely believe me when I declared that we were separated by the sea from both. Then we travelled all night again (I sleep splendidly in these palace cars, so don't be alarmed), and got here to the queen city of Ohio this morning, after the most glorious sunrise I ever saw. This also is a very fine city on the Ohio, with fine hills all round and a magnificent suspension bridge. The most characteristic sight I have seen here, however, was two small boys trotting along together barefooted, with a piece of sugar-cane between them, each sucking one end. I had a note to Force, one of Sherman's generals, now a judge here, who kindly sent us round in a carriage, but was too busy to come with us. To-night we make another long run to Philadelphia. We should have gone to Washington and so worked north, but Philadelphia is the next place where I shall get letters, and I can't do any longer without hearing from you, so that's all about it. I have lots of friends in Philadelphia, so shall probably make two days' stay there.

Continental Hotel, Philadelphia, 23rd September 1870.

Where was I in my narrative? I guess (I am getting a thorough Yankee in my vernacular) I gave you a short account of the queen city, as they call Cincinnati. We left Cincinnati at ten o'clock on Wednesday night and came right away for 600 miles to Philadelphia.

The most interesting part of the road was the crossing the Alleghanies, up which we wound through vast forest tracks for some thirty miles, and down the eastern slopes in the sunset, getting daylight for all the most beautiful parts. As we were rushing up one of the finest gorges, some 200 yards wide, we were suddenly aware of a huge eagle (bigger than those we saw on the Danube as we steamed through the Iron Cates) sailing up on the opposite side, perhaps 100 yards from the train. We were going eighty miles an hour at the least, and the grand old fellow swept along without the least apparent effort, keeping abreast of our car for I should think a couple of miles, when he suddenly turned and settled on a fine pine-tree.

After breakfast we had a real field-day in this splendid city, which rivals Boston in interest and character. Outside it is built of red brick and white marble, the contrast of which materials is to me singularly taking, though I daresay it is very bad art.

Then the chief streets run away long and straight, and as you look down them all seem to dive into groups of trees. Walnut Street, Chestnut Street, and Spruce Street are the names of the oldest and handsomest avenues. Our friend Field, the banker, was all ready for us, and a dozen new friends, including General Meade, the first Federal general who won the battle in the East, and a charming, tall, handsome, grizzled, gentlemanly soldier. We went over the old State House, a pre-revolutionary building, from the top of which there is a splendid view of the town, with the two rivers, the Delaware and Schuylkill, on which it stands. There is the hall in which the Declaration of Independence was signed, and the chair in which Hancock sat, and the table on which it lay for signature. The square is charming, with its old trees and turf, just as it has always stood, and I am happy to say the Pennsylvanians are very proud «of the old place, won't allow it to be touched, and are likely to keep it there till it burns, as I suppose the State House, with all the old-fashioned timbers in wall and roof, will some day. Then we went to the great Normal School for girls here, five hundred strong, the daughters of all sorts of folk, from physicians and lawyers to labourers. I was exceedingly interested and instructed in many classes, especially in the history class. The handsome, self-possessed young woman who was teaching was just beginning the Revolutionary War as we came in, and "felt like" changing the subject as she said, but I begged her to go on, and heard the old story from

Lexington down to Cornwallis's surrender without turning a hair. After classes, at two, the whole school was gathered for Scripture reading and singing a hymn. After the hymn, in compliment to us, they began "God save the Queen"; Rawlins and I got up by a sort of instinct, and to my immense amusement up got the whole company. Then I was asked to say a few words; and talked about the grand education they were getting, referred to the history class and told them no Englishman worth the name now regretted the end of the struggle one hundred years old, but only that any of the bitterness should still be left; spoke of the grand country which has been entrusted to them to be filled with the poor of the whole world, told them that we had a woman's rights movement at home as well as they, which I hoped would not fall into any great absurdities, but there were two rights they would always insist on—the right of every girl in the States to such an education as they were getting, and their own right (they are all being educated as teachers) to go and give this education to those who want it most in West and South. Then the girls all filed out to march music, played by a senior girl, winding in and out of the rows of benches on which they had sat, and so away downstairs and to all parts of the town, the prettiest sight you can imagine. The girls are at the most awkward age, and, of course, many of them plain, but altogether as comely as the same sort would be with us, and not a sign of poverty amongst them, though many were quite plainly dressed. My democratic soul rejoiced at the sight as you may fancy. What a chance for straining the nonsense out of a girl if she has any! We adjourned from the great training-school for girls to the Girard College for orphan boys, founded by a queer old French Voltairian citizen of Philadelphia, who died some forty years ago and left property worth half a million of our money to found this college, with the express *proviso* that no parson of any denomination was ever to be admitted within the walls. I am happy to say, however, that, notwithstanding this provision, which is observed to the letter, the Bible is read and every day's instruction is begun and ended by a religious service. This, by the way, is the case almost everywhere in the States. Notwithstanding all the assertions to the contrary, I have found only one place in which the education is purely secular. This was Cincinnati, where the result is obtained by a combination of the Roman Catholics with the German town population. Well, this college, as it is called, is simply a vast boys' home, just like our own, except that the boys live in a most superb white marble building, copied from the Parthenon. The classes were being taught, and kept in right good order by women, who indeed almost monopolise teaching in this State, and they are in the proportion of more than ten to one. The fault of Girard College is that it is not wanted; the public school system which has grown up since its foundation being open to every one, and offering at least as good an education. If its funds could have been used to support the boys while at the public schools it would have been better. The whole arrangements are decidedly more luxurious than those at Rugby in my time, and they have not yet established workshops. After our round of institutions we were entertained at the Union League Club. The dinner was good and the company better, Mr. MacMichael, the mayor, who had been the chief mover in establishing the club in the dark days of 1861, presided, with General Meade, who commanded at Gettysburg on his left and me on his right. Dear old Field, the most furious and impulsive of Republicans, and the most ardent lover and abuser of England and Englishmen, vice-president, and the rest of the company, staff-officers in the war or marked men in some other way. The club had sent eleven regiments to the war at its own expense, and had exercised immense influence on the Union at the most critical time. At last I was fairly cornered; I had often before had to defend our position in sharp skirmishes, but now, for the first time, was in for a general engagement. Well, I just threw away all defensive arms, and attacked them at once. "You say we were led by our aristocracy, who were savagely hostile to you; I admit they were hostile, though with many notable exceptions, such as the Duke of Argyll, Lord Carlisle, Howards and Cavendishes; but what did you expect? I have taken in three or four American papers for years, and in your debates in Congress, in your newspapers, in every utterance of your public men, I have never heard or read anything but savage abuse of our aristocracy. They don't reply to your insults, but they don't forget them, so when you got into such hard lines they went in heartily for your enemies. Well, you say the South were England's real enemies for the last forty years. True, but aristocracy did not care for that, democracy was represented by you, and that was what they went against." There was an outcry: "Why, here's a pretty business, we thought you were a Democrat."

"So I am, in our English sense, but I am before all things an Englishman. I have nothing to do with our aristocracy (except knowing a few of them), and I fought as hard against them in England through the war as you did against the rebels; but I am not going to allow you to separate them from the nation, or to suppose that they can be punished except through the nation."

"Well, but what do you say for all your great commercial world—bankers, merchants, manufacturers, our correspondents, look how they turned on us!"

"It's no part of my business to defend them; they were mean, I allow, but their business was, as they supposed, and as all of you agree, to make money; besides, after all, who fought your battle better than Cobden, Bright, Forster, and such men as Kirkman-Hodson, and Tom Baring?" Then they fell back on the general position that our Government was hostile to them, and I went through what had really happened in Parliament, and made them admit that if we had listened to Louis Napoleon, and the blockade had been broken, it would have been a narrow squeak for the Union. On the whole, I think, I made a good deal of impression on most of them. General Meade and the soldiers were on my side throughout, and admitted at once that, after all the abuse their press heaped on our governing classes, it was childish to cry out when they proved that they knew of the abuse and didn't love the abusers. We all parted the warmest friends, and I went off to tea at Mrs. W———s', where we met Dr. Mitchell, a scientific man, and his sister, and other very pleasant folk, and heard many interesting stories of the war. The next morning we started for Gettysburg. I had always made a point with myself of seeing this one at any rate of the great battlefields. It was the real turning-point of the war, fought on the 1st, 2nd, and 3rd of July 1863, after the series of defeats and failures under M'Clellan, Pope Hooker, Burnside. I well remember what a long breath we (the Abolitionists) drew in England when the news came of Lee's defeat at the farthest point he had ever made to the North, and felt sure, for the first time, that the war would be put through, and slavery be abolished right down to the Gulf of Mexico. We had the best escort possible in the person of Rosengarten, who was aide-decamp to General Reynolds, commander of the corps which came up first and sustained the whole weight of battle on the first day. Field also "came along," and we had a first-rate time on our journey over the Susquehanna bridge, which the Northern militia burnt behind them as they escaped from Lee's advance. Then we stopped for an hour or two, waiting for a train at York, a nice shady quiet country town of 11,000 inhabitants. The rebels had occupied the place for three days and levied a matter of 80,000 dollars on the people; in all other respects they seem to have behaved excellently and to have been well under command. The old Episcopalian clergyman, a warm friend of England, who had been Rosengarten's tutor, and to whom we paid a visit, gave us a capital description of the three days' occupation, and of the relief the York folk experienced when the poor ragged rebels marched off for Gettysburg, and left the town very little poorer than they had found it. We didn't get to our inn, a huge wooden building on the first day's battlefield, till after sunset. Tea over, we came out on the wooden platform which runs all round the house, and saw the most glorious sight I have ever seen, I think, in the skies. Steaming up Memphremagog we saw the aurora borealis splendidly, but that was nothing to this. In Canada there was no colour in the pure flashes of light which lit and pulsed over the whole sky, but on Saturday the changes of colour were splendid, and I should say for half an hour the heavens were throbbing with the most lovely rose-coloured streamers and sheets and flashes. With my view of the importance to the poor old world of the struggle which was descending there, you can fancy that such an introduction to it was welcome and impressive. Next day we devoted to the battlefield: began at the beginning where, on Thursday the 1st July 1863, Rosengarten himself, as Reynolds's aide-decamp, had ridden forward and placed the first Federal regiments which came on the ground in position between the town of Gettysburg, which contains about 3000 inhabitants and lies in a hollow, and the advancing rebels. Gettysburg is at the junction of three roads and was a point which both armies were bent on seizing. The fight on this the north-east side of the town began early on Thursday. Rosengarten, after carrying out his orders, rode back, and was just in time to see his General fall from his horse, shot through the neck by a sharpshooter, and helped to carry him off the field. After many hours' hard fighting the Federals were driven back through the town with heavy loss. Our friend, General Barlow, who commanded a brigade, was also badly wounded. Luckily, during the day two more corps of the army of the Potomac had come up and been placed in position on a hill just to the south of the town, on part of which the cemetery now stands, which was made immortal by Lincoln's glorious speech at the inauguration. Behind these fresh troops the broken 1st and 11th corps rallied and prepared for the next day. Reinforcements came up to Lee also, and in the town the shopkeepers and other inhabitants heard them making certain of an easy victory in the morning. Meade is evidently a man who gains and holds the confidence of his troops; but as he was slightly outnumbered, and the rebels had the prestige of the first day's victory, I take it he must have been beaten but for the splendid position he had selected. His troops lay along two lines of hills, covered in many places with wood which sloped away from the point overlooking the town, leaving a space between them secure from fire, in which he could move his troops without being seen, while every move of Lee's was open to him. The Confederates began attacks early and kept them up throughout the day, but could not force the position except at one point, where, after dark, they succeeded in making a lodgment and spent the night within Meade's lines. In the morning they were driven out after a desperate struggle, and later in the day Lee made a determined attempt with Longstreet's corps to break the line again. He lost three generals and about 4000 men in the great effort, and when it failed, and he had to fall back to his own lines, the back of the Rebellion was broken and the doom of slavery sealed for ever in North America. At night he went away south, leaving most of his wounded, but Meade was too much exhausted to do more than follow slowly. I am writing in hot haste to catch the post, so can give you no clear idea, I fear, of the great day. The hotel was a nice, clean, reasonable place, with a landlord and servants really civil, and we enjoyed our excursion more than I can tell you.

Next day we came on to Baltimore, drove as usual in the beautiful park and about the town in a carriage sent for us by some patriotic citizen, dined at the Union Club, to which they gave us the *entrée*, and came on to Washington.

Washington, Friday.

You ask whether I read our papers and the news from Europe. No, except just so far as to keep abreast of the bare facts. You know how I hate details of battlefields, and that I have never got over my intense dislike to the glowing and semi-scientific descriptions of "our own correspondents," sitting down in the midst of dying and agonised men to do their penny or guinea a line. The dry report of a general or staff officer, whose sad duty it is to be there, I follow with the deepest interest, and recognise a battlefield as one of the very noblest places from which a true man may make a "bee-line track" to heaven. The noblest death in our times was Robert Shaw's at the attack on Fort Wagner, at the head of his niggers, under whom he was buried; but, for all that, war and its details are a ghastly and horrible evil, which the faith of our Master is going yet to root out of this silly old world, and which none of His servants should touch unless it is the clear path of supreme duty.

I pity the poor French, utterly unmanned as they seem to be by this nineteen years of the rule of Mammon, and heartily wish they could find their manhood again, though I see no glimmer of it yet. Trochu seems a fine fellow, and I can't help believing that many of my acquaintance and the members of the Paris associations, will be found ready to die like men on the walls of the city if they get a chance. By the way, where is N———? I wonder if he has gone back? If so, there is another brave and true man in Paris, and perhaps ten may save it. But I must be getting back to my journal or I shall be dropping stitches. If I don't forget, my last brought you with us to Willard's Hotel, Washington, a great three-hundred-roomed hotel, mixed, if not of Southern proclivities during the war, before the door of which more than one duel was fought in those searching times. At breakfast we found ourselves next the Wards, father and son, G. B———'s friends, to whom I had given some letters. I found they had been even farther west than we; in fact, up to Denver City, in the bosom of the Rocky Mountains, and had also managed to get into four or five Southern states; but they had done it at the sacrifice not only of comfort but of the chance of seeing the home-life of the Americans, and I value the latter infinitely higher than mere sight-seeing, so do not regret the least that we didn't get through the extra 1500 miles, which at the cost of five days' more travel would have let us see the Rocky Mountains and shoot at buffaloes.

We went after breakfast to leave some of my letters, and over the White House, a fine residence of white marble splendidly situated some one and a half miles from the Capitol, with which it is connected by Pennsylvania avenue, wider than Portland Place. I shall keep the details till we meet; the house is as big as the Mansion House I should say, and not very unlike it. Luckily, soon after we got outside we were recognised (at least I was) in the street by Blackie, who was over in England with the Harvard crew. He is in the attorney-general's office, and consequently has the run of all the public apartments, and he took us in hand and lionised us splendidly. The Capitol Patent Office and Treasury I shall bring you photographs of, and describe at leisure in our winter evenings. The view from the top, over the city and Maryland to the north, and across the Potomac over Virginia to the south, is as fine as any I ever saw, General Lee's house at Arlington Heights, now a national cemetery, being the most conspicuous point in the southern view. The thing that struck one most was the staff of women, mostly young and many pretty, serving in the Treasury. They say there are upwards of two thousand, and that for counting, sorting, and repairing the paper currency, they are far superior to men. They earn one thousand dollars (or £200) a year on an average. Fancy the boon to the orphan girls of soldiers and sailors. One of the first we saw was the daughter of a very distinguished Colonel of Marines, who had left her quite destitute, as ladylike, pretty-looking a girl as you ever saw, and she was running over bundles of dollar notes with her fingers as fast as if she were playing the overture to *Semiramide* with you on the piano. It nearly took my breath away, and yet I was assured she never made an error in counting. I wish we could get off a lot of our poor girls in some such way in Somerset House, and send a lot of our Government clerks to till the ground or hammer or do some hard, productive work.

Perhaps, however, the pleasantest part of the day was the end, when he took us off on the street-cars down to the Potomac, where we found a boating club, with their boat-house, etc., just like an Oxford or Cambridge College. There were eight or ten of them down there who received us with open arms, and in a few minutes manned a heavy eight-oared boat with room enough for me and R——— to sit in the stern, and away we went up under the long bridge, over which the armies used to cross in the war time, and saw a glorious sunset on the river, with the stars and stripes floating proudly over our stern. I enjoyed the row vastly and liked the men, who are just training for a race with the Potomac club. Boating flourishes all over the states I have been in, and they have learnt a lesson from their defeat two years ago and pull now in just as good style as our boys. Oxford and Cambridge must mind their hits, for they will have a tough job of it the next time they have to meet a crew from this side.

Next morning I called on our minister after breakfast, having heard by chance that he was in town. I am very glad I did, as I had the pleasure of hearing him praise C———, his ability, willingness, and capacity for work, in a strain which would have rejoiced the heart of poor, dear R. F——— and of the F——— family. He seems to think C——— will come back here, and desires it most earnestly. I got from him Lord Clarendon's last despatch on the Alabama claims, which will be most useful to me in my stump in the

Boston Music Hall on the 11th. It is the room and the course in which Wendell Phillips, Emerson, and all the orators and philosophers figure. I have taken for my subject, "John to Jonathan," suggested by Lowell's famous "Jonathan to John." They won't get any eloquence or oratory out of me, as you know; but I am sure I can say some things in a plain, straightforward way which will do good and help to heal wounded pride and other sorely irritating places in the over-sensitive, but simple and gallant Yankee mind. They have treated me so like a spoilt child from Boston to Omaha and back, that I know they will let me say anything and will listen to it affectionately. I really love them too well to say anything that will really hurt them, and when they see that this kind of feeling and appreciation is genuine, the more thorough John Bull you are the better they like it; that is, all the best of them, who rule the nation in the long run though not directly. When I got back from our embassy, it was just time to be starting for the train to Philadelphia, and lo! there were a dozen folk, from secretaries of state downwards, waiting to offer lodgings, dinners, excursions, lecturings, every sort of kindness in creation. It was hard work to get off, but I managed somehow to make tracks, suppressing, I fear, the fact that I was not likely to get to Washington again. The journey to Philadelphia is very interesting along the coast, though seldom within sight of the sea, but crossing huge inlets and rivers (the abode of canvas-backs) on spider bridges. We didn't change cars at Baltimore, but were dropped by our engine in the outskirts of the town. Six fine horses in a string were then hitched on to each long car, and away we went through the crowded streets along the tramway rails, our driver, or rather, conductor, for he had no reins, blowing his horn loudly to warn all good people, and shouting to the train of horses who trotted along by instinct between the rails. How we missed fifty collisions I can't conceive; at last we had one— crash into a confusion of carts and drays, driven by shouting negroes who had got them all into a hopeless jam as we bore down on them. Bang we went into the nearest; I saw the comical, scared look of the grisly old Sambo who was driving, as he was shot from his seat, but no harm was done except knocking off our own step, and as we shot past I saw his face light up into a broad grin as he sat on the bottom of his cart. We had cleared him right away from his dead-lock with two other vehicles, and he went on his way delighted. At Philadelphia we found our kindest of hosts, Field, waiting supper for us in his delightful house, where he is living for a few days' business as a bachelor. Quiet evening, with talk till eleven o'clock on all manner of places, people, and things, mostly English. Lippincott, the great American publisher, and Rosengarten to breakfast, then a visit from Morrison's friend Welsh, reproachful that we had not occupied his house, and full of interesting stories of the Indian commission, of which he is the moving spirit. Then more schools, workmen's houses, etc., with Rosengarten, and a drive in the park, five miles long on both sides of the river Schuylkill (as broad as the Thames at Putney), and with views combining Richmond Hill and Oxford. The Central Park is nothing to it, or any other I ever saw on heard of. The Quaker city of white marble and red brick fascinated me more and more. A most interesting dinner at Dr. Mitchell's, a scientific man—talk of the war, prairie stories, Yankee stories, wonderful old Madeira and excellent cigars. This morning, after seeing Lippincott's store, and a most interesting talk with Sheridan's adjutant-general on the last campaigns (he came to breakfast), we literally tore ourselves away from Philadelphia and came on here to this splendid, great, empty house, to be received most hospitably by Maria, the big, handsome, good-natured Irishwoman in charge.

Everything is getting so crowded with me that I have hardly time to turn round. All sorts of kind friends urging me to stop just for one day here or there, a few hundred miles making no difference with them, hundreds (almost) of applications for lectures or addresses, and the engagements already made driving me nearly wild to know how I am to get through with them. I shall never get my journal straight. Where was I? With dear old Peter Cooper, the simplest, most utterly guileless of old men who ever made a big fortune in this world or any other, I should think. That I remember, but can't the least get further. Nothing, however, very particular happened, except that I was again caught and had to speak a few words to the Normal Training School of New York, consisting of nine hundred girls. I managed to get out of going with the beautiful Miss P——— to her school, but thought I should be safe in going with the dear old gentleman to the Normal School to be present at the morning service. We were of course on the dais, and Mr. Cooper, after the singing of a hymn, read a chapter of the Bible, then another hymn, and then, instead of the adjournment to their classes at once, as I had expected, I was called upon. You must imagine what I said, for I really don't remember. Then I was photographed alone, and with Mr. Cooper. I enclose a proof of the latter which, I hope, will not quite fade on the way. They tell me the prints will be very good, and I hope to have several to bring home. We left on Wednesday by the afternoon boat to Fall River, the finest boat in the States, the great cabin of which I shall bring you a photograph, all the family grouped round the door breaking one down with their kindness. I slept as usual famously on board the *Bristol,* and waked at Fall River about three, and so on by rail to Boston, and by car up here, where I feel quite at home. Miss Mabel appeared at breakfast, and produced her photographs made at the time of our last visit with great triumph. They are excellent, and I shall bring you lots of them. At eleven was the Harvard memorial ceremony on the laying of the corner-stone of the hall they are building in honour of the members who died in the war. I walked in with Mr A——— and heard a good account of his wife and family. They want me to go out there for a quiet day or two, but, I fear, it is quite impossible. Two of his sons, the Colonel, and our friend Henry, who is just named as one of the lecturers, were there also, and Emerson, Dana, and a number of old and new friends. The ceremony was very simple, Luther's hymn, a short *extempore* prayer, a report, and two addresses, and the benediction, and then we just broke up and left the great tent as we pleased. The point of greatest interest was, of course, the gathering of some seventy or eighty of those who had been in the army, almost all in their old uniforms, and many of them carrying the marks of war about them too plainly. Colonel Holmes amongst them as nice as ever, and young F——— and General M———, with half a dozen other generals.

Lunch afterwards at a very quaint and attractive little club founded in 1792, and recruited by a few of the best fellows in each year, like the Apostles at our Cambridge. Longfellow and our friend Field came to dine here, and the poet was fascinating, full of his English doings, and genial and modest as a big man should be. To-day I have been preparing for my lecture, "John to Jonathan," which comes off next Tuesday, as to which I am considerably anxious, as it is exceedingly difficult to get a line which will have the healing effect I intend. Let us hope for the best. I go for Sunday to Lowell's brother's school, twenty miles away. On Monday evening I meet the Harvard undergraduates, and on Wednesday spend the day with Emerson at Concord. On Thursday I hope to get away, but where? All our plans are changing. We now propose, if it can be so arranged, to go first to Montreal for two or three days to pick up our things, returning to Ithaca to Goldwin Smith for a long day about the 18th, and so to New York, from which we should sail about the 22nd. You will, I daresay, be glad that we don't go from Quebec; but I don't believe there is the least more danger at this time of year by this route than any other. All I have resolved on is, that nothing shall keep me beyond my time.

St. Mark's School, Southborough, Mass.,
Tuesday, 9th October.

We have had a very charming visit to this little village, twenty miles from Boston, in which is established a Church of England boarding-school, modelled as nearly as possible on our public school system, and intended to do for American boys precisely what Eton, Rugby, etc., do for ours. I am not sure that such schools are wanted here.

Were I living here I should certainly try the public schools first for my boys. But they say that the teaching there is too forcing in the earlier stages, and afterwards not liberal enough in the direction of *"the humanities,"* so that the boys get trained more into competitive money-making machines than into thinking cultivated men. There is a very considerable demand at any rate for this kind of school, as this is only one of several in New England. There is an objection too amongst New England mothers. I find that the high schools (as I ought to call them, and not public schools) being open to every one, a large class of Irish and other recent arrivals go there whose manners and language make them dangerous class-mates for their own children. At any rate, St. Mark's school is a successful fact, and seeing how fast they go ahead here I shouldn't be astonished to hear that in a few years it is as big as Rugby. Dr. Lowell is the principal, and a first-rate one, a High Church of England clergyman, not a ritualist. The school is founded as a denominational one, with a little chancel, which opens from the end of the big schoolroom, and in which the doctor, in his robes, reads our prayers morning and evening to the boys. He and his family live entirely with the boys, taking all their meals in the hall, and there is no fagging, the monitors having no power or responsibility, except just to keep order in the schoolroom at certain hours. They have a monthly reception of the friends from the neighbourhood, which took place on Saturday evening. All the boys were there, and handed round ices, cakes, and tea to some thirty ladies and gentlemen who came in, including several of the trustees, a judge whom I had met in England, a neighbouring squire (Boston merchant by profession), who is farming largely down there, reclaiming the stony lands and getting up a most beautiful herd of cattle. Of course I had to "address a few words" to them, all which they took most kindly. On Sunday we had two Church of England services in the pretty parish church, a copy of one in England, the plans of which the Squire, Bartlett, had brought over. We dined in the middle of the day at his house, which would be a good squire's house at home. The family were very nice— a sweet, pretty wife, a strapping great eldest son now at Harvard, and good in all ways. He is bent on going out West as soon as he is through college, and, as a preparation, hired himself out to a farmer this summer vacation, earned ten dollars a week for some two months at hoeing and other hard work, and then had a sporting run to Canada. Two more big sons and any number of younger children. The house was tastefully furnished with some really good pictures, and altogether it was as nice a home as I have seen here. On Monday we got back to dear Elmwood, and I went hard at work on my lecture. Newspaper men came buzzing about all day and seizing my MS. as I got through with it. Also came up Julian H———, one of the Chartist prisoners of 1848. I had known him in the socialist times, and I had always a respect and liking for him, but he had quite slipped out of sight for some eighteen years. His errand touched me. He reminded me (which I had entirely forgotten) that he had applied to Lord R——— in 1851 for a loan of £20 which had been advanced to him through me. He told the long story of his life since, full of interest; I must keep it till we meet. At last he landed in the Massachussets state house, where he is a Government clerk, on a small salary for this country, but out of it he has saved a few hundred dollars, and the object of his visit was to say that he was now anxious to pay his old debt with many hearty thanks to Lord R———. Would I settle whether he should pay for interest, and he would go and draw it out and send it by me? I said I couldn't say whether our friend would take interest, or at what rate, but promised to let him know when I got back, so that he can remit the exact amount to London. Even he has never taken up his citizenship here, but remains an Englishman, and means at any rate to come back and die in the old country. In the evening we went down to a gathering of all the Harvard students who had petitioned me to come and talk to them. They were gathered some five hundred strong in the Massachusetts Hall, and a finer and manlier set of boys I have never seen. I talked to them on Muscular Christianity and its proper limits, as they are likely to run into professional athletics like our boys at home. Told them they lived in a land which had "struck ile" and was so overflowing with wealth that every one was hasting to get rich too quick. Exhorted to patience and thoroughness; read to them Lowell's "Hebe" (you remember the little gem of a poem); told them they ought to take more part in public affairs than their class usually do. All which they swallowed devoutly, and cheered vehemently, like good boys, and then sang a lot of their college songs: "Marching through Georgia" splendid, the rest much like our own. The war has given a magnificent lift to all the young men and boys of this country, and I think the rising generation will put America in a very different place from that which she holds now. Last night I gave my lecture in the Music Hall, which was crammed, and the whole affair a brilliant success. "John to Jonathan" is printed verbatim in the morning newspapers, so you will probably see it before I get back, and I think like it. No more time for the moment.

Ithaca, N.Y., 16th October 1870.

I missed the last mail through stress of work, chiefly on my lecture, which I mentioned in my last. The applications for lectures were so numerous and urgent that I really felt that I ought not to leave the country without giving one at any rate, and all my friends said that the Music Hall at Boston was the place if I only spoke once. It is the largest room in New England, holds nearly three thousand people, is easy to speak in, though it has great deep galleries running round three sides, and in it all the big folk talk and lecture, Wendell Phillips and Sumner follow me, so you see the class of thing at once. Well, as I was in for it much against my will, I was determined to talk out with the whole Yankee nation the controversy which. I had been carrying on already with many of them in private. I was anxious not to leave them with any false impressions, and to let them see clearly that in our national differences I think that we have a very good case, and that even if I didn't think so, I am too good a John Bull not to stand by my own country. Lowell agreed as to the title and object, but I think had serious misgivings as to how the affair might turn out. Mundella thought it very risky and so did most other folk. However, as you know, I don't care a straw for applause, and do care about speaking my own mind, so whether it made me unpopular or not I determined to have my say. In order that I might say nothing on the spur of the moment, I wrote out the whole address carefully, and I am very glad I did, as the reporters all copied from my MS., and consequently I was thoroughly well reported. The *Tribune and Boston Advertiser* printed it in full, and I will bring you home copies. I was a little nervous myself when I got to the hall. Two ex-Governors and the present Governor of the State were on the platform, the two Senators (Sumner and Wilson), Longfellow, Judge Hoare, Dana, Wendell Holmes, Wendell Phillips, Lowell, and, in short, pretty nearly all the Boston big wigs. The great organ played "God save the Queen" as I came in, and the audience, generally, I am told, a very undemonstrative one, cheered heartily. My nervousness, however, wore off at once, when I got on my legs. I found that my voice filled the hall easily, and so was at my ease and got through just within the hour, without once losing the attention of the audience for a minute. They were indeed wonderfully sympathetic and hearty, and gave me three rounds of cheers at the end, far more warmly than at the beginning. Every one came and said that it was a great success; that they had never heard our side fairly stated before; that this and that fact were quite new to them, etc. In fact, if I didn't know how soon the reaction comes in such cases, I should think I had done some good work towards a better understanding between the nations, and, as it is, I am sure I have done no harm, and have at any rate made my own position perfectly clear, and shown them that in the event of a quarrel, they can't reckon upon me for any kind of sympathy or aid. After the lecture whom should I meet as I went out but Craft, the negro who had been the cause of one of the most exciting meetings ever held in that hall some twenty years before, when the attempt was made to seize him and his wife in Boston. I was delighted to see him and to hear a capital account of his experiment at association in Georgia. Then I went to Field's, the publisher, to supper, where were Longfellow, Holmes, Dana, and others, and so home by the last car, thankful that it was all well over. Next morning I got a cheque for 250 dollars (£50). I had, of course, never said a word about any payment, so it was an agreeable surprise. The post brought me I know not how many letters, begging me to lecture in a dozen states on my own terms, so when all trades fail, I can come over here and earn a good living easily enough, which is a consolation. Wednesday, our last whole day with the dear Lowells, I spent peaceably. Went to his lecture in the University on Arthurian legends; Miss Mabel photographed the house and us in groups, and we talked and loafed. In the evening a supper at the house of one of the professors, to meet the whole staff, and a pleasanter or abler set of men I have never come across. Thursday, lunch with Longfellow after packing, then a run down on the car to Boston, to change my cheque, to take a berth on a packet, so as to be armed against any appeals for another day or two in New York, and to get a last look at the favourite points in the old Puritan capital, the place where I should certainly settle if I ever had to leave England. We drove a rather sad party to Mrs. Lowell's sister, and the mother of the beautiful boy whose photograph we have, and who was killed early in the war, to tea, and from her house went to the station and took sleeping-car for Syracuse. I cannot tell you how I like Lowell and all his belongings. It is a dangerous thing to make acquaintance in the flesh with one with whose writings one is so familiar, but he has quite come up to my idea of him, and his wife and Miss Mabel are both very charming in their own ways. I slept well, woke at Albany, breakfasted, and then on to Syracuse, where Mr. Wansey, Mrs. Hamilton's uncle, lives. We got there at two, and I was immediately seized at the station by Wilkinson, the local banker, whom I had just met at Ned's this summer. He drove us all through and round the most characteristic town in America. Great broad streets lined with lovely maple trees, all turned now to clouds of scarlet and gold; down the principal one the railway runs without any fence. Old Mr. Wansey and others came to dine, he a dear old man of eighty, but hale and handsome, rather like my dear old grandfather's picture, the rest pleasant country folk. We played billiards, and told stories after dinner, and had a decidedly good time till nearly midnight. The next morning we breakfasted with Mr. White, the President of this new University, and came on here with him. He is a young man of about thirty-five, and one of the finest scholars America has to boast of at present. By the way, he was a classmate of Smalley at Yale. He is a rich man, and he has nothing whatever to gain by undertaking this work. In short, he is quite worthy of having Goldwin Smith as a fellow-worker, and between them, with the excellent staff of professors and teachers they have got round them, I expect they will make this place in a wondrous short time a great working-men's college. Everything is of course rough at present, as the buildings are still in progress, but two blocks are completed, and there are about seven hundred pupils living in them and in the town at the bottom of the hill on which Cornell stands. It is a most magnificent situation, looking over a large lake, forty miles long, and two splendid valleys, which are now ablaze with the crimson and purple colours of the maples, shumachs, American walnuts, and other trees, which make the hillsides here glow all the later autumn through. We found Goldwin Smith waiting for us at the wharf and looking much stronger than he used to do in England, and quite warm in his welcome. All the professors, with their wives and families, if married, live for the present in a huge square block of buildings originally intended for a hydropathic establishment, in which they have a private sitting-room and bedrooms and dine and take all meals in the hall. You may fancy how much I am interested in this great practical step towards association.

New York, Tuesday.

Here I am in the great city again, to spend the last few days before my start for home. The reception in the great hall, speech, visit to lecture rooms, etc., enthusiasm of boys, baseball games, and football given in my honour, must all keep till we meet. For, alas! I have no time to spend here for writing, as I have another address to give before I start, on Friday evening, and I must write it carefully, as it is to be on the labour question, which is mightily exercising our cousins here. They are getting into the controversy which we are nearly through at home, and if I can give them a little good advice before I come away, I shall be very glad. As I am engaged every evening, it will not be easy to find time to do it as I should like, but I can give the morning, I think, and can at any rate make sure of not talking nonsense.

AMERICA—1880 to 1887

The Cumberland Mountains

East Tennessee, 1st September 1880.

Here I am at my goal, and so full of new impressions that I must put some of them down at once, lest they should slip away like the new kind of recruits, and I should not be able to lay my hand on them again when I want them. The above address is vague, as this range of highlands extends for some 200 miles through this State and Kentucky; but, though fixed as fate myself, I can for the moment put no more definite heading to my letters. The name of the town that is to be, and which is already laid out and in course of building here, is a matter of profound interest to many persons, and not to be decided hastily. The only point which seems clear is that it will be some name round which cluster tender memories in the old Motherland. We are some 1800 feet above the sea, and after the great heat of New York, Newport, and Cincinnati, the freshness and delight of this brisk, mountain air are quite past describing. For mere physical enjoyment, I have certainly never felt its equal, and can imagine nothing finer.

And now for our journey down. We left Cincinnati early in the morning by the Cincinnati Southern Railway, a line built entirely by the city, and the cost of which will probably make the municipality poor for some years to come. But it seems to me a splendid and sagacious act of foresight in a great community, to have boldly taken hold of and opened up at once what must be one, if not the main, artery of communication between North and South in the future. I believe the impelling motive was the tendency of the carrying trade of late years to settle along other routes, leaving the metropolis of the south-west out in the cold. If this be so, the result justifies the prompt courage of the citizens of Cincinnati, for the tide has obviously set in again with a vengeance. The passenger-cars are filled to the utmost of their capacity, and freight, as we know here too well, is often delayed for days, in spite of all the efforts of the excellent staff of the road. Besides its through traffic, the line has opened up an entirely new country, of which these highlands seem likely to prove a profitable, as they certainly are the most interesting, tract. This section has not been open for six months, and already it is waking up life all over these sparsely-settled regions. Down below on the way to Chatanooga I hear that the effect is the same, and that in that great mineral region blast-furnaces are already at work, and coal-mines opening all along the line. At Chatanooga there are connections with all the great Southern lines, so that we on this aerial height are, in these six months, in direct communication with every important seaport from Boston to New Orleans, and almost every great centre of inland population; and the settlers here, looking forward with that sturdy faith which seems to inspire all who have breathed the air for a week or two, are already considering upon which favoured mart they shall pour out their abundance of fruits and tobacco, from the trees yet to be planted and seed yet to be sown. All which seems to prove that Cincinnati, at any rate, has done well to adopt the motto, "L'audace, toujours l'audace," which is, indeed, characteristic of this country and this time.

And the big work has not only been done, but done well and permanently. The engineering difficulties must have been very great; the cuttings and tunnels had to be made through hard rock, and the bridges over streams which have cut for themselves channels hundreds of feet deep. We crossed the Kentucky river, on (I believe) the highest railway bridge in the world, 283 feet above the water; and rushed from a tunnel in the limestone rock right on to the bridge which spans the north fork of the Cumberland river, 170 feet below. The lightness of the ironwork on which these bridges rest startles one at first, but experience has shown them to be safe, and the tests to which they have been put on this line would have tried most seriously the strength of far more massive structures. But it is only in its bridges that the Cincinnati Southern Railway has a light appearance. The building of the line has a solid and permanent look, justifying, I should think, the very considerable sum per mile which has been spent on it above the ordinary cost in this country. And by the only test which an amateur is as well able to apply as an expert, that of writing on a journey, I can testify that it is as smoothly laid as the average of our leading English lines. For the last fifty miles we ran almost entirely through forests, which are, however, falling rapidly all along the side of the line, and yielding place to corn-fields in the rich bottoms, wherever any reasonably level ground bordered the water-courses, up which we could glance as we hurried past. I was surprised, and, I need not say, greatly pleased, to see the apparently excellent terms on which the white and coloured people were, even in the Kuklux regions through which we came. A Northern express man, our companion at this point, denounced it as the most lawless in the United States. About one hundred homicides, he declared, had taken place in the last year, and no conviction had been obtained, the juries looking on such things as regrettable accidents. This may be so, but I can, at any rate, testify, from careful observation of the mixed gangs of workmen on the road, and the groups gathered at the numerous stations, to the familiar and apparently friendly footing on which the races met. As for the decrease of the blacks, it must be in other regions than those traversed by the Cincinnati Southern Railway, for the cabins we passed in the clearings and round the stations swarmed with small urchins, clad in single garments, the most comic little figures of fun, generally, that one had ever seen, as they stood staring and signalling to the train. There is something to me so provocative of mirth in the race, and I have found them generally such kindly folk, that I regret their absence from this same Alpine settlement,—a regret not shared, doubtless, by the few householders, to whom their constant small peculations must be very trying.

About five we stopped at the station from which this place is reached, and turning out on the platform were greeted by four or five young Englishmen, who had preceded us, on one errand or another, every one of whom was well known to me in ordinary life, but whom for the first moment I did not recognise. I had seen them last clothed in the frock-coat and stove-pipe hat of our much-vaunted civilisation, and behold, here was a group which I can compare to nothing likely to be familiar to your readers, unless it be the company of the *Danites*, as they have been playing in London. Broad-brimmed straw or felt hats, the latter very battered and worse for wear; dark-blue jerseys, or flannel shirts of varying hue; breeches and gaiters, or long boots, were the prevailing, I think I may say the universal costume, varied according to the taste of the wearer with bits of bright colour laid on in handkerchief at neck or waist. And tastes varied deliciously, two of the party showing really a fine feeling for the part, and one, our geologist, 6 ft. 2 in. in his stockings, and a mighty Etonian and Cantab, in brains as well as bulk, turning out, with an heroic scorn of all adornment, in woefully battered nether-garment and gaiters, and a felt which a tramp would have looked at several times before picking it out of the gutter. There was a light buggy for passengers and a mule waggon for luggage by the platform; but how were nine men, not to mention the manager and driver, both standing over 6 feet, and the latter as big at least as our geologist, to get through the intervening miles of forest tracks in time for tea up here? Fancy our delight when a chorus of "Will you ride or drive?" arose, and out of the neighbouring bushes the Danites led forth nine saddle-horses, bearing the comfortable half-Mexican saddles with wooden stirrups in use here. Our choice was quickly made, and throwing coats and waistcoats into the waggon, which the manager good-naturedly got into himself, surrendering his horse for the time, we joined the cavalcade in our shirts.

A lighter-hearted party has seldom scrambled through the Tennessee mountain roads on to this plateau. We were led by a second Etonian, also 6 ft. 2 in. in his stockings, whose Panama straw hat and white corduroys gleamed like a beacon through the deep shadows cast by the tall pine trees and white oaks. The geologist brought up the rear, and between rode the rest of us—all public schoolmen, I think, another Etonian, two from Rugby, one Harrow, one Wellington—through deep gullies, through four streams, in one of which I nearly came to grief, from not following my leader; but my gallant little nag picked himself up like a goat from his floundering amongst the boulders, and so up through more open ground till we reached this city of the future, and in the dusk saw the bright gleam of light under the verandahs of two sightly wooden houses. In one of these, the temporary restaurant, we were seated in a few minutes at an excellent tea (cold beef and mutton, tomatoes, rice, cold apple-tart, maple syrup, etc.); and during the meal the news passed round that the hotel being as yet unfurnished and every other place filled with workpeople, we must all (except the geologist and the Wellingtonian, who had a room over the office) pack away in the next cottage, which had been with difficulty reserved for us. If it had been a question of men only, no one would have given it a thought; but our party had now been swollen by two young ladies, who had hurried down by an earlier train to see their brother and brother-in-law, settlers on the plateau, and by another young Englishman who had accompanied them. A puzzle, you will allow, when you hear a description of our tenement. It is a four-roomed timber house, of moderate size, three rooms on the ground floor, and one long loft upstairs. You enter through the verandah on a common room, 20 ft. long by 14 ft. broad, opening out of which are two chambers, 14 ft. by 10 ft. One of these was, of course, at once appropriated to the ladies. The second, in spite of my remonstrances, was devoted to me, as the Nestor of the party, and on entering it I found an excellent bed (which had been made by two of the Etonians), and a great basin full of wild-flowers on the table. There were four small beds in the loft, for which the seven drew lots, and two of the losers spread rugs on the floor of the common room, and the third swung a hammock in the verandah. Up drove the mule waggon with luggage, and the way in which big and little boxes were dealt with and distributed filled me with respect and admiration for the rising generation. The house is ringing behind me with silvery and bass laughter, and jokes as to the shortness of accommodation in the matter of washing appliances, while I sit here writing in the verandah, the light from my lamp throwing out into strong relief the stems of the nearest trees. Above, the vault is blue beyond all description, and studded with stars as bright as though they were all Venuses. The katydids are making delightful music in the trees, and the summer lightning is playing over the Western heaven; while a gentle breeze, cool and refreshing as if it came straight off a Western sea, is just lifting, every now and then, the corner of my paper. Were I young again,—but as I am not likely to be that, I refrain from bootless castle-building, and shall turn in, leaving windows wide open for the katydid's chirp and the divine breeze to enter freely, and wishing as good rest as they have all so well earned to my crowded neighbours in this enchanted solitude.

Rugby, Tennessee, 10th September 1880.

I take it I must have "written you frequent" (as they say here), at this time of year, in the last quarter-century on this theme, but, if you let me, should like to go back once more on the old lines. "Loafing as she should be taken" is likely, I fear, to become a lost art, though to my generation it is the one luxury. A country without good loafing-places is no longer a country for a self-respecting man in his second half-century. The rapid deterioration of our poor dear old England in this respect fills me with forebodings far more than the Irish Question, which we shall worry through on the lines so staunchly advocated by you. No fear of that, to my thinking; but, alas! great fear of our losing the power and the means of loafing. Time was when John Bull, in his own isle, was the best loafer in Christendom—(I may say in the world, the Turk and Otaheitan loafer doing nothing else, and he who does nothing but loaf loses the whole flavour of it)—and I can remember the time when at the seaside—for instance, Cromer, and inland, Betwys-y-Coed, Penygurd, and the like—the true loafer might be happy, gleaning "the harvest of a quiet eye," and far from any one who wanted to go anywhere or do anything in particular. The railway has come to Cromer, and I hear that the guardian phalanx of Buxtons, Hoares, Gurneys, and Barclays, all good loafers in the last generation, have thrown up the sponge and gone with the stream. I was at Betwys and Penygurd last year, and at the former there were three or four long pleasure-vans meeting every train; at the latter, three parties came in, in a few hours, to do Snowdon and get back to dinner at Capel Curig or Bethgellert. Indeed, I was sore to mark that even Henry Owen, landlord and guide, once a good loafer, has succumbed., Over here it is still worse in the Atlantic States; but this is a big country, in which oases *must* be left yet for many a long year for the loafer, of which this is one. It lies on a mountain plateau, seven miles from the station, to which a hack goes twice daily to meet the morning and evening mails (once too often, perhaps, for the highest enjoyment of the loafer); but otherwise the outer world, its fidgets and its businesses, no more concern us than they did Cooper's jackdaw. I am conscious that regular work here must be done by some one, as daily meals at 7 A.M., and 12.30 and 6 P.M., never fail, with abundance of grapes and melons—the peaches, alas! were cut off by frosts when the trees were in blossom. But beyond this, and the presence of a young Englishman in the house, who, in blue shirt and trousers, tends and milks the cows, and puts in six or eight hours' work a day at one thing or another in the neighbouring fields, there is nothing to remind one that this world doesn't go on by itself, at any rate in these autumn days. Almost every cottage, or shanty, as they call these attractive wooden houses, has a deep verandah (from which you get a view, over the forest, of the southern range of mountains, with Pilot Knob for highest point), and, in the verandah, rocking-chairs and hammocks, in one or other of which a chatty host or hostess is almost sure to be found, enjoying air, view, rocking, and the indescribable depth of blue atmosphere which laps us all round. There is surely something very uplifting in finding the sky twice as far off as you know it at home. I felt this first on the Lower Danube and in Greece; but I doubt if Bulgarian or Greek heavens are as high as these. Every now and again, a merry group of young folk go by in waggon or on horseback; but even they are loafers, as they have no object in view beyond enjoying one another's company, and possibly lunch or tea at the junction of the two mountain-streams, the only lion we have within a day's journey. Their parents may be found for the most part in and round the hotel, for they are wise enough to let the young ones knock about very much as they please, while they take their own ease in the verandahs or shady grounds of "The Tabard." That hostelry of historic name stands on an eminence next to this shanty, and my "loaf-brothers," when I get any, are generally saunterers from amongst its guests, and the one who comes oftenest is perhaps the best loafer I have ever come across. He is a rancheman on the Rio Grande, and has been out here ever since he left Marlborough, some fourteen years ago. Since then I should think he has done as hard work as any man, in the long drives of 2000 miles which he used to make from Southern Texas up to Colorado or Kansas, before the railway came. Even now, I take it that for ten months in the year he covers more ground and exhausts more tissue than most men, which makes him such a model loafer when he gets away. Yesterday, for instance, he started after lunch from "The Tabard," 300 yards off, under a sort of engagement, as definite as we make them, to spend the afternoon here. On the way he came across a hammock swinging unoccupied in the hotel grounds, and a volume of Pendennis, and only arrived here after supper, in the superb starlight (the moon is objectionably late in rising just now), to smoke a pipe before bed-time. His experience of Western life is as racy as a volume of Bret Harte. Take the following, for instance:—At a prairie-town not far from his ranche, as distances go in the West, there is a State Court of First Instance, presided over by one Roy Bean, J.P., who is also the owner of the principal grocery. Some cowboys had been drinking at the grocery one night, with the result that one of them remained on the floor, but with sense enough left to lie on the side of the pocket where he kept his dollars. In the morning, it appeared that he had been "rolled"—*Anglicè*, turned over and his pocket picked— whereupon a court was called to try a man on whom suspicion rested. Roy Bean sat on a barrel, swore in a jury, and then addressed the prisoner thus: "Now, you give that man his money back." The culprit, who had sent for the lawyer of the place to defend him, hesitated for a moment, and then pulled out the money. "You treat this crowd," were Roy's next words; and while "drinks round" were handed to the delighted cowboys at the prisoner's expense, Roy pulled out his watch and went on: "You've got just five minutes to clear out of this town, and if ever you come in again, we'll hang you." The culprit made off just as his lawyer came up, who remonstrated with Roy, explaining that the proper course would have been to have heard the charge, committed the prisoner, and sent him to the county town for trial. "And go off sixty miles, and hang round with the boys [witnesses] for you to pull the skunk through and touch the dollars!" said Roy scornfully; whereupon the lawyer disappeared in pursuit of his client and unpaid fee.

It occurs to one to ask how much of the litigation of England might be saved if Judges of First Instance might open with Roy's formula: "Now, you give that man his money back." I am bound to add that his practice is not without its seamy side. When the railway was making, two men came in from one of the gangs for a warrant. A brutal murder had been committed. Roy told his clerk (the boy in the grocery, he being no penman himself) to make out the paper, asking: "Wot's the corpse's name?" "Li Hung," was the reply. "Hold on!" shouted Roy to his clerk; and then to the pursuers: "Ef you ken find anything in them books," pointing to the two or three supplied by the State, "about killin' a Chinaman, it ken go," and the pursuers had to travel on to the next fount of justice.

Here is one more: my "loaf-brother" heard it himself as he was leaving Texas, and laughed at it nearly all the way up. A group of cowboys at the station were discussing the problem of how long the world would last if this drought went on, the prevailing sentiment being that they would rather it worruted through somehow. A cowboy down on his luck here struck in: "Wall, if the angel stood right thar," pointing across the room, "ready to sound, and looked across at me, I'd jest say, 'Gabe! toot your old horn!'"

Rugby, Tennessee.

I was roused at five or thereabouts on the morning after our arrival here by a visit from a big dog belonging to a native, not quite a mastiff, but more like that than anything else, who, seeing my window wide open, jumped in from the verandah, and came to the bed to give me goodmorning with tail and muzzle. I was glad to see him, having made friends the previous evening, when the decision of his dealings with the stray hogs who came to call on us from the neighbouring forest had won my heart; but as his size and attentions somewhat impeded my necessarily scanty ablutions, I had to motion him apologetically to the window when I turned out. He obeyed at once, jumped out, laid his muzzle on the sill, and solemnly, and, I thought, somewhat pityingly, watched my proceedings. Meantime, I heard sounds which announced the uprising of "the boys," and in a few minutes several appeared in flannel shirts and trousers, bound for one of the two rivers which run close by, in gullies 200 feet below us. They had heard of a pool ten feet deep, and found it too; and a most delicious place it is, surrounded by great rocks, lying in a copse of rhododendrons, azaleas, and magnolias, which literally form the underwood of the pines and white oak along these gullies. The water is of a temperature which allows folk whose blood is not so hot as it used to be to lie for half an hour on its surface and play about without a sensation of chilliness. On this occasion, however, I preferred to let them do the exploring, and so at 6.15 went off to breakfast.

This is the regular hour for that meal here, dinner at twelve, and tea at six. There is really no difference between them, except that we get porridge at breakfast and a great abundance of vegetables at dinner. At all of them we have tea and fresh water for drink, plates of beef or mutton, apple sauce, rice, tomatoes, peach pies or puddings, and several kinds of bread. As the English garden furnishes unlimited water and other melons, and as the settlers— young English, who come in to see us—bring sacks of apples and peaches with them, and as, moreover, the most solvent of the boys invested at Cincinnati in a great square box full of tinned viands of all kinds, you may see at once that in this matter we are not genuine objects either for admiration or pity. I must confess here to a slight disappointment. Having arrived at an age myself when diet has become a matter of indifference, I was rather chuckling as we came along over the coming short-commons up here, when we got fairly loose in the woods, and the excellent discipline it would be for the boys, especially the Londoners, to discover that the human animal can be kept in rude health on a few daily crackers and apples, or a slap-jack and tough pork. And now, behold, we are actually still living amongst the flesh-pots, which I had fondly believed we had left in your Eastern Egypt; and I am bound to add, "the boys" seem as provokingly indifferent to them as if their beards were getting grizzled. One lives and learns, but I question whether these states are quite the place to bring home to our Anglo-Saxon race the fact that we are an overfed branch of the universal brotherhood. Tanner, I fear, has fasted in vain.

Breakfast was scarcely over, when there was a muster of cavalry. Every horse that could be spared or requisitioned was in demand for an exploring ride to the west, and soon every charger was bestrid by "a boy" in free-and-easy garments, and carrying a blanket for camping out. Away they went under the pines and oaks, a merry lot, headed by our geologist, who knows the forest by this time like a native, and whose shocking old straw blazed ahead in the morning sun like, shall we say, "the helmet of Navarre," or Essex's white hat and plumes before the Train Bands, as they crowned the ridge where Falkland fell and his monument now stands, at the battle of Newbury. Charles Kingsley's lines came into my head, as I turned pensively to my table in the verandah to write to you:—

When all the world is young, lad, and all the trees are green;

And every goose a swan, lad, and every lass a queen;

Then hey for boot and horse, lad, and round the world away;

Young blood must have its course, lad, and every dog his day.

Our two lasses are, undoubtedly, queens out here. The thought occurs, are our swans—our visions, already so bright, of splendid crops, and simple life, to be raised and lived in this fairyland—to prove geese? I hope not. It would be the downfall of the last castle in Spain I am ever likely to build.

On reaching our abode, I was aware of the Forester coming across from the English garden, of which he has charge, followed by a young native. He walked up to me, and announced that they were come across to tidy up, and *black the boots*. Here was another shock, that we should be followed by the lumber of civilisation so closely! Will boots be blacked, I wonder, in the New Jerusalem? I was at first inclined to protest, while they made a collection, and set them out on the verandah, but the sight of the ladies' neat little high-lows made me pause. These, at any rate, it seemed to me, *should* be blacked, even in the Millennium. Next minute I was so tickled by a little interlude between the Forester and the native, that all idea of remonstrance vanished. The latter, contemplating the boots and blacking-pot and brushes—from under the shapeless piece of old felt, by way of hat, of the same mysterious colour as the ragged shirt and breeches, his only other garments—joined his hands behind his back, and said, in their slow way, "Look 'ere, Mr. Hill, ain't this 'ere pay-day?" The drift was perfectly obvious. This citizen had no mind to turn shoe-black, and felt like discharging himself summarily. Mr. Hill, who was already busily sweeping the verandah, put down his broom, and after a short colloquy, which I did not quite catch, seized on a boot and brush, and began shining away with an artistic stroke worthy of one of the Shoeblack Brigade at the London Bridge Station. The native looked on for a minute, and then slowly unclasped his hands. Presently he picked up a boot and looked round it dubiously. I now took a hand myself. If there was one art which I learned to perfection at school, and still pride myself on, it is shining a boot. In a minute or two my boot was beginning "to soar and sing," while the Forester's was already a thing of beauty. The native, with a grunt, took up the spare brush, and began slowly rubbing. The victory was complete. He comes now and spends two hours every morning over his new accomplishment, evidently delighted with the opportunity it gives him for loafing and watching the habits of the strange occupants, for whom also he fetches many tin pails of water from the well, in a slow, vague manner. He has even volunteered to fix up the ladies' room and fill their bath (an offer which has been declined, with thanks), but I doubt whether he will ever touch the point of a genuine "shine."

They are a curious people, these natives, as the Forester (an Englishman, reared in Lord Denbigh's garden at Newnham Paddocks, and thirty years out here) told me, as we walked off to examine the English garden, but I must keep his experiences and my own observation for separate treatment. The English garden is the most advanced, and, I think, the most important and interesting feature of this settlement. If young Englishmen of small means are to try their fortunes here, it is well that they should have trustworthy guidance at once as to what are the best crops to raise. With this view, Mr. Hill was placed, in the spring of this year, in charge of the only cleared space available. All the rest is beautiful, open forest-land. You can ride or drive almost anywhere under the trees, but there is no cultivated spot for many miles, except small patches here and there of carelessly sown maize and millet, and a rood or two of sweet potatoes. The Forester had a hard struggle to do anything with the garden at all this season. He was only put in command in May, six weeks at least too late. He could only obtain the occasional use of a team, and his duties in the forest and in grading and superintending the walks interfered with the garden. Manure was out of the question, except a little ashes, which he painfully gathered here and there from the reckless log-fires which abound in the woods. He calls his garden a failure for the year. But as half an acre which was wild forest-land in May is covered with water-melons and cantalupes, as the tomatoes hang in huge bunches, rotting on the vines for want of mouths enough to eat them, as the Lima beans are yielding at the rate of 250 bushels an acre, and as cabbages, sweet potatoes, beets, and squash are in equally prodigal abundance, the prospect of making a good living is beyond all question, for all who will set to work with a will.

In the afternoon, I inspected the hotel, nearly completed, on a knoll in the forest, between the English garden and this frame-house. It is a sightly building, with deep verandahs prettily latticed, from which one gets glimpses through the trees of magnificent ranges of blue forest-covered mountains. We have named it "The Tabard," at the suggestion of one of our American members, who, being in England when the old Southwark hostelry from which the Canterbury Pilgrims started was broken up, and the materials sold by auction, to make room for a hop store, bought some of the old banisters, which he has reverently kept till now. They will be put up in the hall of the new Tabard, and marked with a brass plate and inscription, telling, I trust, to many generations of the place from which they came. The Tabard, when finished, as it will be in a few days, will lodge some fifty guests; and, in spite of the absence of alcoholic drinks, has every chance, if present indications can be trusted, of harbouring and sending out as cheery pilgrims as followed the Miller and the Host, and told their world-famous stories five hundred years ago.

The drink question has reared its baleful head here, as it seems to do all over the world. The various works had gone on in peace till the last ten days, when two young natives toted over some barrels of whisky, and broached them in a shanty, on a small lot of no-man's land in the woods, some two miles from hence. Since then there has been no peace for the manager. Happily the feeling of the community is vigorously temperate, so energetic measures are on foot to root out the pest. A wise state law enacts that no liquor store shall be permitted under heavy penalties within four miles of an incorporated school; so we are pushing on our school-house, and organising a board to govern it. Meantime, we have evidence of unlawful sale (in quantities less than a pint), and of encouraging gambling, by these pests, and hope to make an example of them at the next sitting of the county court. This incident has decided the question for us. If we are to have influence with the poor whites and blacks, we must be above suspicion ourselves. So no liquor will be procurable at the Tabard, and those who need it will have to import for themselves.

A bridle-path leads from the hotel down to the Clear Fork, one of the streams at the junction of which the town site is situate. The descent is about 200 feet, and the stream, when you get to it, from thirty feet to fifty feet wide,—a mountain stream, with deep pools and big boulders. Your columns are not the place for descriptions of scenery, so I will only say that these gorges of the Clear Fork and White Oak are as fine as any of their size that I know in Scotland, and not unlike in character, with this difference, that the chief underwood here consists of rhododendron (called laurel here), azalea, and a kind of magnolia I have not seen before, and of which I cannot get the name. I passed huge faggots of rhododendron, twelve feet and fourteen feet long, lying by the walks, which had been cleared away ruthlessly while grading them. They are three miles long and cost under £100, a judicious outlay, I think, even before an acre of land has been sold. They have been named the Lovers' Walks, appropriately enough, for no more well-adapted place could possibly be found for that time-honoured business, especially in spring, when the whole gorges under the tall pines and white oak are one blaze of purple, yellow, and white blossom.

On my return to the plateau, my first day's experiences came to an end in a way which no longer surprised me, after the boot-blacking and the Lovers' Walks. I was hailed by one of "the boys," who had been unable to obtain a mount, or had some business which kept him from exploring. He was in flannels, with racquet in hand, on his way to the lawn-tennis ground, to which he offered to pilot me. In a minute or two we came upon an open space, marked, I see on the plans, "Cricket Ground," in which rose a fine, strong paling, enclosing a square of 150 feet, the uprights being six feet high, and close enough to keep, not only boys out, but tennis-balls in. Turf there was none, in our sense, within the enclosure, and what there must have once been as a substitute for turf had been carefully cleared off on space sufficient for one full-sized court, which was well marked out on the hard, sandy loam. A better ground I have rarely seen, except for the young sprouts of oak, and other scrub, which here and there were struggling up, in a last effort to assert their "ancient, solitary reign." At any rate, then and there, upon that court, I saw two sets played in a style which would have done credit to a county match (the young lady, by the way, who played far from the worst game of the four, is the champion of her own county). This was the opening match, the racquets having only just arrived from England, though the court has been the object of tender solicitude for six weeks or more to the four Englishmen already resident here or near by. The Rugby Tennis Club consists to-day of seven members, five English and two native, and will probably reach two figures within a few days on the return of the boys. Meantime the effect of their first practice has been that they have resolved on putting a challenge in the Cincinnati and Chatanooga papers offering to play a match—best out of five sets—with any club in the United States. Such are infant communities, in these latitudes!

You may have been startled by the address at the head of this letter. It was adopted unanimously on our return in twilight from the tennis-ground, and application at once made to the State authorities for registration of the name and establishment of a post-office. It was sharp practice thus to steal a march on the three Etonians, still far away in the forest. Had they been present, possibly Thames might have prevailed over Avon.

A Forest Ride, Rugby, Tennessee.

There are few more interesting experiences than a ride through these southern forests. The scrub is so low and thin, that you can almost always see away for long distances amongst pine, white oak, and chestnut trees; and every now and then at ridges where the timber is thin, or where a clump of trees has been ruthlessly "girdled," and the bare, gaunt skeletons only remain standing, you may catch glimpses of mountain ranges of different shades of blue and green, stretching far away to the horizon. You can't live many days up here without getting to love the trees even more, I think, than we do in well-kempt England; and this outrage of "girdling," as they call it—stripping the bark from the lower part of the trunk, so that the trees wither and die as they stand—strikes one as a kind of household cruelty, as if a man should cut off or disfigure all his wife's hair. If he wants a tree for lumber or firewood, very good. He should have it. But he should cut it down like a man, and take it clean away for some reasonable use, not leave it as a scarecrow to bear witness of his recklessness and laziness. Happily not much mischief of this kind has been done yet in the neighbourhood of Rugby, and a stop will now be put to the wretched practice. There is another, too, almost as ghastly, but which, no doubt, has more to be said for it. At least half of the largest pines alongside of the sandy tracts which do duty for roads have a long, gaping wound in their sides, about a yard from the ground. This was the native way of collecting turpentine, which oozed down and accumulated at the bottom of the gash; but I rejoice to say it no longer pays, and the custom is in disuse. It must be suppressed altogether, but carefully and gently. It seems that if not persisted in too long, the poor, dear, long-suffering trees will close up their wounds, and not be much the worse: so I trust that many of the scored pines, springing forty or fifty feet into the air before throwing out a branch, which I passed in sorrow and anger on my first long ride, may yet outlive those who outraged them. Having got rid of my spleen, excited by these two diabolic customs, I can return to our ride, which had otherwise nothing but delight in it.

The manager, an invaluable guest from New York, a doctor, who had served on the Sanitary Commission through the war, and I, formed the party. The manager drove the light buggy, which held one of us also, and the handbags 3 while the other rode by the side, where the road allowed, or before or behind, as the fancy seized him. We were bound for a solitary guest-house in the forest, some seventeen miles away, in the neighbourhood of a cave and waterfall which even here have a reputation, and are sometimes visited. We allowed three and a half hours for the journey, and it took all the time. About five miles an hour on wheels is all you can reckon on, for the country roads, sandy tracts about ten feet broad, are just left to take care of themselves, and wherever there is a sufficient declivity to give the rain a chance of washing all the surface off them, are just a heap of boulders of different sizes. But, after all, five miles an hour is as fast as you care to go, for the play of the sunlight amongst the varied foliage, and the new flora and fauna, keep you constantly interested and amused. I never regretted so much my ignorance of botany, for I counted some fourteen sorts of flowers in bloom, of which golden-rod and Michaelmas-daisy were the only ones I was quite sure I knew,—and by the way, the daisy of Parnassus, of which I found a single flower growing by a spring. The rest were like home flowers, but yet not identical with them— at least, I think not—and the doubt whether one had ever seen them before or not was provoking. The birds—few in number—were all strangers to me; buzzards, of which we saw five at one time, quite within shot, and several kinds of hawk and woodpecker, were the most common; but at one point, quite a number of what looked like very big swifts, but without the dash in their flight of our bird, and with wings more like curlews', were skimming over the tree-tops..1 only heard one note, and that rather sweet, a cat-bird's, the doctor thought; but he was almost as much a stranger in these woods as I. Happily, however, he was an old acquaintance of that delightful insect, the "tumble-bug," to which he introduced me on a sandy bit of road. The gentleman in question took no notice of me, but went on rolling his lump of accumulated dirt three times his own size backwards with his hind legs, as if his life depended on it. Presently his lump came right up against a stone and stopped dead. It was a "caution" to see that bug strain to push it farther, but it wouldn't budge, all he could do. Then he stopped for a moment or two, and evidently made up his small mind that something must be wrong behind, for no bug could have pushed harder than he. So he quitted hold with his hind legs, and turned round to take a good look at the situation, in order, I suppose, to see what must be done next. At any rate, he presently caught hold again on a different side, and so steered successfully past the obstacle. There were a number of them working about, some single and some in pairs, and so full of humour are their doings that I should have liked to watch for hours.

We got to our journey's end about dusk, a five-roomed, single-storied, wooden house, built on supports, so as to keep it off the ground. We went up four steps to the verandah, where we sat while our hostess, a small, thin New Englander, probably seventy or upwards, but as brisk as a bee, bustled about to get supper. The table was laid in the middle room, which opened on the kitchen at the back, where we could see the stove, and hear our hostess's discourse. She boiled us two of her fine white chickens admirably, and served with hot bread, tomatoes, sweet potatoes, and several preserves, of which I can speak with special praise of the huckleberry, which grows, she said, in great abundance all round. *The boys*, we heard, had been there to breakfast, after sleeping out, and not having had a square meal since they started. Luckily for us, her white chickens are a very numerous as well as beautiful family, or we should have fared badly. She and her husband supped after us, and then came and sat with us in the balcony, and talked away on all manner of topics, as if the chances of discourse were few, and to be made the most of. They had lived at Jamestown, close by, a village of some eight or ten houses, all through the war, through which the Confederate cavalry had passed again and again. They had never molested her or hers in any way, but had a fancy for poultry, which might have proved fatal to her white family, but for her Yankee wit. She and her husband managed to fix up a false floor in one of their rooms in which they fed the roosters, so whenever a picket came in sight, her call would bring the whole family out of the woods and clearing into the refuge, where they remained peacefully amongst corn-cobs till the danger had passed. She had nothing but good to say of her native neighbours, except that they could make nothing of the country. The Lord had done all He could for it, she summed up, and Boston must take hold of the balance. We heard the owls all night, as well as the katydids, but they only seemed to emphasise the forest stillness. The old lady's beds, to which we retired at ten, after our long gossip in the balcony, were sweet and clean, and I escaped perfectly scatheless, a rare experience, I was assured, in these forest shanties. I was bound, however, to admit, in answer to our hostess's searching inquiries, that I had seen, and slain, though not felt, an insect suspiciously like a British B flat.

The cave which we sought out after breakfast was well worth any trouble to find. We had to leave the buggy and horses hitched up and scramble down a glen, where presently, through a tangle of great rhododendron bushes, we came on a rock, with the little iron-stained stream just below us, and opposite, at the top of a slope of perhaps fifteen or twenty feet, was the cave, like a long black eye under a red eyebrow, glaring at us. I could detect no figure in the sandstone rock (the eyebrow), which hung over it for its whole length. The cave is said to run back more than 300 feet, but we did not test it. There would be good sitting-room for 300 or 400 people along the front, and so obviously fitted for a conventicle, that I could not help peopling it with fugitive slaves, and fancying a black Moses preaching to them of their coming Exodus, with the rhododendrons in bloom behind. Maidenhair grow in tufts about the damp floor, and a creeping fern, with a bright red berry, the name of which the doctor told me, but I have forgotten, on the damp, red walls. What the nook must be when the rhododendrons are all ablaze with blossom, I hope some day to see.

We had heard of a fine spring somewhere in this part of the forest, and in aid of our search for it presently took up a boy whom we found loafing round a small clearing. He was bare-headed and bare-footed, and wore an old, brown, ragged shirt turned up to the elbows, and old, brown, ragged trousers turned up to the knees. I was riding, and in answer to my invitation he stepped on a stump and vaulted up behind me. He never touched me, as most boys would have done, but sat up behind with perfect ease and balance as we rode along, a young centaur. We soon got intimate, and I found he had never been out of the forest, was fourteen, and still at (occasional) school. He could read a little, but couldn't write. I told him to tell his master, from me, that he ought to be ashamed of himself, which he promised to do with great glee; also, but not so readily, to consider a proposal I made him, that if he would write to the manager within six months to ask for it, he should be paid $1. I found that he knew nothing of the flowers or butterflies, of which some dozen different kinds crossed our path. He just reckoned they were all butterflies, as indeed they were. He knew, however, a good deal about the trees and shrubs, and more about the forest beasts. Had seen several deer only yesterday, and an old opossum with nine young, a number which took the doctor's breath away. There were lots of foxes in the woods, but he did not see them so often. His face lighted up when he was promised $2 for the first opossum he would tame and bring across to Rugby. After guiding us to the spring, and hunting out an old wooden cup amongst the bushes, he went off cheerily through the bushes, with two quarter-dollar bits in his pocket, an interesting young wild man. Will he ever bring the opossum?

We got back without further incident (except flushing quite a number of quail, which must be lovely shooting in these woods), and found the boys at home, and hard at lawn-tennis and well-digging. The hogs are becoming an object of their decided animosity, and having heard of a Yankee notion, a sort of tweezers, which ring a hog by one motion, in a second, they are going to get it, and then to catch and ring every grunter who shows his nose near the asylum. Out of this there should come some fun, shortly.

The Natives, Rugby, Tennessee.

When all is said and sung, there is nothing so interesting as the man and woman who dwell on any corner of the earth; so, before giving you any further details of our surroundings, or doings, or prospects, let me introduce you to our neighbours, so far as I have as yet the pleasure of their acquaintance. And I am glad at once to acknowledge that it *is* a pleasure, notwithstanding all the talk we have heard of "mean whites," "poor, white trash," and the like, in novels, travels, and newspapers. It may possibly be that we have been fortunate, and that our neighbours here are no fair specimens of the "poor whites" of the South. This, and the next three counties, are in the north-western corner of Tennessee, bordering on Kentucky. They are entirely mountain land. There are very few negroes in them, and they were strongly Unionist during the war. At present, they are Republican, almost to a man. There is not one Democratic official in this county, and I am told that only three votes were cast for the Democratic candidates at the last State elections. They are overwhelmed by the vote of western and central Tennessee, which carries the State with the solid South; but here Union men can speak their minds freely, and cover their walls with pictures in coloured broad-sheet of the heroes of the war,—Lincoln, Governor Brownlow, Grant and his captains. They are poor almost to a man, and live in log-huts and cabins which, at home, could scarcely be rivalled out of Ireland. Within ten miles of this place there are possibly half a dozen (I have seen two) which are equal in accommodation and comfort to those of good farmers in England. The best of these belongs to our nearest neighbour, with whom a party of us dined, at noon, the orthodox hour in the mountains, some weeks since. He is a wiry man, of middle height, probably fifty-five years of age, upright, with finely cut features, and an eye that looks you right in the face. He has been on his farm twenty years, and has cleared some fifty acres, which grow corn, millet, and vegetables, and he has a fine apple orchard. We should call his farming very slovenly, but it produces abundance for his needs. He sat at the head of his table like an old nobleman, very quiet and courteous, but quite ready to speak on any subject, and especially of the five years of the war through which he carried his life in his hand, but never flinched for an hour from his faith. His wife, a slight, elderly person, whose regular features showed that she must have been very good-looking, did not sit down with us, but stood at the bottom of the table, dispensing her good things. Our drink was tea and cold spring water; our viands, chickens, ducks, a stew, ham, with a profusion of vegetables, apple and huckleberry tarts, and several preserves, one of which (some kind of cherry, very common here) was of a lovely gold colour, and of a flavour which would make the fortune of a London pastry-cook; a profusion of water-melons and apples finished our repast; and no one need ask a better,—but I am bound to add that our hostess has the name for giving the best square meal to be had in the four counties. It would be as fair to take this as an average specimen of the well-to-do farmers' fare here, as that of a nobleman with a French cook of the gentry at home. Our host is a keen sportsman, and showed us his flint-lock rifle, six feet long, and weighing 16 lbs.! He carries a forked stick as a rest, and, we were assured, gets on his game about as quickly as if it were a handy Westley-Richards, and seldom misses a running deer. The vast majority of these mountaineers are in very different circumstances. Most, but not all of them, own a log cabin and minute patch of corn round it, probably also a few pigs and chickens, but seem to have no desire to make any effort at further clearing, and quite content to live from hand to mouth. They cannot do that without hiring themselves out when they get a chance, but are most uncertain and exasperating labourers. In the first place, though able, to stand great fatigue in hunting and perfectly indifferent to weather, they are not physically so strong as average English or Northern men. Then they are never to be relied on for a job. As soon as one of them has earned three or four dollars, he will probably want a hunt, and go off for it then and there, spend a dollar on powder and shot, and these on squirrels and opossums, whose skins may possibly bring him in ten cents as his week's earnings. It is useless to remonstrate, unless you have an agreement in writing. An Englishman who came here lately, to found some manufactures, left in sheer despair and disgust, saying he had found at last a place where no one seemed to care for money. I do not say that this is true, but they certainly seem to prefer loafing and hunting to dollars, and are often too lazy, or unable, to count, holding out their small change and telling you to take what you want. Temperate as a rule, they are sadly weak when wild-cat whisky or "moonshine," as the favourite illicit beverage of the mountains is called, crosses their path. This is the great trouble on pay nights at all the works which are starting in this district. The inevitable booth soon appears, with the usual accompaniment of cards and dice, and probably a third of your men are thenceforth without a dime and utterly unfit for work on Mondays, if you are lucky enough to escape dangerous rows amongst the drinkers. The State laws give summary methods of suppressing the nuisance, but they are hard to work, and though public sentiment is vehemently hostile to whisky, the temptation proves in nine cases out of ten too strong. The mountaineers are in the main well-grown men, though slight, shockingly badly clothed, and sallow from chewing tobacco; suspicious in all dealings at first, but hospitable, making everything they have in the house, including their own beds, free to a stranger, and generally refusing payment for lodging or food. They are also very honest, crimes against property (though not against the person) being of very rare occurrence. The other day, a Northern gentleman visiting here expressed his fears to a native farmer, who, after inquiring whether there were any prisons and police in New England, what these were for, and whether his interrogator had locks to his doors and his safes, and bars to his window-shutters, remarked, "Wal, I've lived here man and boy for forty year, and never had a bolt to my house, or corn-loft, or smoke-house, and I'll give you a dollar for every lock you can find in Scott county." The cattle, sheep, and hogs wander perfectly unguarded through the forest, and I have not yet heard of a single instance of a stolen beast.

There is a rough water-mill on a creek close by, called Back's Mill, which was run by the owner for years—until he sold it a few months ago—on the following system. He put the running gear and stones up, and above the latter a wooden box, with the charge for grinding meal marked outside. He visited the mill once a fortnight, looked to the machinery, and took away whatever coin was in the box. Folks brought their corn down the steep bank if they chose, ground it at their leisure, and then, if they were honest, put the fee in the box; if not, they went off with their meal, and a consciousness that they were rogues. I presume Buck found his plan answer, as he pursued it up to the date of sale.

In short, sir, I have been driven to the conclusion, in spite of all traditional leanings the other way, that the Lord has much people in these mountains, as I think a young English deacon, lately ordained by the Bishop of Tennessee, will find, who passed here yesterday on a buggy, with his young wife and child, and two boxes and ten dollars of the goods of this world, on his way to open a church mission in a neighbouring county. I heard yesterday a story which should give him hope as to the female portion, at any rate, of his possible flock. They are dreadful slatterns, without an inkling of the great Palmerstonian truth that dirt is matter in its *wrong* place. A mountain girl, however, who had, strange to say, taken the fancy to go as housemaid in a Knoxville family, gave out that she had been converted, and, upon doubts being expressed and questions asked as to the grounds on which she based the assurance, replied that she knew it was all right, because now she swept underneath the rugs.

When one gets on stories of quaint and ready replies in these parts, one "slops over on both shoulders." Here are a couple which are current in connection with the war, upon which, naturally enough, the whole mind of the people is still dwelling, being as much occupied with it as with their other paramount subject, the immediate future development of the unbounded resources of these States, which have been really opened for the first time by that terrible agency. An active Secessionist leader in a neighbouring county, in one of his stump speeches before the war, had announced that the Southerners, and especially Tennessee mountain men, could whip the white-livered Yanks with pop-guns. Not long since, having been amnestied and reconstructed again to a point when he saw his way to running for a State office, he was reminded of this saying at the beginning of his canvas. "Wal, yes," he said, "he owned to that and stood by it still, only those mean cusses [the Yanks] wouldn't fight that way."

The other is of very different stamp, and will hold its own with many world-wide stories of graceful compliments to former enemies by kings and other big-wigs. General Wilder, one of the most successful and gallant of the Northern corps commanders in the war, has established himself in this State, with whose climate and resources he became so familiar in the campaign which ended under Look-out Mountain, and has built up a great iron industry at Chatanooga, in full sight of the battlefields from which 14,000 bodies of Union soldiers were carried to the national cemetery. Early in his Southern career he met one of the most famous of the Southern corps commanders (Forrest, I believe, but am not sure as to the name), who, on being introduced, said, "General, I have long wished to know you, because you have behaved to me in a way for which I reckon you owe me an apology, as between gentlemen."

Wilder replied in astonishment that to his knowledge they had never met before, but that he was quite ready to do all that an honourable man ought. "Well now, General," said the other, "you remember such and such a fight (naming it)? By night you had taken every gun I had, and I consider that quite an ungentlemanly advantage to take, anyhow." By the way, no man bears more frank testimony to the gallantry of the Southern soldiers than General Wilder, or admits more frankly the odds which the superior equipment of the Federals threw against the Confederate armies. His corps, mounted infantry, armed with repeating rifles, were equal, he thinks, to at least three times their numbers of as good soldiers as themselves with the ordinary Southern arms. There are few pleasanter things to a hearty well-wisher, who has not been in America for ten years, than the change which has taken place in public sentiment, indicated by such frank admissions as the one just referred to. In 1870, any expression of admiration for the gallantry of the South, or of respect or appreciation of such men as Lee, Jackson, Longstreet, or Johnson, was received either silently, or with strong disapproval. How it is quite the other way, so far as I have seen as yet, and I cannot but hope that the last scars of the mighty struggle are healing up rapidly and thoroughly, and that the old sectional hatred and scorn lie six feet under ground, in the national cemeteries:—

No more shall the war-cry sever,

Or the inland rivers run red;

We have buried our anger for ever,

In the sacred graves of the dead.

Under the sod and the dew,

Waiting the Judgment Day;

Love and tears for the blue!

Tears and love for the gray!

No man can live for a few weeks on these Cumberland Mountains, without responding with a hearty "Amen!"

Our Forester, Rugby, Tennessee.

Nothing would satisfy our Forester but that some of us should ride over with him, some nine miles through the forest, to see Glades, the farm upon which he has been for the last eight years. He led the way, on his yellow mare, an animal who had nearly given us sore trouble here. The head stableman turned all the horses out one day for a short run, and she being amongst them, and loving her old home best, went off straight for Glades through the woods, with every hoof after her. Luckily, Alfred, the Forester's son, was there, and guessing what was the matter, just rode her back, all the rest following. The ride was lovely, glorious peeps of distant blue ranges, and the forest just breaking out all over into golds, and vermilions, and purples, and russets. We only passed two small farms on the way, both ramshackle, and so the treat of coming suddenly on some one hundred acres cleared, drained, with large, though rough, farm buildings, and bearing the look of being cared for, was indescribably pleasant. Mrs. Hill and her son Alfred received us, both worthy of the head of the house; more I cannot say. They run the farm in his absence with scarcely any help, Alfred having also to attend to a grist and saw mill in the neighbouring creek. There were a fine mare and filly in the yard, as tame as pet dogs, coming and shoving their noses into your pockets and coaxing you for apples. The hogs are good Berkshire breed, the sheep Cotswolds. The cows (it is the only place where we have had cream on the mountains), Alderney or shorthorns. The house is a large log-cabin, one big room, with a deep, open fireplace, with a great pine-log smouldering at the back across plain iron dogs, a big hearth in front, on which pitch-pine chips are thrown when you feel inclined for a blaze. The room is carpeted and hung with photographs and prints, a rifle and shot gun, and implements of one kind or another. A small collection of books, mostly theological, and founded on two big Bibles, two rocking and half a dozen other chairs, a table, and two beds in the corners furthest from the fire, complete the furniture of the room, which opens on one side on a deep verandah, and on the other on a lean-to, which serves for kitchen and diningroom, and ends in a small, spare bedroom. A loft above, into which the family disappeared at night, completes the accommodation. I need not dwell on our supper, which included tender mutton, chickens, apple-tart, custard pudding, and all manner of vegetables and cakes. Mrs. Hill is as notable a cook as her husband is a forester. After supper we drew round the big fireplace, and soon prevailed on our host to give us a sketch of his life, by way of encouragement to his three young countrymen who sat round, and are going to try their fortunes in these mountains:—

"I was born and bred up in one of Lord Denbigh's cottages, at Kirby, in Warwickshire. My father was employed on the great place, that's Newnham

Paddocks, you know. He was a labourer, and brought up sixteen children, not one of whom, except me, has ever been summonsed before a justice, or got into any kind of trouble. I went to school till about nine, but I was always longing to be out in the fields at plough or birdkeeping; so I got away before I could do much reading or writing. But I kept on at Sabbath School, and learnt more than I did at the other. The young ladies used to teach us, and they'd set us pieces and things to learn for them in the week. My Cæsar (the only ejaculation Amos allows himself; he cannot remember where he picked it up), how I would work at my piece to get it for Lady Mary! I've fairly cried over it sometimes, but I always managed to get it, somehow. After a bit, I was taken on at the house. At first, I did odd jobs, like cleaning boots and carrying messages; and then I got into the garden, and from that into the stable, and then for a bit with the keepers, and then into livery, to wait on the young ladies. So you see I learnt something of everything, and was happy, and earning good wages. But I wanted to see the world, so I took service with a gentleman who was a big railway contractor. I used to drive him, and do anything a'most that he wanted. I stayed with him nine years, and 'twas while going about with him that I met my wife here. We got married down in Kent, thirty-six years ago. Yes (in answer to a laughing comment by his wife), I wanted some one to mind me in those days. That poaching trouble came about this way. I had charge for my master of a piece of railway that ran through Lord————'s preserves, in Wales. There were very strict rules about trespassing on the lines then, because folks there didn't like our line, and had been putting things on it to upset the trains. One day I saw two keepers coming down the line, with a labourer I knew between them. He was all covered with blood, from a wound in his head. 'Why,' said I, 'what's the matter now?' 'I've been out of work,' he said, 'this three weeks, and I was digging out a rabbit to get something to eat, when they came up and broke my head.' From that time the keepers and I quarrelled. I summonsed them, and got them fined for trespassing on the line; and then they got me fined for trespassing on their covers. We watched one another like hawks. I'd often lie out at night for hours in the cold, in a ditch, where I knew they'd want to cross the line, and then jump up and catch them; and they'd do the same by me. Once they got me fined £3: 10s. for poaching. I remember it well. I was that riled, I said to the justices right out, 'How long do you think it'll take me, gentlemen, to pay all that money, with hares only 1d. apiece?' Then I went in for it. I remembered the text, 'What thy hand findeth to do, do it with thy might.' I did it. I used to creep along at night, all up the fences, and feel for the places where the hares came through, and set my wires; and I'd often have ten great ones screaming and flopping about like mad. And that's what the keepers were, too. I've given a whole barrowful of hares away to the poor folk of a morning. Well, I know (in answer to an interpellation of Mrs. Hill), yes, 'twas all wrong, and I was a wild chap in those days. Then I begun to hear talk about America, and all there was for a man to see and do there, so I left my master, and we came over, twenty-seven years ago. At first I took charge of gentlemen's gardens, in New York and New Jersey. Then we went to Miscejan, where I could earn all I wanted. Money was of no account there for a good man in those days, but the climate was dreadful sickly, and we had our baby; the first we had in twelve years, and wanted to live on bread and water, so as we could save him. So we went up right amongst the Indians, to a place they call Grand Travers, a wonderful healthy place, on a lake in the pine-forest country, as it was then. I went on to a promontory, where the forest stood, not like it does here, but the trees that thick, you had scarce room to swing an axe. Well, it was a beautiful healthy place, and we and baby throve, and I soon made a farm; and then folk began to follow after us, and before I left, there were twenty-three saw-mills, cutting up from 80,000 to 150,000 feet a day, week in and out. They've stripped the country so now, that there's no lumber for those mills to cut, and most of them have stopped. I used to have a boat, with just a small sail, and I'd take my stuff down in the morning, and trade it off to the lumber-men, and then sail back at night, for the wind always changed and blew back in the evenings, most part of the year. Well, then, the war came, and for two years I kept thinking whether I oughtn't to do my part to help the Government I'd lived under so long. Besides, I hated slavery. So in the third year I made up my mind, and 'listed in the Michigan Cavalry. I took the whole matter before the Lord, and prayed I might do my duty as a soldier, and not hurt any man. Well, we joined the Cavalry, near 60,000 strong down in these parts; and I was at Knoxville, and up and down. It was awful, the language and the ways of the men, many of them at least, swearing, and drinking, and stealing any kind of thing they could lay hands on. Many's the plan for stealing I've broken up, telling them they were there to sustain the flag, not to rob poor folks. I spoke very plain all along, and got the men, many of them any way, to listen. I got on famously, too, because I was never away plundering, and my horse was always ready for any service. An officer would come in, after we had had a long day's work, to say a despatch or message must go, and no horse in our company was fit to go but mine, so the orderly must have him; but I always said no, I was quite ready to go myself, but would not part company from my horse. The only time 1 took what was not mine was when we surprised a Confederate convoy, and got hold of the stores they were carrying. There they were lying all along the roads, greatcoats and blankets, and meal bags, and good boots, with English marks on them. My Cæsar, how our men were destroying them! I got together a lot of the poor, starving folk out of the woods that both sides had been living on, and loaded them up with meal and blankets. My Cæsar, how I loved to scatter them English boots! They never had seen such before. No, sir (in reply to one of us), I never fired a shot all that time, but I had hundreds fired at me. I've been in the rifle-pits, and now and again seen a fellow drawing a bead on me, and I'd duck down and hear the bullet ping into the bank close above. They got to employ me a good deal carrying despatches and scouting. That's how I got took at last. We were at a place called Strawberry Plains, with Breckenridge's division pretty near all round us. I was sent out with twelve other men, to try and draw them out, to show their force and position; and so we did, but they were too quick for us. Out they came, and it was a race back to our lines down a steep creek. My horse missed his footing, and down we rolled over and over, into the water. When I got up, I was up to my middle, and, first thing I knew, there was a rebel, who swore at me for a G—d d———Yankee, and fired his six shooter at me. The shot passed under my arm, and before he could fire again an officer ordered him on, and gave me in charge. I was taken to the rear, and marched off with a lot of prisoners. The rebels treated me as if I'd been their father, after a day or two. I spoke out to them about their swearing and ways, just as I had to our men; and I might have been tight all the time I was a prisoner, only I'm a temperance man. They put me on their horses on the march, and I was glad of it, for I was hurt by my roll with my horse, and had about the chest. After about six days I got my parole, with five others. They were hard pressed then and didn't want us toting along. Then we started north, with nothing but just our uniforms, and they full of vermin. The first house we struck I asked where we could find a Union man about there. They didn't know any one, didn't think there was one in the county. I said that was bad, as we were paroled Union soldiers,—and then all was changed. They took us in and wanted us to use their beds, which we wouldn't do, because of the vermin on us. They gave us all they had, and I saw the women, for I couldn't sleep, covering us up with any spare clothes they'd got, and watching us all night long. They sent us on to other Union houses, and so we got north. I was too ill to stay north at my old work, so I sold my farm, and came south to Knoxville, where I had come to know many kind, good people, in the war. They were very kind, and I got work at the improvements on Mr. Dickenson's farm (a model farm we had gone over), and in other gentlemen's gardens. But I didn't get my health again, so eight years ago I came to this place on the mountains, which I knew was healthy, and would suit me. Well, they all said I should be starved out in two years and have to quit, but before three years were out I was selling them corn and better bacon than they'd ever had before. Some of 'em begin to think I'm right now, and there's a deal of improvement going on, and if they'd only, as I tell 'em, just put in all their time on their farms, and not go loafing round gunning, and contented with corn-dodgers and a bit of pork, and give up whisky, they might all do as well as I've done. I should like to go back once more and see the old country; but I mean to end my days here. There's no such country that I ever saw. The Lord has done all for us here. And it seems like dreams, that I should live to see a Rugby up here on the mountains. I mean to take a lot in the town, or close by, and call it Newnham Paddocks. So I shall lay my bones, you see, in the same place, as it were, that I was reared in."

I do not pretend that these were his exact words,—the whole had to be condensed to come within your space,—but they are not far off. It was now past nine, the time for retiring, when Amos told us that he always ended his day with family prayers. A psalm was read, and then we knelt down, and he prayed for some minutes. Extemporary prayers always excite my critical faculty, but there was no thought or expression in this I could have wished to alter. Then we turned in, I, after a pipe in the verandah, in one clean white bed, and two of the boys in the big one in the opposite corner. There I soon dozed off, watching the big, smouldering, white pine-log away in the depth of the chimney-nook, and the last flickerings of the knobs of pitch pine in front of it, between the iron dogs, and wondering in my mind over the brave story we had just been listening to, so simply told (of which I fear I have succeeded in giving a very poor reflection), and whether there are not some—there cannot, I fear, be many—such lives lying about in out-of-the-way corners, on mountain, or plain, or city. My last conscious speculation was whether the Union would have been saved if all Union soldiers had been Amos Hills.

I waked early, just before dawn, and was watching alternately the embers of the big log, still aglow in the deep chimney, and the white light beginning to break through the honeysuckles and vines which hung over the verandah, and shaded the wide, open window, when the clock struck five. The door opened softly, and in stepped Amos Hill in his stockings. He came to the foot of our beds, picked up our dirty boots, and stole out again, as noiselessly as he had entered. The next minute I heard the blacking brushes going vigorously, and knew that I should appear at breakfast with a shine on in which I should have reason to glory, if I were preparing to walk in Bond Street, instead of through the scrub on the Cumberland Mountains. I turned over for another, hour's sleep (breakfast being at 6.30 sharp), but not without first considering for some minutes which of us two—if things were fixed up straight in this blundering old world—ought to be blacking the other's boots. The conclusion I came to was that it ought *not* to be Amos Hill.

The Negro "Natives", Rugby, Tennessee, 30th October 1880.

There is one inconvenience in this desultory mode of correspondence,—that one is apt to forget what one has told already, and to repeat oneself. I have written something of the white native of these mountains; have I said anything of his dark brother? The subject is becoming a more and more interesting and important one every day, through all these regions. In these mountains, the negro, perhaps, can scarcely be called a native. Very few black families, I am told, were to be found here a year or two since. My own eyes assure me that they are multiplying rapidly. I see more and more black men amongst the gangs on roads and bridges, and come across queer little encampments in the woods, with a pile of logs smouldering in the midst, round which stand the mirth-provoking figures of small black urchins, who stare and grin at the intruder on horseback, till he rides on under the gold and russet and green autumnal coping of hickories, chestnuts, and pines.

I am coming to the conclusion that wherever work is to be had, in Tennessee, at any rate, there will the negro be found. He seems to gather to a contractor like the buzzards, which one sees over the tree-tops, to carrion. And unless the white natives take to "putting in all their time," whatever work is going will not long remain with them. The negro will loaf and shirk as often as not when he gets the chance, but he has not the same craving for knocking off altogether as soon as he has a couple of dollars in his pocket; has no strong hunting instinct, and has not acquired the art of letting his pick drop listlessly into the ground with its own weight, and stopping to admire the scenery after every half-dozen strokes. The negro is much more obedient, moreover, and manageable,—obedient to a fault, if one can believe the many stories one hears of his readiness to commit small misdemeanours and crimes, and not always small ones, at the bidding of his employers. There is one thing, however, which an equally unanimous testimony agrees in declaring that he will not do, and that is, sell his vote, or be dragooned into giving it for any one but his own choice; he may, indeed, be scared from voting, but cannot be "squared," a singular testimony, surely, of his prospective value as a citizen. Equally strong is the evidence of his resolute determination to get his children educated. In some Southern States the children are, I believe, kept apart, but in the only school I have had the chance of seeing, black and white children were together. They were not in class, but in the front of the barn-like building, used both for church and school, having just come out for the dinner hour. There was a large, sandy, trampled place under the trees, by no means a bad play-ground, on which a few of the most energetic, the blacks in the majority, were playing at some game as we came up, the mysteries of which I should have liked to study. But the longer we stayed, the less chance there seemed of their going on, and the game remains a mystery to me still. Where these children, some fifty in number, came from, is a problem; but there they were, from somewhere. And everywhere, I hear, the blacks are forcing the running, with respect to education, and great numbers of them are showing a thrift and energy which are likely to make them formidable competitors in the struggle for existence in all states south of Kentucky, at any rate.

In one department (a very small one, no doubt), they will have crowded out the native whites in a very short time, if I may judge by our experience in this house. We number two ladies and six men, and our whole service is done by one boy. Our first experiment was with a young native, who "reared up" on the first morning at the idea of having to black boots. This prejudice, I think I told you, was removed for the moment, and he stayed for a few days. Where it was he "weakened on us" I could not learn for certain, but incline to the belief that it was either having to carry the racquets and balls to the lawn-tennis ground, or to get a fire to burn in order to boil the water for a four-o'clock tea. Both these services were ordered by the ladies, and I thought I saw signs (though I am far from certain) that his manly soul rose against feminine command. Be that as it may, off he went without warning, and soon after Amos Hill arrived, with almost pathetic apologies and a negro boy, short of stature, huge of mouth, fabulous in the apparent age of his garments, named Jeff. He had no other name, he told us, and did not know whether it signified Jefferson or Geoffrey, or where or how he got it, or anything about himself, except that he had got our place at $5 a month,—at which he showed his ivory, "some!"

From this time all was changed. Jeff, it is true, after the first two days, gave proofs that he was not converted, like the white housemaid who had learned to sweep under the mats. His sweeping and tidying were decidedly those of the sinner, and he entirely abandoned the only hard work we set him, as soon as it was out of sight from the Asylum. It was a path leading to a shallow well, which the boys had dug at the bottom of the garden. The last twenty yards or so are on a steeper incline than the part next the house, so Jeff studiously completed the few feet that were left to the brow, and never put pick or shovel on the remainder, which lay behind the friendly brow of the slope. But in all other directions, where the work was mainly odd jobs, a respectable kind of loafing, Jeff was always to the fore, acquitting himself to the best, I think, of his ability. We did not get full command of him till the arrival of a young Texan cattle-driver, who taught us the peculiar cry for the negro, by appending a high "Ho" to his name, or rather running them together, so that the whole sounded, "Hojeff!" as nearly as possible one syllable. Even the ladies picked up the cry, and thenceforward Jeff's substitute for the "Anon, anon, sir!" of the Elizabethan waiter was instantaneous. He built a camp-oven, like those of the Volunteers at Wimbledon, and neater of construction, from which he supplied a reasonably constant provision of hot water between six and six, of course cutting his own logs for the fire. His highest achievement was ironing the ladies' cotton dresses, which they declared he did not very badly. Most of us entrusted him with the washing of flannel shirts and socks, which at any rate were faithfully immersed in suds, and hung up to dry under our eyes. The laundry was an army tent, pitched at the back of the Asylum, where Jeff spent nearly all his time when not under orders, and generally eating an apple, of which there was always a sack, a present from some ranche-owner, or brought over from the garden, lying about, and open to mankind at large. I never could find out whether he could read. One evening he came up proudly to ask whether his mail had come, and sure enough when the mail arrived there was a post-card, which he claimed. We thought he would ask one of us to read it for him, but were disappointed. He had a habit of crooning over and over again all day some scrap of a song. One of these excited my curiosity exceedingly, but I never succeeded in getting more than two lines out of him—

Oh my! oh my! I've got a hundred dollars in a mine!

One had a crave to hear what came of those 100 dollars. It seems it is so almost universally. The nearest approach to a complete negro ditty which I have been able to strike is one which the Texan gives, with a wonderful roll of the word "chariot," which cannot be written. It runs:—

The Debbie he chase me round a stump,

Gwine for to carry me home;

He catch me most at ebery jump,

Gwine for to carry me home.

Swing low, sweet chay-o-t,

Gwine for to carry me home.

The Debbie he make one grab at me,

Gwine, etc.,

He missed me, and my soul goed free,

Gwine, etc.

Swing low, etc.

Oh! won't we have a gay old time,

Gwine, etc.

A eatin' up o' honey, and a drinkin' up o' wine.

Gwine, etc.

Swing low, etc.

This, sir, I think you will agree with me, though precious, is obviously a fragment only. It took our Texan many months to pick it up, even in this mutilated condition. But after all, Jeffs character and capacity come out most in the direction of boots. It. is from his attitude with regard to them that I incline to think that the Black race have a great future in these States. You may have gathered from previous letters that there is a clear, though not a well marked, division in this settlement as to blacking. Amos Hill builds on it decidedly, and would have every farmer appear in blacked boots, at any rate on Sunday. The opposition is led by a young farmer of great energy and famous temper, who, having been "strapped," or left without a penny, 300 miles from the Pacific coast, amongst the Mexican mines, and having made his hands keep his head in the wildest of earthly settlements, has a strong contempt for all amenities of clothing, which is shared by the geologist and others. How the point will be settled at last, I cannot guess. It stands over while the ladies are still here, and I have actually seen the "strapped" one giving his wondrous boots a sly lick or two of blacking on Sunday morning. But, anyhow, the blacks will be cordially on the side of polish and the aristocracy. This one might, perhaps, have anticipated; but what I was not prepared for, was Jeffs apparent passion for boots. I own a fine, strong pair of shooting-boots, which he worshipped for five minutes at least every morning. As my last day in the Asylum drew on, I could see he was troubled in his mind. At last, out it came. Watching his chance, when no one was near, he sidled up, and pointing to them on the square chest in the verandah which served for blacking-board, he said, "I'd like to buy dem boots." After my first astonishment was over, I explained to him that I couldn't afford to sell them for less than about six weeks of his wages, and that, moreover, I wanted them for myself, as I could get none such here. He was much disappointed, and muttered frequently, "I'd like to buy dem boots!"—but my heart did not soften.

Perhaps I ought rather to be giving your readers more serious experiences, but somehow the negro is apt to run one out into chaff. However, I will conclude with one fact, which seems to me a very striking confirmation of my view. All Americans are reading the *Fool's Errand,* a powerful novel, founded on the state of things after the war in the Kuklux times. It is written by a Southern judge, a fair and clever man, clearly, but one who has no more faith in the negro's power to raise himself to anything above hewing wood and drawing water for the "Caucasian" than C. J. Taney himself. In all that book there is no single instance of the drawing of a mean, corrupt, or depraved negro; but the negroes are represented as full of patience, trustfulness, shrewdness, and power of many kinds.

The Opening Day, Rugby, Tennessee.

Our opening day drew near, not without rousing the most serious misgivings in the minds of most of us whether we could possibly be ready to receive our guests. Invitations had been issued to our neighbours—friends, as we had learnt to esteem them—in Cincinnati, Knoxville, Chatanooga, whose hospitalities we had enjoyed, and who had expressed a cordial sympathy with our enterprise, and a desire to visit us. We looked also for some of our own old members from distant New England, in all probability seventy or eighty guests, to lodge and board, and convey from and back to the railway, seven miles over our new road,—no small undertaking, under our circumstances. But the hotel was still in the hands of the contractor, from whom, as yet, only the upper floors had been rescued. The staircase wanted banisters, and the hall and living-rooms were still only half-wainscotted, and full of carpenters' benches and plasterers' trays; while the furniture and crockery lumbered up the big barn, or stood about in cases on the broad verandah. As for our road, it was splendid, so far as it went, but some two miles were still merely a forest track, from which all trees and stumps had been removed, but that was all; and the bridge over the Clear Fork stream, by which the town site is entered, had only the first cross timbers laid from pier to pier, while the approaches seemed to lie in hopeless, weltering confusion, difficult on horseback, impossible on wheels. However, the manager declared that we should drive over the bridge on Saturday afternoon, and that the contractor should be out of the hotel by Monday midday. With this we were obliged to be content, though it was running things fine, as we looked for our guests on that Monday afternoon, and the opening was fixed for the next morning. And so it came to pass, as the manager said. Bridge and road were declared passable by the named time, though nervous persons might well have thought twice before attempting the former in the heavy omnibuses hired for the occasion; and we were able to get possession and move furniture and crockery into the hotel, though the carpenters still held the unfinished staircase.

So far so good; but still everything, we felt, depended on the weather. If the glorious days we had been having held, all would be well. The promise was fair up to Sunday evening, but at sunset there was a change. Amos Hill shook his head, and the geologist's aneroid barometer gave ominous signs. They proved only too correct. Early in the night the rain set in, and by daybreak, when we were already astir, a steady, soft, searching rain was coming down perpendicularly, which lasted, with scarcely a break, clear through the day, and till midnight. With feelings of blank despair we thought of the new road, softened into a Slough of Despond, and the hastily thrown-up approaches to the bridge giving way under the laden omnibuses, and waited our fate. It was, as usual, better than we looked for. The morning train from Chatanooga would bring our southern guests in time for early dinner, if no break-down happened; and sure enough, within half an hour of the expected time up came the omnibuses, escorted to the hotel door by the manager and his son on horseback; and the Bishop of Tennessee, with his chaplain, the Mayor of Chatanooga, and a number of the leading citizens of that city and of Knoxville, descended in the rain. In five minutes we were at our ease and happy. If they had all been Englishmen on a pleasure-trip, they could not have taken the down-pour more cheerily as a matter of course, and pleasant, rather than otherwise, after the long drought. They dined, chatted, and smoked in the verandah, and then trotted off in *gum* coats to look round at the walks, gardens, streets, and cots, escorted by "the boys." The manager reported, with pride, that they had come up in an hour and a quarter, and without any kind of *contretemps*, though, no doubt, the new road *was* deep, in places.

All anxiety was over for the moment, as the Northern train, bringing our Cincinnati and New England friends, was not due till after dark. We sat down to tea in detachments from six to eight, when, if all went well, the northerners would be about due. The tables were cleared, and relaid once more for them, and every preparation made to give them a warm welcome. Nine struck, and still no sign of them; then ten, by which time, in this early country, all but some four or five anxious souls had retired. We sat round the stove in the hall, and listened to the war-stories of the Mayor of Chatanooga, and our host of the Tabard, who had served on opposite sides in the terrible campaigns in the south of the State, which had ended at Missionary Ridge, and filled the national cemetery of Chatanooga with 14,000 graves of Union soldiers. But neither the interest of the stories themselves, nor the pleasure of seeing how completely all bitterness had passed out of the narrators' minds, could keep our thoughts from dwelling on the pitch-dark road, sodden by this time with the rain, and the *mauvais pas* of the bridge. Eleven struck, and now it became too serious for anything but anxious peerings into the black night, and considerations as to what could be done. We had ordered lanterns, and were on the point of starting for the bridge, when faint sounds, as of men singing in chorus, came through the darkness. They grew in volume, and now we could hear the omnibuses, from which came a roll of, "John Brown's body lies mouldering in the grave," given with a swing and precision which told of old campaigners. That stirring melody could hardly have been more welcome to the first line waiting for supports, on some hard-fought battle-ground, than it was to us. The omnibuses drew up, a dense cloud rising from the drenched horses and mules, and the singers got out, still keeping up their chorus, which only ceased on the verandah, and must have roused every sleeper in the settlement. The Old Bay State, Ohio, and Kentucky had sent us a set of as stalwart good fellows as ever sang a chorus or ate a beef-steak at midnight; and while they were engaged in the latter operation, they told how from the break-down of a freight-train, theirs had been three hours late, how the darkness had kept them to a foot's-pace, how the last omnibus had given out in the heavy places, and had to be constantly helped on by a pair of mules detached from one of the others. "All's well that ends well," and it was with a joyful sense of relief that we piloted such of our guests as the hotel could not hold across to their cots in the barracks at one in the morning. By nine, the glorious Southern sun had fairly vanquished rain and mist, and the whole plateau was ablaze with the autumn tints, and every leaf gleaming from its recent shower-bath. Rugby outdid herself and "leapt to music and to light" in a way which astonished even her oldest and most enthusiastic citizens, some half dozen of whom had had something like twelve months' experience of her moods and tempers. Breakfast began at six, and ended at nine, and for three hours batches of well-fed visitors were turned out to saunter round the walks, the English gardens, and lawn-tennis grounds, until the hour of eleven, fixed by the Bishop for the opening service. The church being as yet only some six feet above ground, this ceremony was to be held in the verandah of the hotel. Meantime, Bishop and chaplain were busy among "the boys," organising a choir to sing the hymns and lead the responses. The whole population were gathering round the hotel, some four or five buggies, and perhaps twenty horses, haltered to the nearest trees, showed the interest excited in the neighbourhood. In addition to the seats in the verandah, chairs and benches were placed on the ground below for the surplus congregation, behind whom a fringe of white and black natives regarded the proceedings with grave attention. Punctual to time, the Bishop and his chaplain, in robes, took their places at the corner of the verandah, and gave out the first verses of the "Old Hundredth." There was a moment's pause, while the newly-organised choir exchanged glances as to who should lead off, and the pause was fatal to them for the moment. For on the Bishop's left stood the stalwart New Englander who had led the pilgrims of the previous evening in the "John Brown" chorus. He, unaware of the episcopal arrangements, and of the consequent vested rights of "the boys," broke out with "All people that on earth do dwell," in a voice which carried the whole assembly with him, and at once reduced "the boys" to humble followers. They had their revenge, however, when it came to the second hymn at the end of the service. It was "Jerusalem, the golden," which is apparently sung to a different tune in Boston to that in use in England, so though our musical guest struggled manfully through the first line, and had almost discomfited "the boys" by sheer force of lungs, numbers prevailed, and he was brought into line. The service was a short one, consisting of two psalms, "Lord, who shall dwell in thy tabernacle?" and "Except the Lord build the house," the chapter of Solomon's prayer at the dedication of the Temple, half a dozen of the Church collects, and a prayer by the Bishop that the town and settlement might be built up in righteousness and the fear and love of God, and 'prove a blessing to the State. Then, after the blessing, the gathering resolved itself into a public meeting after American fashion. The Board spoke through their representatives, and Bishop, judge, general manager, and visitors exchanged friendly oratorical buffets, and wishes and prophecies for the prosperity of the New Jerusalem in the Southern highlands. A more genuine or healthier act of worship it has not been our good-fortune to attend in these late years.

Dinner began immediately afterwards, and then the company scattered again, some to select town lots, some to the best views, the Bishop to organise a vestry, and induce two of "the boys" to become lay readers, pending the arrival of a parson (in which he was eminently successful); the chaplain to the Clear Fork with one of "the boys'" fishing-rods, after black bass; and a motley crowd to the lawn-tennis ground, to see some set played which would have done no discredit to Wimbledon, and excited much wonder and some enthusiasm amongst natives and visitors. A cheerful evening followed, in which the new piano in the hotel sitting-room did good service, and many war and other stories were told round the big hall stove. Early the next morning the omnibuses began carrying off the visitors, and by night Rugby had settled down again to its ordinary life, not, however, without a sense of strength gained for the work of building up a community which shall know how to comport itself in good and bad times, and shall help, instead of hindering, its sons and daughters in leading a brave, simple, and Christian life.

Life in an American Liner

It is some years since I addressed you last over this signature—indeed I should doubt if five per cent of your present readers will remember the "harvests" of a quiet (ought I to say "lazy" rather than "quiet"?) eye, which I was wont in those days, by your connivance, to submit to them in vacation times. Somehow to-day the old instinct has come back on me, possibly because I happen to be on an errand which should be of no small interest to us English just now; possibly because the last days of an Atlantic crossing seem to be so naturally provocative of the instinct for gossiping, that one is not satisfied with the abundant opportunities one gets on board the vessel in which one is a luxurious prisoner for ten days.

We have been going day and night since we left Queenstown harbour at an average rate of 18 (land) miles an hour. We are more than 1300 passengers (roughly 200 saloon, and the rest steerage), whose baggage, when added to the large cargo of dry goods we are carrying, sinks our beautiful craft till she draws 24 feet of water. She herself is more than 150 yards long, and weighs as she passes Sandy Hook,—well, I am fairly unable to calculate what she weighs, but as much, at any rate, as half a dozen luggage-trains on shore. We have had our last, or the captain's dinner, at which fish, to all appearance as fresh as if the sailors had just caught them over the side, and lettuces, as crisp as if the steward had a nursery garden down below, have been served as part of a dinner which would have done no discredit to a first-class hotel; beginning with two sorts of soup, and ending with two sorts of ices. Similar dinners, with other meals to match—four solid ones in the twenty-four hours, besides odds and ends—have been served day by day, without a hitch, in a cabin kept as sweet as Atlantic air, constantly pumped into it by the engine, can make it.

By the way, sir, I may remark here, in connection with our feeding, that if we might be taken as average specimens of our race, there is no ground whatever for anxiety as to the Anglo-Saxon digestion, of which some disagreeable philosophers have spoken with disrespect and foreboding in recent years. There were, perhaps, ten persons whose native tongue was not English, and yet we carried our four solid meals a day with resolution bordering on the heroic. The racks were never on the tables, and we had only for a few hours a swell, which thinned our ranks for two meals; and yet when I look round, and make such inquiry as I can, I can see or hear of nothing more than a very slight trace of dyspepsia here and there. The principal change I remarked in the manners and customs on the voyage was the marked increase of play and betting on board. When I first crossed, ten years ago, there was nothing more than an occasional game at whist in the saloon or smoking-room. This voyage it was not easy to get out of the way of hard play except on deck. The best corner of the smoking-room was occupied from breakfast till "Out lights" by a steady poker party, and other smaller and more casual groups played fitfully at the other tables. There were always whist and other games going on in the saloon, but of a soberer and (in a pecuniary sense) more innocent character. There were "pools" of a sovereign or a half sovereign on every event of the day, "the run" being the most exciting issue. The drawer of the winning number seldom pocketed less than £40, when it was posted on the captain's chart at noon. I heard that play is rather favoured now than otherwise on all the lines, as a percentage is almost always paid to the funds of the Sailors' Orphan Asylum, for which excellent charity a collection is also legitimately made during every passage. We were good supporters, and collected nearly £70 at our entertainment, which I attribute partly to the fact that we had on board a leading American actor, who most good-naturedly "turned himself loose" for us, and that the plates at the two doors were held by the daughters of an English earl, and an (late, alas!) American ambassador of great eminence. The countries could not have been more characteristically or charmingly represented, and the charity owes them its best thanks.

There was the usual mine of information and entertainment, to be struck with ease by the merest novice in conversational shaft-sinking. Why is it that folk are so much more ready to talk on an Atlantic steamer than elsewhere? I myself "struck ile," in several directions, one of a sad kind—Scotch farmers of the highest type going out to select new homes, where there will be no factors. The most remarkable of these appeared to have made up his mind finally when he had been told that he would not be allowed a penny at the end of his lease for the addition of three rooms he was obliged to make to his house, as his family were growing up. Have landlords and factors gone mad, in face of the serious times which are on them?

There were quite an abundance of parsons, of many denominations, and all of mark. Prayers on Sunday were read by a New England Episcopalian, and the sermon preached by a Scotch Free Kirk minister. All were men of broad views, in some cases verging on Latitudinarianism to a point which rejoiced my heretic soul, e.g. a Protestant minister in a great American western city, whose church had recently been rebuilt. Looking round to find where his flock could be best housed on Sundays, pending reconstruction, he found the neighbouring synagogue by far the most convenient, and proposed to go there. His people cordially agreed, and despite the furious raging of the (so-called) religious press, into the synagogue they went for their Sunday services, stayed there six months, and when they left, were only charged for the gas by the Rabbi. An intimacy sprung up. It appeared that the Rabbi looked upon our Lord as the first of the inspired men of his nation, greater than Moses or Samuel, and in the end the two congregations met at a service conducted partly by the Rabbi and partly by my informant!—a noteworthy sign of the times, but one at which I fear many even of your readers will shake their heads.

There were some Confederate officers, ready to talk without bitterness of the war, and I was very glad to improve the occasion, having never had the chance of a look from that side the curtain. Anything more grim and humorous than the picture of Southern society during those awful four years I never hope to meet with. The entire want of regular medicines, especially bark, was their greatest trouble in his eyes. In his brigade their remedy for "the shakes" came to be a plaster of raw turpentine, just drawn from the pine woods, laid on down the back. Some one suggested that pills were very portable, and easily imported. "Pills!" he said scornfully; "pills, sir, were as scarce in our brigade as the grace of God in a grog shop at midnight." Nothing so much brought out to me the horrors of civil war as his account of the perfect knowledge each side had of the plans and doings on the other. A Northern officer, he had since come to know, was leaning against a post within three yards of Jeff. Davis when he made his famous speech announcing the supersession of Joe Johnson as the general fronting Sherman. Sherman had heard it in a few hours, and was acting on the news before nightfall. The most terrible example was that of the mining of the Richmond lines. The defenders knew almost to a foot where the mines were, and when they were to be fired. Breckenbridge's division, in which he fought, were drawn up in line to repel the attack when the earthworks went up in the air, and the assailants rushed into the great gap which had been made, and which was nearly filled, before they fell back, with the bodies of Northern soldiers. For the last two years, in almost every battle he had all he could do to hold his own against the front attack, knowing and feeling all the while that the enemy was overlapping and massing on both flanks, and that he would have to retire his regiment before they could close. And yet they held together to the last!

I pity mothers, too, down South,

Altho' they sat amongst the scorners.

It is a curious experience, and one well worth trying, this ten days' voyage. When you go on board at Liverpool, and look round at the first dinner, there are probably not half a dozen faces you ever saw before. By the time you walk out of the ship, bag in hand, on to the New York landing-place, there are scarcely half a dozen with» whom you have not a pleasant speaking acquaintance; while with a not inconsiderable number you feel (unless you have had singularly bad luck) as if you must have known them intimately for years, without having been aware of it. As you touch the land, the express men and hotel touts rush on you, and the spell is broken. The little society resolves itself at their touch into separate atoms, which are whirled away, without time to wish one another God-speed, into the turbulent ocean of New York life, never again to be gathered together as a society in this world, for worship, for food, or fun. "The present life of man, 0 king!" said a Saxon thane in Edwin's Witenagemot, when they were consulting whether Augustine and his priests should be allowed to settle at Canterbury, "reminds me of one of your winter feasts where you sit with your thanes and counsellors. The hearth blazes in our midst, and a grateful heat is spread around, while storms of rain and snow are raging without. A little sparrow enters at one door and flies delighted around us, till it departs through the other. Such is the life of man, and we are as ignorant of the state which went before us as of that which will follow it. Things being so," went on the thane, "I feel that if this new faith can give us more certainty, it deserves to be received,"—which last sentiment has, I allow, no bearing on the present subject, nor, perhaps you will say, has the rest of it. But somehow the old story came into my head so vividly as I was leaving the steamer, that I feel like tossing it on to your readers, to see what they can make of it; though I own, on looking at it again, I am not myself clear as to the interpretation, or whether I am the sparrow or the thane.

New York is more overwhelming than ever,—surely the most tremendous human mill on this planet; but I must not begin upon it at the end of a letter.

Life in Texas, Ranche on the Rio Grande, 16th September 1884.

It must be many years now (how they do shut up in these latter days like a telescope) since I confided to you in these columns the joy—not unmixed with reverence—of my first interview with that worthy small person (I am sure he must be a person) the tumble-bug of the U.S.A. I looked upon him in those days as on the whole the most industrious and athletic little creature it had ever been my privilege to encounter. I am obliged now to take most of that back, for to-day I have discovered that he isn't a circumstance to his Mexican cousin on this side the Rio Grande. At any rate, the specimens I have met with here are not only bigger, but work half as hard again, and about twice as quick. I was sitting just now in the verandah in front of this ranche cabin, waiting for the horses to be saddled-up at the corral just below, and looking lazily, now eastward over the river and the wide Texan plains beyond, fading away in the haze till the horizon looked like the Atlantic in a calm, now westward to the jagged outline of the Sierra Nevada, gleaming in the sunshine sixty miles away, when I became aware of something moving at my feet. Looking down I found that it was a tumble-bug rolling a ball of dirt he had put together, till it was at least four times as big as himself, towards the rough stony descent just beyond the verandah, at a pace which fairly staggered me. In a few seconds he was across the floor, and in amongst the stones which lay thickly over the slope beyond. Here his troubles began. First he pushed his ball backwards over a big stone, on the further side of which it fell, and he with it, headlong—no, not headlong, stern foremost—some five inches, rolling over one another twice at the bottom. But he never quitted hold, and began pushing away merrily again without a moment's pause. Then he ran the ball into a *cul-de-sac* between two stones, some inches high. After two or three dead heaves, which lifted the ball at least his own length up the side of the stones—and you must remember, to judge of the feat, that he was standing on his head to do it—he quitted hold, turned round, and looked at the situation. I am almost certain I saw him scratch his ear, or at least the side of his head, with his fore-claw. In a second or two he fixed on again with his hind-claws, pushed the ball out of the *cul-de-sac*, and continued his journey. If that bug didn't put two and two together, by what process did he get out of that *cul-de-sac?* "Cogito, ergo sum." Was I wrong in calling him a person? Well, I won't trouble you further with particulars of his journey, but he ran his big ball into his hole under a mesquite-bush, 19 1/2 yards from the spot on the verandah where I first noticed him, in eleven minutes and a few seconds by my watch. I made a calculation before mounting that, comparing my bug with an average Mexican, five feet eight inches high, and weighing ten stone, the ball of dirt would be at least equal to a bale of cotton, eight feet in diameter, and weighing half a ton, which the man would have to push or carry 2 1/2 miles in eleven minutes, to equal the feat of his tiny fellow-citizen. In the depressed condition of Mexico, might not this enormous bug-power be utilised somehow for the benefit of the Republic?

I had barely finished my ciphering when I was called to horse, and in a few minutes was riding across a vast plain, nearly bare of grass in this drought, but dotted with mesquite-bushes, prickly pear, and other scrub, so that the general effect was still green. The riding was rough, as much loose stone lay about, and badgers', "Jack Rabbits'" and other creatures' holes abounded; but the small Mexican horse I rode was perfectly sure-footed, and I ambled along, swelling with pride at my quaint saddle, with pummel some eight inches high, and depending lasso, showing that for the time I was free of the honourable fraternity of "gentlemen cow-punchers." Besides myself, our party consisted of the two ranche-men—an Englishman and an American, aged about thirty, old comrades on long drives 1000 miles away to the North, but now anchored on this glorious ranche on the Bio Grande—and a cowboy. The Englishman's yellow hair was cropped close to his head, and his fair skin was burnt as red, I suppose, as skin will burn; the Marylander's black hair was as closely cropped, and his skin burnt an equally deep brown. The cowboy, an English lad of about twenty, reconciled the two types, having managed to get his skin tanned a deep red, relieved by large dark brown freckles, from the midst of which his great blue eyes shone out in comical contrast. I fear—

The very mother that him bare,

She had not known her child.

They were all attired alike, in broad felt sombreros, blue shirts, and trousers thrust into boots reaching to the knees. Each had his lasso at pummel, and between them they carried a rifle, frying-pan, coffee-pot, big loaf, and forequarter of a porker—for we were out for a long day. A more picturesque or efficient-looking group it would be hard to find. I must resist the temptation of telling all we did or saw, and come at once to our ride home shortly before sunset. The ranche-men and I were abreast, and the cowboy a few yards behind, when we came across a bunch of cattle, conspicuous amongst which strode along a stalwart yearling bull calf, whose shining brindle hide and jaunty air showed that he, at least, was not suffering from the scanty food which the drought has left for the herds on these wide plains. He was already as big as his poor raw-boned mother, who went along painfully picking at every shrub and tuft in her path, to provide his evening meal at her own expense. Now these dude calves (who insist on living on their parents, and will do nothing for their own livelihood) can only be cured by the insertion of a horse-ring in the upper lip, so that they cannot turn it up to take hold of the maternal udder, and it is often in bad times a matter of life or death to the cows to get them ringed. After a conference of a few seconds, the Marylander shifted the rifle to the saddle of the Englishman (already ornamented with the frying-pan and the coffee-pot), and calling to the cowboy, dashed off for the bunch of cattle. Next moment the cowboy shot past us at full speed, gathering up his lasso as he went; the bull-calf was "cut out" of the bunch as if by magic, and went straight away through mesquite-brush and prickly pears, at a pace which kept his pursuers at their utmost stretch not to lose ground. It was all they could do to hold it, never for a full mile getting within lasso-reach of Boliborus, the ranche-man following like fate, upright from shoulder to toe (they ride with very long stirrups), bridle hand low, and right hand swinging the lasso slowly round his head, awaiting his chance for a throw; the cowboy close on his flank; ranche-man number two clattering along, pot, kettle, and rifle "soaring and singing" round his knees, but availing himself of every turn in the chase, so as to keep within thirty or forty yards. I, a bad fourth, but near enough to see the whole and share the excitement (if, indeed, I hadn't it all to myself, the sport being to the rest a part of the daily round). The crisis came just at the foot of a mound, up which Boliborus had gained some yards, but in the descent had slackened his pace and the pursuers were on him. The lasso flew from the raised hand, and was round his neck, a dexterous twist brought the rope across his forelegs, and next moment he was over on his side half, throttled. I was up in some five seconds, during which his lassoer had him by the horns, ranche-man number two was prone with all his weight upon his shoulders, and the cowboy on his hind quarters, catching at his tail with his left hand. That bull calf's struggle to rise was as superb as Bertram Risingham's in *Rokeby*, and as futile; for the cowboy had caught his tail and passed it between his hind legs, and by pulling hard kept one leg brandishing aimlessly in the air, while the weight of the ranche-men subdued his forequarters. The ring was passed through his upper lip, and the lasso was off his neck in a few seconds more, and the ranche-men turned to mount, saying to the cowboy, "Just hold on a minute." The cowboy passed the tail back between the hind legs, grasped the end firmly, and stood expectant. Boliborus lay quiet for a second or two, and then bounded to his feet, glaring round in rage and pain to choose which, of his foes to go for, when he became aware of something wrong behind, and looking round, realised the state of the case. Down went his head, and round he went with a rush for his own tail end, but the tail and boy were equal to the occasion, and the latter still holding on tight by the former, sent back a defiant kick at the end of each rush, which, however, never got within two feet of the bull's nose, and could be only looked upon as a proper defiance. Then Boliborus tried stealing round to take his tail by surprise, but all to as little purpose, when the ranche-men, who were now both mounted, to end the farce, rode round in front of the beast, caught his eye, and cried, "Let go." Whisking his freed tail in the air he made a rush, but only a half-hearted one, at the nearest, who just wheeled his horse, and as he passed administered a contemptuous thwack over his loins with a lasso. Boliborus now stood looking down his nose at the appendant ring, revolving his next move, with so comic an expression that I burst into a roar of laughter, in which the rest joined out of courtesy. This was too much for him, as ridicule proves for so many two-legged calves, so he tossed his head in the air, gave a flirt with his heels, and trotted off after his mother, a sadder, and let us hope, wiser bull-calf; in any case, a ringed one, and bound in future to get his own living.

On my ride home my mind was much occupied by that cowboy, who rode along by me—telling how he had been reading *Gulliver's Travels* again (amongst other things), found it wasn't a mere boy's book, and wanted to get a Life of Swift—in his battered old outfit, for which no Jew in Rag-Fair would give him five shillings. The last time I had seen him, two years ago, he had just left Hallebury, a bit of a dandy, with very tight clothes, and so stiff a white collar on, that on his arrival he had been nicknamed "the Parson."

At home he might by this time be just through responsions by the help of cribs and manuals, having contracted in the process a rooted distaste for classical literature. Possibly he might have pulled in his college boat, and won a plated cup at lawn tennis, and all this at the cost of, say, £250 a year. As it is, besides costing nothing, he can cook a spare-rib of pork to a turn on a forked stick, hold a bull-calf by the tail, and is voluntarily wrestling (not without certain glimmerings of light) with *Sartor Resartus*. Which career for choice? How say you, Mr. Editor?

Crossing the Atlantic, 4th September 1885.

A mug-wump! I should like to ask you, sir—not as Editor, not even as English gentleman, but simply as vertebrate animal—what you would do if a stranger were all of a sudden to call your intimate friends "mug-wumps," not obscurely hinting that you yourself laboured under whatever imputation that term may convey? I don't know what the effect might have been in my own case, but that the story of O'Connell, as a boy, shutting up the voluble old Dublin applewoman by calling her a "parallelopiped," rushed into my head, and set me off laughing. I haven't been able to learn more of the etymology of the word than that it is said over here to have been first used in a sermon (?) by Mr. Ward Beecher, and now denotes "bolters" or "scratchers," as they were called last autumn, or in other words, the Independents, who broke away from the party machine of Republicanism and carried Cleveland. More power to the "mug-wump's" elbow, say I; and I only wish we may catch the "mugwumps," "mug-wumpism," or whatever the name for the disease may be, in England before long. One of the groups on the deck of the liner, amongst whom I first heard the phrase, was a good specimen of the machine-politician, a democrat of the Tammany Hall type. "You bet" I stuck to him till I got at his candid account of the campaign of last autumn, most interesting to me, but I fear not so to the general English reader, so I will only give you his concluding sentence:—"Well," with a long suck at the big cigar he was half-eating, half-smoking, "I tell you it was about the thinnest ice you ever saw before we were over,—but, *I got to land!*" From what I heard on board and since, I believe the President is doing splendidly; witness his peremptory order for the great ranche-men to clear out of the Reserves which they had leased from the Indians, and fenced to the extent of some millions of acres; the righteousness of which presidential action is proved (were proof needed) by the threatened resistance of General B. Butler, one of the largest lessees. I can see too clearly looming up a determined opposition to the President's Civil Service reform from politicians of both parties, mainly on the ground that he is "establishing a class" in these U.S.—a policy which "the Fathers" abhorred and guarded against, and which their only legitimate heirs, the machine politicians, will fight to the death. You may gauge the worth of this opposition by contrasting their two principal arguments—(1) Nine-tenths of the work of the Departments (Post Office, Customs, etc.) can be learnt just as well in three months as in ten years; and (2) the other tenth, requiring skilled and experienced officers, has never been interfered with by either side. But, if argument two is sound, *cadit quostio*, as there is *ex hypothesi* already a permanent class of civil servants, I conclude that were I an American I would accept "mug-wump" as a title of honour instead of resenting it, and help to get up a "Mug-wump" club in every great city.

We had a splendid crossing, deck crowded all the way, and the company gloriously cosmopolitan and communicative during the short intervals between the orthodox four full meals a day. There is surely no place in the world where that universal instinct, the desire to get behind the scenes of one's neighbours' lives, is so easily and abundantly gratified. Here is one of my rather odd discoveries. On reaching the deck, after my bath on the first morning, for the tramp before breakfast, I was joined by a fine specimen of an old Yorkshireman. It seems we had met years ago, at some political or social gathering, and as he looked in superb health and fit to fight for his life, I congratulated. Yes, he said, it was all owing to his having discovered how to pass his holiday. He used to go to some northern seaside place, one as bad as the other, for "whenever the wind blew on shore you might as well be living in a sewer." So he saved enough one year to buy a return-ticket on a Cunard liner, calculating that whatever way the wind blew he must be getting sea-air all the time. He has done it every year since, having found that besides sea-air he gets better food and company than he could ever command at home. My next "find" was a pleasant soldierly-looking man who called to me from the upper deck to come up and see a sword-fish chasing a whale. Alas! I arrived too late. The uncivil brutes had both disappeared by the time I got up; but I was much consoled by the talk which ensued with my new acquaintance. He was a Lieutenant of Marines in the Admiral's flag-ship off Palermo in King Bomba's last days, and was sent ashore to arrest and bring on board all sailors found with the Garibaldini. He seems to have found it necessary to be present himself at the battle of Metazzo (I think that was the name) and at the storming of the town afterwards, in which the Garibaldini suffered severely. The dead were all laid out before the gate after the town was taken, and he counted no less than seventy bluejackets amongst them! They used to drop over the sides of the ships and swim ashore, or smuggle themselves into the bum-boats which came off to the fleet with provisions. No wonder that we have been popular in Italy ever since.

Then, attracted by a crowd on the fore part of the deck, roped off to divide steerage from saloon passengers, I became one of a motley group assisting at a sort of moral "free-and-easy," got up for the 300 steerage folk by two ecclesiastics, whom I took at first for Romish priests from their costume. I found I was mistaken, and that they were the Principal and a Brother of "the Fraternity of the Iron Cross," an order of the American Episcopal Church, which, it seems, has taken root in several of the large cities. The Brethren are vowed to "poverty, purity, and temperance" (or obedience, I am not sure which); and these two were crossing in the steerage to comfort and help the poor folk there—no pleasant task, even in so airy a ship and such fine weather. One can imagine what power this kind of fellowship must give the Iron Cross Brethren with their rather sad fellow-passengers, to whom they could say—one of them, indeed, did say it—"We are just as poor as the poorest of you, for we own no property of any kind, and never can own any till our deaths." This Brother (a strapping young fellow of twenty-five, who I found had been an athlete at Oxford) waxed eloquent to them on his experiences in Philadelphia, especially on the working-men Brethren there. One of these, a big, rough chap, with a badly broken nose, he had rather looked askance at, first, till he found that the broken nose had been earned in a rough-and-tumble fight with a fellow who was ill-using a woman. Now they were the closest friends, and he looked on the broken nose as more honourable than the Victoria Cross, and hoped none of the men there would fail to go in for that decoration if they ever got the same chance.

In melancholy contrast to the Iron Cross Brethren were two other diligent workers in quite another kind of business. They haunted the smoking-room from breakfast till "lights out," officious to help to arrange the daily sweepstakes on the ship's run; gloating over, and piling caressingly as they rattled down on the table, the dollars and half-crowns; always on the watch and ready to take a hand at cards, just to accommodate gents with whom time hung heavily. Bagmen, they were said to be; but I doubt if they travel for any industry except plucking pigeons on their own account— unmistakable Jews of a low type, who never looked any man in the face:—

In their eyes that stealthy gleam,

Was not learned of sky or stream,

But it has the hard, cold glint

Of new dollars from the mint.

Their industry was pursued cautiously, as the fine old captain is known to hold strong views about gambling, and there was less on this ship than any other I have crossed on. No baccarat-table going all day, with excited youngsters punting their silver (gold, too, now and then) over the shoulders of the players,—only a quiet hand at euchre or poker at a corner table, in the afternoon and after dinner; but even with such straitened opportunities, youngsters may be plucked to a fairly satisfactory figure. From £10 to £20 was often at stake on one deal at poker, and, I was told, not seldom much higher sums. I saw myself one mere boy inveigled into blind-hookey for a minute or two while the poker party was gathering. He won the first cut; and two minutes later I saw "Iscariot Ingots, Esq., that highly respectable man," looking abstractedly across the room, and dreamily gathering up a large handful of silver which the boy rattled down as he flung off to take his seat at the poker-table; and so on, and so on.

It occurs to one to ask, not without some indignation, why this sort of thing is allowed on these Atlantic steamers. My own observation confirms the general belief that professionals cross on nearly every boat; and, on every boat, there are youngsters fresh from school or college, out of leading-strings for the first time, and with considerable sums in their pockets. It is a bad scandal, and might be stopped with the greatest ease. Prohibit all cards, except whist for small points in the smoking-room; and let it be the purser's or some other officer's duty to see the rule enforced. As things stand, I do not know of a more dangerous place for youngsters—American or English—than an Atlantic steamer.

One never gets past Sandy Hook, I think, without some new sensation. This time, for me, it was the harbour buoys, each of which carried a brilliant electric lamp. They are lighted from the shore!

Notes from the West, Cincinnati, 24th September 1886.

I never come to this country without stumbling over some startling differences between our kin here and ourselves, which it puzzles me to account for. Take this last. Some days ago, I met a young Englishman from a Western ranche. He had run down some six hundred miles, from Kansas City, into which he had brought a "bunch" of steers from the ranche. As he would not be wanted again for a fortnight, he had taken the opportunity of looking in on his friends down South. In our talk the question of railway fares turned up. "Oh, yes," he said, "the fare is $25; but I only paid $16."

"How is that?"

"Why, I just went to the 'ticket-scalpers',' right opposite the railway dépôt—here is their card (handing it to me); and, you see, my ticket is to Chatanooga; so I might go on for another hundred and fifty miles if I wanted to." There was the business card, "Moss Brothers, ticket-brokers, opposite central dépôt, Kansas City, members of the Ticket Brokers' Union." It went on to say that every attention is paid to travellers, inquiries made, and information given, by these enterprising Hebrews; and on the back, a list of the towns to which they could issue tickets, including nearly every important centre in the Northern and Western States. Since then I have made inquiries at several towns, and find that the "scalper" is an institution in every one of them; and, apart from the saving of money, is much in favour with the travelling public, on account of his civility and intelligence. The ordinary railway clerk is a remarkably short-tempered and ill-informed person, out of whom you can with difficulty extract the most trifling piece of information, even as to his own line; while the despised "scalper" across the road (generally a Jew) will take any amount of trouble to find out how you can "make connections," while furnishing you with a ticket, which he guarantees, at a third less, on the average, than his legitimate but morose rival in "the dépôt." But the strangest thing of all is, that even the railway directors seem to think it all right; or, at any rate, that it is not worth their while to try to stop this traffic. One friend, a first-rate business man, actually said that he should have no scruple what, ever in going to the "scalpers" when off his own system, over which, of course, he is "dead-headed." I heard several explanations of the phenomenon, the only plausible one being that it is impossible to control the enormous issues of cheap excursion tickets which are made by all the main lines. But surely, then, the question occurs, "Why impossible!" At any rate, the average Briton is inclined to think that if such establishments appeared opposite the Euston Square or Waterloo termini, they would soon hear something from Mr. Moon and Mr. Ralph Dutton not to their advantage.

I gleaned other items of information from my young friend from Kansas which may be useful to some of your readers, now that there is scarcely a family in England (so it seems to me, at least) which is not sending out one or more of its younger members to try their fortunes in the Far West. This, for instance, seems worth bearing in mind: When a young fellow comes out from home, he shouldn't go and hire himself out at once to a farmer. If he does, he'll find they'll make the winter jobs for an Englishman pretty tough. He'll get all the hardest work laid out for him, and mighty poor pay at the end. Let him go and board with a farmer. Any one will be glad to take him for a few dollars. Then he can learn all he wants, and they'll be glad of his help, because they'll see it's a picnic. If you like it, you can buy and settle down. If not, you can just pull out, and go on somewhere else.

The administration of justice on the plains is still in a primitive condition. The difficulty of getting a jury of farmers together makes a gaol delivery a troublesome matter. Another youngster from Dakota illustrated this from his section. There was a turbulent member of the community who, after committing other minor offences, at last got lodged in the shanty which does office for a gaol, on the serious charge of a murderous attack on a girl who refused any longer to receive his attentions, and on her father when he came to the rescue. He had lain in gaol for some weeks, waiting for a judge and jury, when 4th July came round. The Sheriff-Constable, with all the rest of the neighbours, was bound for the nearest railway-station, some ten miles off, where the anniversary of "the glorious Fourth" was to be commemorated, with trotting marches and other diversions. He had one other prisoner in charge, and so, after weighing the matter well, and taking the length of their incarceration into account, came to the ingenious conclusion to let them out for the day, each going bail for the return of the other on the following day. On the morrow, however, it was found that the chief culprit had not turned up, and the fathers of the little community gathered in indignant council to consider what was to be done. After some debate the Sheriff-Constable gave it as his opinion that, on the whole, Dogberry's advice was sound, and they should let him go, and thank God they were rid of a knave, "the country having spent too much already over the darned cuss." To this the *patres conscripti* agreed, and went home to their farms. Even stranger is another well-authenticated story from one of the most active and important of the new cities in the North-West. Amongst the first settlers there was one who had dabbled in real estate, and grown with the growth of the city, until he had become "one of our principal citizens." No one seemed to know whether he was a lawyer by profession, and he never conducted a case in Court. But one thing was quite clear, that he was intimate with all the judges, had the *entrée* to their private rooms, and, especially in the case of the Judges of the Supreme Court, scarcely ever failed to avail himself of this privilege when the Courts were sitting. He had a capital cook and good horses, which were always freely at the service of the representatives of justice. Gradually it began to be quietly understood, no one quite knew how, amongst suitors, that it was possible, and very desirable, to interest the gentleman in question in their cases. He was ready, it would seem, to accept a retaining-fee. His charge was fixed at a very moderate percentage on the value of the property in dispute, which nobody need pay unless they thought it worth while. Moreover, the system was one of "No cure, no pay." He gave every one an acknowledgment in writing of the amount paid in their respective cases, with an undertaking to return the full sum in the event of their proving unsuccessful. It therefore naturally appeared to the average Western suitor about as profitable an investment as he could make. Strange to say, this queer practice seems to have gone on for years, and no shadow of suspicion ever fell on this "principal citizen," whatever might have been the case as to his friends the judges. The strong individuality and secretiveness which marks the Western character may probably account for the fact that during his life no one would seem to have taken any public notice of this peculiar industry. If a suitor was successful, he was content; if not, he got back his money, and it was nobody's affair but his own. Well, the good man died, and was buried, and his executors, in administering his estate, were astonished to find bundles of receipts from suitors of all classes and degrees, acknowledging the repayment to them of sums varying in amount from $5 and upwards "in the case of Brown v. Jones," "in the matter of United States v. Robinson," "*ex parte* White," etc. This led to further inquiry, and the facts came ~ gradually to light. The sagacious testator had, in fact, taken his percentage *from both sides* in almost every case of any importance which had been heard in the Courts for years. He had never mentioned suit or suitor to any of the judges, his visits to them being simply for the purpose of asking them to dinner, offering them a drive, or a bed if they were on circuit away from home, or interchanging gossip as to stocks, railways, or public affairs. And so for years five honest men had been presiding in the different Courts, entirely innocent of the fact that almost every suitor was looking upon each of them as a person who had received valuable consideration for deciding in his favour. I own that my experience, though, of course, narrow, is decidedly favourable as to the ability and uprightness of the judges in out-of-the-way districts; so that nothing but what I could not but regard as quite unimpeachable evidence would have satisfied me that a whole-community of litigants should have gone on paying black-mail in this egregiously stupid manner.

I was considerably astonished, and a little troubled, to find so many of my friends among Northern Republicans—men who had gone through and borne the burden of the War of Secession—not, indeed, sympathising with the Irish, whom they dislike and distrust more than we do, but saying: "Oh, you had better let them have their own way. Look at our experience of twenty years after the war. Until we let the Southern States have their own way, and withdrew the troops, and threw over the carpetbaggers, we had no peace; and now they are just as quiet as New England." To which, of course, I made the obvious reply: "Let the seceding States have their own way, did you? Why, I had always understood that they went out because you elected a free-soil President, pledged to oppose any further extension of their peculiar institution, and that at the end of the war that institution had not only been confined within its old limits, but had absolutely disappeared. The parallel would have held if you had said to Mr. Jefferson Davis and his backers in the spring of 1861, 'Do what you please as to your negroes; take them where you will; it is a purely domestic matter for you to settle in your own way.' Instead of this, you said, 'You shall not take your slaves where you please, and you shall not go out of the Union.' In the same way, we have to say now to the Irish, 'You shall not do what you please with the owners of property in Ireland, and you shall not go out of the Union.'"

You will be glad to hear that, wherever I went, there seemed to be the expectation of a revival of trade in the near future. I can see no ground myself for the expectation, so long as all industry remains in its present competitive phase, and the power of production goes on increasing instead of diminishing. Why should men not desire as eagerly to take each other's trade this next year as they did last year? But the knowing people think otherwise, and I suppose that is good for something.

Westward Ho! 2nd April 1887.

It must be nearly thirty years since I first wrote to you over this signature, but never before except in long vacations, and from outlandish parts. Why not keep to a good rule? you may ask, at this crowded time of year. Well, the fact is I really want to say something as to this "Westward Ho!" gadfly, which seems to have bitten young England with a vengeance in these last months. I am startled, not to say alarmed, at the number of letters I get from the parents and guardians—generally professional men—of youngsters eagerly bent on cattle-ranches, horse-ranches, orange-groves in Florida, vineyards, peach and strawberry-raising, and I know not what other golden dreams of wealth quickly acquired in the open air, generally with plenty of wild sport thrown in. I suppose they write from some fancy that I know a good deal about such matters. That is not so; but I do know a very little about them, and may possibly do some good by publishing that little just now in your columns.

First, then, as to cattle and horse-raising on ranches. This is practically a closed business on any but a small scale, and as part of farm work. All the best ranche-grounds are in the hands of large and rich companies, or millionaires, with whom no newcomer can compete. It will, no doubt, be a valuable experience for any young man to work for a year or two on a big ranch as a cowboy; but he must be thoroughly able to trust his temper, and to rough it in many ways, or he should not try it. At the end, if prudent, he will only have been able to save a few hundred dollars. But this is not the kind of thing, so far as I see, that our youngsters at all expect or want. Orange-groves are excellent and profitable things, no doubt, and there are parts in Florida and elsewhere where there is still plenty of land fit for this purpose, though the choice spots are probably occupied. But an orange-grove will not give any return till the sixth year, cautious people say the seventh.

Vineyards may, with good luck, be giving some return in the third or fourth year; but the amount of hard work which must be put into the soil in breaking up, clearing out stumps, and ploughing, even if there is no timber to fell, is very serious; and the same may be said of peach-orchards and early, fruit and vegetable-rearing. Moreover, the choice places for such industry, such as Lookout Mountain, are for the most part occupied. In a word, though it is quite possible to do well in other industries, and in ordinary farming, nothing beyond a decent living can be earned, without at any rate as free an expenditure of brain and muscle as high farming requires at home. On the other hand, sport, except for rich ranche-men who can command waggons, horses, and men, and travel long distances for it, is not to be had generally, and apt to disappoint where it can be had.

So much for the working side of the problem. The playing side—outside whisky-shops, which I will assume the young Englishman means to keep clear of—ought also to be looked fairly in the face before the experiment is tried. Perhaps the most direct way to bring it home to inquirers will be to quote from the letter of a young English public-school boy who has lately finished his first year as a cowboy on the cattle-ranche of one of the big companies:—

Friday night we had quite a time. We went to an exhibition of the home talent of——, and really of all shows this was the worst I ever saw. One man, the town barber, and our greatest "society man," played a nigger, and played it so well that one could not help fancying he has at one time been a "profesh." The rest were so dull and such sticks that it made him shine more than ever. After the home talent, there was a "social hop," at which Jerry and I shone as being the "bored young men." You can, of course, see why I was bored; and Jerry, he is from Ohio, and of course——— cannot compete with Ohio. However, as Jerry was somewhat of a great man, the quadrilles being all called by him—i.e. he stood on the stage and shouted, "balance all," "swing your partners," "lady's chain," at the right time—we had to stay, and more or less to dance. Jerry took great pains to find me partners worthy of a man who had danced in a dress-coat. He did not succeed but once, when he introduced me to a very lively little school-lady, "marm," I should say; the rest were very wooden in movement and conversation. The school-marm amused me very much. She had not long returned from the————— University, where all the young ladies, though they met the other sex at school, were not allowed to speak to them at other times. The girls were allowed to give dances, but she and three or four others thought that a "hen-pie" dance was too much of a fraud, so they contrived a plan by which they could get three or four dancing men in without going to the door. They fastened a pulley on to the beam where the bell hung, and with the aid of a clothes-basket and a rope they spoiled the "hen-pie" with two or three young men. This plan worked well several times, till one night three or four of them were exerting themselves to get a very heavy boy up, when instead of a boy they perceived the bearded face of the head-master. In horror they turned loose the rope and fled, leaving him twelve feet from the ground, hanging on by his fingers to the window-sill, from which, as no one would respond to his call for help, he finally dropped. The young lady told it much better than I have. Jerry was very popular as a "caller." I noticed he understood his audience well, and whenever they got a figure they didn't know, he came in with "grand chain," which they all knew and performed very nicely; so you would see a whole set lost in the intricate feat of "visiting" (say) and all muddled up, when you would hear the grand voice of Jerry, "grand chain," and all the dancers would smile and go to it, and Jerry was quite the boss. We however lost our reputation as good young men, as towards midnight we were overcome with a great thirst; so wicked I, a hardened sinner, persuaded the social barber to let me have half-a-pint of whisky; and J——— and I were caught in the barber's shop, eating tinned oysters with our pocket-knives, and biscuits, and indulging in whisky-and-water. We were caught by three young men who had "got religion" last fall, and who were, of course, highly shocked; but I think they would have overcome all their scruples but for the stern mothers in the background, and they not only envied us our whisky-and-water, but also our mothers. Half the fight in drinking, I think, is to have been "raised" to look upon it as an every-day luxury, and not as a thing to be had as a great treat on the sly. Well, good-bye! I have written a lot of rubbish, but beyond that am fatter than I have ever been in America.

This will probably give readers a pretty clear notion of the social life available in the West. It is, as they will see at a glance, utterly unlike anything they have been used to. If this kind of social life (and there is something to be said for it) is what they want, in the interludes of really hard manual labour and rough board and lodging, let them start by all means, and they may do very well out West. Otherwise they had better look the thing round twice or thrice before starting. In any case, no young man ought to take more ready money with him than will just keep him from starving for about a month.

If he cannot make his hands keep him by that time, he has no business, and will do no good, in the West.

The Hermit, Rugby, Tennessee, 19th September 1887.

I have always had a strong curiosity about hermits—remember I paid a shilling as a small boy, when I could ill afford it, to see one, somewhere up by Hampstead, a cruel disappointment—used to make shy approaches to lonely turnpike keepers before they were abolished, with no success; finding them always, like Johnson's "hoary sage," inclined to cut sentiment short with, "Come, my lad, and drink some beer," I came to the conclusion long since that the genuine hermit is as extinct as the dodo in the British Isles. I was almost excited, therefore, the other morning, to get a note on a dirty scrap of paper here, asking for the loan of a book on geology, for, on inquiry, I found it came from "the Hermit." He had suddenly appeared to the man who drives the hack, and sent it in by him. No one could tell me anything more except that the writer was "the Hermit," and lived, no one knew how, in a shanty four miles away in the forest. I got the book out of the library, "loaned" a pony, and in due course found myself outside a dilapidated snake-fence, surrounding some three acres of half-cleared forest, and the rudest kind of log-hut; evidently the place I was in search of, but no hermit. While I was meditating my next move, a dismal howl, like, I should think, the "lulilooing" of Central Africa, came from out the neighbouring bush. I shouted myself, and in a few moments "the Hermit" appeared, and certainly at first glance "filled the bill" satisfactorily. His head was a tangled mass of long hair and beard, out of which shone two big, blue eyes; a long, lean figure, slightly bent, and clothed in a tattered shirt, and trousers which no old Jew clothesman would have picked off a dunghill. I explained my errand and produced the book.

He thanked me, excused his dress; had other clothes, he said, in the house, which he would have put on had he expected me; was rather excited, so I must excuse him, as his "buck" had gone right off, in disgust, he believed, at the smallness of his flock, as he had only eight ewes. "Buck" I found to be *Anglice* "ram," and that it was in the hope of luring back the insufficiently married lord of his flock that he had been howling when I came up. On my doubting whether such a call would not be more likely to speed the flight of the truant "buck," he rushed away in the other direction and uplifted it again; and in two or three minutes the eight ewes, with several lambs, were all round him, rubbing against his legs, while an Angora goat looked on with dignity from some yards off. From our talk I found that he was a Shrewsbury man, knew three or four languages, and mathematics up to the differential calculus; found England "too noisy," and, moreover, could get no land there; had come out and gone to the agricultural class at Cornell University; had now bought this bit of land, on which he could live well, as he was a vegetarian (pointing round to some corn, turnips, etc., in his enclosure); had indigestion at first, but now had found out how to make bread which agreed with him. His trouble was the forest hogs, which were always watching to get at his crops, and his fence, having weak places, would not keep them out, so he had to be always on the watch. If he had any one to keep out the hogs, he could go and find his "buck," he said, wistfully. The better man within me here was moved to offer to keep watch and ward against hogs while he sought his "buck"; but, on the whole, as the sun was already westering, and I had doubts as to when he might think of relieving guard, my better man did not prevail, and I changed the subject to the book I had brought. He glanced at the title-page, was pleased to find that it was of recent date, as his geology was rusty. Then, as he did not invite me into his log-hut, I rode away. Next evening, as I was strolling down our street, my attention was called to the noticeboard outside the chief store, kept by an excellent, kindly New Englander, Tucker by name, who very liberally allows any of his neighbours to use it. Here I found the following notice from "the Hermit," which had been sent up by the hackman, to be posted. It opens, you will remark, in the true prophetic style. It ran: "Ho! all ye passers by! Strayed—like a fool!—a Ram (a male sheep,) butts like a nipper, and runs after! God will bless the seer if he lets Isaac Williams, of Sedgemoor Road, know. That is all. Please, Mr. Tucker, post this. Oh, I forgot,—Buy of Tucker!" I think you will agree that I have struck a *bona fide* hermit in my old age.

But to return to my loafing idyll. Perhaps, if I had to select out of several the ideal loafing haunt in these parts, it would be the verandah of our doctor, another bright New Englander, a graduate of Harvard, and M.D., who, after fourteen years' practice at Boston, was driven South by threatenings of chest troubles, and happily pitched on this tableland amongst the mountains. Not that he is a loaf-brother, except on rare occasions; a man diligent in his business, and prompt to answer any professional call; but as nobody seems ever to be ill, his leisure is abundant. The greater part of this he spends in the study and practice of grape-culture, in which he has, in the five years since he took it up, earned a high reputation. But in these autumn months, all the pruning, thinning, and tending are over in the forenoon, and in the hours which follow, which are delightfully hot and enjoyable to all sun-lovers, he is generally to be found in his verandah, well supplied with rocking-chairs. In front of the verandah is his principal vineyard, sloping south, and at the bottom of the slope, right away to the distant mountain-range (with Pike's Peak soaring to the clouds, the centre of the military telegraph system in the war, from which messages were flashed to Look-out Mountain, over Chattanooga, in the critical days of battle, before Sherman started on his march to the sea), wave beyond wave, as it were, of many-coloured forest, each taking fresh tints as clouds flit over, and the triumphant old sun slopes to the West. There one may find the doctor in his rocker, his feet higher than his head on one of the verandah supports—and all who have learnt to appreciate the rocking-chair will agree that "heels up" is half the battle—his tobacco and a book on vines on a small table by his side, and over his head, within easy reach, a rope depending from the verandah roof. At first I took it for the common domestic bell-pull, but soon discovered its more subtle bearing on the luxury of loafing. The doctor had been much exercised by the visits of birds of outrageous appetite to his "Norton's Virginia," and other precious vines. At first he had resorted to his double-barrelled gun and small shot—indeed, it yet stood in a corner of the balcony, loaded—but had soon abandoned it. Its use was compatible neither with his love for birds nor the enjoyment of his rocking-chair. So, by an ingenious arrangement, he had hung bells at five or six points in the vineyard, connecting each and all with the depending-rope, so that no sooner did a bird settle with a view to lunch or dinner, than it was saluted by a peal from a bell close by, which sent it skirling back to the forest, while the doctor had neither to lower his heels nor take the pipe from his mouth.

Watching the entire discomfiture of the birds adds, I must own, a keener zest even to the delicious view and air, and to the racy stories of Western life poured out by one or another of the loaf-brethren. A specimen or two may amuse your readers. Placard over the piano in a favourite resort of Texan cowboys: "Don't shoot the musician; he is doing his best." Cowboy entering the cars at midnight, thermometer below zero, after snorting for a minute, lets down a window, is remonstrated with, and replies, "Wal, I'd as soon sleep with my head in a dead horse as in this car with the windows shut!" Another tale I repeat with hesitation, though it was seriously vouched for by the narrator as going on in his neighbourhood, and within his own cognisance. An eccentric settler, who played the fiddle powerfully, and lived next a man who had thrown a bridge over a creek, in respect of which the knotty question of "right of way" had arisen between them, read, or discovered somehow, that excessive vibration was the cause of the fall of bridges, and that a well-known railway iron bridge had been distinctly felt to vibrate to the notes of a fiddle, all that was necessary being to find the right chord and play up. Thereupon he set himself on the peccant bridge, and fiddled till he had hit on the sympathetic chord to his own satisfaction; since which he has put in all his spare time at the bridge, fiddling on the right chord and looking for the signs of a crash and the discomfiture of his neighbour. A mad world, my masters! And lucky for the world, say I. But for the cracked fellows going up and down, what a dull place it would be!

The whole neighbourhood, or, at any rate, the men of hunting age, have suddenly been roused into unwonted excitement and activity by the presence of a specimen of the larger carnivora close to this town. It is either a large panther or what they call a Mexican lion—at any rate, as big a beast of this kind as are bred over here, as his footprint, seen of many persons, clearly proves. He has been heard to roar by numbers, and Giles, the saw-mill man, who, passing along wholly unarmed, saw him gliding through the bush close by, puts him at five feet from nose to tail (root, not tip) at least. Giles adds that, at the sight, his hair stood up and distinctly lifted his straw hat—so perhaps his evidence must be discounted considerably. Any way, a party, now collecting dogs to bring him to bay, start to-morrow at dawn to give an account of him. It is more than a year since one has ventured down this way. A slaughter-house which has lately been set up in the woods near by would seem to have drawn him. Let us hope that no cunning old sportsman will watch there to-night and bag him single-handed, and I may possibly have to tell you of a memorable hunt next week.

American Opinion on the Union, SS. Umbria, 5th October 1887.

That panther-hunt went off in a "fizzle." Our contingent of determined sportsmen kept tryst at daylight, fully armed, but some neighbours who were to bring the proper dogs failed. The sun rose, broad and bright, and so, after a short advance in skirmishing order over the ground where the sawmill man had been so scared—just to save their credit as Nimrods—the chase was abandoned; wisely, I should think, for I can scarcely imagine a more hopeless undertaking than the pursuit of a panther in a Tennessee forest in broad daylight without dogs. Whether Sawyer Giles had grounds for his scare, and what was the length of that panther, must now remain for all time in that useful category of insoluble questions—like the identity of "Junius," and Queen Mary's guilt—which innocently employ so much of the spare time of the human race.

I have been back for the last fortnight "in amongst the crowd of men," and if the things they have done are but "earnest of the things that they shall do," well, our grandchildren will have a high old time of it! At any rate, our cousins hold this faith vigorously. Take, for instance, the case of a leading dry-goods man who has been sitting by me in the smoking-room of this ship, which has been carrying us for the last four days against a head-wind at the average rate of twenty miles an hour. Recollect, sir, that this ship is about 400 feet in length, of 8800 tons register, with engines of 14,000 horse-power, and must at this moment be as heavy as (say) lour big luggage-trains. I ventured to suggest that, whatever may be in store for us in the way of flying, science has about said her last word in the direction of driving steam or any other ships on the Atlantic. I felt almost inclined to resent the pity tinged with scorn with which he said, "Why, *sir!* this is the hundred and twenty-eighth time I have crossed this ocean. The first time it took me twenty-two days. This vessel does it in six days and a half, and I shall do it in half that time yet,—yes, *sir!*" My friend must be at least sixty!

The New York hotels were crammed as I came through with men who had come from all parts of the States for the yacht-race. I went out on a friend's steam-yacht on the Thursday, when the second day's race should have come off. There was fog and no wind off Sandy Hook, so after lying-to in a lopping sea for a couple of hours, we just steamed back, some hundred of us. But the game had been well worth the candle. Anything so beautiful as the movements of those two yachts in and out amongst the expectant fleet of sightseers, I never beheld. There were several old yachtsmen (Americans) on board, who seemed rather to think the *Thistle* the more perfect of the two, and when the second and deciding race had been sailed, still guessed that if their Commodore, Pain, or Malcolm Forbes had sailed the *Thistle*, she would not have been twelve, or any, minutes behind.

As to more serious matters, you may be sure I lost no chance of talking on our crisis with every intelligent American or Canadian,—and I happened upon a great number of the latter. Amongst the majority of Americans I was much struck, and, I own, surprised, to find a sort of lazy fatalism prevailing, so far as they troubled their heads at all about the Irish question. Not a man of them believed in the tyranny of the British Government or the wrongs of the Irish; but they seemed to think it was somehow destiny. They knew the Irish—were likely to have at least as bad a time with them as we are having—but, unless you made up your minds to shoot, there was no putting them down or bringing them to reason. They had had to shoot—in New York during the war, and at other times—and might probably have to shoot again \ but then, that was over vital matters. We should never make up our minds to shoot over letting them have a Parliament at Dublin, and so they would get it by sheer insolence and intrigue. Such views would have depressed me had I not found, on the other hand, that the few men who had mastered the situation, without a single exception saw that it was a matter, nationally, of life or death, and hoped our Government would shrink from no measure necessary to restore the rule of law, and preserve the national life.

Amongst the Canadians, on the other hand, I did not happen upon a single Home-ruler—in fact, was obliged to own to myself that they seemed to set more store by the unity of the Empire than we do in the as-yet-United Kingdom. Indeed, if my acquaintances are at all representative of the views of our Canadian fellow-subjects, I feel very sure that the slight bond which holds the Dominion to us would part within a few months of the triumph of the Home-rule agitation. This possible fiasco, however, did not seem to them much worth thinking about; but what was really exercising them was the probability of a more intimate union or federation with the Mother-country. For defensive purposes, I was glad to find that they saw no difficulty whatever; believed, indeed, that that question was already solved. But all felt that the really difficult problem was a commercial union, which, nevertheless, must be managed somehow, if the Empire is to hold together. On this there were wide differences of opinion, but, on the whole, a decided inclination to a plan which I will endeavour to put in a few words. It is, that every portion of the Empire shall be free, as at present, to impose whatever tariff of customs it might think best for raising its own revenue; but an agreed discount (say, ten per cent) should be allowed on all goods the manufacture or product of the Mother-country, or any of its possessions. Inasmuch, it was argued, as such à plan would allow the free admission of all food and raw material, it ought not to hurt the Free-trade susceptibilities of England, while leaving the self-governing Colonies and India free to raise their own revenue as might suit their own views or circumstances. On the other hand, it would give an equal and moderate advantage to all subjects of the Empire. A similar advantage might also, under this plan, be given to importations made in ships belonging to any portion of the Empire.

You, sir, may very probably have heard of and considered this plan, as I have been told that it, or one almost identical, has been submitted both to the London Chamber of Commerce, and to the Colonial Office, by Sir Alexander Galt. I do not remember, however, to have ever seen it discussed in your columns, as I think it might be with advantage. One's brain possibly is not so fit for the examination of political problems on even such a magnificent ship as the *Umbria* as on shore; but "after the best consideration I can give it," it does seem to me to be a solution which might go far to satisfy the scruples of all but fanatics of the "buy in the cheapest and sell in the dearest market" gospel.

We have run 435 miles in the teeth of the wind, in the last twenty-four hours.

EUROPE—1876 to 1895

A Winter Morning's Ride

The proverb that "The early bird gets most worms" has no truer application than in travelling, considered as a fine art. Of course to him who uses locomotion as a mere method of getting from one place to another, it matters nothing whether he starts at 3 A.M. or at noon. But to the man who likes to get the most he can out of his life, and looks upon a journey as an opportunity for getting some new insight into the ways and habits and notions of his fellowmen, there is no comparison between their value. The noonday travelling mood, like noonday light, is commonplace and uniform; while the early morning mood, like the light when it first comes, is full of colour and surprise. Such, at any rate, has been my experience, and I never made an out-of-the-way early start without coming upon one or more companions who gave me a new glimpse into some corner of life, and whose experience I should have been the poorer for having missed. My last experience in this matter is very recent. In the midst of the wild days of last December I received an unexpected summons on business to the north. My appointment was for eleven o'clock on the morrow, 200 miles from London. It was too late to make arrangements for leaving home at once, so I resolved to start by the first morning train, which leaves Euston Square at 5.15 A.M. Accordingly, soon after four next morning I closed the house door gently behind me, and set out on my walk, not without a sense of the self-approval and satisfaction which is apt to creep over early risers, and others who pride themselves on keeping ahead of their neighbours.

It was a fine wild morning, with half a gale of wind blowing from the north-west, and driving the low rain-clouds at headlong speed across the deep clear sky and bright stars. The great town felt as fresh and sweet as a country hillside. Not a soul in the streets but an occasional solitary policeman, and here and there a scavenger or two, plying their much-needed trade, for the wet mud lay inches deep. I was early at the station, where a sleepy clerk was just preparing to open the booking-offices, and a couple of porters were watering and sweeping the floor of the big hall. Soon my fellow-passengers began to arrive, labouring men for the most part, with here and there a clerk, or commercial traveller, muffled to the eyes.

Amongst them, as they gathered round the fire, or took short restless walks up and down the platform, was one who puzzled me not a little. He had arrived on foot just before me, indeed I had followed him for the last quarter of a mile through Euston Square, and had already begun to speculate as to who he could be, and on what errand. But now that I could get a deliberate look at him under the lights in the hall, my curiosity was at once raised and baffled. He was a strongly built, well-set young fellow of five feet ten or eleven, with clear gray eyes, deep set under very straight brows. His hair was dark, and would have curled but that it was cropped too short. He was clean shaved, so that one saw all the lower lines of his face, which a thick nose, slightly turned up, just hindered from being handsome. He wore a high sealskin cap, a striped flannel shirt with turn down collars, and a slipknot tie with a rather handsome pin. His clothes were good enough, but had a somewhat dissipated look, owing perhaps to the fact that only one button of his waistcoat was fastened, and that his boots, good broad double-soled ones, were covered with dry mud. His whole luggage consisted of the travelling-bag he carried in his hand, one of those elaborate affairs which generally involve a portmanteau or two to follow, but swelled out of all gentility and stuffed to bursting point.

An Englishman? I asked myself. Well, yes,—at any rate more like an Englishman than anything else. A gentleman? Well, yes again, on the whole; though not of our conventional type—at any rate a man of some education, and apparently a little less like the common run of us than most one meets.

Here my speculations were cut short by the opening of the ticket-window by the sleepy clerk, and the object of them marched up and took a third-class ticket for Liverpool. I followed his example. My natural aversion to eating money raw in railway travelling inclining me to such economy, apart from the interest which my problem was exciting in my mind. I am bound to add that nothing could be more comfortable than the carriages provided on the occasion for the third-class passengers of the N.W.K. I followed the sealskin cap and got into the same carriage with its owner. As good luck would have it, no one followed us. He put his bag down in a corner, and stretched himself along his side of the carriage with his head on it. I had time to look him well over again, and to set him down in my own mind as a young English engineer, who had been working on some continental railway so long as to have lost his English identity somewhat, when he started up, rubbed his eyes, took a good straight look at me, and asked if any one coming from abroad could cut us off in the steamer that met this train. I found at once that I was mistaken as to nationality.

I answered that no one could cut us off, as there was no straighter or quicker way of getting to Liverpool than this; but that he was mistaken in thinking that any steamer met the train.

Well, he didn't know about meeting it, but anyway there was a steamer which went right away from Liverpool about noon, for he had got his passage by her, which he had bought at the tobacco-store near the station.

He handed his ticket for the boat to me, as if wishing my opinion upon it, which I gave to the effect that it seemed all right, adding that I did not know that tickets could be bought about the streets as they could be in America.

Well, he had thought it would save him time, perhaps save the packet, as she might have sailed while he was after his ticket in Liverpool, which town he didn't know his way about. But now, couldn't any one from the Continent cut her off? He had heard there was a route by Chester and Holyhead, which would bring any one who took it aboard of her at Queenstown.

I answered that this was probably so, beginning to doubt in my mind whether my companion might not, for all his straightforward looks and ways, have come by the bag feloniously. Could it be another great jewel robbery?

I don't know whether he noticed any doubtful look in my eyes, but he added at once that he was on the straight run from Heidelberg. He had come from there to London in twenty-six hours.

I made some remark as to the beauty of Heidelberg, and asked if he knew it well.

Why, yes, he said he ought to, for he had been a student at the University there for the last nine months.

Why then was he on the straight run home? I ventured to ask. Term wasn't over?

No; term wasn't over; but he had been arrested, and didn't want to go to prison at Strasburg, where one American student was in for about two years already.

But how did he manage to get off? I asked, now thoroughly interested in his story.

Well, he had just run his bail. When he was arrested he had sent for the doctor at whose house he lodged to bail him out. That was what troubled him most. He wouldn't have the Herr Doctor slipped up anyway. He was going to send the money directly he got home, and there were things enough left of his to cover the money.

What was he arrested for?

For calling out a German student.

But I thought the German students were always fighting duels.

So they were, but only with swords, which they were always practising. They were so padded when they fought that they could not be hurt except just in the face, and the sword arm was so bandaged that there was no play at all except from the wrist. You would see the German students even when out walking, miles away from the town, keeping playing away with their walking-sticks all the time, so as to train their wrists.

What was his quarrel about?

Well, it was just this. The American students, of whom there were a large number there, kept pretty much to themselves, and no love was lost between them and the Germans. They had an American Club to which they all belonged, just to keep them together and see any fellow through who was in a scrape. He and some of the American students were sitting in the beer garden, close to a table of Germans. Forgetting the neighbourhood, he had tilted his chair and leant back in it, and so come against a German head. The owner jumped up, and a sharp altercation followed, ending in the German's calling him out with swords. This he refused, but sent a challenge to fight with pistols by the President of the Club, a real fine man, who had shot his two men down South before he went to Heidelberg. The answer to this was his arrest, and arrest was a very serious thing now. For some little time since, a German and an American fought, with swords first and then with pistols. The American had his face cut open from the eye right down across the mouth, but when it came to pistols he shot the German, who died in an hour. So he was in jail, and challenging with pistols had been made an offence punishable by imprisonment, and that was no joke in a German military prison.

Did he expect the University authorities would send after him then?

No; but his folk were all in Germany for the winter. He had a younger brother at Heidelberg who had taken his bag down to the station for him, and would have let his father know, as he had told him to do. If he had telegraphed the old gentleman might come straight off and stop him yet, but he rather guessed he would he so mad he wouldn't come. No; he didn't expect to see his folk again for three or four years.

But why? After all, sending a challenge of which nothing came was not so very heinous an offence.

Yes, but it was the second time. He had run from an American university to escape expulsion for having set fire to an outhouse. Then he went straight to New York, which he wanted to see, and stopped till his money was all gone. His father was mad enough about that.

I said plainly that I didn't wonder, and was going to add something by way of improving the occasion, but for a look of such deep sorrow which passed over the boy's face that I thought his conscience might well do the work better than I could.

He opened his bag and took out a photograph, and then his six-shooter—a self-cocking German one, he said, which was quicker and carried a heavier ball than any he had seen in America; and then his pipes and cigar tubes; and then he rolled a cigarette and lighted it; and, as the dawn was now come, began to ask questions about the country. But all in vain; back the scene he was running from came, do what he would. His youngest brother, a little fellow of ten, was down with fever. He had spoilt Christmas for the whole family. It would cut them up awfully. But to a suggestion that he should go straight back he could not listen. No, he was going straight through to California, the best place for him. He had never done any good yet, but he was going to do it now. He had got a letter or two to Californians from some of his fellow-students, which would give him some opening. He wouldn't see his people for four or five years, till he got something to show them. He would have to pitch right in, or else starve. He would go right into the first thing that came along out there, and make something.

As we got further down the line the morning cleared, and we had many fellow-passengers; but my young friend, as I might almost call him by this time, stuck to me, and seemed to get some relief by talking of his past doings and future prospect. I found that he had been at Würzburg for a short time before going to Heidelberg, so had had a student's experience of two of the most celebrated German Universities. My own ideas of those seats of learning, being for the most part derived from the writings of Mr. Matthew Arnold, received, I am bound to own, rather severe shocks from the evidently truthful experience of one medical student.

He had simply paid his necessary florins (about £1 worth) for his matriculation fee, and double that sum for two sets of lectures for which he entered. He had passed no matriculation examination, or indeed any other; had attended lectures or not, just he pleased—about one in three he put as his average—but there was no roll-call or register, and no one that he knew of seemed to care the least whether he was there or not. However, he seemed to think that but for his unlucky little difficulty he could easily at this rate have passed the examination for the degree of doctor of medicines. The doctor's degree was a mighty fine thing, and much sought after, but didn't amount to much professionally, at least not in Germany, where the doctor has a State examination to pass after he has got his degree. But in America, or anywhere else, he believed they could just practise on a German M.D. degree, and he knew of one Herr Doctor out West who was about as fit to take hold of any sick fellow as he was himself. Oh, Matthew, Matthew, my mentor! When I got home I had to take down thy volume on Universities in Germany, and restore my failing faith by a glance at the Appendix, giving a list of the courses of lectures by Professors, Privabdocenten, and readers of the University of Berlin during one winter, in which the Medical Faculty's subjects occupy seven pages; and to remind myself, that the characteristics of the German Universities are "*Lehrfreiheit und Lernfreiheit*," "Liberty for the teacher, and liberty for the learner"; also that "the French University has no liberty, and the English Universities have no sciences; the German Universities have both." Too much liberty of one kind this student at any rate bore witness to, and in one of his serious moments was eloquent on the danger and mischief of the system, so far as his outlook had gone.

By the time our roads diverged, the young runaway had quite won me over to forget his escapades, by his frank disclosures of all that was passing in his mind of regret and tenderness, hopefulness and audacity; and I sorrowed for a few moments on the platform as the sealskin cap disappeared at the window of the Liverpool carriage, from which he waved a cheery adieu.

As I walked towards the carriage to go on my own way, I found myself regretting that I should see his ruddy face no more, and wishing him all success "in that new world which is the old," for which he was bound, with no possessions but his hand-bag and self-reliance to make his way with. I might have sat alone for thrice as long with an English youngster, in like case, without knowing a word of his history; but then, such history could never have happened to an Englishman, for he never would have run his bail, and would have gone to prison and served his time as a matter of course.

How much each nation has to learn of the other! But I trust that by this time my young friend has seen to it that the good-natured Herr Doctor who went bail for him hasn't "slipped up anyway."

Southport, 22nd March.

I wonder if you will care to take a seaside letter, at this busiest time of the year? Folk have no business to be "on the loaf" before Easter, I readily admit. Still, there is much force and good-sense, I have always held, in that tough, old regicide Major-General Ludlow's action, when he found England under Cromwell too narrow to hold him. He migrated to Switzerland, and characteristically changed his family motto to *"Ubi libertas, ibi patria"* ("Where I can have my own way, there is my country") or (if I may be allowed a free rendering to fit the occasion), "Whenever man can loaf, then is long vacation."

But my motive for writing is really of another kind. In these later years, a large and growing minority of my personal friends and acquaintances seem to be afflicted with that demon called Neuralgia,—some kind of painful affection connected with the nerves of the head and face, which makes the burden of life indefinitely heavier to carry than it has any right to be. To all such I feel bound to say, Give this place a trial in your first leisure. In one case, at any rate, and that an apparently chronic one, in which every east wind, and almost every sudden change of temperature, brought with it acute suffering, I have seen with my own eyes a complete cure effected by a few days in this air. The experiment was tried three months since, and from that time the demon seems to have been exorcised, and has been quite unable to return, though we have had a full average in these parts of sudden changes of temperature,—east winds, cold rains, and the other amenities of early spring in England.

Can I account for this? Well, so far as I can judge, the peculiar conformation of the shore must have much to say to it. From the open window where I am sitting, there lies between me and the sea (it being low water) an almost level stretch of sand of more than half a mile in depth. Beyond that there is a narrow strip of sea, on which a fleet of tiny fishermen's craft, with their ruddy-brown sails, are plying their trade; and again, beyond that, between channel and open sea, is another long sand-bank. Now I am told, and see no reason to doubt, that the evaporation from this great expanse of wet sand is charged with double the amount of ozone which would rise from the like area of salt-water. But whatever the cause, the fact stands as I have stated above. In another hour or two the sea will be close up to these windows, lapping against the sea-wall, and spoiling the view for the time, but, happily, only for a short time. For while it is up, there is nothing but very shallow, muddy water to be seen, on which the faithful old sun, try as he will, can paint no pictures. Whereas at low tide, the colours of these sandy wastes— the steely gleam of the wet parts, the bright yellow of the dry, and the warm and rich tints of brown of the intermediate, and the quaint, black line of the pier, running out across them all till it reaches the pale blue of the channel, where the fishing-boats all lie at anchor round the pier-head at sunset—are one perpetual feast, even to the untrained eye. What the delight must be to a painter, when the level sun turns the blacks into deep purples, and glorifies all the yellows and browns, and gives the steely gleams a baleful and cruel glint, I can only guess, unless, indeed, it should make him hang himself, in despair of reproducing them on mortal canvas. That long, black pier is our favourite place of resort. Probably the ozone is stronger there than elsewhere. It is three-quarters of a mile long, and at the end, at noon, a most attractive, daily performance comes off gratis. At that hour the gulls are fed by an official of the pier company, and afterwards, at intervals, by children, who bring scraps of viands in their pockets for this purpose.

I am not defending the practice, which tends, no doubt, to pauperise a number of these delightful birds. I have watched them carefully, and never seen one of them go off to earn his honest, daily fish. There they sit lightly on the water, with heads turned to the pier-head, and float past with the tide, rising for a short flight back again, as it carries them too far past to see when the doles are beginning to be served. When these begin, they are all in the air, wheeling and crossing each other in perfect flight to get the proper swooping-point. It seems to be a rule of the game that they pick up the fragments in their swoop, for when this is neatly done by any one, the rest leave him alone, though he may carry off a larger prize than he is able to swallow on the wing. But in a high wind there is trouble. Not one in a dozen of them can then be sure of his prey in his swoop, and after one or two attempts the greedy ones alight and attack the viands on the water. But this seems to be against the rules of the game, and instantly others alight by the side of the transgressor, and strive eagerly for whatever of the desired morsel is still outside his yellow beak. I noted with pleasure that there are generally a few who will take no part in these squabbles, but if they failed in their swoop, soared up again with dignity, to wait for another chance. These must, I take it, be undemoralised gulls, from a distance. Always play your game fair, or there will be trouble, whether amongst birds or men.

At other seaside places the shallowness of the sand limits the pure delight of children in their castle-building. Here it seems boundless. I saw one sturdy urchin yesterday throwing out stoneless sand from a hole some four feet deep. The castles and engineering works are therefore on a splendid scale, several of them from five to ten yards across, inside which bits of old spars (portions, I fear, of wrecks) are utilised for causeways and bridges. The infant builders are ambitious, for I have seen frequent attempts, not wholly unsuccessful, at putting sand steeples on the churches. These higher efforts were all made by girls, who, indeed, I regret to say, seemed to do not only the decorative, but the substantial work. The boys employed themselves mainly in creeping through the holes which the girls had dug under the spars, to represent bridges, and in knocking down the boundary walls. Is this a sign of our topsy-turvy times? In my day, we boys did all the building and engineering, and the girls used to come and sit on our walls, and destroy our castles. On this highest part of the sands, the children's playground, there stand also certain skeletons of booths, to be covered with canvas, I presume, in the summer, for the sale of ginger-beer and cakes. These, the largest especially, some nine feet high, attracted the boys, several of whom essayed to reach the highest cross-bar. Only one succeeded while I watched, a born sailor-boy, who was not to be foiled, and succeeded in getting on to it. There he sat, and looked scornfully down on the sand-diggers, in the temper, no doubt, of the chorus of the old sea song—

We jolly sailor boys a-sitting up aloft,

And the land-lubbers funking down below.

After a time he descended, and, looking for a few moments at the diggers, went straight away across the sands towards the sea. I saw that he had only a wooden spade, while most of theirs had iron heads.

There is another kind of amusement which is strange to me, being necessarily confined to great expanses of sand. A boat on wheels, called the *Flying Dutchman*, careers along at a splendid pace when there is wind enough, and I am told can tack handily, and never runs into the sea. If it did, it would not matter, as it must at once upset in such case in very shoal water. When the Royal Society was here, several eminent philosophers were reported to be disporting themselves in the *Flying Dutchman*, when the President, Professor Cayley, called on them to read papers, or make promised speeches.

This flat sandy coast is far from being so innocent as it looks. There are the wrecks of two vessels in sight even now. One of these, I hear, it took the lifeboat fourteen hours' *continuous hard work* to reach, and they brought off every man of the crew, twenty-five in number—a feat deserving wider fame than it has attained. They must be glorious sea-worthies, these Lancashire fishermen! Of the fine public buildings, the four-miles tramway, the Free Library, Botanic Gardens, and the rest, I need not speak. Lord Derby's *mot* on opening the Botanic Gardens is enough,—that the Southport folk can skate on real ice in July, and sit under palm-trees at Christmas. But I may say that the esplanade is a grand course for tricyclers and bicyclers, who seem fond of challenging and running races with tradesmen's carts—a somewhat risky operation for other vehicles and passengers.

One word, however, before I close, about the most striking of the churches, St. Andrew's. I was attracted to it by its good proportions, and the stone tracery of several of the windows, reminding one of the patterns of the early decorated period of Gothic art. It can seat some 1500 people on the floor, there being no galleries. I am sorry to say, however, that appearances are deceitful. It is of no use to have fine proportions and good decoration if they won't stand; and unhappily, although the church is only twelve years old, the cleristory walls have been blown out of the perpendicular, so that the whole nave roof has to come off that they may be solidly rebuilt. What would an old monkish architect have said to such a catastrophe? The more's the pity, inasmuch as the necessary closing of the church is going to shelve, probably for months, the most striking preacher I have heard this month of Sundays. I first learnt, sir, in your columns the golden rule, that during prayers the worshipper is responsible for keeping up his own attention, while at sermon-time it is the parson's business. Well, I have been to St. Andrew's for the last three Sundays, and during sermons, none of which have lasted less than half an hour, have neither gone to sleep, nor thought about anything but what the preacher was saying. I suspect it is (as Apollo says of Theodore Parker, in the "Fable for Critics") that—

This is what makes him the crowd-drawing preacher,

There's a background of God to each hard-working feature,

Every word that he speaks has been fierily furnaced

In the blast of a life that has struggled in earnest.

Whatever be the cause, however, there is the fact; and I own I am somewhat surprised, being rather curious about such matters, that I had never heard the name of Prebendary Cross before I happened to come to this place.

A Village Festival

Pan is dead! So, at least, those who claim to be teachers of us English on such subjects have told us; and if our poets cannot be trusted about them, who can? The present writer, at any rate, does not pretend to an opinion whether Pan is dead, or, indeed, whether he was ever alive. But if so, he ought to have kept alive, for never surely was his special business so flourishing in our country as in these last days. All round the Welsh border on both sides there is not a hamlet which is not indulging in its "Lupercalia" in these summer days, in spite of the cold and wet which have inopportunely come upon us. For the most part, these "feasts of Pan" are almost monotonously like one another; but I have just returned from one which had characteristics of its own—a pleasing variety, and creditable, I think, to gallant little Wales, for the scene of it was over the border. My attention was called to it by a large red bill at our station, announcing that, on the 9th inst. the annual festival of the Gresford Ladies' Club would be held, for which return tickets might be had at tempting rates; and further, that "no rifle-galleries, or stalls used for the sale of nuts and oranges, will be allowed to be put up in the village or highways on the day." Why should a ladies' club invite me, and all men, by large red bill, to be present at their festival, and at the same time deprive me of the chance of indulging in the favourite feast pastime of these parts? I resolved to satisfy myself; and reaching the pretty station, in due course found myself on the platform with perhaps a dozen women of all ranks and ages—evidently members of the club, for each of them wore a white scarf over the right shoulder, and carried a blue wand with a nosegay at the top. Following admiringly up the steep hill with other spectators, I saw them enter a wicket-gate under an arch of flowers, and remained outside, where the brass band of the county yeomanry were making most energetic music. Presently the gate opened, and a procession of the members emerged two-and-two, and, headed by the band in full blast, marched, a dainty procession, each one white-scarfed and carrying a nosegay-topped wand, to the parish church hard by on the hill-top. It was a unique procession, so far as my experience goes. First came the squire's wife, the club President, with the senior member, followed by another lady, I believe from the rectory, with the member next in seniority. These two, both past eighty, I remarked, instead of the white scarf crossing the shoulder and looped at the waist with blue, wore large white handkerchiefs, trimmed with blue, over both shoulders, shawl-wise. This I found was the old custom, the regular members formerly wearing the shawl, the honorary members the scarf, for distinction's sake. Now, all members, regular and honorary alike, wear the scarf. We are levelling up fast, and I own I regret it, in this matter of dress. As a boy, I was in this part of Wales, and almost every woman on holidays wore the red cloak and high black hat, and looked far better, I think, than their descendants at this

Gresford Club fête, though several of these were as well dressed as the squire's wife and daughters. I followed the procession into church, as did most of the crowd through which they passed, one man only refusing to join in my hearing, on the ground that he had been already to one service too many. He had got married there, his neighbour explained, and his wife was in the procession. The service was short and well chosen, with a good, sound ten-minutes sermon at the end, and then the procession re-formed, the band still leading, and marched to tea in the big schoolroom facing the churchyard. "Scholæ elymosynæ Dominæ Margarettæ Strode, fundatæ 1725, ad pauperes ejus sumptibus erudiendos," I read over the door. I notice that the Welsh are rather given to Latin inscriptions can it be in token of defiance to vernacular English?

During the tea-hour I had the pleasure of exploring church and churchyard, the former a large and fine specimen of the later perpendicular, but containing relics of painted glass of a much earlier date, probably thirteenth century. Portions of this, of a fine straw-colour, the Rector says, are invaluable, the art being lost. I wonder what Mr. Powell would say to that? The churchyard is glorious with its yews, more than twenty grand trees, and the grandfather of them the largest but one, if not the largest, in the Kingdom. He measures 29 feet 6 inches round 6 feet from the ground, and is confidently affirmed by Welsh experts (who have duly noted it in the parish register) to be 1400 years old. Without supposing that Merlin reposed in his shade, one cannot look at him in his glorious old age and doubt that he must have been a stout tree in Plantagenet times, and furnished bow-staves for Welshmen who marched behind Fluellen to the French wars.

Presently the band struck up again, and the procession returned to the wicket-gate, through which I now gained an entrance on payment of 1s. towards the club funds, one of the best investments of the kind I have ever made, for inside is the most perfect miniature village green I should think in the world, take it all in all. It is a natural terrace about one hundred yards long, by (perhaps) forty broad, on the side of the steep, finely wooded hill, with the station down below, and the church and village above. The valley, which runs up into the Welsh hills to the west, is here narrow, with a bright trout-stream dancing along between emerald meadows out into the great Cheshire plain, over which, in the distance, rise the cathedral towers and the castle and spires of Chester. One can fancy the hungry eyes with which many a Welshman has looked over that splendid countryside from this perch on the hillside when Hugh Lupus and his successors were keeping the border, with short shrift for cattle-lifters. It is well worth the while of any of your readers who may be passing Gresford Station this autumn, to stop over a train, and go up and spend an hour there. But I must get back to the ladies' club, who now, at 6 P.M., opened the three hours' dance on the green, the great feature of the gathering. It began with a country-dance, at which we males could only gaze and admire. As before, the squire's wife and the senior member led off, and went down the thirty or forty couples. What wonderful women are these Welsh! I was fascinated by the next senior, a dear old soul, who had only missed this dance twice in more than sixty years, and was in such a hurry to get under way, that she started before the leading couple had got properly ahead, rather thereby confusing the subsequent saltations. When the music at last stopped, she sat herself on a bench, a picture of joyous old age, and declared that if she had been a rich woman, she should have spent all her substance in keeping a band. After the country-dance came polkas, in which I noted that for some time the men, by way of reprisals, I suppose, danced together; but this did not last long, and presently the couples were sorted in the usual manner, and when the station-bell warned me to speed down the hill, I left them all as busy on the green as the elves (perhaps) may be in the moonlight, or Pan's troop in the days before his lamented decease. On my way home I mused on the cheering evidence the day had afforded of the healthy progress of the great task which has been laid on this generation, and' which it seems to be taking hold of so strenuously and hopefully. I do not know that I ever saw so entirely satisfactory a blending of all classes in common enjoyment, which to some extent I attribute to the custom of the procession, and the sorting of honorary and regular members above noticed. During the whole afternoon I never heard a word which might not have been spoken in a drawing-room, and in spite of the rigorous exclusion of tobacco, there was no lack of young men. I question whether it would be possible to see the like in any exclusive gathering, either of the classes or the masses. The club is as prosperous financially, I am glad to hear, as it is socially, having a reserve fund of some £600, while the subscriptions are very moderate. No doubt the political and industrial atmosphere is dark with heavy clouds both' at home and abroad; but I do begin to think that this white lining of a truer and fuller blending of our people than has ever been known before in England, or anywhere else, is going to do more than compensate for whatever troubles may be in store for us from wars or other convulsions, and that we shall be in time to meet them as a united people.

Then let us pray that come it may—

As come it will for a' that—

That man to man, the warld o'er,

Shall brithers be for a' that.

The "Victoria," New Cut.

Of all the healthy signs of real social progress in this remarkable age, I know of none more striking, or, I will add, more thankworthy in a small way, than the contrast of the present condition of the big People's Theatre in Southwark with that which middle-aged men can remember. Probably many of my readers who in the fifties and sixties held it to be part of the whole duty of man to attend the University boat-race at Putney, or the Oxford and Cambridge match at Lord's, will be able to call up in their memories the "Vic." of those days. For my own part, I always felt that the big costermonger's theatre suffered unfairly in reputation—as many folk and places before it have done—for the casual notice of a man of genius. "Give us the Charter," Charles Kingsley makes his tailor-hero exclaim in 1848, "and we'll send workmen into Parliament who shall find out whether something better can't be put in the way of the boys and girls in London who live by theft and prostitution, than the tender mercies of the Victoria." I do not pretend to anything more than a casual acquaintance with the "Vic." in those days; but my memory would not bear out Parson Lot in denouncing it as "a licensed pit of darkness.", That description would far better designate the Cider Cellars, the Coal Hole, and other fashionable resorts on the north side of the Thames, in which a working man's fustian jacket and corduroys were never seen. I should say that one evening spent at Evans's in those days, or at the mock Court (the judge and jury) presided over by Baron Nicholson, as that rotund old cynic was called, would have done any youngster far more harm than half a dozen at the "Vic." At the one you might sit smoking cigars and drinking champagne, if you were fool enough, and hear everything that was sacred and decent slily or openly ridiculed and travestied, in the company of M.P.'s, barristers, and others, all well-dressed people. At the "Vic." you could rub shoulders with costers and longshoremen, noisy, rowdy, and prone to fight on the slightest provocation, while the entertainment was more than coarse enough, but quite free from the subtle poison of a crim.-con. trial presided over by Baron Nicholson. With this saving, however, I am bound to admit that the old "Vic." was not a place which could have been looked on without serious misgivings by any one in the remotest degree responsible for peace or decency in South London. The influence which it exercised, to put it mildly, though undoubtedly powerful, could by no possibility have had any elevating effect on the intellect or morals of any human being; but for all that, it was always a favourite place of resort, and had a strong hold on the dense population who earn a scanty and precarious living in the New Cut and the Old Kent Road. How it was that the lease of the old "Vic.," with seventeen years still to run, came into the market some eight years back, I am not aware; but so it happened, and it was purchased by a financial Company, who, with the best intentions, embarked on the risky experiment of running the "Royal Victoria Hall," as it was now called, as a coffee-tavern and place of entertainment, against the neighbouring music-halls in which drink was sold. In eight months the Company lost £2800, and the Victoria was closed, with every chance of drifting back, on the next change of ownership, into the old ruts. Happily for South London, a better fate was in store for the "Vic.," for there were those who had eyes to see its value if properly handled, not, indeed, as a commercial speculation, but as a power for lifting the social life of the neighbourhood on to a higher level. A committee was formed, with the late Mr. Samuel Morley as chairman, and Miss Cons as honorary secretary and manager, a guarantee fund was raised, and the Hall reopened. It has been a hard fight; but with a chairman whose speech in the darkest hour rang, "We don't mean to let this thing fall to the ground," and a lady of unsurpassed experience and devotion amongst the poor, whose whole life was from the first freely and loyally given to the work, the field has been won. I say deliberately "won," and if any one doubts my word, let him walk over Waterloo Bridge any evening (for the "Vic." is always open), and look at this thing fairly; let him go into the coffee-tavern, the theatre, the big billiard and smoking-rooms, the reading and class-rooms at the top, and the gymnasium in the basement, and keep his ears and eyes wide open all the time,—and then go home and thank God that such work is going on in the very quarter of our huge city in which the need is sorest. I say, let him go any evening, but for choice I would advise a Tuesday, for on Tuesdays the "Penny Science Lectures" are given, which are, of course, less popular than the variety entertainments and the ballad concerts which occur whenever the funds allow, or some first-rate artist, such as Sims Beeves, volunteers to come and sing to the Hew Cut. To return to the "Penny Science Lectures," the wonder is, not that eminent men should be ready to go over to Southwark and give them without payment—that note of our day has become too common to surprise—but that an average of over five hundred, mostly of the *gamin* age, from the Hew Cut, should be ready to pay their penny and come, and listen, and appreciate.

It was on May Day that I visited the old "Vic.," almost by chance, and without a notion of what I was likely to see or hear. The lecture was on "The Foundation-Stones of London," and proved to be a geological, not an archæological one. Mr. H. Kimber, M.P. for the neighbouring division of South London, was in the chair, and the lecturer was Professor Judd, F.R.S., who, in a clear, terse address, aided by excellent dissolving views projected by limelight on the huge drop-scene of the stage, showed the gravel, clay, chalk, and lower strata, with the fossils found in each, with admirable clearness. The big theatre was not, of course, full, but there was a large audience, quite up to the average of upwards of five hundred, and any one at all used to such scenes could see how keenly interested they were, and how quick to seize the lecturer's points. Most of the men were in their working clothes, but clean and brushed up, and no lecturer could have wished for a better audience. The only thing that brought back to my mind the slightest remembrance of the old "Vic." was, that by a coster in the centre of the front row of the pit sat a big brindled bull-terrier of the true fighting type. Strange to say, he remained looking at the views with perfect gravity till the lecturer made his bow, when he jumped quietly down at once, and trotted about the pit to find friends, as though he had learned all he could, and wanted to talk it over with pals, but was not interested in the formal vote-of-thanks business. On the three following Tuesdays, as the bills informed me, "The Moon," "The Circulation of the Blood," and "The Backbone of England," were the subjects, all, again, illustrated by dissolving views. And these lectures are kept up on every Tuesday, such speakers as the Dean of Westminster, Sir John Lubbock, Professor Seeley, taking their turn with the purely scientific men, and drawing as good attendances.

You must find room for one specimen of the quick humour of this New Cut audience. Dr. Carpenter, in one of his experiments, dispensed with a prism, explaining to his audience that the objects would now appear inverted, and they must "put them right way up" in their minds,—"or stand on yer 'eds," came the prompt suggestion from the gallery. Out of these lectures science-classes have grown in the last three years, encouraged by a committee, selected from the Council, of some hundred ladies and gentlemen. Of these I have no space to speak; but one fact will indicate the thoroughness of the work done at them. Dr. Fleming's report for 1887 tells us that out of forty students who went in for examination in the several classes, seven obtained first-class, and eighteen second-class certificates. I have only touched on what, after all, is an outgrowth, which has developed naturally from the original scheme, but was no part of it. This was rational and hearty and clean amusement. The Council were determined to test whether an answer could not be found to the straight question of "Poor Potlover" in Punch:—

"Where's this cheap and respectable fun

To be spotted by me? There's the kink!

Don't drink? All serene, if you'll p'int me to summat that's better

than drink.

To that "summat" the Victoria Hall Council, all honour to them, have pointed with quite encouraging success. There is no department of the Hall which is not in a healthy condition, and the fact that £1800 was taken in pennies and twopences for admissions during 1887, though the Hall was closed in the summer for repairs, may well encourage the Council and their devoted manager to take courage and persevere in their present effort to purchase the freehold as a fitting memorial to Mr. Samuel Morley. There was no part of his wide work of philanthropy which that fine old English merchant valued more than this. He supported it lavishly during his life, and had he lived till the freehold came into the market, there would have been little difficulty in raising the necessary sum, £17,000. Of this, £3500 has already been promised by members of the Council, and I cannot believe that the opportunity will be allowed to slip, and the deposit-money of £500 already paid to be forfeited. It seems that the Charity Commissioners have let it be known that the old "Vic." will be accepted by them as one of the People's Palaces for South London, if the freehold can only be obtained; and I cannot for a moment doubt that this will be done if the facts are only fairly known. The teetotalers ought to do all that remains to be done, in gratitude for the best story in their quiver, which they owe to the "Vic." A short meeting is held, called the "Temperance Hour," *outside* the house on Friday nights, at which working men are the speakers. One of them, a carter, stuck fast at the bottom of a hill in the suburbs one day. Another man who was passing, unhitched his own team and helped him up. On an offer to pay being made, the good Samaritan declared he had been paid beforehand. "Why, I never saw you before in my life, did I?" "I've seen you, though," said the other; "I heard you speak one night outside the 'Vic.' and I went in and took the pledge—me and my family has been happy ever since!"

Whitby and the Herring Trade, 30th August 1888.

Any fresh herrings for breakfast, sir? Four a penny this morning, sir!" Such was my greeting this day, as I turned out of my lodgings for an early lungs'-full of this inspiring air. I had almost broken out on that fish-wife with, "Why, you abominable old woman, you asked me twopence for three yesterday"; but restraining my natural, if not righteous indignation, I replied meekly, "Four a penny! Why, what makes them so cheap, ma'am?"

"'T' boats all full—ha'n't had sech a catch this summer," which news gladdened me almost as much as if the catch had been my own. No one can watch these grand fellows, the Dogger Bank fishermen, and not feel, a sort of blood-relationship to them, and the keenest sympathy with their heroic business on the great waters. So, thinks I, I'll go down to the quay directly after breakfast, and see them all at their best, those hard-handed, big-bearded, soft-hearted sea-kings from all the East and South Coast towns of England, from Sunderland to Penzance. When they are such grand, silent, kindly creatures on every day in the week, even when the catch has been poor and light, what will they be to-day?

I had spent most of my mornings for some days on the quay, watching the fish-market there with much interest. It goes on nearly all the forenoon on the pavement, just above that part of the harbour-wall to which the herring-boats run when they come in from their night's work on the Dogger Bank. A simple, hand-to-mouth kind of business, the auction; but well adapted, at any rate, to clear the boats, and get their daily contents to market in the quickest and cheapest way. As soon as a boat comes to the quay, one of the crew (generally numbering five men, or four men and a boy) comes on shore with a basket half-full of herrings, and turns them out on the pavement. The fish-broker who acts for that boat comes up, looks at the sample, and makes an offer for the ship's take by "the lash" or ten thousand. If this is accepted, the unloading begins at once; but if not, as is oftenest the case, the take is put up to auction. The broker rings a bell, which soon brings round him the seven or eight other brokers like himself, and other buyers (if any) who are within hearing. Up goes the first last of ten thousand at once, and no time is lost or talk thrown away. In very few minutes the whole is sold, and a cart or lorry from the railway is standing by to carry off the barrels in which the herrings are packed then and there. Now, on the previous day I had heard the prices ranging from £7: 10s. to £8 for "the last," and had not remarked that only some six boats of the whole fleet had come back from the fishing-grounds, and that none of these had made anything like a big catch. Consequently, I came down prepared to hear something like the same prices ruling, and to see most of the crews drawing at least from £15 to £20 for their night's work.

Well, in a long life I don't remember ever to have been more hopelessly wrong or unpleasantly surprised. I could see at once that all was not right by the faces of the men and women in the small groups scattered about the market, which now drew together as the broker's bell rang for the sale of the herrings, which lay, a lovely, gleaming mass, at least three feet deep in the uncovered hold of the *Mary Jane*, as she rocked gently on the harbour swell, some twenty feet down below us. I could scarcely believe my ears as I heard the bids slowly rising by 5 s. at a time till they reached 30s. the last, and there stopped dead. The hammer fell, and the whole catch of the *Mary Jane* passed to the purchaser in about two minutes at that figure. The next boat, and next but one, did no better. Broker after broker knocked his client's catch down at 30s. Once only I heard an advance on that figure, and this was by private contract. The handsome Hercules, in long leather boots and blue jersey, who represented one of the Whitby boats, appealed in my hearing to the broker, who relented with no very good grace, and agreed to give £2 per last of ten thousand of the catch of Hercules's boat.

It was a depressing sight, I must own, even in the bright sunshine of this most picturesque of English harbours, and Sam Weller's earnest inquiry to his master, "Ain't somebody to be wopped for this?" rose vividly in my mind as the fittest comment on the whole business. Just then a tug which had been getting up steam was ready to leave the harbour, and two Hartlepool smacks, whose freights of herrings were still unsold, hitched on, to be towed out to sea and then run home, in the hope of finding a better market in the Durham port. An old salt stood next me, whose fishing days were well over, and who had just taken a good bite of the blackest kind of pigtail to comfort himself. I looked inquiringly at him as the tug steamed out between the two lighthouses, with the smacks in tow; but he shook his head sorrowfully. "Well, but they can't do worse than here," I remonstrated; "herrings maybe scarcer in the colliery district." He jerked his head towards the little group of brokers and buyers,—"They'd know the prices at Hartlepool in five minutes," he said. This telegraphing was to his mind the worst thing that had happened for fishermen in his time. "Did prices often go up and down like this?" I asked. "Yes," and worse than this. He had known them as low as 15s. and as high as £15 within a few days. No, he couldn't see what was "to odds it" much for the better. Last time he was across at Liverpool he had stopped at a big fish-shop where he saw barrels standing which he recognised. "What's the price of those herrings?" he asked. "Eight for 6d." the man answered. "So I told him I saw they was from Whitby, and that he got them at Whitby for 6d. a hundred."

Whitby and the Herring Trade, 31st August 1888.

I had got thus far last night, and posted down again early this morning to the market, which has a sombre kind of attraction for me. Only two boats in, with light catches of from one and a half to two lasts each. The first sold at £5: 5s., which price the second boat refused. Theirs were a first-rate lot, and they shouldn't go under £6, for which they were holding out when I had to leave, and there seemed to be a general belief that they would get it. This was puzzle enough for any man, to see under his own eyes the same fish sold on three consecutive summer days for £7:10s., £1:10s., and £5:5s.!—a sort of thing no fellow can understand. To add to my bewilderment, I learnt that at Great Grimsby yesterday (the £1:10s. day here) the last had sold for upwards of £15! So that my old salt's view as to the telegraph doesn't quite hold water, and the two smacks which shook the water off their bows and sailed for Hartlepool, may have made a good day's work of it, after all. Indeed, a sailor on the quay declared that they had sold at £5, so that, after paying £2 apiece for the tug, which had towed them all the way, they still got £3 a last, or double the price they would have realised at Whitby. "So it comes to this, that the more fish you catch, the less pay you get," I said to my informant. "Yes," he seemed to think that was mostly the case, adding that to his mind it was the railways that made all the money out of fish—

Sic vos non vobis mellificatis apes.

It is an old story enough, but scarcely less true or sad in 1888 than when most of the world's hardest work was done by slaves. However there are, happily, signs in the air that, here in England at any rate, we are waking up to the truth, that if we can find no better way of organising industry than competition run mad, we are going to have real bad times. Royal Commissions on the sweating system; Toynbee Hall interventions in great strikes; co-operative effort springing up all over the country, and finding its most zealous and devoted advocates at least as much amongst those who don't work with their hands as those who do,—all go to prove that the reign of king *laissez faire*, with his golden rule of "cash payment the sole *nexus* between man and man," is over. Indeed, our danger may soon be from too much meddling with and mothering industry. Nevertheless, no one can spend a few hours on the quay here in the herring season and not long for some one—scholar, philanthropist, political economist (new style), co-operator—to come along and teach these fine fellows to read their sphinx riddle. It would not be, surely, such a difficult task as it looks at first sight. There is no need to begin with the vast herring-fishing industry, with its distant markets at Billingsgate, Liverpool, and Manchester. The reform might begin at once on a modest scale. Beside the herrings, one sees every morning other fish lying on the quay—skate, cod, ling, whiting, rock-salmon—brought in by the smaller and less venturesome boats by dozens, not by lasts of ten thousand. Take the cod as the most valuable of these fish. I saw four fine cod-fish sold by auction yesterday on the quay for 5s. 3d. Within a few hundred yards, and all over the town, cod was selling at the shops at 6d. the pound. Surely a very moderate amount of organising ability would enable those who catch these fish to get the retail prices prevailing on the same day in the home market, and then the experience gained might assist materially in the solution of the larger problem.

Meantime, besides the almost unique interest and beauty of its surroundings,—the steep cliffs, on which the quaint old red-roofed houses, with their wooden balconies, are piled in most picturesque and unaccountable groups; the grand old abbey ruin looking down from the highest point; the swing-bridge between the two harbours, and the estuary beyond, running up into a fine amphitheatre of green meadow and dark wood, dotted with village churches and old windmills, and backed by the high moors,—there is a joyous side to Whitby harbour, even on days when the market goes most against the Dogger Bank fishermen. If the fathers have too often to eat sour grapes, their children's teeth are not set on edge,—such merry, well-fed, bare-footed urchins of both sexes I never remember to have seen elsewhere. They swarm, out of school hours, along the quays; skim up and down the water-worn harbour-walls wherever there is a rope hanging; run over the herring boats lying side by side, as soon as the freights are cleared; and toboggan down the boat slides at the gangways, dragging themselves along on their stomachs when these are not slippery enough for the usual method of descent. There seems, too, to be a large supply of old rickety tubs kept for their special use; for all day long you see two or three of them scrambling into one of these, and sculling about the harbour, no man hindering or apparently noticing them. Finer training for their future life would be hard to find, and one cannot help doubting as one sees their straight toes, as handy almost as fingers in their climbing feats, whether the last word has been spoken as to clothing the human foot, at any rate up to the age of ten or twelve. It is not often, I think, that one comes on early surroundings and heroes entirely suited to each other; but Whitby's hero—patron saint I had nearly called him—could have found no such suitable place to have been raised in all the world round. James Cook was born in a neighbouring village, but first apprenticed on board a Whitby collier, and to the last days of his life retained a most loving remembrance of the old town. Every one of his famous ships, the *Endeavour*, the *Resolution*, and the *Discovery*, were built at Whitby. The house, of his master, Mr. Walker, with whom he lived during his apprenticeship as a sailor lad, and to whom most of his letters were written after he had mapped the Quebec reaches of the St. Lawrence under the fire of the French guns, and was a gold-medallist of the Royal Society and the most famous of eighteenth century navigators, is still fondly pointed out in a narrow street running down to the inner harbour.

Sunday by the Sea, Whitby, 7th September 1888.

We saw something of the industrial life of Whitby last week. The spiritual is quite as interesting, and certainly, so far as my observation goes, has a character of its own, distinct from that of any other of our popular seaside resorts. It may be the presence of so large a seagoing element; at any rate, unless appearances are quite misleading, there is an earnest and deep though quiet religious impulse working amongst the harbour-folk and townspeople, not without its influence in the new quarter which has grown on to the old town, and with its casino and large cricket and lawn tennis grounds, is becoming a popular—though, happily, not a fashionable—summer resort. This is, of course, most apparent on Sundays, on which the absence of anything like the annoyances, both religious and secular, which spoil the day of rest at so many health-resorts, is very noteworthy. Not that Whitby is without its open-air services. On the contrary, they are at least as frequent as elsewhere, on quays, shore, cliffs; but after watching them with some care I do not remember anything fanatical or startling, or in the bad taste of coarse familiarity with mysteries which so often revolts one in street and field preaching elsewhere. One of these I had never seen the like of before, and am inclined to think it may interest your readers. On my first Sunday afternoon I was watching a crowded service on the quay, at the foot of the West Cliff, from above. As it ended, and began to disperse, a man in sailor's Sunday suit of thick blue cloth severed himself from the crowd, and came leisurely up the stone steps, with a Bible and hymn-book in his hand. At the top of the steps is a public grass-plot, some thirty by twenty yards in size, the only part of the sea-front which has escaped enclosure on this cliff. Round it are some fifteen or sixteen benches, very popular with those who will not pay to go into the casino enclosure. They were all occupied by people chatting, smoking, courting, looking at the view, when the newcomer walked into the middle of the plot, took off his fur-trimmed sailor's cap, opened his Bible, and looked round. He was good to look at, with his strong, weather-beaten, bronzed features, short-cropped, grizzled hair, and kindly blue eye, part-owner and best man in one of the Penzance boats, I heard. On looking at him, passages in the lives of Drake and Hawkins, and Wesley and Whitfield, and Charles Kingsley's loving enthusiasm for the Cornish sailor-folk, became clearer to me. Not a soul noticed him or moved from their seats, and the talking, smoking, courting went on just as though he were not there, standing alone on the grass, Bible in hand. I quite expected to see him shut his book and depart. Not a bit of it. Clearly he had come up there to deliver his testimony. That was his business; whether any one chose to listen to it or not, was theirs. So he read out two or three verses from the Epistle to the Romans, and began to preach. His subject was Paul's conversion, which he described almost entirely in St. Luke's and the Apostle's own words, which he quoted without referring to his Bible, and then urged roughly, but with an earnestness which made his speech really eloquent, that the same chance was open to every one. He himself had heard the call thirty years ago, and had been happy ever since. He had been in peril of death again and again since then, had seen boats founder with all hands, but had no fear, nor need any man have, by sea or land, who would just hear and follow that call. Then he stopped, wiped his brow, and looked round. The sitters had all become silent, but not a soul of them moved or spoke. I was standing, with one or two others, behind the high rails of the enclosure, or I think we should have gone and stood by him as he gave out a hymn; but we knew neither words nor tune, so were helpless. He sang it through by himself, made a short prayer "that the word that day might not have been spoken in vain," and then put on his cap, and went down the steps into the crowd below. One voice from the benches said "Thank you!" as he left the plot.

The next service I came across was a strange contrast. Under the cliff, in front of the Union Jack planted in the sands, was a large gathering, composed mostly of children sitting in rows, with mothers and nurses interspersed, and a number of men and women standing round the circle. As I came up, I was handed a leaflet of hymns, which explained that it was a gathering of the "Children's Special Service Mission," which has its head-quarters, it seems, in London, and is presided over by Mr. Stuart, the vicar of St. James's, Holloway. The service was conducted by a young man not in orders, with a strong choir to help him. He, too, did his preaching earnestly and well; and though it seemed to me above the younger children's heads, who for the most part made sand-castles or mud-pies furtively, was evidently listened to sympathetically by the elder part of the audience who stood round. But if the teaching scarcely touched the children, they all left their mud-pies and enjoyed the singing. The Mission, I was told, holds these services on the sands through the seaside season, at all the chief resorts on the coast. The leaders and organisers are mostly young men and women, and all, I believe, volunteers. A noteworthy sign of our time the Mission seemed to me, and I was glad to hear that it is countenanced, if not actively supported, by the resident Church clergy.

If we turn from the volunteer to the regular side of Church work, Whitby still has an almost unique attraction for the student of the religious movement in England. The late Dean Stanley, who loved every phase of the historical development of the life of the National Church, and mourned over the thoroughness of recent restorations, which, as he thought, threaten the entire disappearance of the surroundings and forms of the worship of the Georgian era, would have thanked God and taken courage if he could have visited Whitby Parish Church in 1888, for church and service are a perfect survival. The wave of Victorian ecclesiastical reform, without destroying anything, seems to have gently removed all that was really objectionable, and breathed new life into the dry bones of Georgian worship. I am not sure that I should say "everything objectionable," for probably the vast majority of even truly Catholic church-goers would not agree as to the big shield with the national arms which hangs over the centre of the chancel arch, dividing the two tables of the Ten Commandments. I am prepared to admit that this particular lion and unicorn are not good specimens of discreet beasts of their respective kinds. But even as they stand they are national symbols, and no reminder that Church and nation are still one can be spared nowadays; and they are not half so grotesqile as most of the gurgoyles you will see in the noblest Gothic cathedrals. And then they vividly remind my generation of the days when they first toddled to church in the family procession. The church itself is a gem, though with no orthodox architectural beauty, for it retains traces of the handiwork of thirty generations in its walls, pillars, galleries, and stunted square tower,—from the round arches (there are still two, though the best, a fine Norman window, has been bricked up) of its earliest builders in the twelfth, to the white-washed walls and ceilings and square-paned windows of eighteenth century churchwardens. I should think the three-decker (I am obliged to use the profane name, having forgotten the correct one), the clerk's desk, reading-desk, and pulpit rising one above the other in front of the chancel, must be unique, the last of its race. The clerk has, indeed, retired into the choir; but the rector still reads the prayers and lessons admirably from his desk, and ascends the pulpit, where he is on a level with the faculty pew of the squire, and the low galleries, to deliver his excellent short discourses. Long may he and his successors do so. One is only inclined to regret that he does not take off his surplice in the reading-desk, and ascend to preach in his black gown. Curious it is to remember that less than thirty years ago Bryan King and others excited riots in many parishes by preaching in the surplice. The pews on the floor are all high oaken boxes with doors, though the great majority of them are now free. The visitor in broadcloth is put into one of the larger ones, lined with venerable baize, once green. These are somewhat narrow parallelograms with seats round the three sides, so that it requires caution in kneeling to avoid collision with your opposite neighbour. And the body of the church being nearly square by reason of the addition of side aisles at different periods, and the "three-decker" well out on the floor, the pews have been planned so that they all face towards it, and consequently all the congregation can see each other. This is supposed to be a drawback to worship; probably is—must be, where people have been always used to looking all one way. That it really hinders a hearty service, no one would maintain who has attended one in Whitby Parish Church. It was quite full, when I was there, of a congregation largely composed of men, and the majority of these sailors and other working folk. Let any reader who still goes to church make a point of ascending the 190 stone steps which lead up to it from the old town, and looking at the matter with his own eyes, if ever he should be within reach. The rector is a sort of successor to the old abbots of St. Hilda, with ecclesiastical jurisdiction over the whole town, wherein are five or six churches worked by curates, all in the modern style, seats facing eastward, no three-deckers, surpliced choirs, and chanted psalms, and canticles. Indeed, in one place of worship, those who have a taste for gabbled prayers, bowings and posturings, lighted candles, and the rest of the most modern ritual, can find it, but in a proprietary chapel not under the jurisdiction of the rector.

Singing-Matches in Wessex, 28th September 1888.

I remember, sir, that some quarter of a century ago, you were interested in the popular songs of our English country-folk, and so may possibly think gleanings in this field still worthy of notice. In that belief, I send this note of some "singing-matches," which, by a lucky chance, I was able to attend last week in West Berks. The matches in question were for both men and women, a prize of half a crown being offered in each case. The occasion was the village "veast," or annual commemoration of the dedication of the parish church, still the immemorial day of gathering and social reunion in every hamlet of this out-of-the-way district. I was glad to find the old word still in use, for as a Wessex man it would have been an unpleasant shock to me to find the "veast" superseded by a "festival," habitation, or other modern gathering. In some respects, however, I must own that the character of the "veast" has changed; these singing-matches, for instance, being a complete novelty to me. There used to be singing enough after the sports, as the sun went down, and choruses, rollicking and sentimental, came rolling out of the publicans' booths—for the most part of dubious character—but singing-matches for prizes I never remember. I suppose the craze for competitive examination in every department of life may account for this new development; anyhow, there were the matches to come off—so the bills assured us—in the village schoolroom, of all places, which was thrown open for this purpose, and for dancing, at sunset. Hither, then, I repaired from the vicar's fields, where the sports had been held, in the wake of a number of rustic couples and toffee-sucking children. The school is a lofty room, fifty feet long, with a smaller class-room as transept at the upper end, along which ran a temporary platform. Upon this the Farringdon Blue-Ribbon Band, in neat uniforms, were already playing a vigorous polka. Presently this first dance ended, the band stood back, and the three judges coming to the front, announced the terms of the competition, the men to begin, and a dance to be interpolated after every two songs, every singer, one at a time, to come up on the platform. There was no hesitation amongst the singers, the first of whom stepped up at once, and so the matches went on, two songs and a dance alternately, until all who cared to compete had sung. Then, at about 9 P.M., the prizes were awarded, and I left, the dancing going on merrily for another two hours.

I was amused by the award of the men's prize to the singer of a vociferously applauded ditty, entitled "The Time o' Day," for it showed that the keenest zest of the Wessex rustic is still, as it was thirty years ago, to get a rise out of—or, in modern slang, to score off—"thaay varmers." It began:—

A straanger wunst in Worcestershèer,

A gen'lman he professed,

He lived by takin' o' people in,

He wuz so nicely dressed.

Wi' my tol-de-rol, etc.

This stranger, having a gold chain round his neck, swaggers in the farmers' room on market-day, till—

He zets un in a big arm-cheer,

And, bein' precious deep,

Sticks out his legs, drows back his arms,

And "gammots" off to sleep.

The farmers canvas him, and doubt if he has any watch to his chain. His friend, "by them not understood," pulls out the chain, shows a piece of wood at the end, and puts it back. The stranger wakes; the farmers ask him "the time o' day"; he excuses himself, on the plea that last night, having taken a glass too much, he did not wind up his watch. At this—

The varmers said, and did protest,

Ez sure ez we're alive,

Thet thee dost not possess a watch

Of pounds we'll bet thee vive.

The stranger covers the bets, pulls out a piece of wood, touches a spring, and shows a watch inside:—

'Bout vifty pounds thaay varmers lost,

Which in course thaay hed to paay,

And the bwoys run arter'em down the street,

Wi' "Gee us the time O' daay."

Wi' my tol-de-rol, etc.

I did not, however, concur in the award myself. I should have given the prize for a love-song, a sort of rustic rendering of "Phyllis is my only Joy," the chorus of which ran:—

For ef you would, I'm sure you could

Jest let a feller know;

Ef it strikes you as it likes you,

Answer yes or no.

The judges, however, followed, if (two being "varmers") they did not thoroughly sympathise with, the obvious feeling of the crowded room. The patriotic songs, I noticed, had quite changed their character. They never were of the vulgar jingo kind in Wessex, but there used to be much of the old Dibdin and tow-row,-row ring about them. "The Poor Little Soldier Boy" may be taken as a specimen of the new style. His father dies of wounds; he 'lists; comes home; is discharged; wanders starving, till, opposite a fine gate, he sinks down, asking the unknown inmates how they will like to find him, "dead at their door in the morn." At this crisis a lady appears, who takes him in and provides for him for life. The only lines I carried away were from a song even more pacific in tone than "The Poor Little Soldier Boy." They ran:—

Ef I wur King o' France,

Or, better, Pope o' Rome,

I'd hev no fightin' men abroad,

Nor weepin' maids at home.

But there was an approach to "waving the flag" amongst the women, one of whom, a strapping damsel, sang:—

We've got the strength of will,

And old England's England still,

And every other nation knows it—"rather"!

which word "rather" ended every verse of a somewhat vulgar ditty. She did not get the prize, nor did the matron whom I fixed on as the winner, who sang without a hitch a monotonous and, I began to think, never-ending ballad on the rivalries of "young Samuèl" and one "Barnewell" for the graces of an undecided young woman. The attention with which this somewhat dreary narrative was listened to deceived me, for the prize went, without public protest, to a young woman of whose song I could not catch a line, though I could just gather that it was feebly sentimental. My impression is that it was her bright eyes, and pretty face and figure, that carried it with the judges, rather than her singing. If I am right, it will neither be the first nor last time that the prizes in this world fall to *tes beaux yeux*.

The school faces the upper end of the village green, and I left it so crowded that it was a wonder how the dancers could get along at all with their polkas and handkerchief dances, the latter a kind of country dance, which were the only ones in vogue. When I got out, I saw lighted booths at the other end of the green, and went down to inspect. It was a melancholy sight.

There was the publican's dancing-booth without a soul in it. One swing only was occupied in the neighbouring acrobatic apparatus, and the round-about was motionless. The gipsies were there, ready and eager to tell fortunes, and with a well-lighted alley for throwing at cocoa-nuts with bowls rather larger than cricket-balls—the most modern and popular substitute, I am told, for skittles. There they were, but not a customer in sight, the only human being but myself being the solitary county policeman, who patrolled the green with most conscientious regularity, only slackening his pace for a moment or two as he passed under the bright open windows of the schoolroom, from which the merry dance-music came streaming out into the moonlight. I could almost find it in my heart to pity the publican and gipsies, so overwhelming did their defeat seem, for not a glass of beer had been allowed all day in the vicar's fields, where the cricket-match had been played and all the races run, on milk, tea, or aerated waters. The whole stock of these last beverages, supplied from the "Hope Coffee Room," which has faced the public-house on the village green now for about three years, was drunk out before the dancing ended and the school closed on "veast" night, to the exceeding joy of the vicar's niece and her lieutenants, two bright Cornish damsels, handy, devoted, and ardent teetotalers. These three have been fighting the publicans since 1886, when they started the "Hope Coffee Room," supplied with bread, butter, and cakes from the vicarage, and aerated drinks and light literature, all, I take it, at something under cost price, though this the three ardent damsels will by no means admit. The vicar, who is no teetotaler himself, shrugs his shoulders laughingly, plays his fiddle, pays the bills, and lets them have their own way, with an occasional protest that some night he shall have his barn and ricks burnt. There is, however, no real danger of this, as he has lived with and for his poor for more than thirty years with scarcely one Sunday's break, and gipsy or publican would get short shrift who damaged him or anything that is his. I found him quite ready to admit the great improvement which is apparent in the "veast," as in many other phases of rustic life, though he cannot get over, or look with anything but dislike and distrust at, the cramming and examining system, which, as he mourns, embitters the only time in the lives of his poor children which used to be really happy, when they could play about on the village green and in the lanes regardless of Inspector and Government grant. Nor am I sure that he does not look with regret at the disappearance of cudgel-playing and wrestling out of the programme of the yearly "Veast-Sports." Cricket, fine game as it is, does hot bring out quite the same qualities. No doubt there were now and then bad hurts in those sports, and fights afterwards; but these came from beer, and might happen just as easily over cricket. So he muses, and I rather sympathise. As has been well sung by the ould gamester:—

Who's vor a bout O' vrendly plaay,

As never should to anger move,

Sech spworts be only meant for thaay

As likes their mazzards broke for love.

But I should be sorry to believe that there are fewer youngsters to-day in the West country who "likes their mazzards broke for love" than there used to be half a century ago.

The Divining-Rod, 21st September 1889.

About a quarter of a century ago, I had the chance of seeing some experiments in the search for water by the use of "the divining rod" on a thirsty stretch of the Berkshire chalk range. Oddly enough (what a lot of odd things there are lying all round us!) at the highest points of this very range you might come on "dew-ponds," which never seemed to run dry, though how the white chalky water got there, or kept there, no one, I believe, has ever been able to explain from that day to this. But these "dew-ponds" were of no use, of course, to the cottages scattered along the hillside, and whoever wanted spring-water, had to go down about 400 feet for it. Well, I neglected that chance, and ever since have been regretting it.

My notion of the water-diviner was gathered from Sir Walter's famous portrait of Dousterswivel in the *Antiquary*; a fellow "who amongst fools and womankind talks of the Cabala, the divining-rod, and all the trumpery with which the Rosicrucians cheated a darker age, and which, to our eternal disgrace, has in some degree revived in our own." I was resolved that the revival should in no case be forwarded by me, and so lost my opportunity, and have been ever since tantalised by reports of marvels wrought by the hazel-wand, as to which I was quite at a loss to form any reasonable opinion. It was with no little satisfaction, therefore, that I received, and accepted, an invitation to assist at a water-search about to be undertaken by a diviner of considerable reputation in the outskirts of Deer Leap Wood, in the parish of Wootton, Surrey.

This wood, notable even amongst the loveliest of that favoured county, belongs to the worthy representative of the author of *Sylva* and the *Memoirs*, who, having built some excellent cottages on its confines, desires to find the occupants a good supply of spring-water *in situ*. Accordingly a group of us, men and women of all ages, and of all degrees of scepticism—for I doubt if there was a single believer in the efficacy of the rod, though the squire himself and a friend preserved a judicious silence—gathered last Friday after breakfast on the lawn before Wootton House, to await the arrival of the water-doctor, whom the agent had gone to meet at the station. It was agreed on all hands that a preliminary test should be applied, and that the lawn on which we stood offered quite admirable facilities for this purpose. For, more than two hundred years ago, John Evelyn had diverted a portion of the stream, which runs down the valley in which the house stands, for the purpose of making a fountain on the terraces. (Let it be noted in passing, that the lead-work of that fountain has needed no repair from that day to this! There *were* plumbers in those days!) From this fountain two pipes carry the water into the house, under the lawn on which we stood. Now the lawn turf is as smooth as a billiard-table, without the slightest indication of the whereabouts of these pipes, which indeed was only known vaguely to the squire, and not at all to any one else of those present. If the divining-rod could discover these, the experiment at "Deer Leap Wood" might be undertaken with good hope.

Well, the doctor, conducted by the steward, arrived in due course, a stout middle-aged man, of the stamp of a high-class mechanic; plain and straightforward in speech, and with no pretence whatever to mystery. In answer to our questions, he said: "He couldn't tell how it came about; but of this he was sure, that he could find springs and running water. Thirty years ago he was working as a mason at Chippenham, with a Cornish miner amongst others. He saw this man find water with the rod; had then tried it himself, and found he could do it. That was all he knew. Any one*of us might have the same power. Why, two young gentlemen who saw him working at Warleigh, near Bath, had copied him, and found a spring right under their father's library." We listened, and then proposed that he should just try about the lawn. He produced a hazel twig shaped like a Y, the arms, each some eighteen inches long; the point, perhaps, six inches. I may note, however, that the dimensions can be of no consequence, for he used at least half a dozen in his trials, cutting them at random out of the hazel-bush as we walked along, and taking no measure of any of them. Taking an arm of the Y between the middle fingers of each hand, he walked across the lawn slowly, stooping slightly forward, so as to keep the point downwards, about a foot from the ground. He had not gone a dozen yards before the rod quivered, and then the point rose at once straight up into the air. "There's running water here," he said, "and close to the surface." We marked the spot and followed him, and some twenty-five yards further the point of the Y again sprang up into the air. The steward, who knew the plans accurately, was appealed to, and admitted that these were the precise spots under which the pipes ran. In answer to the suggestion that the point sprang up by pressure of his fingers, voluntary or involuntary, he asked two of us to hold the arms beyond his fingers, and see if we could prevent the point rising. We did so (I being one), and did all we could to keep it pointed downwards, but it rose in spite of us, and I watched his hands carefully at the same time and could detect no movement whatever of the muscles. Then he broke one of the arms, all but the bark, and still the point rose as briskly as ever. Lastly, he proposed that each of us should try if we had the power. We did so, but without success, except that in the case of Mrs. Evelyn and another lady the point trembled, and seemed inclined, though unable, to rise. He then took hold of their wrists, and at once it rose, nearly as promptly as it had done with him. This was enough; and we started in procession, on ponies, in carriage^, or walking, to Deer Leap Wood, where in the course of an hour he marked with pegs some half dozen spots, under which running water will be found at from 70 feet to 100 feet. He did not pretend to be able to give the exact depth, but only undertook to give the outside limits. And so we all went back to lunch, and Mullins took his fee and departed. I know, sir, that you have many scientific readers, and can picture to myself the smile tinged with scorn with which they will turn to your next page when they get thus far. Well, I own that the boring remains to be done, the results of which I hope to send you in due course. Meantime, let me remind them of a well-known adventure of one of the most famous of their predecessors towards the end of last century. Sir Joseph Banks, botanising on the downs on a cloudless June day, came across a shepherd whom he greeted with the customary "Fine day,"—"Ees," was the reply, "but there'll be heavy rain yet, afore night." Sir Joseph passed on unheeding, and got a thorough drenching before he reached his inn. Next morning he went back, found the shepherd, and put a guinea in his hand, with "Now, my man, tell me how you knew there was going to be rain yesterday afternoon."

"Whoy," said Hodge, with a grin, "I zeed my ould ram a shovin' hisself back'ards in under thuck girt thornin bush; and wenever a doos that there'll sartin sure be heavy rainfall afore sundown."

Note.—Water was found where it was expected by the Diviner, and this well is now used by the tenants of the Deer Leap Cottages.—October 1895.

Sequah's "Flower of the Prairie," Chester, 26th March 1890.

"Why, what on earth can this be?" I asked of the man who stood next me in the Foregate some ten days ago, as we paused at a crossing to allow the strange object which had drawn from me the above ejaculation to pass on, with its attendant crowd. It was a mighty gilded waggon, certainly fourteen feet long by six feet or seven feet broad. It was drawn by four handsome bays. On two raised seats at the front sat eight men, English, I fancy, every man of them, but clad over their ordinary garments in long leather coats with fringes, such as our familiar Indians wear in melodrama, and in the broad-brimmed, soft felts of the Western cowboy. They were all armed with brass instruments and made the old streets resound with popular airs. Behind these raised seats, in the body of the waggon, rode some half dozen, including three strapping brown men, Indians, I fancy they pose for, but they looked to me more like the half-castes whom one sees on the Texan and Mexican ranches on the Bio Grande. They also were clad in fringed leather coats, and wore sombreros over their long black locks. The sides of the waggon, where not gilt, were panelled with mirrors, on which were emblazoned the Stars and Stripes and other coloured devices. Altogether, the thing seemed to me well done in its way, whatever it might mean; and I turned inquiringly to my neighbour and repeated my question, as the huge gilded van and its jubilant followers passed away down the station road. "Oh! 'tis the 'Merikin chap, as cures folks's rheumatics and draws their teeth."

"He must draw something more than their teeth," I said, "to keep up all that show." My neighbour grinned assent. "He've drawed pretty nigh all the loose money as is going hereabouts already," he said as we parted. "One more quack to fleece the poor," I thought, as I walked on. "Well, anyhow, they get a show for their shillings; that van beats Barnum!"

In this mind I reached the vicarage of one of our biggest city parishes to which I was bound. "I don't know about quack," said the vicar, when I had detailed my adventure on the way, using that disparaging phrase; "but this I do know, that I have given over writing certificates for my poor from downright shame, the demand is so great." And then he explained that the "medicineman," whose stage name was Sequah, made no charge to any patient who brought a clergyman's certificate of poverty; that the van had now been in the town above a week; and at first he, the vicar, had given such certificates freely, both for treatment (tooth-drawing) and for the medicines, but now refused except in the case of the very poorest. No! not because Sequah was an impostor; on the contrary, he had done several noteworthy cures—at any rate temporary cures—on some of the vicar's own parishioners: notably in the case of one old man who had been drawn up to the van in a wheel-chair. He had had rheumatism for two years, which had quite disabled him, and was in great pain when he got on the platform. After he had been treated he walked down the steps without help, and wheeled his chair home himself. Unluckily, Sequah had advised him to get warm woollen underclothing, and on his pleading that he had not the money to buy it, had given him a sovereign. This so elated him that he felt quite a new man, and could not help breaking his sovereign on the way home to give the new man a congratulatory glass at a favourite pot-house. This had thrown him back, and his knees were a little stiff again, but the pain had not returned even in this case.

After such testimony from a thoroughly trustworthy and matter-of-fact witness, I resolved to see this strange thing with my own eyes, and went off straight from the vicarage to the scene of action, to which the vicar directed me. This was an old tan-yard about half an acre in extent, and was full of people when I arrived, the space immediately round the waggon being densely crowded. It was drawn up in the middle of the plot. The eight brass-bandsmen had wheeled round so as to look down from their raised benches on the floor of the waggon, on which was a large leather chair. In front of the chair, speaking to the crowd from the end of the waggon, stood a tall figure, in a finer kind of leather-fringed coat, ornamented with rows of blue, red, and white beads. At first glance I thought it was a woman from the fineness of the features, and masses of long, light hair falling on the shoulders. A second glance, however, showed me that it was a man, and a vigorous and muscular one too. He was explaining that the medicines he was going to sell presently were not "scientific," but "natural" medicines, "compounded of the water of a Californian spring and certain botanic ingredients"! I will not trouble you with a list of all the ailments they will cure if taken steadily and in sufficient doses, but get on at once to the performance. Having finished his speech, he put on his sombrero, took up a pair of forceps from a table on which a row of them were displayed, and stood by the chair. Upon this, advanced an apparently endless line of men, women, and children, marshalled by the Indians who stood at the foot of the steps. One by one they came up, sat down in the chair, passed under Sequah's hands, and descended the steps on the other side of the waggon into the wondering crowd, while the band discoursed vigorous and continuous music. I watched him draw at least fifty teeth in less than as many minutes. The patient just sat down, opened his mouth, pointed to the peccant tooth, and it was out in most cases before he could wink. There were perhaps three or four cases (of adults) in which things did not go quite so smoothly, and one— that of a young woman, who seized her bonnet and rushed down the steps in evident pain and rage—after which he stopped the band, and explained to us that her tooth was so decayed that he had had to break the stump in the jaw. This he had done, and should have taken the pieces out without causing any further pain, if she had just waited a few more seconds. There are rumours flying round that the infirmary is crowded daily with patients in agonies from broken fangs which have been left in by Sequah. On the other hand, two of our doctors whom I have met admit that he is a very remarkable "extractor," and has first-rate instruments.

There were still crowds waiting their turn when he finished his tooth-drawing for the day, and announced that he would now treat a case of rheumatism. Thereupon, an elderly man—who gave his name and address, and stated that he had been rheumatic for twelve years, unable to walk for two, and was now in great pain—was carried up the steps and put in the chair. Then buffalo-robes were brought by the Indians, two of whom held them up so as to conceal Sequah and the third, a rubber, who remained inside with the patient. Then the brass band struck up boisterously, the buffalo-robe screen was agitated here and there, and a strong and very pungent smell (not unlike hartshorn) spread all round. I timed them, and at the end of eighteen minutes the buffalo-robes were lowered, and there was the old man dressed again and seated in the chair. The band stopped. Sequah asked the old man if he felt any pain now. He replied, "No," and then was told to walk to the front of the platform, which he did; then to get down the ladder, walk round the waggon amongst the crowd, and come up on the other side, which he did, looking, I must say, as astonished as I was, at his own performance. Then six or seven men, mostly elderly, came up and declared that they had been similarly treated, and were wonderfully better, some of them quite cured and at work again. Then Sequah invited any person who had been treated by him or taken his medicines and were none the better, to come up into the waggon and tell us about it, as that was their proper place and not below. This offer seemed quite *bona fide*, but it did not impress me, as I doubt whether any protesting patient would have had much chance of ascending the steps, which were kept by the Indians and their able-bodied confederates. No one answering, two big portmanteaus were brought up, out of which he began to sell his medicines at a dollar (4s.) the set—two bottles and two small packets. The rush to be served began, people crushing and struggling to get near enough to hand up their hats or caps with 4s. in them, which were returned with the medicines in them. I watched for at least ten minutes, when, there being apparently no end to the purchases, I strolled away, musing on the strange scene, and wondering what the attraction can be in the Bohemian life which could induce a man of this evident power to wander about the world in a gilded waggon, in a ridiculous costume, and talking transparent clap-trap, to sell goods which apparently want no lies telling about them.

I may add that I went again last Saturday, when there was even a greater crowd, and an older and more severe case of rheumatism was treated with quite as great (apparent) success.

French Popular Feeling, 15th August 1890.

I doubt if any of your readers has less sympathy than I with the yearning to go back twenty, thirty, or forty years (as the case may be), which seems to be a note of contemporary literature, and therefore, I take it, of the average mind of the men and women of our day, who have passed out of their first youth. "The Elixir of Life," which Bulwer dreamed and wrote of, which should restore youth, with its bounding pulses and golden locks, its capacity for physical enjoyment, and for building castles in Spain, I think I may say with confidence I would not drink four times a day, with twenty minutes' promenade between the glasses (as I am just now drinking of the *source Cosar* here), even if an *elixir vito source* were to come bubbling up to-morrow in this enchanting Auvergne valley, and our English doctor here at Royat—known to all readers of Mr. *Punch's* "Water Course"—were to put it peremptorily on my treatment-paper to-morrow morning. It is not surely the "*good fellows* whose beards are gray," who sigh over the departure of muscular force, and sure quickness of eye and nerve, which enabled them in years gone by to jump five-barred gates or get down to leg-shooters. They are glad to see the boys doing these things, and rejoicing in them; but, for themselves, do not desire any more to jump five-barred gates or get down to leg-shooters. They have learned the wise man's lesson, that there is a time for all things, and that those who linger on life's journey and fancy they can still occupy the pleasant roadside places after their part of the column has passed on ahead, will surely find themselves in the way of, and be shouldered out by, the next division, without a chance of being able to regain their place in the line, side by side with old comrades and contemporaries.

But it is one thing to fall out of the line of march of one's own accord, from an unwise hankering after roadside pleasures, and quite another to have to fall out because one can no longer keep one's old place in the column by reason of failing wind, or muscle, or nerve; and the man of sense who feels his back stiffening, or his feet getting tender, will do well to listen to such hints betimes, and betake himself at once to whatever place or regimen holds out the best hope of enabling him to keep step once more, till the day is fairly over and the march done. It is for this reason, at any rate, that I find myself at Royat, from which I have been assured by more than one trustworthy friend who has tested the waters, that I shall return after three weeks "with new tissues," and "fit to fight for my life." I don't see any prospect of having to fight for my life in my old age, though one can't be too confident with the new Radicalism looming up so menacingly, and am very well content with my old tissues, if they can' only be got into fair working order again, of which I already begin to think there is good prospect here, though my experience of the *sources* "Eugénie" and "Cæsar" is as yet not a week old.

It is more than twenty years since I have written to you from France over this signature, and since that time I have only been once in Paris, for two days on business. The gay city is much less changed than I expected to find it, so far as one can judge from a drive across it from the Gare de l'Ouest to the Gare de Lyon, and a stroll (after depositing luggage at the latter station) along the Rue de Rivoli and the Quais, and through the streets of the old city. The clearance which has left an open space in front of Notre Dame, so that one can get a good view of the western front, seemed to me the most noteworthy improvement. The great range of public buildings and offices which have been added to the Louvre are stately and impressive, but cannot make up for the disappearance of the Tuileries. The Eiffel Tower is a great disappointment. All buildings should be either beautiful or useful; but it is neither, and only seems to dwarf all the other buildings. But one change impressed me grievously. Where are all the daintily dressed women and children gone to? Perhaps the world of fashion may be out of town; but there must be some two millions of people left in Paris, a quarter of them at least well-to-do citizens, and able to give as much care as of old to their toilets. Nevertheless, I assure you, I sought in vain for one really dainty figure such as one used to meet by the score in every street. Can twenty years of the true Republic have made La Belle France dowdy? It is grievous to think of it, and I hope to be undeceived before I get back amongst the certainly better got-up women of my native land.

For my nine hours' journey south, I bought a handful of the cheap illustrated papers—*Le Grelot, Le Troupier*, and others—which seem to be as much the daily intellectual fare of the French travelling public as (I regret to say) *Tit-Bits* and its congeners are, at any rate in my part of England. Of course it is always difficult to know what "the people" are thinking or caring about; but to get at what they read must be not a bad test. A perusal of these certainly surprised me favourably, especially in this respect, that they were almost entirely free from the pruriency which is so generally supposed to be the characteristic of modern French literature.

I wish I could speak half as favourably of the attitude of France, so far as these journals disclose it, towards her neighbours; but this is about as bad as it can be, touchy, jealous, and unfair, all round. Take, for instance, the *Troupier*, which is specially addressed to the Army. The cartoon represents the "Grand Jeu de Massacre," at which all passers-by are invited to join free of charge. The *jeu* consists of throwing at a row of puppets, citizens of Alsace-Lorraine, in which a brutal German soldier is indulging, while the French "Ministre des Affaires (qui lui sont) Etrangères" slumbers peacefully on a neighbouring seat. But we come off at least as badly as Germany. In a vigorous leader, entitled "Une Reculade," on the Zanzibar Question, after a very bitter opening against England—"il n'y a guère de pays qui n'ait été roulé dupé et volé par elle,"—the *Troupier* breaks into a song of triumph over the backing-down of England, "flanquée d'Allemagne et de ses alliés," before the resolute attitude of France. "Cette reculade," it ends, "de nos ennemis indique suffisamment que La France a repris la place et le rang qui lui conviennent, et qu'elle est de taille à se faire respecter partout et par tous. C'est tout ce que nous desirions." In all commercial and industrial matters we are equally grasping and unscrupulous. There seems to be just now a great stir in the sardine industry, and, so far as I can make out, English and American Companies seem to be competing for a monopoly of that savoury little fish. It is, however, upon the English "Sardine Union Company, Limited"—"qui s'appelle en France, Société Générale de l'Industrie Sardinière de France"—that the vials of journalistic wrath are being emptied. "Sept polichinelles," it would seem, have subscribed for one share each, and the whole scheme is utterly rotten. Nevertheless, this bogus Company threatens to buy up all the sardine manufactories in France at fancy prices, and, the control being in England, will manufacture there all the metal boxes, and will build all the fishing-boats over there, "au détriment de nos constructeurs Français," and so on, and so on. I was getting quite melancholy over all these onslaughts on my native country, when I came upon a topic which alone seems to excite the petit-journaliste more than the sins of the long-toothed Englishman—viz. those of priests and their followers and surroundings. Here is a comic example, over which the Grelot foams in trenchant and sarcastic but incredibly angry sentences. A Belgian Council has decided to divide the 500 fr. which it has voted to the "Institut Pasteur," the vote being "pour M. Pasteur et pour St. Hubert." This remarkable vote was carried on the pleading of a Deputy, who, after paying homage to M. Pasteur, added: "C'est un grand homme qui a opéré des cures merveilleuses; seulement il y a un autre grand homme, qui depuis onze cent soixante-trois années a opéré des miracles, c'est St. Hubert—M. Pasteur devra travailler longtemps avant d'en arriver là." I am afraid you will have no room for more than one of the scathing sentences in which the writer tosses this unlucky vote backwards and forwards: "M. Pasteur acceptera-t-il de partager les 500 fr. avec St. Hubert (adresse inconnue), ou St. Hubert refusera-t-il de partager avec M. Pasteur (adresse connue)?—'That is the question/ comme disait le nommé Shakespeare."

It was in the midst of such instructive if not entirely pleasant reading, that I arrived at Clermont, the old capital of Auvergne, by far the most interesting town I have been in this quarter of a century, not excepting Chester. From thence, one comes up to Roy at, about three miles, in an electric tramway, or by 'bus or cab.

Royat les Bains, 23rd August 1890.

Some thirty years ago, more or less, I remember reading with much incredulous amusement Sir Francis Head's "Bubbles of the Brunnen." It was in the early days of the Saturday Review, when the infidel Talleyrand gospel of surtout jooint de zèle was being preached to young England week by week in those able but depressing columns. I, like the rest of my contemporaries, was more or less affected by the cold water virus, and was certainly inclined to look from the superior person standpoint on what I could not but regard as the outpourings of the second childhood of an eccentric septuagenarian, who was really asking us to believe that the Schwalbach waters were as miraculously potent as the thigh-bone of St. Glengulphus, of which is it not written in *The In-goldsby Legends*:—

And cripples, on touching his fractured *os femoris*,

Threw down their crutches and danced a quadrille.

I need scarcely say to you, sir, that it is many years since I have been thoroughly disabused of this depressing heresy; but perhaps one never quite recovers from such early demoralisation. At any rate, now that I find myself approaching Sir Francis's age, and much in his frame of mind when he blew his exhilarating bubbles, I can't quite make up my mind to turn myself loose, as he did, and in Lowell's words, "pour out my hope, my fear, my love, my wonder," upon you and your readers. The real fact, however, stated in plain (Yankee) prose is, that Schwalbach (I have been there) "is not a circumstance" to this refuge for the victim of gout, rheumatism, eczema, dyspepsia, and I know not how many more kindred maladies, amongst the burnt-out volcanoes of the Department Puy-de-Dome. Nevertheless, you may fairly say, and I should agree, that my ten days' experience of the effect of the waters is scarcely sufficient to make me a trustworthy witness as to the healing properties of these springs. Twenty-one days is the prescribed course, and as I am as yet but half through, I will not "holloa till I am out of the wood," but will try in the first place to give you some idea of this Royat les Bains and its surroundings.

Let us look out from this third-floor window at which I am writing, on the highest guest-floor of the topmost hotel in Royat, to which a happy chance (or my good angel, if I have one) led me on my arrival. I look out across a narrow valley, from three to four hundred yards wide, upon a steep hill which forms its opposite side. They say this hill is a burnt-out volcano. However that may be, it is now clothed with vineyards on all but the almost precipitous places where the rock peeps out. On the highest point, against the sky-line, stands out a small white house, calling itself the Hôtel de l'Observatoire, from which there must be a magnificent view; but how it is to be reached I have not yet learned, for there is no visible road or footpath, and the peasants object to one's attempting the ascent through the vineyards. The valley winds up round this hill, taking a turn to the north, our side widening out and sweeping back behind Royat Church and village, to which the retreating hill behind forms a most picturesque background. For, on the lower slope, just above the houses, are stretches of bright green meadow, interspersed amongst irregular clumps of oak; above this comes a brown-red belt of rough ground, growing heather and wild strawberries; and, again above that, all along the brow, are dense pine woods. The constant changes of colour which this southern sun brings out all day long on this hillside make it difficult to break away from one's window and descend to the *établissement* to drink waters and take baths. This institution lies down at the bottom of the valley I have been describing, some 200 feet below this window, and 150 feet below the broad terrace which is thrown out from the ground-floor of this hotel. From the terrace a rough zigzag path leads down to the brook, which rushes down from Royat village in a succession of tiny waterfalls, sending up to us all day the murmur of running water. On reaching the brook's bank, we have about one hundred yards to walk by its side, when, crossing a good road which runs round it, we reach the low wall of the park, in which lies the bathing establishment. From this point the electric tram-cars run to Clermont, carrying backwards and forwards for two sous baigneurs and holiday-folk enough, I should say, to pay handsome dividends. This park occupies the whole breadth of the valley, pushing back the houses on either side against the hillsides. Its main building, a handsome structure, built of lava, with red-tiled roof, contains all the separate baths and a *piscine*, or swimming bath, besides a good-sized hall for sanitary gymnastics, and a *salle d'escrime*, in which a professor instructs pupils daily in fencing and *le boxe*. The broad path runs from top to bottom of this park, having this *établissement* building on its left or northern side, and on its right two parallel terraces, one above the other. On the lower of these is the great *source*, the "Eugénie," which bubbles up here in magnificent style, sending up some millions of gallons daily. Over the Eugénie *source* is a pavilion, with open sides and striped red and white curtains. A second pavilion on the same terrace, a little lower down, is devoted to the band, which plays every afternoon for two or three hours; and below that again, the casino. On the second or upper terrace are a few favoured *châlet* shops, for the sale of books, pictures, photographs, and the pottery and *bijouterie* of Auvergne. Then, above again, comes the road which encloses the park, on the opposite side of which are the row of large hotels built against the rocky side of the valley, and communicating at the back from their upper stories with the road which runs up to Royat village.

The rest of the park is laid out in lawns and garden-beds, full of bright flowers and walks, amongst which are found three other sources—the Cæsar, the St. Mart, and the St. Victor, each of which has its small drinking-pavilion. In front of these several pavilions and along the terraces are a plentiful supply of seats, and chairs which you can carry about to any spot you may select under the shade of the plane-trees and acacias which line the terraces and walks, with weeping-willows, chestnuts, and poplars happily interspersed here and there. The abundant water-supply which the brook brings down is well utilised, so that the whole park, some six acres in extent, is kept as fresh and green, and the flower-beds as luxuriant and bright with colour, as if it were in dear, damp England. At the bottom of the park, a handsome viaduct of arches, built of lava, spans the valley, seeming to shut Royat in from the outer world, and beyond, the valley broadens out into a wide plain, with Clermont, the capital of Auvergne, in the foreground, and beyond the city, stretching right away to Switzerland, a splendid sea (as it were) of corn and maize and vines and olives, the richest, it is said, in the whole of *la belle* France. It is stated in all the guidebooks, and by trustworthy residents, that on a clear day you may see Mont Blanc from Royat, but as yet I have not been lucky enough.

Unless I have failed altogether in describing the view which lies constantly before me—from the pine-clad hillside over Royat village, with its gray church and white red-roofed houses to the west, away down over the park and surrounding hotels and shops, and viaduct and city and plain to the far east—you can now fancy what it must be in the early morning, when the light mist is lying along the hillsides until the sun has had time to dispose of the clouds in the upper air, or at night, when the clear sky is thick with stars, and the Northern Lights flame up behind the silent volcano opposite this Hôtel de Lyon. There is no place on earth, from the back-slums of great cities to the mountain-peak or mid-ocean, to which early morns and evening twilights do not bring daily, or almost daily, some touch of the beauty of light-pictures which sun and moon and stars paint for us so patiently, whether we heed them or no; but to get them in their full perfection, one should be able to look at them in the light, dry, warm air of such places as these volcanic highlands of Auvergne.

And now for the life we lead in this air and scenery. Every morning at six I arrive at the Cæsar spring and drink two glasses, with twenty minutes' interval between them. Then I climb the hill to *café au lait* and two small rolls and butter on the terrace, which comes off about 7 A.M., as soon as the last of our party of four has come up from the park. Rest till eleven follows, when we have *déjeûner à la fourchette*, which, as we sit down about a hundred, lasts for an hour. In the afternoon I drink two glasses at the St. Mart spring, and between them have twenty minutes in the *piscine*, which is my great treat of the day. Going punctually at two, when the ladies surrender this swimming-bath to the men, I almost always get it to myself, and enjoy it as I used to do years ago, when my blood was warm enough, lying about amongst the waves on the English coast, and letting them just tumble and toss me about as they would. This water comes warm from the Eugénie spring daily, and is so buoyant that one can lie perfectly still on the top of it with one's hands behind one's head; and if there were no roof to the *piscine*, and one could only look straight up all the time into the deep-blue sky, twice as high, so it looks, as ours in England, the physical enjoyment would be perfect. It is not far from that as it is, and I thoroughly sympathise with Browning's Amphibian:—

From worldly noise and dust,

In the sphere which overbrims

With passion and thought—why, just

Unable to fly, one swims.

Royat les Bains, 30th August 1890.

I suppose there never was a garden since Eden (unless, perhaps, in the early days of the Jesuit settlements in the Paraguay) in which the devil has not had a tree or a corner somewhere; and it would be well for us all if he were no more in evidence in other health and holiday resorts than he is here in the *parc*. His booth is at the end of the middle terrace, a small pavilion, well shaded by tall acacias, in which in the afternoons you can risk a franc, occasionally two, every minute on the *course des petits chevaux*. The *course* is a round table, with eight or ten concentric grooves, in each of which a small horse and jockey runs. Outside this *course*, with room for a page-boy to move round between the two, there is a slight railing with a flat top, at which the players sit round and post their stakes. These are collected by the page, who lets each player draw a number in exchange for the francs. As soon as he has made his circuit, the croupier gives a turn to a handle which works the machinery. The first turn brings all the horses into line, and the next starts them round the course, each in his own groove. After another turn or two, the croupier lets go the handle, and the puppets begin to scatter, the winner being the one which passes the post last before the machine stops, and they all come to a standstill.

Then the croupier calls out the winning number, and the owner gets all the stakes, except one, which goes to the table. Beyond this, the Company has no interest whatever, so it is said. Of course one looks with jealousy at every such game of chance, and I was inclined to think at first that the croupier was in league with two women, one spectacled, who sat steadily at one end of the players, playing in partnership, and seeming to win oftener than any of the others; but the longer I watched, the weaker grew my suspicions. Most of the players, by the way, are women, though there are a few men who come and sit for hours, playing and smoking cigarettes. Besides the sitters many strollers come up, stake their francs for a course or two, and then move on, not unfrequently with a handful of silver. On the whole, if play is to be allowed at all, it can scarcely take a more harmless form, if only the good-natured French papa could be kept from letting his children play for him. He comes up with a child of ten or twelve years, lets them sit down, and supplies them from behind with the necessary francs, and after a round or two the little faces flush and hands shake, especially if they be girls, in a way which is painful to see. A child gambling is as sad a sight, for every one but the devil and his elect, as this old world can show.

Next to the *courses des petits chevaux*, at some thirty yards' distance, comes the large pavilion in which the excellent band sit and play for an hour in the forenoon and afternoon, and again at 8 P.M. Round the pavilion is a broad space, gravelled and well shaded, and furnished with chairs which are occupied all the afternoon by *baigneurs* and visitors, mostly in family groups, the women knitting or sewing, and the children playing about in the intervals of the music, and before and after the regular concerts. Occasionally they have a *bal d'enfants* in this space, controlled by a master of the ceremonies, a dancing-, master, I am told. Under him the children, boys and girls of thirteen or fourteen, down to little trots who can scarcely toddle, may enjoy polkas, galops, and the *taran-tole des postilions*, as well as the gravel allows; and now and again comes a *défilé*, in which, in couples carefully graduated according to size and age, the children march round the walks, and in and out amongst the approving sitters. A very pretty, and to me rather a curious sight, as I much doubt if the English boy could be induced to perform such a march, even in the hope of small packets of bonbons at the end, which are distributed to the best performers.

The big orchestral platform in this pavilion is often occupied, when the band is not playing, by itinerant performers, who (I suppose) hire it from the Company in the hope of getting a few francs out of the sitting and circulating crowd. The performances are poor, so far as I have seen, though one conjurer certainly played a trick which entirely beat me at the time, and for which I am still quite unable to account. He produced what he called a *garotte*, made of two stout planks which shut one upon another (like our old stocks), and in which was a central hole for the neck, and two smaller ones for the wrists. This garotte he handed round, and though I did not get hold of it, I inspected it in the hands of a youth who was standing just in front of me, and satisfied myself that the planks were solid wood. Then he placed it on a stand, and called up a stout damsel in the flesh-coloured tights which seem to be *de rigueur* for all female performers, who knelt down and laid her neck in the big hole, and a wrist in each of the smaller ones. The conjurer then let down the upper plank upon her, and having borrowed a signet ring from an elderly *décoré* Frenchman who was sitting near the platform, proceeded to encircle the two planks with strips of stout paper or tape, which he sealed with the ring. Then he held up a screen for the space of twenty seconds, and on lowering it the damsel was posturing in her tights, while the *garotte* remained *in situ*, with the tapes still there and the seals unbroken. By what trick she got her head and hands out I was utterly unable to guess, and strolled away with the rather provoking sense of having been fooled through my eyes. I hope a green parrot who flew down and sat on the railing close to the *garotte*, with his head wisely on one side, flew off better satisfied.

Below, on the lowest terrace, at the end of the *établissement* buildings, is the *salle d'escrime*, which is open daily in the afternoons, when you may see through the big windows the "Maître d'Escrime, Professeur de S.A.R. le Prince des Galles," sitting ready to instruct pupils, or, so it seemed, to try a friendly bout with all comers. The former were generally too much of mere beginners to make any show worth seeing, but on one day an awkward customer turned up who ran the professor, so far as I could judge, very hard. Indeed, I am by no means sure that he acknowledged several shrewd hits, but my knowledge of fencing is too small to make my judgment worth much. Le boxe is also announced to go on here, but I have never seen the gloves put on yet. Indeed, I much doubt whether young Frenchmen really like having their heads punched for love. It is an eccentricity which does not seem to spread out of the British Isles. There was a tempting *assaut d'armes* last Sunday, presided over by General Paquette, at which eleven *maîtres d'escrime* of regiments in this department, and one professor from Paris were to fence. I was sorely tempted to go, but as the thermometer stood at 80° in the shade, and so reinforced my insular prejudices as to the day, abstained.

Again, beyond the Casino, on the upper terrace, is a good croquet-ground on the broad gravel space at the lower end of the *parc*. I should think it a difficult ground to play on, but as a rule the French boys are decidedly good players, and seem to enjoy the game thoroughly, and to get round the hoops quicker than any of ours could do on a lawn like a billiard-table. The Casino, besides a restaurant and reading-room, contains a theatre, at which there are performances five nights in the week, and generally a ball on the off-nights. These are often fancy-balls, and always, I hear, very lively; but I cannot speak from experience, never having as yet descended either to them or to the plays and operettas. When one can sit out on a terrace and see the lights coming out in the valley, and the Milky Way and all the stars in the heaven shining as they only do down South, even the artists of the Théâtre Français, and the other theatrical stars who visit the Casino in the season, cannot get me indoors o' nights, even at Casino prices. These are very reasonable, the *abonnement* for a seat being only 1 franc a night, or 2 francs for a *fauteuil*. Your readers may perhaps be able to judge of the kind of entertainment given by a specimen. To-night there are two operettas,—*Violonnaux*, music by Offenbach; and *Les Charbonneurs*, music by G. Coste. I own I never heard of either of the pieces.

I think, sir, you will allow that there are attractions enough of all kinds provided by the Compagnie Anonyme des Eaux Minérales de Royat, who own the *parc* and run the business. They can well afford it, as every visitor pays 10 francs as an *abonnement* for drinking the waters, and the charges for baths are high, e.g. 2.50 francs for a separate bath, and 2 francs for the swimming-bath, decidedly more than any of our English watering-places, not excepting Bath; but one has so much more fun, if one wants it, for the money. And then there is this immense thing to be said for this Royat Company,— their park is entirely free and open to any one who cares to walk through it. I have seen scores of peasants in blouses, and their wives, sitting about during the concerts, not on the same terrace with the band, where a sou is charged for chairs, but near enough to hear the music perfectly; and one meets them all about the garden, walking and chatting amongst the—I was going to write "well dressed," but that they are not, but eminently respectable, if rather dowdy—crowds of bathers and visitors. I do not, of course, mean that there are no exceptions, either in the case of dowdiness or respectability, but they are rare enough to prove the rule. On the other hand, the number of religious of both sexes is remarkable who come to use the waters, principally for throat ailments. Sisters of several kinds, some wearing black hoods with white breastplates, others in large white head-dresses, with long flaps, like a bird's wings, which flap as they walk, are frequent in the early mornings and other quiet times; and besides the regular clergy, there are three monkish orders represented. Of these the most striking are two Franciscans, I believe, clad in rough, ruddy-brown flannel gowns, reaching to the ground, with large rosaries hanging before and cowls behind, and girt with knotted ropes. Peter the Hermit preached the First Crusade in the neighbouring Church of St. Mary of the port at Clermont, assisted doubtless by many a friar clad precisely as these are, except that the modern monk or friar (as I was disappointed to note, at any rate in one case) does not go bare-footed, or even in sandals, but in substantial shoes and trousers! I was much struck by the quiet, patient, and reverent expression on all the faces, very different from what I remember in past years. Persecution may very well account, however, for this. There is no branch, I take it, of the Church Universal which does not thrive under it, in the best sense.

Auvergne en Fête, 6th September 1890.

These good folk of Auvergne seem to get much more fun, or at least much more play, out of life than we do; at any rate, they have been twice *en fête* in the three weeks we have been here. I suppose it is because we have in this business cut down our saints till we have only St. Lubbock left, with his quarterly holiday, while they, more wisely, have stuck to the old calendar. But it seems all wrong that they, who get five times as much sun as we, should also get three or four times as many holidays; for sunshine is surely of itself a sort of equivalent for a holiday. Perhaps, however, if we had lots of it, the national "doggedness as does it" might wear out. That valuable, but unpleasant characteristic could scarcely have leavened a nation living in a genial climate; but, with about half Africa on our hands, in addition to Ireland and other trifles all round the world, the coming generation will need the "dogged as does it" even more than their fathers. So let us sing with Charles Kingsley, "Hail to thee, North-Easter," or with the old Wiltshire shepherd, claim that the weather in England must be, anyhow, "sech as plaazes God A'mighty, and wut plaazes He plaazes I."

Determined to see all the fun of the fair, a friend and I started for Clermont from Royat by the electric tramway, and reached the Place de Jaude in a few minutes—the "Forum Clermontois," as it is called in the local guidebooks—the largest open space in the ancient capital of Auvergne. It is a famous place for a fair, being nearly the size and shape of Eaton Square, with two rows of plane-trees running round it, but otherwise unenclosed. As we alighted from the tram-car, we could see a long line of booths, with prodigious pictures in front of them, and platforms on which bands were playing and actors gesticulating; but before starting on our tour, we were attracted by a crowd close to the stopping-place of the cars. It proved to be a ring, four or five deep, round the carpet of athletes. They were two, a man and a woman, both in the usual flesh-coloured tights, the latter without any pretence of a skirt. The man was walking round, changing the places of the weights and clubs, until sufficient sous had been thrown on to the carpet, the woman screening her face from the sun with a big fan, and talking with her nearest neighbours in the ring. She was a remarkably fine young woman, with well-cut features, and a snake-head on a neck like a column; and, strange to say, her expression was as modest and quiet as though pink tights were the ordinary walking-dress on the Place de Jaude. The necessary sous were soon carpeted, and the performance began. It was just the usual thing, lifting and catching heavy weights, wielding clubs, etc., the only novelty being that a woman should be one of the performers. She followed the man, doing several feats with heavy weights which were painful to witness, and we passed on to the row of booths. The average price for entrance was 2 1/2 sous, but after experimenting on the two first, we agreed that in such a temperature the outside was decidedly the best part of the show. These two were some Indian dancers, male and female, who stood up one after another and postured from the hips, and waved scarfs, the rest beating time on banjos; and a *"Miss* Flora, *dompteuse,"* a snake-tamer. From this announcement over the booth entrance we rather expected to find a countrywoman, but the performer was a squat little Frenchwoman, in the same skirtless tights, who took some sleepy snakes out of a box, put them round her neck, and then wanted to make us pay a second time, which we declined to do. The next booth ought to have been amusing, but no boys came to play while we stopped. It was announced as "Le Massacre d'Innocents." A number of these "Innocent" puppets looked out of a row of holes in a large wooden frame, not more than eight feet from the rail in front of it. Standing behind this rail the player, on paying 5 centimes, is handed a soft ball, which he can discharge at any one of the Innocents he may select, and "chaque bonhomme renversé gagne une demi-douzaine de biscuits." I suppose the biscuits were bad, as otherwise the absence of boys seemed incredible. Any English lower-school boy would have brought down a *bonhomme* at that distance with every ball, unless the balls were somehow doctored. But no boy turned up; so we passed on to the biggest booth in the fair, with pictures of wondrous beasts and heroic men and women over the platform, on which a big drum and clarionet invited entrance, in strains which drowned those of all the neighbouring booths. We read that inside a "Musée historique, destructive, et amusant" was on show, but contented ourselves with the pictures outside.

Facing the other side of the place, with their backs to the larger booths along which we had come, were a row of humbler stalls and booths, most of the latter being devoted to some kind of gambling. There were three or four *courses des petits chevaux*, not so well appointed as the permanent one in the Royat Park, but on the same lines, and a number of hazard-boards-and other tables, about the size of those which the thimble-riggers used to carry about at English fairs. These last were new to me. They have a hollow rim round them, into which the player puts a large marble, which runs out on to the face of the table, which is marked all over with numbers, six or eight towards the centre being red, and the rest black. If the marble stops on one of these red numbers, the player wins; if on a black one, the table wins. The odds seemed to be more than twenty to one against the player; but if so, the tables would surely be less crowded. As it was, they did a merry trade, never for a moment wanting a player while we looked on. Most of these were soldiers of the garrison, interspersed with peasants in blouses, who dragged out their sous with every token of disgust and resentment, but seemed quite unable to get away from the tables. On the whole, after watching for some time, I was confirmed in the belief that we are right in putting down gambling in all public places. Nothing, I suppose, can stop it; but there is no good in thrusting the temptation under the noses of boys and fools.

After making the round of the fair, we strolled up the hill to the Cathedral, which dominates the city, and looks out over as fair and rich a prospect as the world has to show. Brassey, when he was building one of the railways across La Limagne, the plain which stretches away east of Clermont, is reported to have said that if France were utterly bankrupt, the surface value of her soil would set her on her legs again in two years; and one can quite believe him. The streets of the old town, which surrounds the Cathedral, are narrow and steep, but full of old houses of rare architectural interest. Many of them must have belonged to great folk, whose arms are still to be seen over the doors, inside the quiet courts through which you enter from the streets. In these one could see, as we passed, little groups of gossips, knitting, smoking, "*causer*-ing." The *petit bourgeois* has succeeded to the noble, and now enjoys those grand, broad staircases and stone balconies. They form an excellent setting to the Cathedral, itself a grand specimen of Norman Gothic, begun by Hugues de la Tour, the sixty-sixth bishop, before his departure for the Crusades, and finished by Viollet-le-Duc, who only completed the twin spires in 1877. But interesting as the Cathedral is, it is eclipsed by the Church of Notre Dame du Port, the oldest building in Clermont. It dates from the sixth century, when the first church was built on the site by St. Avitus, eighteenth bishop. This was burnt 853 A.D., and rebuilt by St. Sigon, forty-third bishop, in 870. Burnt again, it was again rebuilt as it stands to-day, in the eleventh century. In it Peter the Hermit is said to have preached the First Crusade, when the Council called by Pope Urban II. was sitting at Clermont. Whether this be so or not, it is by far the most perfect and interesting specimen of the earliest Gothic known to me; and the crypt underneath the chancel is unique. It is specially dedicated to St. Mary du Port, and over the altar is the small statue of the Virgin and Child, around and before which votive offerings of all kinds—crosses and military decorations, bracelets, jewels, trinkets, many of them, I should think, of large value—hang and lie. The small image has no beauty whatever—in fact, is just a plain black doll— but of untold value to many generations of Auvernois, who regard it as a talisman which has, again and again, preserved their city from sword and pestilence. I am not sure whether, amongst the small marble tablets which literally cover the walls, one may not be found in memory of the great fight of Gergovia, in which Vercingétorix, if he did not actually defeat Cæsar, turned the great captain and his Roman legions away from this part of Gaul. At any rate, amongst the most prominent, is one inscribed with the names "Coulmiers," "Patay," "Le Mans," the battles which in 1870-71 stayed the German advance on Clermont, and saved the capital of Auvergne. The rest are, for the most part, private tablets, thanksgivings for the cure of all manner of sickness and disease to which flesh is heir. To this shrine all sufferers have come in the faith which finds a voice all round these old walls,—"Qu'on est heureux d'avoir Marie pour mère"! That human instinct which longs for a female protectrix and mediator "behind the veil," speaks here, too, as it did 2000 years ago, when the [Greek phrase] guarded the shrines of Athens and her colonies.

Scoppio Del Carro, Florence, Easter Eve, 1891.

I have just come back from witnessing an extraordinary, and, I should think, a unique ceremony, which is enacted here on Easter Eve; and, on sitting down quietly to think it over, can scarcely say whether I am most inclined to laugh, or to cry, or to swear. In truth, the "Scoppio del Carro"—or "explosion of the fireworks"—as it is called, is a curious comment on, or illustration of, your last week's remarks on Superstitions. "The carefully preserved dry husk of outward observance" in this case undoubtedly speaks, to those who have ears to hear, of a heroic time, and the spectator rubs his eyes, and feels somehow—

As though he looked upon the sheath

Which once had clasped Excalibur.

At any rate, that is rather how I felt, as, standing at noon in the dense crowd in the nave of the Duomo, I saw the procession pass within a few feet of me, on their way from the great entrance up to the high altar, which was ablaze already with many tall candles. Although within a few feet, the intervening crowd was so thick that I could only see the heads and shoulders of the taller choristers and priests as they passed; but I saw plainly enough, though the wearer was low of stature, the tall mitre—it looked like gold—which the Archbishop wore as he walked in the procession. Our bishops, I am told, are wearing or going to wear them (Heaven save the mark!), which made me curious. They threaded their way slowly up to the high altar; and presently we heard in the distance intoning and chants; and then, after brief pause, the dove (so called) started from the crucifix, I think, at any rate from a high point on the altar, for the open door. But in order to be clear as to what the dove carries and is supposed to do, we must go back to the Second Crusade.

I give the story as I make it out by comparing the accounts in various guide-books with those of residents interested in such matters. These differ much in detail, but not as to the main facts. These are, that in 1147 A.D. a Florentine noble of the Pazzi family, Raniero by name, joined, some say led, the 2500 Tuscans who went on the Crusade. In any case, he greatly distinguished himself by his courage, and is said to have planted the first standard of the Cross on the walls of Jerusalem. For this he was allowed to take a light from the sacred fire on the Holy Sepulchre, which he desired to carry back to his much-loved F'orence. An absurd part of the legend now comes in. Finding the wind troublesome as he rode with the light, he turned round, with his face to his horse's tail (as if the wind always blew in Crusaders' faces), and so at last brought it safely home, where his ungrateful fellow-citizens, when they saw him come riding in this fashion, called out, "Pazzo!" "Pazzo!" or "Mad!" which his family forthwith wisely adopted as their patronymic.

The sacred fire was housed in a shrine in St. Biagio, built by Raniero, and has never been allowed to go out since that day—so it is said—and from it yearly are relighted all the candles used in Florentine churches at the Easter festival. It is a striking custom. Gradually, during the Good Friday services, the lights are extinguished in the Duomo, and all the churches, till at midnight they are in darkness, and are only relit next day by fire brought even yet by a Pazzi, a descendant of Raniero, from St. Biagio. This is, however, doubtful, some authorities asserting that the family is extinct, others that it not only exists, but still spends 2000 lire a year in preserving the sacred fire. A stranger has no means that I know of, of sifting out the fact. Anyhow, I can testify that somehow the fire is in the Duomo before noon, as any number of candles were alight on the high altar when I got there at 11.30, half an hour before the procession. Anything more orderly than the great crowd I have never seen. It was of all nations, languages, and ranks, though the great majority were Tuscan peasants with their families from all the surrounding country, waiting in eager expectation for the flight of the dove from the high altar, through the doors to the great car which stands waiting outside at the bottom of the broad steps in front of the Duomo. If the dove makes a successful flight, and lights the fireworks which are hung round the car, there will be a good harvest and abundance of wine and oil, and of oranges and lemons. This year the faces of the peasants and their wives and children—and most attractive brown faces they were—were anxious, for it had been raining hard in the morning, and still drops were falling. However, all went well. At about 12.10 the chanting ceased, and the dove—a small firework of the rocket genus—rushed down the nave, some ten feet over our heads, along a thin wire which I had not noticed before, and set light promptly to the fireworks on the car, which began to turn and explode, not without considerable fizzing and spluttering, but on the whole successfully. Then the dove turned and came back, still alight, and leaving a trail of sparks as it sped along, to the high altar. How it was received there, and what became of it, I cannot say, as I was swept along in the rush to the doors which immediately followed, and had enough to do to pilot my companion, a lady, to the new centre of interest. This was the car to which the sacred fire had now been transferred, and which was about to start on its round to the other churches. It is chocolate-coloured, and spangled with stars, some twenty feet high, surmounted by a large crown and Catherine-wheel. As our crowd swept out of the Duomo and down the steps, to mingle with the still larger crowd outside, men were rehanging the car with fresh fireworks, and putting-to four mighty white oxen, gaily garlanded. I remarked that the conductor, a tall, six-foot man, could not look over the shoulder of one of these shaft-oxen as he was harnessing him in the shafts!

There could be no question as to the very best place for spectators. It was the centre of the top step leading up to the Duomo façade; and, finding ourselves there, we stopped and let the crowd surge past us. Almost at once I became aware that this favoured spot was occupied by the English-speaking race almost exclusively, the accent of cousin Jonathan, I think, on the whole predominating. Two Italian boys looked up at us with large, lustrous brown eyes; otherwise the natives were absent. It seems like a sort of law of social gravitation, that in these latter days the speakers of our language should get into all the world's best places, and having got there should stop. One cannot much wonder that the speakers in other tongues should feel now and then as if they were being rather crowded out. We did not pursue the car as it lumbered away under the glorious campanile, surrounded by the rejoicing multitude, for the sun had now got the upper hand, and the whole city and plain right away to the lower hills, and the snow-capped Apennines in the background, were aglow with the sort of subdued purple or amethyst light which seems to me to differentiate Tuscany from all other countries known to me. Now, gradually to put out all the lights in the churches on Good Friday, and to relight them from fire from the Holy Sepulchre next day, seems to me a worthy and pathetic custom; but this mixing it up with the firework business, and having the Bishop and all the strength of the Cathedral out to help in this dove trick, spoils the whole thing, and makes one wish one had not gone to see it, recalling too forcibly, as it does to an Englishman, the Crystal Palace on a fireworks' night, and the similar "dove" which travels from the Royal Gallery, where too-well-fed citizens and others sit smoking, to light the great "concerted piece" in the grounds below. It was like inserting "Abracadabra!" in the middle of the "Miserere." P.S.—Since writing the 'above, we have had an arrival in Florence which will interest your readers,— to wit, fifty young persons of both sexes from Toynbee Hall, with Mr. Bolton King as conductor; and the English community are doing all they can to make their stay pleasant. On the morrow of their arrival Lady Hobart entertained them at her villa of Montauto, the one in which Hawthorne wrote *Transformation.* It is a thirteenth-century house, or, I should rather say, that the villa, with its large, airy suite of rooms, with vaulted ceilings, has grown round a machicolated tower* of that date, the highest building on the Bellosquardo Hill, to the south-west of the city. From the top of it, reached by rather rickety and casual old stairs, there is, I should think, as glorious a view as the world can show,—a perfect panorama, with Florence lying right below, and beyond, Fiesole and Vallombrosa, and the village of stone-cutters on the slope of the Apennines, which reared the greatest of stonecutters, Michael Angelo, and beyond, the highest Apennines, still snow-covered; and to the north, the rich plain of vineyards, and olive-groves, and orange and lemon gardens, thickly sprinkled with the bright white houses of the peasant cultivators and the graceful campaniles of village churches, beyond which one could see clearly on this "white-stone" day the snow-clad peaks of the Carrara Mountains in the far north. I can hardly say whether the Toynbee visitors, or those who were gathered to welcome them by the hospitable hostess, enjoyed the unrivalled view most; but this we soon discovered, that the visitors were about as well acquainted with the story of each point of interest, as it was pointed out to them, as the oldest resident. Surely the schoolmaster is at last abroad with us in England in many ways of which we have good right to feel proud, and for which we may well be thankful.

A Scamper at Easter, 8th April 1893.

No one can dislike more than I the habit which has become so common of late years amongst us—thanks, or rather no thanks, to Mr. Gladstone—of running down our own English ways of dealing with all creation, from Irishmen to black-beetles. I believe, on the contrary, that on the whole there is not, nor ever was, a nation that kept a more active conscience, or tried more honestly to do the right thing all round according to its lights. Nevertheless, I am bound to admit that our methods don't always succeed, as, for instance, with our treatment of our "submerged tenth," if that is the accepted name for the section of our people which Mr. G. Booth, in his excellent *Life and Labour in London*, places in his A and B classes (and which, by the way, are only 8.2, and not 10 per cent), or with our seagulls. Some years ago I called your readers' attention to the rapid demoralisation of these beautiful birds at one of our northern watering-places; how they just floated past the pier-heads hour after hour, waiting for the doles which the holiday folk and their children brought down for them in paper-bags. Our sea-going gulls, I regret to note, are now similarly affected. At any rate, some forty of them diligently followed the steamer in which I sailed for my Easter holiday, from the Liverpool docks till we dropped our pilot and, turned due south off Holyhead. By that time our last meal had been eaten and the remains cast into the sea. The gulls seemed to be quite aware of this; and we left them squabbling over the last scraps of fish and potatoes, or loafing slowly back to Liverpool. Thirty-six hours later we entered the Garonne, and steamed sixty miles up it to Bordeaux. For all that distance there were plenty of French gulls on the water or in the air, but, so far from following us, not one of them seemed to take the least notice of us, but all went on quietly with their fishing or courting; and yet our cook's mate must have thrown out as much broken victuals after breakfast in the Garonne as he did after luncheon or dinner on the Welsh coast. It cannot be because the French gulls are Republicans, for the Republic has, if anything, increased the national appetite for unearned loaves and fishes. It is certainly very odd; but, anyhow, I hope our gulls will not take to more self-respecting ways of life, for it is a real treat to watch them in the ship's wake, without effort, often without perceptible motion of the wings, keeping up the fourteen knots an hour. The Captain and I fraternised over the gulls, whom he loves, and will not allow to be shot at from his ship. "I'll shoot whether you like it or not," insisted a sporting gent on a recent voyage. "If you do, I'll put you in irons," retorted the Captain; whereupon the sporting gent collapsed—a pity, I think, for an action for false imprisonment would have been interesting under the circumstances. I fancy the Captain is right, but must look up the law after Easter.

I am surprised that this route is not more popular with the increasing numbers of our people who like a short run to the south of France in our hard spring weather. You can get by this way to Bordeaux quicker than you can by Dover or Folkestone from any place north of Trent, unless you travel day and night, and sleep on the trains, and for about half the money. The packets are cargo-boats, but with excellent cabins and sleeping accommodation for twelve or fourteen passengers, including as good a bath as on a Cunard or White Star liner. And yet I was the only passenger last week. There can scarcely be a more interesting short voyage for any one who is a decent sailor; but I suppose the fourteen or sixteen hours "in the Bay of Biscay, oh!" scares people. As far as my experience goes, the Atlantic roars like a sucking-dove in the Channel and the Bay at Easter-time. There was not wind enough to dimple the ocean surface, and until we passed Milford Haven, no perceptible motion on the ship. Then, as we crossed the opening of the Bristol Channel, she began to roll—quite unaccountably, as it seemed at first; but on watching carefully, one became aware that, though the surface was motionless, the great deep beneath was heaving with long pulsations from the west, which lifted us in regular cadence every thirty or forty seconds. I have often crossed the Atlantic, but never seen the like, as always before there has been a ripple on the calmest day, which gave the effect, at any rate, of surface motion. The best idea I can give of it is, if on a long stretch of our South Downs the successive turf slopes took to rising and falling perpendicularly every minute. The Captain said there must have been wild weather out west, and these were the rollers. It was a grand sight to watch the great heave pass on till it reached the Land's End, and ran up the cliffs there. We passed near enough to see the mining works, close to the level of high-tide, and the villages on the cliff-tops above, or clinging on to the slopes wherever these were not too precipitous. One can realise what manner of men and sailors this Far West has bred of old, and, I hope, still breeds. I pity the Englishman whose pulse does not quicken as he sails by the Land's End, and can see with a glass some of the small harbours out of which Drake and Frobisher and Hawkins sailed, and drew the crews that followed and fought the Armada right away to the Straits of Dover.

As the Land's End light receded, we became aware of another light away some twenty miles to the south-west. It is on a rock not fifty yards across, the Captain says, at high tide, and often unapproachable for weeks together—"The Hawk," by name, on which are kept four lighthouse-men, who spend there alternate months, weather permitting. I was glad to hear that there are four at a time, as the sight of "The Hawk" brought vividly to my mind the gruesome story of fifty years back, when there were only two men, who were known not to be good friends. One died, and his companion had to wait with the dead body for weeks before his relief came.

I noticed, before we were two hours out, that there was something unusually smart about the crew, quite what one would look for on the *Umbria* or *Germanic*, but scarcely on a 700-tons cargo-boat plying to Bordeaux. Several of the young hands were fine British tars, with the splendid throats and great muscular hands and wrists which stand out so well from the blue woollen jerseys; but the one who struck me most was the ship's carpenter, a gray, weather-beaten old salt, who was going round quietly, but all the time with his broad-headed hammer, setting little things straight, helping to straighten the tarpaulins over the hatches and deck-cargo, and sounding the well. I caught him now and then for a few words, as he passed my deck-chair, and got the clue. Most of the crew were Naval Reserve men, and followed the Captain, a lieutenant in the R.N.R., who could fly the blue ensign in foreign ports, which they liked. Besides, he was a skipper who cared for his men, looked after their mess and berths, and never wanted to make anything out of them; charged them only a shilling a pound for their baccy, the price at which he could get it out of bond, while most skippers charged 2s. 6d., the shop price. He had come to this boat while his big ship was laid up in dock, to oblige the owners, so they had followed him. Besides, he never put them to any work he wouldn't bear a hand in; had stood for hours up to his waist last year in the hold when they were bringing five hundred cattle and seven hundred hogs from Canada, running before a heavy gale. The water they shipped was putting out the engine fires, and the pumps wouldn't work till they had bailed for ten hours. However, they got in all right, and never lost a beast. Of course I was keen to hear the Captain on this subject, and so broached it at his table. Yes, it was quite true; they had run before a heavy gale from off Newfoundland, and the pumps gave out off the Irish coast. They got the sludge bailed out enough for all the fires to get to work just about in time, or would have drifted on the rocks and gone all to pieces in a few minutes. Yes, it was about the nastiest piece of work he had ever had to do; the sludge, for it was only half water, was above his waist, and had quite spoiled his uniform. The deck engineer—a light-haired man, all big bones and muscle, whom he pointed out to me—was in the deepest part of the hold up to his arm-pits, and had worked there for ten hours without coming up! He was a R.N.R. man, like the old carpenter and most of the rest. The old fellow was one of the staunchest and best followers, probably because he was tired of going aground. He had been aground seventeen times! for the Captain in his last ship had a way of charging shoals, merely saying, "Oh, she'll jump it!" which she generally declined to do. The Captain is a strong Churchman, but shares the prejudice against carrying ministers. "The devil always has a show" when you're carrying a minister. The first time he tried it, he was taking out his own brother, and they were twenty-two days late at Montreal. It was an awful crossing, a gale in their teeth all the way; most of the ships that started with them had to put back. I suggested that if he hadn't had his brother on board, he mightn't have got over at all; but he wouldn't see it. Next time, a man fell from the mast-head and was killed; and the next, a man jumped overboard. He would never carry a minister again if he could help it.

One pilot took us out to Holyhead, but it took three French ones to take us up to Bordeaux. The Garonne banks are only picturesque here and there; but the flat banks have their own interest, for do we not see the choicest vineyards of the claret country as we run up? There was the Chateau Lafitte and the Chateau Margaux. I suppose one ought within one's heart, or rather, within one's palate perhaps, "to have felt a stir"—

As though one looked upon the sheath

Which once had clasped Excalibur.

But I could not tell the difference between Margaux and any decent claret with my eyes shut, so I did not feel any stir—unless, perhaps, as a patriot, when we passed much the most imposing establishment, and the Captain said, "That is Chateau Gilbey"! I looked with silent wonder, for did I not remember years ago, when the Gladstone Grocers' Licences Bill was young, and the Christie Minstrels sung scoffingly—

Ten little niggers going out to dine,

One drank Gilbey, and then there were nine?

And here was Gilbey with the finest "caves" and the choicest vineyard in the Bordelaise! Who can measure the competitive energy of the British business-man?

I must end as I set out, with the birds. As we neared the mouth of the Garonne, sixteen miles from land, the Captain said, two little water-wagtails flitted into the rigging. There they rested a few minutes, and then, to my grief, started off out to sea, but again and again came back to the ship. At last a sailor caught one, and the Captain secured it and took it to his cabin, but thought it would be sure to die. It was the hen-bird. She did not die, but flitted away cheerfully when he brought her out and let her fly on the quay of Bordeaux. But I fear she will never find her mate.

Lourdes, 15th April 1893.

The farthest point south in our Easter scamper was Lourdes, to which I found that my companions were more bent on going than to any other possible place within our range. The attractions even of the Pass of Ronces-valles, of St. Sebastian, and the Pyrenean battle-fields of 1814, faded with them before those of the nineteenth-century Port Royal. At first I said I would not go. The fact is, I am one of the old-fashioned folk who hold that some day the kingdoms of this world are to become the kingdoms of Christ, and that all peoples are to be gathered "in one fold under one Shepherd." It has always seemed to me that one of the surest ways of postponing that good time is to be suspicious of other faiths than our own; to accuse them of blind superstition and deliberate imposture; even to walk round their churches as if they were museums or picture-galleries, while people are kneeling in prayer. So I said "No"; I would stop on the terrace at Pau, with one of the most glorious views in the world to look at, and carefully examine Henry IV.'s château, or go and get a round of golf with my hibernating fellow-countrymen. I thought that the probable result of visiting Lourdes might be to make me more inclined to think a large section of my fellow-mortals dupes, and their priests humbugs—conclusions I was anxious to avoid. However, I changed my mind at the last moment, and am heartily glad I did. It is an easy twenty miles (about) from Pau, from which you run straight to the Pyrenees, and pull up in a green nook of the outlying lower mountains, where two valleys meet, which run back towards the higher snow-capped range. They looked so tempting to explore, as did also the grim old keep on the high rock which divides them and completely dominates the little town, that twenty years ago I couldn't have resisted, and should have gone for an afternoon's climb. But I am grown less lissom, if not wiser, and so took my place meekly in the fly which my companions had chartered for the grotto. We were through the little town in a few minutes, the only noteworthy thing being the number of women who offered us candles of all sizes to burn before the Madonna's statue in the grotto, and the number of relic-shops. Emerging from the street, we found ourselves in front of a green lawn, at the other end of which was a fine white marble church, almost square, with a dome—more like a mosque, I thought, than a Western church; and up above this another tall Gothic church, with a fine spire, to which the pilgrims ascend by two splendid semi-circular flights of easy, broad steps, one on each side of the lower church, and holding it, as it were, in their arms. We, however, drove up the steep ascent outside the left or southern staircase, and got down at the door of the higher church, which is built on the rock at the bottom of which is the famous spring and grotto. We entered by a spacious porch, where my attention was at once arrested by the mural tablets of white marble, each of which commemorated the cure of some sufferer: "Reconnaissance pour la guérison de mon fils," "de ma fille," etc., being at least as frequent as those for the cure of the person who put up the tablet. I thought at first I would count them, but soon gave it up, as not only this big vestibule, but the walls of all the chapels, and of the big church below (built, I was told, and hope, by the Duke of Norfolk at his own cost), are just covered with them. This upper church was a perfect blaze of light and colour, much too gorgeous for my taste; but what the decorations were which gave this effect I cannot say, as I was entirely absorbed in noting the votive offerings of all kinds which were hung round each of the shrines, both here and in the lower church. The most noteworthy of these, to my mind, are the number of swords, epaulettes, and military decorations, which their owners have hung up as thank offerings. I do not suppose that French officers and privates differ much from ours, and I am bold to assert that Tommy Atkins would not part with his cross or medal, or his captain, for that matter, with his epaulettes or sword, if they had gone away from Lourdes no better in body than when they went there hobbling from wounds, or tottering from fever or ague.

When we had seen the upper church we went down a long flight of circular stairs, and came out in the lower (Duke of Norfolk's) church,—much more interesting, I think, architecturally, and decorated in better, because quieter, taste than the upper one. From this we went round to the grotto in the rock, on which the upper church stands, and in which the famous spring rises, and over it a not unpleasant (I cannot say more) statue of the Madonna; and all round candles alight of all sizes, from farthing-dips to colossal moulds, many of which had been burning, they said, for a week. A single, quiet old priest sat near the entrance reading his Missal, but only speaking when spoken to. In front were ranged long rows of chairs, on which sat or knelt some dozen pilgrims with wistful faces, waiting, perhaps for the troubling of the waters. These are carried from the grotto to a series of basins along the rock outside, at one of which two poor old crones with sore eyes were bathing them, and talking Basque (I believe)—at any rate some unknown tongue to me. I should have liked to hear their experiences, but they couldn't understand a word of my Anglican French. Here, again, the most striking object is the mass of crutches of all shapes and sizes, and fearsome-looking bandages, which literally cover the rock on each side of the entrance to the grotto, for the space (I should guess) of fourteen or fifteen feet on one side, and ten or twelve on the other.

And so we finished our inspection, and went back to our fly, which we had ordered to meet us at the end of the lawn above mentioned, which lies between the churches and the town; and so to the railway station, and back to Biarritz by Pau. I daresay that people who go there at the times when the great bodies of pilgrims come, may carry away a very different impression from mine. All I can say is, that I never was in a place where there was less concealment of any kind; and there was no attempt whatever to influence you in any way by priest or attendant. There were all the buildings and the grotto open, and you could examine them and their contents undisturbed for any time you chose to give to them, and draw from your examination whatever conclusions you pleased. So I, for one, can only repeat that I am heartily glad that I went; and shall think better of my Roman Catholic brethren as the result of my visit for the rest of my life.

Of course, the main interest of Lourdes lies in the world-old controversy between the men of science and the men of faith, as to the reality of the alleged facts—miracles, as many folk call them—of the healing properties which the waters of this famous spring, or the air of Lourdes, or the Madonna, or some other unknown influence, are alleged to possess, and to be freely available for invalid pilgrims who care to make trial of them. Every one in those parts that I met, at Lourdes itself, at Pau, Biarritz, Bayonne, is interested in the question and ready to discuss it. Perhaps I can best indicate the points of the debate by formulating the arguments on each side which I heard, putting them into the mouths of representative men—a doctor and a priest. I was lucky enough to fall in with an excellent representative of the scientific side, an able and open-minded M.D. on his travels. I had no opportunity of speaking to one of the priests; but their side of the argument is stoutly upheld by at least half of the people one meets.

Dr.—They are nothing but what are called faith-cures, akin to those which the Yankee Sequah effects when he goes round our northern towns in his huge car, with his brass band and attendant Indian Sachems in the costume of the prairie. Of course, here the surroundings are far more impressive and serious; but the cures are the same for all that—some action of the nerves which makes patients believe they are cured, when they are not really. Probably nine-tenths are just as bad again in a few months.

Priest.—Well, don't we say they are faith-cures? We don't pretend that we can do them, as this Sequah you talk about does. You allow that great numbers *think* they are cured, and walk about without crutches or bandages, or pains in their bodies, and enjoy life again for a time at any rate; which is more than you can do for them, or they wouldn't come here to be healed.

Dr.—How long do they walk about without crutches or pains in their limbs? Why don't you take us behind the scenes, and let us test and follow up some of these cures?

Priest.—We can't take you behind the scenes, for there are no scenes to go behind. We tell you *we* don't do the cures, or know precisely how they are done. We can't hinder your inquiries, and don't want to hinder them if we could. There are the tablets of "reconnaissance," with names and addresses;

you can go to these, if you like, or talk to the patients whom you see at the spring or in the chapels.

Dr.—Come, now! You don't really mean to say you believe that our Lord's Mother appeared to this girl on 23rd March 1858, and told her that this Lourdes was a specially favourite place with her; and that she has since that time given these special healing qualities to the water or air of Lourdes, or whatever it is that causes these effects at this place?

Priest.—We mean to say that the girl thoroughly believed it, and we hold that her impression—her certainty—didn't come from the devil, as it must if it was a lie; that it wasn't the mere dream of a hysterical girl, and was not given her for nothing. Else, how can one account for these buildings, costing, perhaps, as much as one of your finest cathedrals, all put up in thirty-five years?

Dr.—Yes; but that doesn't answer my question. Did the Mother of our Lord appear to this girl, and is it she who works the cures.

Priest.—If you mean by "appear," "come visibly," we don't know. But you should remember always that the French have a very different feeling about the Madonna from you English. Perhaps you can't help connecting her with another French girl, Joan of Arc, who believed the Madonna had appeared to her and told her she should turn you English out of France, which she did—a more difficult and costly job even than building these churches.

Dr.—Well, we won't argue about the Madonna, and I am quite ready to admit that the evidence you have here, in the tablets and votive offerings, the crutches and bandages, are *primâ-facie* proof that numbers of pilgrims have gone away from Lourdes under the impression that they were cured. What I maintain is, that you have not shown, and cannot show, that your cures are not merely due to the absorption of diseased tissue as the result of strong excitement—an effect not at all common, but quite recognised as not unfrequent by some of the highest authorities in medical science.

There the controversy rests, I think; at any rate, so far as I heard it debated; and I must own that the scientific explanation does not seem to me to hold water. To take one instance, would the absorption of diseased tissue drive a piece of cloth out of a soldier's leg or body? Perhaps yes, for what I know; but would the excitement of a mother cure the disease of her child? These two classes of cures (of which there are a great number) struck me, perhaps, more than any of the rest. But I must not take up more of your space, and can only advise all your readers who are really interested in this problem to take the first opportunity they can of going to Lourdes, and, if possible, as we did, at a time when the great bodies of pilgrims are not there, and they can quietly examine the facts there, for—*pace* the doctors and men of science—these tablets, swords, crutches, etc., are facts which they are bound to acknowledge and investigate. I shall be surprised if they do not come away, as I did, with a feeling that they have seen a deeply interesting sight for which it is well worth while to come from England, and that there are two sides to this question of the Lourdes miracles (so-called), either of which any reverent student of the world in which he is living may conscientiously hold.

Fontarabia, 22nd April 1893.

Every year the truth of Burns's "the best-laid schemes o' mice and men gang aft a-gley," comes more home to me. From the time I was ten the Pass of Roncesvalles has had a fascination for me. Then the habit of ballad-singing was popular, and a relative of mine had a well-deserved repute in that line. Amongst her old-world favourites were "Boland the Brave" and "Durandarté." The first told how Boland left his castle on the Rhine, where he used to listen to the chanting in the opposite convent, in which his lady-love had taken the veil on the false report of his death, and "think she blessed him in her prayer when the hallelujah rose"; and followed Charlemagne in his Spanish raid, till "he fell and wished to fall" at Boncesvalles. The second, how Durandarté, dying in the fatal pass, sent his last message to his mistress by his cousin Montesinos. In those days I never could hear the last lines without feeling gulpy in the throat:—

Kind in manners, fair in favour,

Mild in temper, fierce in fight,—

Warrior purer, gentler, braver,

Never shall behold the light.

They may not be good poetry, but Monk Lewis, the author, never wrote any others as good. Then Lockhart's *Spanish Ballads* were given me, and in one of the best of those stirring rhymes, Bernardo del Carpio's bearding of his King, I read—

The life of King Alphonso I saved at Roncesval,

Your word, Lord King, was recompense abundant for it all;

Your horse was down, your hope was flown; I saw the falchion

shine

That soon had drunk thy royal blood had I not ventured mine, etc.

Then, a little later, a family friend who had been an ensign in the Light Division in July 1813, used to make our boyish pulses dance with his tales of the week's fighting in and round Roncesvalles, when Soult was driven over the Pyrenees and Spain was freed. And again, later, came the tale of Taillefer, the Conqueror's minstrel, riding before the line at the battle of Hastings, tossing his sword in the air, and chanting the "Song of Roland," and of the "Peers who fell at Roncesvalles." So you will believe, sir, that my first thought when I got to Biarritz, with the Pyrenees in full view less than twenty miles off, was, "Now I shall see the pass where Charlemagne's peers, and five hundred British soldiers as brave as any paladin of them all, had fought and died." The holidays galloped, and one day only was left, when at our morning conference I found that my companions were bent on Fontarabia and San Sebastian, and assured me we could combine the three, as Roncesvalles, they heard, was close to Fontarabia. Then my faith in Sir Walter—combined, I fear, with my defective training in geography—led me astray, for had he not written in the battle-canto of Marmion:—

Oh, for one blast of that dread horn,

On Fontarabian echoes borne,

That to King Charles did come,

When Roland brave, and Oliver,

And every Paladin and Peer,

At Roncesvalles died, etc.

Now, of course, if Charlemagne could hear the horn of Roland on the top of the pass where he turned back, "borne on Fontarabian echoes," then Fontarabia must be at the foot of the pass, where Roland and the rear-guard were surrounded and fighting for their lives. In a weak moment I agreed to Fontarabia and San Sebastian, and so shall most likely never see Roncesvalles. It is fourteen miles distant as the crow flies, or thereabouts; and I warn your readers that the three can't be done in one long day from Biarritz.

However, I am bound to admit that Fontarabia and San Sebastian make a most interesting day's work. I had never been in Spain before, and so was well on the alert when a fellow-passenger, as we slowed on approaching the station, pointed across the sands below us and said, "There's Fontarabia!" There, perhaps two miles off, lay a small gray town on a low hill with castle and church at the top, and gateway and dilapidated walls on the side towards*us, looking as though it might have gone off to sleep in the seventeenth century—a really curious contrast to bustling Biarritz from which we had just come. We went down to the ferry and took a punt to cross the river, which threaded the broad sands left by the tide. It was full ebb; so our man had to take us a long round, giving us welcome time for the view, which, when the tide is up, must be glorious. Our bare-footed boatman, though Basque or Spaniard, was quite "up to date," and handled his punt pole in a style which would make him a formidable rival of the Oxford watermen in the punt race by Christ Church meadow, which, I suppose, is still held at the end of the summer term. A narrow, rough causeway led us from the landing-place to the town-gate in the old wall, where an artist who had joined the party was so taken with the view up the main street that he sat down at once to about as difficult a sketch as he will meet in a year's rambles. For from the gateway the main street runs straight up the hill to the ruined castle and church at the top. It is narrow, steep, and there are not two houses alike all the way up. They vary from what must have been palaces of the grandees—with dim coats-of-arms still visible over the doorways, and elaborately carved, deep eaves, almost meeting those of their opposite neighbours across the street—to poor, almost squalid houses, reaching to the second story of their aristocratic neighbours', but all with deep, overhanging, though uncarved eaves, showing, I take it, how the Spaniard values his shade. Up we went to the church and castle, the ladies looking wistfully into such shops as there were, to find something to buy; but I fancy in vain. Not a tout appeared to offer his services; or a shopkeeper, male or female, to sell us anything. Such of the Fontarabians as we saw looked at us with friendly enough brown eyes, which, however, seemed to say, "Silly souls! Why can't you stop at home and mind your own business?" Even at the end of our inspection, when we spread our lunch on a broad stone slab near the gate— the tombstone once, I should think, of a paladin—there being no houses of entertainment visible to us, we had almost a difficulty in attracting three or four children and a stray dog to share our relics.

The old castle is of no special interest, though there were a few rusty old iron tubes lying about, said to have once been guns, which I should doubt; and Charles V. is said to have often lived there during his French wars. The church is very interesting, from its strong contrast with those over the border—square, massive, sombre, with no attempt at decoration or ornament round the high brass altars, except here and there a picture, and small square windows quite high up in the walls, through which the quiet, subdued light comes. The pictures, with one exception, were of no interest; but that one exception startled and fascinated me. The subject is the "Mater Dolorosa," a full-length figure standing, the breast bare, and seven knives plunged in the heart,—a coarse and repulsive painting, but entirely redeemed by the intense expression of the love, the agony, grid the sorely shaken faith which are contending for mastery in the face. The painter must have been suddenly inspired, or some great master must have stepped in to finish the work. San Sebastian does not do after Fontarabia; a fine modern town, with some large churches and a big new bull-ring, but of little interest except for the fort which dominates the town on the sea-front. How that fort was stormed, after one repulse and a long siege of sixty-three days; how, in the two assaults and siege, more than four thousand gallant soldiers of the British and allied army fell; and the fearful story of the sack and burning of the old town by the maddened soldiers, is to me almost the saddest episode in our military history. I was glad when we had made our cursory inspection and got back to the station on our return to Biarritz. That brightest and most bustling of health resorts was our head-quarters, and I should think for young English folk must be about the most enjoyable above ground. I knew that it was becoming a formidable rival of the Riviera for spring quarters, but was not at all prepared for the facts. Almost the first thing I saw was a group of young Englishmen in faultless breeches and gaiters, just come back from a meet of the pack of hounds; next came along some fine strapping girls in walking costume, bent, I should think, on exploring the neighbouring battlegrounds; next, men and youths in flannels, bound for the golf links, where a handicap is going on (I wonder what a French caddie is like?); then I heard of, but did not see, the start of the English coach for Pau (it runs daily); and then youths on bicycles, unmistakable Britons,—though the French youth have taken kindly, I hear, to this pastime. There are four gigantic hotels at which friends told me that nothing is heard but English at their *tables d'hôte*; and in the quiet and excellent small "Hôtel de Bayonne," at which we stayed, having heard that it was a favourite with the French, out of the forty guests or thereabouts, certainly three-fourths were English, and the other one-fourth mostly Americans. On Easter Monday there was a procession of cars, with children in fancy dresses representing the local industries; but the biggest was that over which the Union Jack waved, and a small and dainty damsel sat on the throne surrounded by boys in the orthodox rig of a man-of-war's-man and Tommy Atkins. In fact, a vast stream of very solvent English seem to have fairly stormed and occupied the place, to the great delight of the native car-drivers and shopkeepers; and so grotesque was it that Byron's cynical doggerel kept sounding in my head as, at any rate, appropriate to Biarritz:

The world is a bundle of hay,

Mankind are the asses that pull;

Each tugs in a different way,

And the greatest of all is John Bull.

But, apart from all the high jinks and festive goings-on, there is one spot in Biarritz which may well prove a magnet to us, and before which we should stand with uncovered heads and sorrowfully proud hearts; and that is the fine porch of the English church. One whole side of it is filled by a tablet, at the head of which one reads: "*Pristinæ virtutis memor.* This porch, dedicated to the memory of the officers, non-commissioned officers, and men of the British army, who fell in the south-west of France from 7th October 1813 to 14th April 1814, was erected by their fellow-soldiers and compatriots, 1882." Then come the names of forty-eight Line regiments, and the German Legion, followed in each case by the death-roll, the officers' names given in full. Let me end with a few examples. The 42nd lost ten officers—two at Nive, one at Orthez, and seven at Toulouse; the 43rd—five at Nivelle and Bayonne; the 57th—six at Nivelle and Nive; the 79th—five at Toulouse, of whom three bore the name of Cameron; the 95th—six at the Bidassoa, Nivelle, and Nive. Such a record, I think, brings home to one even more vividly than Napier's pages the cost to England of her share in the uprising of Europe against Napoleon; and it only covers six months of a seven years' struggle in the Peninsula! At the bottom of the tablet are the simple words:—

Give peace in our time, oh Lord!

Echoes from Auvergne, La Bourboule, 2nd July 1893.

We had heard through telegrams and short paragraphs in the French papers of the sinking of the *Victoria* before the *Spectator* of 1st July came to us here, in these far-away highlands of Auvergne; but yours was the first trustworthy account in any detail which reached us. I am sure that others must have felt as thankful to you as I did, for your word was worthy the occasion, and told as it should be told, one of the stories which ennoble a nation, and remain a [Greek phrase] for all time. The lonely figure on the bridge is truly, as you say, a subject for a great pictorial artist, and belongs "rather to the poet than the journalist"; and one trusts that Sir George Tryon's may stand out hereafter in worthy verse as one of "the few clarion names" in our annals. But it was surely the noble steadfastness of all, from admiral to stoker, which has once more given us all "that leap of heart whereby a people rise" to a keener consciousness of the meaning of national life. I think one feels it even more out here amongst strangers than one would have felt it at home, and can give God thanks that the old ideal has come out again in the sinking of the *Victoria* as it did in that of the *Birkenhead* forty years ago, when the ship's boats took off all the women and children, and the big ship went down at last "still under steadfast men."

Those are, as you know, the words of Sir Francis Doyle, who gave voice to the mixed anguish and triumph of the nation in worthy verse. I heard the great story from the lips of one of the simplest of men, Colonel Wright, who as a subaltern had formed the men up on the deck of the *Birkenhead* under Colonel Seton, and stood at his place on the right of the line when she broke in two. He was entangled for some moments in the sinking wreck, but managed to free himself, and, being a famous swimmer, rose to the surface, and struck out for the shore amongst a number of the men. It must have been one of the most trying half hours that men ever went through; for, as they swam and cheered one another, now and again a comrade would suddenly disappear, and they knew that one of the huge sharks they had seen from the deck, passing backwards and forwards under the doomed ship, was amongst them. When they had all but reached the shore the man who swam by Wright's side was taken. When I heard the tale he was Assistant-Inspector of Volunteers under Colonel M'Murdo, and going faithfully through his daily work. Strange to say, neither Horse Guards nor War Office had taken any note of that unique deck-parade and swim for life, and Ensign Wright had risen slowly to be Major and Sub-Inspector of Volunteers. Stranger still, he seemed to think it all right, and there was no trace of resentment or jealousy in his plain statement of the facts—which, indeed, I had to draw out by cross-questioning on our march from the Regent's Park to our headquarters in Bloomsbury. I was so moved by the story that I wrote it all to Mr. Cardwell, then at the War Office, and had the pleasure of seeing Major Wright's name in the next *Gazette* amongst the new C.B.'s.

Well, well! It does one good now and then to breathe for a little in a rarer and nobler atmosphere than that of everyday, into which we must after all sink, and live there for nine-tenths of our time,—like the old fish-wife, Mucklebackit, going back to mending the old nets and chaffering over the price of herrings which have been bought by men's lives. And here we have great placards just out, announcing "Fêtes de jour et de nuit," with donkey-races and all manner of games, and fireworks, including an "embrasement général," whatever that may forebode. "This life would be quite endurable but for its amusements," said Sir G. Cornewall Lewis, a wise man and excellent Minister of the Crown.

Our first Sunday at La Bourboule has been edifying from the Sabbatarian point of view, and I shouldn't wonder if the good little parson who is taking the duty here during the bathing-season holds it up to us for instruction next Sunday, if he can get a room for service, and a congregation. There is no English church, and from what I hear not much prospect of an arrangement for joint worship in the French Protestant church, which was almost concluded, being carried out. Unfortunately, a succession of young Ritualists have managed to alarm the French Protestant pastor and his small flock, by treating them as Dissenters, and making friends ostentatiously with the Roman Catholic priests. However, happily the present incumbent (or whatever he should be called) is a sensible moderately broad Churchman, who it may be hoped will bring things straight again. But to return to my Sabbatarian story. An English lady fond of equestrian exercise hired horses for herself and a friend, and invited the able and pleasant young Irishman who doctors us all, and is also churchwarden, to accompany them for a ride in these lovely mountains. They started from this hotel, and, as it happened, just as the parson was coming by; so, not being quite easy in their consciences (I suppose), asked him if he saw any harm in it. To this he replied, sensibly enough, that it was their fight, not his; and if they saw none, he had nothing to say. So off they rode, meaning certainly to be back by 8 P.M. for supper. I was about till nearly nine, when they had not turned up; and next morning I heard the conclusion of the whole matter. The doctor's horse cast a shoe, and had to be led home, limping slightly; while the lady's horse came back dead-lame, and her companion's steed with both knees broken! Judging by the unmistakable talent of these good Bourboulais for appreciating the value to their guests of their water and other possessions, I should say that this Sunday ride will prove a costly indulgence to the excursionists.

La Bourboule, 10th July 1893.

Currency questions are surely amongst the things "which no fellow can understand,"—a truth for which. I think, sir, I may even claim you as a witness, after reading your cautious handling of the silver question in recent numbers. But so far as my experience goes, there are no questions as to which it is more difficult to shake convictions than those which have been arrived at by unscientific persons. For instance, in this very charming health-resort, the authorities at the Établissement des Bains, where one buys bath-tickets, are under the delusion that 20 fr. (French money) are the proper equivalent for the English sovereign. On my first purchase of six tickets, amounting to 15 fr. (each bath costs 2 fr. 50 c., or 50 c. more than at Royat), the otherwise intelligent person who presided at the *caisse d'établissement*, tendered me a single 5 fr. piece; and on my calling his attention to the mistake, as I supposed it to be, and demanding a second 5 fr., calmly informed me that 20 fr. was the change they always gave, and he could give no other. Whereupon, I carried off my sovereign in high dudgeon, and—there being neither bank nor money-changer's office in this place, though more than twenty large hotels!—applied to two of the larger shops only to find the same delusion in force. In short, I only succeeded in getting 25 fr. in exchange for my sovereign as a favour from our kind hostess at this hotel. Wherefore, as I hear that a great crowd of English are looked for next month, I should like to warn them to bring French money with them. This experience reminded me of a good story which I heard Thackeray tell thirty years ago. (If it is in *The Kicklebury's on the Rhine*, or printed elsewhere, you will suppress it). Either he himself or a friend, I forget which, changed a sovereign on landing in Holland, put the change in one particular pocket, and on crossing each frontier on his way to the South of Italy, before that country or Germany had been consolidated, again exchanged the contents of that pocket for the current coin of the Kingdom, Duchy, or Republic he was entering. On turning out the contents at Naples he found them equivalent to something under 5s. of English money.

Before I forget it, let me modify what I said last week as to the ecclesiastical position of the Protestants here.

The Anglicans are now represented by the "Colonial and Continental Society." They sent a clergyman, who has managed so well that we are now on excellent terms with our French Protestant brethren, though we have as yet no joint place of worship. This, however, both congregations hope to secure shortly,—indeed, as soon as they can collect £400, half of which is already in hand. Then the municipality, or the "Compagnie d'Établissement des Bains," I am not sure which, give a site, and another £400, which will be enough to pay for a small church sufficient for the present congregations.

These will hold the building in common, and, let us hope, will adjust the hours for the services amicably. At present, the French Protestants worship in the *buvette*, where we all drink our waters; and we Anglicans in an annex of the establishment—a large room devoted during the week to Punch and Judy and the marionettes. This rather scandalises some of our compatriots; I cannot for the life of me see why. Indeed, it seems to me a very healthy lesson to most of us, who are accustomed to the ritual which prevails in so many of our restored, or recently built, English churches,—the lesson which Jacob learnt on his flight from his father's tents, when he slept in the desert with a stone for pillow, "Surely the Lord is in this place, and I knew it not." Our congregation yesterday was something over thirty. I believe it rises to one hundred, or more, next month. The service was thoroughly hearty, and I really think every one must have come meaning to say their prayers. I felt a slight qualm as to how we should get on with the singing, and could not think why the parson should choose about the longest hymn in the book, for there was no organ, harmonium, or other musical instrument, and no apparent singing-men or singing-women. However, my qualms vanished when our pastor led off with a well-trained tenor voice which put us all at our ease.

The rest of our Sunday was by no means so successful, for the *fête du jour et du soir* began soon after our 11 A.M. *déjeûner*, and lasted till about 10 P.M., when the lights in most of the paper-lanterns had burnt out, and people had gone home from the Casino and the promenade to their hotels or lodgings. I am old-fashioned enough to like a quiet Sunday; but here, when the place is *en fête*, that is out of the question,—at any rate, if you are a guest at one of the hotels which, as they almost all do, faces on the "Avenue Gueneau de Mussy." That name will probably remind some of your readers of the able and popular doctor of the Orleans family, who accompanied their exile, lived in England during the Empire in Mortimer Street, Cavendish Square, and was popular in London society. After 1870 he returned to France, and, it seems, rediscovered these waters, or, at any rate, made them the fashionable resort of patients in need of arsenical treatment. In gratitude, his name has been given to this main avenue of La Bourboule, which runs the whole length of the town, parallel to the River Dordogne, which comes rushing down the valley from Mont Dore at a pace which I have never seen water attain except in the rapids below Niagara, in which that strongest and rashest of swimmers, Captain Webb, lost his life. The Avenue, though parallel with, is some fifty yards from the river, and the intervening space is planted with rows of trees, under which many donkeys and hacks stand for the convenience of visitors. The opposite bank of the Dordogne, which is crossed by two bridges, rises abruptly, and is crowned by the two rival casinos, with the most imposing hotel of the place between them, where (I am told) you pay 5 fr. a day extra for the convenience of the only lift in La Bourboule! The fête of last Sunday was given by the old Casino, and commenced directly after *déjeûner* with a gathering in the rooms and in front of the Casino on the terrace, where the guests sat at small tables consuming black coffee, absinthe, and other drinks, and strolling now and then into the billiard-room, or the room in which the *jeu aux petits chevaux*, and some other game of chance which I did not recognise, were in full swing. There is an inner room where baccarat and roulette are going on, supposed to be only open to tickets bought from the^ authorities, but which a young Englishman, my neighbour at the *table d'hôte*, tells me he found no difficulty in entering without a ticket. The rest of the fête, consisting chiefly of donkey-races, climbing greasy poles, and fishing half-francs out of meal tubs with the mouth, came off in a small park and plateau on the hillside above the Casino.

I used to enjoy donkey-races as a boy, when at our country feasts each boy rode his neighbour's donkey, and the last past the post was the winner, and should probably have gone up the hill to witness a French race, but that I found that here each boy rides his own donkey, and the first past the post wins. This takes all the fun out of the race, so I abstained. There were a few second-rate fireworks after dark, and the Casino and most of the hotels were prettily lighted, and the trees hung with yellow paper lanterns which looked like big oranges, but to the Englishman, more or less accustomed to the great Brock's performances, the illumination business was very flat.

Comité des Fêtes. 17th July 1893.

An Englishman can scarcely avoid the danger of having his national vanity fed in this La Bourboule. A new hotel is being built on a fine site above the Dordogne, just beyond the new Casino, and I hear on the best authority that the proprietor means to have it furnished from top to bottom by Messrs. Maple. As this will involve paying a duty of from 30 to 50 per cent on the articles imported, it is not easy to see where the profit can come in, as the most prejudiced John Bull will scarcely deny that native French furniture is about as good, and not very much dearer than English. I can only account for it by the desire of all purveyors here—from the chief hotel-keepers to the dealers in the pretty Auvergne jewellery and the donkey-women—to get us as customers,—not, perhaps, so much from love or admiration for us, as because we have so much less power of remonstrance or resistance to their charges. Unless he sees some flagrant overcharge in his hotel bill, the Briton does not care to air his colloquial French in discussing items with the former, who only meet him with polite shrugs; and as for the others, they at once fall back upon an Auvergnese *patois*, at least as different from ordinary French as a Durham miner's vernacular is from a West countryman's. What satisfaction can come of remonstrating about 2 fr., even in faultless grammatical French, when it only brings on you a torrent of explanation of which you cannot understand one word in ten?

But the desire to make us feel at home has another—I may almost say a pathetic—side. Thus the *Comité des fêtes* spares no effort to meet our supposed necessities, and has not only provided tennis-grounds and other conveniences for *le sport*, but for the last ten days has been preparing for a grand *chasse au renard*, as a special compliment, I am told, to the English visitors. The grand feature of the hunt is a *recherché* luncheon in an attractive spot in the forest, at the end of the run, at which the Mayor presides, and to which the other civic dignitaries go in full costume, accompanied by a chief huntsman and two *chasseurs* with *tridents*—of all strange equipments for a fox-hunt! For this luncheon the charge is 5 fr.; but, so far as I can learn, you may join the chase without partaking. The question naturally occurs: "How if Renard will not run that way, or consent to die within easy distance of the luncheon?" and the answer of the Mayor would, I suppose, be Dogberry's: "Let him go, and thank God you are rid of a knave." But, in any case, the *Comité des fêtes* are prepared for such a mishap, for they have had four foxes ready for some days, *in a large oven*—of all places in the world! and one of these will surely be induced to take the proper course, which is carefully marked out. As two of them have come from Switzerland, and there cannot be much to occupy or amuse Swiss foxes in an oven, except quarrelling with their French cousins, I should doubt as to the condition of the lot on the day of the hunt, even if all survive to that date. This, I am sorry to say, cannot be fixed as yet, for it seems that no English visitor has been found who will take a ticket; so I fear my "course" may be over before the *chasse* comes off. In that case I shall always bear a grudge against your lively contemporary, the *Daily Graphic*, who, it seems, printed an illustrated account of the *chasse* of last summer, to which the present abstinence of the British sportsman to-day is generally attributed. Can we wonder at the want of understanding between the two peoples when one comes across such strange pieces of farce as this, meant, I believe, for a genuine compliment and advance towards good-fellowship?

I wish I could speak hopefully upon more serious things than the *chasse au renard*; but in more than one direction things seem to me to be drifting, or going back, under the Republic. E.g. a friend of mine, who prefers smoking the cigars he is used to, ordered a box from his tobacconist in Manchester, who entrusted them to the Continental Parcels Delivery Company on 15th June. Next day, though notice had been given of payment of all charges on delivery, they were stopped at the Gare du Nord, at Paris, where the station-master refused to forward them until he got an undertaking in writing from my friend to pay all charges. This was sent at once, but produced no effect for three days, when another letter arrived—not now from the station-master, but from a person signing himself "Contributions Agent"—saying that undertaking No. 1 was not in proper form. Thereupon, undertaking No. 2 is sent; but still nothing happens, and my friend had almost given up hope of getting his cigars when he bethought him of advising with a deputy, who was luckily staying here in the same hotel. That gentleman seemed not at all surprised, but offered to write to his secretary in Paris to go to the Gare du Nord and look after the box. The offer was, of course, thankfully accepted, with the result that the cigars were sent on at once, with the following bill: "Droit d'entrée, 38 fr. 77 c.; timbre d'acquit à caution, 7 c.; toile d'emballage—consignation, 40 fr. 27 c.: total, 79 fr. 11 c."—which about doubled the original cost. This instance of the slovenliness (if not worse) of a railway company and the Customs has been quite eclipsed, however, by the Post Office. Another friend posted a letter here to his sister in England, but unluckily in the forenoon, when the next departure was for Bordeaux. To that town, accordingly, his letter went, and thence to America, whence in due course—i.e. at the end of three weeks—it reached its destination in England. Again, a lady here received several dividends more than a week ago, which she forwarded to her husband in England in a registered letter. This has never reached him; and the Post-Office officials here are making inquiries (very leisurely ones) as to what has become of it. Then the clergyman of the church here, having a payment to make in his parish in England, sent the money, and got the official receipt several posts before he received a reminder from the same official (dated a week earlier than the receipt) that the payment was due; and lastly, *pour comble*, as they say here, a county J.P. has never received at all the formal summons from his High Sheriff, sent some weeks since, to serve on the grand jury at the coming Assizes! Whatever the consequences may be of utterly ignoring such summons, he has thus incurred them, which, for all I know, may be equal to the penalties of præmunire. But seriously, I fear the incubus of the Republican superstition, as you have defined it, is spreading fast and far in this splendid land. The centralisation fostered by the Second Empire, and favoured by the Republic for the last twenty years, seems to have demoralised the national nerve-centre at Paris under the shadow of the Eiffel Tower—which,

Like a tall bully, lifts its head and lies,

—and to be spreading its baleful influence through the Departments. At any rate, that is the only explanation I can suggest for the marked deterioration and present flabbiness of all Government departments with which the foreign visitor comes in contact. I am glad to be able, however, to record, before closing this, that the registered letter containing dividend warrants mentioned above has reached its destination in England.

Dogs and Flowers, La Bourboule, 24th July.

During the greater part of our stay, the theatre here was devoted to comic and other operatic performances, which I did not care for, and so scarcely glanced at the play-bills, posted up daily in our hotel; and was not even tempted by the announcement of "une seule représentation extraordinaire" of Le Songe d'une Nuit d'Eté, as I did not like to have my idea of A Midsummer Night's Dream disordered by a French metrical version. When too late, I sorely regretted it, as, had I even read the caste, I should have gone, and been able to give you a trustworthy report,—for the three principal characters were William Shakespeare—by M. Dereims, of the opera (who would sing his great song of *La Reine de Saba*)—Falstaff, and Queen Elizabeth! Next morning I catechised a young Englishman, whose report was, as near as I can recollect, as follows: "Well, there wasn't much of our *Midsummer Night's Dream* in it, no Oberon and Titania, or Bottom, or all that fairy business. Queen Elizabeth and one of her ladies went out at night disguised, to a sort of Casino or Cremorne Gardens" [what would Secretary Cecil have said to such an escapade?], "and coming away they met Shakespeare and Falstaff, and had a good time; and Falstaff sang a song which brought the house down. Then, as the Queen falls in love with Shakespeare, they get some girl to marry him right away." One more lost opportunity, and to think that I shall probably never get another chance!—

There is a flower that shines so bright,

They call it marigold-a:

And he that wold not when he might,

He shall not' when he wold-a.

As you are fond of dog-lore, here is a sample from Auvergne. Just opposite our hotel lives the young Scotch (not Irish, as I think I called him last week) doctor. His wife owns a clever pug, whose friendship any self-respecting dog would be anxious, I should say, to cultivate. One of the rather scratch-pack gathered for the coming fox-chase, who wandered as they pleased about the town, seems to have shared my view, for every morning, between *café* and *déjeûner*, he came and paid a visit of about five minutes to Mrs. Gilchrist's pug, in the doctor's vestibule, always open to man and dog. At the end of his call, he trotted off down the avenue to whatever other business he might have in hand. Now, his visits could not have been amatory, as both are of the masculine sex, nor could they have been gastronomic, for he invariably refused the food which Mrs. Gilchrist offered him. What other conclusion is possible than that he came to talk over the gossip afloat in the dog-world of La Bourboule?

Lastly, as to the excursions. These are numerous, and very interesting in all ways, for you drive through great, sad pine-forests (in which I was astonished to see many of the trees gray with the weeping moss which makes the Louisiana and Texas forests so melancholy) and breezy heaths all aglow with wild flowers, getting every now and then indescribably glorious glimpses of the rich plain which stretches away from this backbone of Central France to the Alps. The flora is quite beyond me, but I recognised many varieties of heart's-ease, fox-gloves, gentians, amongst them an exquisite blue variety, and the air was often scented with meadow-sweet or wild-thyme. Then almost every mountain-top is crowned by a peculiarly shaped block of dark rock, which looks as if some huge saurian, disgusted with a changing world, had crawled up there to die and get petrified. They must, however, have been even bigger than the *Atlanlosaurus immanis*, the biggest of the family yet found, I believe. I well remember the delight of Dr. Agnew, of New York, when the American geologists came upon its thigh bone, two feet longer than that of any European monster. It had become agate, and I have a scarf-pin made of a polished fragment, and presented to me by the triumphant doctor. I cannot tell you what these rocks really are, as I made no ascent, preferring nowadays, like dear Lowell, "to make my ascents by telescope."

But the human interest of the excursions, as usual, far exceeds the botanical or geological. The chief of these is the "Tour d'Auvergne," the seat of the Count who enlisted to repel invasion, but never would take a commission from Republic or Napoleon, and died in battle, the "premier grenadier de la France." There is nothing left of his tower except the foundations, and a dungeon on the high rock, on which a native woman sells photographs and relics, quite as genuine, I should say, as most such. Opposite, across a deep valley, rises another rock crowned by a chapel, which is approached by a steep path, up which once a year goes a procession, past the seven stations, at each of which there is a crucifix, and on the lowest a figure the size of life. Christianity, they say, has died down very low in Auvergne. I should doubt it, as I saw no sign of defacement, either here or on any of the roadside crosses, which are everywhere. I fear we could hardly say as much if we had them—as I wish we had—on every English high-road. On the walls of the village which clusters round the side of the keep, a placard (of which I enclose a copy) interested me much. The three Municipal Councillors there give their reasons for resigning their seats on the Council. On the whole, I think they were wrong, and should have stayed and "toughed it out." I should like to know how it strikes you. You will see that the poster bears a stamp. Might not our Chancellor of the Exchequer raise a tidy sum that way? What a lump Pears, Hudson, Epps, or Van Houten and Co. would have to pay, and earn the thanks of a grateful country too! But I must not try your patience or space further, so will only note the Roman remains at Mont Dore, another health-resort of the Dordogne Valley, four miles above La Bourboule, which are worth going all the way to see, as I would advise any of your readers to do who are looking out for an interesting countryside, with as fine air as any in the world, in which to spend their coming holidays.

Dutch Boys, The Hague, 1st May 1894.

Much may be said both for and against breaking one's good resolutions, but no one, I should think, will deny the merit of making them. Well, sir, before starting for my Whitsuntide jaunt this year, I resolved firmly that nothing should induce me to send you any more letters over this signature. Have I not been trying your patience, and the long-suffering of your readers any time these thirty years, with my crude first impressions of cities and their inhabitants, from Constantinople to the Upper Missouri? "Surely," I said to myself, "sat prata biberunt." What can young England in the last decade of the century—who enjoy, or at any rate read, *Dodo, and The Fabian Essays, and The Heavenly Twins*—care or want to know about the notions of an old fogey, whose faiths—or fads, as they would call them—on social and political problems were formed, if not stereotyped, in the first half? What, then, has shaken this wise resolve? You might guess for a week and never come within miles of the answer. It was the sight of a group of Dutch boys playing leap-frog in front of this hotel, and the contrast which came unbidden into my head between the chances of Dutch and English boys in this matter, and the different use they make of them.

In front of this hotel lies the large open space, now planted with trees, and about the size of Grosvenor Square, which is called "Tournooiveld," and was in the Middle Ages the tilt-yard of the doughty young Dutch candidates for knighthood. The portion of this square immediately in front of the hotel, about 40 yards deep and 150 broad, is marked off from the rest by a semicircular row of granite posts, rather over three feet in height, and three to four yards apart, two of them being close to lampposts, but the line otherwise unbroken. No chain connects these posts, and they have no spike on the top of them. As I stood at the door the morning after my arrival, admiring the fine linden-trees in full foliage, enter four Dutch boys from the left, who, without a word, broke at once into single file, and did "follow my leader" over all the posts till they got to the end on the extreme right, and disappeared quietly down a side street. Well, you will say, wouldn't four English boys have done just the same % and I answer, Yes, certainly, so far as playing leap-frog over the posts goes; but they would have to come out here to find such a row of posts in the middle of a city. At any rate, in the city with which I am best acquainted in England, the few posts there fit for leap-frog are connected with chains and have spikes on their tops. Moreover, do I not pass daily up a flight of steps, fenced on either side by a broad iron banister, which was obviously intended by Providence for passing boys to get a delicious slide down 1 But, sir, no English boy on his way to school or on an errand has ever slid down those banisters, for the British Bumble has had prohibitory knobs placed on them at short intervals for no possible reason except to prevent boys sliding down. The faith that all material things should be made to serve the greatest good of the greatest number is surely as widely held in England as in Holland, and yet, here are the tops of these Dutch posts *culotté*, if I may say so, worn smooth and polished by the many generations of boys who have enjoyed leap-frog over them, while the British posts and banisters have given pleasure to no human being but Bumble from the day they were put up.

But it was not of the Dutch posts but the Dutch boys that I intended to write, for they certainly struck me as differing in two particulars from our boys, thus. Two of the posts, as I have said, are so close to the lamp-posts that you can't vault over them without coming full butt against the lamp-post on the other side. When the leader came to the first of them he did not pass it, as I expected, but just vaulted on to the top, and sat there while he passed his leg between the-post and the lamp-post, and then jumped down and went on to the next. Every one of the rest followed his example gravely and without a word; whereas, had they been English boys, there would have been a bolt past the leader as soon as he was seated, and a race with much shouting for the lead over the remaining pillars. I have been studying the Dutch boy ever since, and am convinced that he is the most silent and most "thorough" of any of his species I have ever come across; and the boy is father to the man in both qualities. On Whit-Monday this city was crowded, all the citizens and country-folk from the suburbs being in the streets and gardens; the galleries and museums, oddly enough, being closed for the day. Walking about amongst them the silence was really rather provoking. At last I took to counting the couples we met who were obviously just married, or courting, and ought at any rate to have had something to say to each other. Out of eleven couples in one street, only one were talking, though all looked quite happy and content. It is the same everywhere. As we neared the landing-place at the Hook of Holland, our steamer's bows were too far out, and a rope had to be thrown from the shore. There were at least twenty licensed porters waiting for us, in clean white jackets,—one of these, without a word, just coiled a rope and flung it. It was missed twice by the sailor in our bows, and fell into the water, out of which the thrower drew it, and just coiled and threw it again without a word of objurgation or remonstrance, and the third time successfully. Not one of the white-jacketed men who stood round had uttered a syllable of advice or comment; but what a Babel would have arisen in like case at the pier-heads of Calais or Dieppe, or for that matter at Dover or Liverpool. No wonder that William the Silent is the typical hero of Dutchmen; there are two statues of him in the best sites in this city, and half a dozen portraits in the best places in the galleries. Hosea Biglow's—

Talk, if you keep it, pays its keep,

But gabble's the short road to ruin.

'Tis gratis (gals half price), but cheap

At no price when it hinders doing,—

ought to be put into Dutch as the national motto. Then as to thoroughness. Take the most notable example of it first. We have been driving all round for some days, and have only once come to a slope up which our horse had to walk. When we got to the top, there was the sea on the other side, obviously even to the untrained eye at a considerably higher level than the green fields through which we had just been driving. Of course it is an old story, the Dutchman's long war with the German Ocean, but one never realises it till one comes to drive uphill to the sea, and then it fairly takes one's breath away. I was deeply impressed, and took advantage of a chance that offered of talking the subject over with an expert, who, like most Dutchmen, happily speaks English fluently. Far from expressing any anxiety as to the land already won, he informed me that they are seriously contemplating operations against the Zuider Zee, and driving him permanently out of Holland! And I declare I believe they will do it, and so win the right, alone, so far as I know, amongst the nations, of saying to the sea: "Hitherto shalt thou come and no further, and here shall thy proud waves be stayed." One more example,— their thoroughness as to cleanliness. Not only the pavements of the main thoroughfares, but all the side-streets are thoroughly well washed and cleansed daily. When you walk out in the early morning you might eat your breakfast anywhere with perfect comfort on the sidewalks. We had to look for more than a quarter of an hour to find a bit of paper in the streets, and the windows in the back streets, even of houses to let, are rubbed bright and polished to a point which must be the despair of the passing English housewife. Why are Dutch house-maidens so incomparably more diligent and clean than English? Can it be their Puritan bringing-up? In short, ten days' residence here—I have never before done anything but rush through the country on my way east—seems likely to make me review old prejudices, and to exclaim, "If I were not an Englishman, I would be a Dutchman!" One may read and enjoy Motley without really appreciating this silent and "thorough" people, or understanding how it came to pass that by them, in this tiny and precarious corner of Europe, "the great deliverance was wrought out."

"Poor Paddy-Land!"—I—6th Oct. 1894.

Six weeks ago, when I was considering where I should go for my autumn holiday, some remarks of yours decided me "to give poor Paddy-land a turn" (the phrase is not mine, but that of the first housemaid I came across in Dublin). When one has been talking and thinking for the last eight years of little else than that "distressful country," it certainly seemed a fair suggestion that one might as well go and look at it when one got the chance. So I have scrambled round from Dublin to Kerry, and from Cork to the Giant's Causeway, and can bear hearty witness to the soundness of your advice. For a flying visit of a few weeks, though insufficient for any serious study of a people or country, may greatly help one in judging both of them from one's ordinary standpoint at home.

Of course, the first object of an Englishman who has not lost his head must be to ascertain whether the Irish people really long for a separate Parliament, and a severance of all connection with the rest of the Empire. Well, sir, I was prepared to find that the men in the street—car-drivers, boatmen, waiters, and fellow-travellers on the railways—would, to a great extent, adapt their opinions to whatever they might think would please their questioner, but certainly was quite unprepared for the absolute unanimity with which I was assured that Home Rule is dead. It is only the American-Irish, and especially the "Biddys of New York," so my informants protested, "who want to break up the Union." I was warned, however, as to the man in the street. "You must remember that our people are full of imagination, and you must take off a large discount from all they tell you; but you'll always find a groundwork of fact at the bottom of their stories." A good piece of advice, which a professional friend in Dublin started me with, and which I found to be true enough, except that where local politics or the land came in, the groundwork of fact was apt to be too minute to be easily discerned. Take, as an example, a story which was told me on the spot by a thoroughly trustworthy witness. Towards the end of Mr. Forster's Chief-Secretaryship a sensation message was flashed to New York that a Government stronghold had been taken by the Invincibles, the garrison having surrendered with all the guns and stores. This announcement produced a liberal response in dollars from the other side, particularly from "the Biddys of New York." Now for the "groundwork of fact" underlying this superstructure. The Government have, it seems, on their hands a number of Martello towers on the southern coast which are useless for military purposes. A band of some dozen "bhoys," headed by a notorious Invincible, came out of Cork one summer evening and summoned the garrison of one of these Martello towers. The garrison (an elderly pensioner), who was at tea with his wife and children, wisely surrendered at discretion; whereupon the patriots took possession of the single cannon and some old muskets and ammunition, which latter they carried off next morning, when they abandoned the tower and cannon on the approach of the police. But though the groundwork of fact as to the condition of the Home Rule agitation may be infinitesimal, there is very serious apprehension still on the Land Question, upon which I found it difficult to draw the man in the street. I was fortunate enough, however, to come across several resident landlords and professional men, both Catholic and Protestant, who, one and all, look with the gravest distrust at the operation of recent land legislation. The Commissioners who administer these Acts have, unfortunately, the strongest interest in prolonging the present state of uncertainty. Their appointments will end with the cessation of appeals by tenants for further reductions of rent, which, under the circumstances, does not seem likely to come about before the landlords' interest has been pared down bit by bit till it touches prairie-value. The present utter confusion and uncertainty is at any rate a striking object-lesson as to the dangers of meddling with freedom of contract by Acts of Parliament.

When I landed in Ireland, I was under the impression—for which I think you, sir, and perhaps the late Lord Beaconsfield, with his dictum about the "melancholy ocean," were responsible—that there is a note of sadness underlying the superficial gaiety of the Irish character, as is the case with most Celts. Well, whether it be from natural incapacity, and that each observer only brings with him a limited power of seeing below the surface in such matters, in any case I wholly failed to discern any such characteristic in Central or South Ireland, though there may be a trace of it perhaps in the North, where, by the way, they are not Celts. On the contrary, the remark of a friendly and communicative Killarney carman, "Shure, sir, we always try to get on the sunny side of the bush, like the little birds," seemed to me transparently true. And next to this desire for the sunny side of the bush, a happy-go-lucky, hand-to-mouth temper struck me as the prevailing characteristic, as Sir Walter saw it when he wrote "Sultan Solomon's Search after Happiness." Look at the national vehicle, the outside car—far more national and popular than our hansom. Did any race ever invent a conveyance so easy to mount and dismount from, or which offers the same chances of being shot off at every street corner or turn in the road? If any reader doubts, let him go over to the next horse-show at Dublin, and watch the crowd breaking up at the end of the show. The roads into the city are certainly unusually broad, but the sight of a dozen jaunting-cars coming along, two or three abreast, as hard as their horses can trot, the driver lolling carelessly, with a loose rein, on one side, and a couple of Irishmen on the other, is a sight to make the Saxon "sit up," though he may be accustomed to the fastest and most reckless West End hansoms. Like one of your recent correspondents, I could distinguish natives from visitors, as each of the latter had a tight hold of the bar—a precaution which the native scorned. I managed to extract from an enthusiastic admirer—a young Irish subaltern who had ridden on them all his life—the confession that he had left a car involuntarily (or, *Anglid*, had been shot out) three times in the last eighteen months; but then, as he explained, he always fell on his feet! I was touched again and again by the almost pathetic craving for English appreciation,—quite as strong, I think, as, and certainly much pleasanter than, that of our American cousins. I was exploring the Killarney Lakes, in the first-rate four-oared boat of a cadet of the MacGrillicuddy family, who, with his English wife, exercises a very delightful hospitality almost under the shadow of "The Reeks," which bear his name. It was a perfect day, the changing lights and tints on mountains and woods and lakes being more delicately lovely than any I could recall, except, perhaps, at the head of the Lake of Geneva. We had been talking of the Scotch lakes, and I could not help saying, "Why, this beats Loch Katrine and Ellen's Isle out of the field."

"Ah," said our host, with a sigh, "if only Sir Walter Scott had been an Irishman!" and then he went on to speak of the neglect of Ireland by the Royal Family and English governing people—e.g. Lord Beaconsfield had never set foot in her, and Mr. Gladstone only once, for an hour or two, to receive the freedom of Dublin. But why had the Queen made her favourite home in Scotland, and left poor Ireland out in the cold? Why did the English flock to Scotch rivers and moors and golf-links in crowds every autumn when only a stray sportsman or tourist found his way to Killarney or Connemara or Donegal? It was all owing to the Wizard of the North, who had made Scotland enchanted ground.

Without ignoring other and deeper causes, I think one cannot but feel what a difference it would have made if Sir Walter had been Irish. The Siege of Derry is a more heroic and pathetic story than any in Scotch annals of the struggle for the Stuarts, and the genius which has made us intimate friends of the Baron of Bradwardine and Dugald Dalgetty, of Dandie Dinmont, Edie Ochiltree, Jeanie Deans, Cuddie and Mause Headrigg, and a dozen other Scotch men and women, would surely have found as good materials for character-painting among the Irish peasantry. But the speculation, though interesting, is too big to deal with at the end of a paper.

"Poor Paddy-Land!"—II

I suppose every one expects to find Ireland the land of the unlooked-for. I did, at any rate, but was by no means prepared for several of the surprises which greeted me. For instance, the best arranged, and for its size and scope the most interesting, National Gallery I have ever seen. It is only forty years old (incorporated in 1854), a date since which one would have thought it scarcely possible to get together genuine specimens of all the great schools of art, from the well "picked-over" marts of England and the Continent. But the feat has been accomplished, mainly, I believe, by the entire devotion and fine taste and judgment of the late director, Mr. Henry E. Doyle. His untimely death in the spring of this year has left a blank, social and artistic, which it will be hard to fill; but happily his great work for Irish art was done, and all that his successors will have to do will be to follow his lead faithfully. Irish Art owes much to his family, for he was the son of H. B., and the younger brother of the immortal "Dicky," while, I believe, Mr. Conan Doyle is his nephew.

But it is not the general collection of pictures, remarkable as that is, which differentiates the Irish from other national galleries known to me. It is the happy arrangement which has set apart a fourth of the whole space for a collection of portraits, and authentic historical pictorial records, comprising not only the portraits of eminent Irishmen and Irishwomen, but also of statesmen and others who were politically or socially connected with Ireland, or whose lives serve in any way to illustrate her history, or throw light on her social or literary or artistic records. I think I may safely venture the assertion—for I spent the greater part of two afternoons in this historical and portrait department—that there is Scarcely a man or woman, from the time of Elizabeth to that of O'Connell and Lord Melbourne, of whom one would be glad to know more, with whom one does not leave it, feeling far better acquainted. And then they are so admirably and often pathetically grouped, e.g. Charles I., Cromwell, and R. Cromwell, on a line, all full of character, and Strafford hard by, with the look of "thorough" on his brow and mouth as no other portrait I have ever seen has given. Then there are "Erin's High Ormonde," Sir Walter Raleigh, by Zuccaro, painted between his two imprisonments, and coming down later, Lords Wellesley and Hastings, and groups of great nobles and Lords-Lieutenant. For fighting men, William III. as a boy; Walker, the defender of Derry; the Duke, the Lawrences, Lord Gough, and a score of other gallant Irishmen. The terrible Dean stands out amongst the literary men, and near him Sir R. Steele and Sterne, and (*longo intervallo*, except on shelves) Tom Moore, Croker, Lever, etc. Then come the "patriots" of all schools: Lord E. Fitzgerald, and Grattan, and E. Hudson, Secretary of the United Irishmen in 1784; Wolfe Tone, and Daniel

O'Connell; half a dozen Ponsonbys of different ranks, and several pictures of Burke, one of which especially (said to be by Angelica Kauffmann) is, to my mind, quite invaluable. Burke stands upright, his side-face towards you, sublime, as he looked, I am sure, when he was making his immortal speech at Bristol. By his side, at right angles, so that you get his full face, is Charles Fox, one hand on Burke's shoulder, the other on a table on which he is leaning. You can hear him saying as plainly as if you were there one hundred years ago, "Now, my dear Edmund, if you say that in the House, you'll upset the coach." Fox has evidently dined well, and Burke is fasting from all but indignation. The portraits of women are as interesting, such as Miss Farren, afterwards Lady Derby; Mrs. Norton, by Watts, which is worth a visit to Dublin to see, etc. But I must not run on, and will only note one lesson I carried away. There are two portraits, and three engravings from portraits, by N. Hone, R.A., an Irishman, but one of our original Royal Academicians. You will remember what Peter Pindar says of that painter in his *Odes to the Royal Academicians*":—

And as for Mr. Nathan Hone,

In portraits he's as much alone

As in his landscape stands the unrivalled Claude.

Of pictures I have seen enough,

Vile, tawdry, execrable stuff,

But none so bad as thine, I vow to God.

I have always till now maintained that Peter, with all his cynicism, was the best art critic, the Ruskin, shall we say, of his time. Now I give him up. N. Hone was no doubt quarrelsome and disagreeable, but he was a very considerable portrait-painter.

I had noted Derry as one of the places to be seen on account of the siege, and accordingly went there, to get another startling sensation. Like most other folk, I suppose, I had always looked on the story as interesting and heroic, and had wondered in a vague way how some 30,000 men, commanded by a distinguished French soldier, and a considerable part of them at any rate well-equipped regular troops, could have been kept at bay for ten months by a mere handful of regulars, backed by the 'prentice boys of the town and neighbourhood. Religious zeal was no doubt a strong factor on the side of the town, and Parson Walker, a born leader of men, "with a bugle in his throat," like "Bobs." But when one remembers that no provision had been made for a siege, that many of the leading men were for opening the gates, and indeed that the French officers and James's deputy were actually within 300 yards in their boats, to accept the surrender, when the 'prentices rushed down and shut and manned the gates, and then looks at the scene on the spot, one is really dumbfounded, and wanders back in thought to King Hezekiah and Jerusalem. From the Cathedral, which dominates the city, you can trace distinctly the line of the old walls, and can hardly believe your eyes. The space enclosed cannot be more than a quarter of a mile in length, by some 300 yards in breadth (I could not get exact measurements), and in it, including garrison and the country folk who had flocked in, were more than 30,000 people. It was bombarded for eight months, during at least the last four of which famine and pestilence were raging. No wonder that the parish registers tell of more than 9000 burials in consecrated ground, while "the practice of burial in the backyards became unavoidable!" Where can such another story be found in authentic history? Parson Walker, let us say, fairly earned his monument.

I must own to grievous disappointment as to the farming in Ulster. All through the South and Centre I had seen the hay in the fields in small cocks in September, and the splendid ripe crops of oats and barley uncut, or, if cut, left in sheaf, or being carried in a leisurely fashion, which was quite provoking, while tall, yellow ragweed was growing in most of the pastures in ominous abundance. That will all be altered, I thought, when I cross "Boyne Water." Not a bit of it! Here and there, indeed, I saw a good rick-yard and clean fields, but scarcely oftener than about Cork or Killarney, and no one seemed to mind any more than the pure southern Celts. One man said, when I mourned over the ragweed three feet or four feet high, that he did not mind it, as it showed the land was good! As to leaving hay in cock, well that was the custom—they would get it into stack after harvest, any way before Christmas; as to dawdling over cutting and carrying, well, with prices at present rates, what use in hurrying? There was a comic song called "Clear the Kitchen," popular half a century ago, which ran—

I saw an old man come riding by.

Says I, "Old man, your horse will die";

Says he, "If he dies I'll tan his skin,

And if he lives I'll ride him agin."

It fits the Irish temper, North and South, pleasant enough to travel amongst, but bad, I should think, to live with.

"Panem et Circenses", Rome, 21 st April 1895.

I have been asking myself at least a dozen times a day during the last fortnight, why Rome should be (to me, at any rate) the city of surprises, far more than Athens or Constantine, for instance, or any other city or scene of world-wide interest in Europe or America. Jerusalem and the Nile cities I have never seen (and fear I never shall now). Surely, to what I take to be the majority of your readers, who have gone through, as I have, the orthodox educational mill—public school and college—precisely the contrary should be true. We spent no small part of from six to ten years of the most impressionable time of our lives in studying the story of the Mistress of the Old World, from Romulus and Remus to the Anto-nines. Even the idlest and most careless of us could scarcely have passed his "greats" without knowing his geography well enough to point out on the map the position of each of the seven hills, the Forum, the Janiculum, the Appian Way, the Arch of Titus, the Colosseum, etc., and must have formed some kind of notion in his own mind of what each of them looked like. At any rate, I had no excuse for not knowing my ancient Rome better than I knew any modern city, both as to its geography and the politics, beliefs, and habits of its citizens; for I was for two years in the pupil-room of a teacher (Bishop Cotton) who spared no pains, not only on the texts of Livy, Horace, Sallust, and Juvenal, and the geography, but in making the Rome of the last years of the Republic and the first Caesars live again for us. For instance, he would collect for us all the best engravings then to be had (it was before the days of photographs) of Rome, and show us what remained of the old buildings and monuments, and where the Papal city had encroached and superseded them; and again, would take infinite pains to explain the changes in the ordinary life of the Roman citizen, which had been creeping on since the end of the third Punic war, when her last formidable rival went down, and the struggle between patrician and plebeian had time and opportunity to develop and work itself out, till it ended in the Augustan age, when the will of the Cæsar remained the sole ultimate law, in Rome, and over the whole Empire. Of course the explanation of the phrase "Panem et circenses," and the growth of the system, in the shape of public feastings, shows, baths, and other entertainments, with which each successful Tribune or General, as he came to the front, and the Cæsars after them, tried to bribe and sway the mob of the Forum, formed no small part of this instruction. One item of the list will best illustrate my text—that of public baths—which came most directly home to me, as I was devoted to swimming in those days, and so had great sympathy with the poor citizen of Imperial Rome who desired to have baths in the best form and without payment.

I do not know that there is any trustworthy evidence as to the public baths of Rome before Imperial times, but we can estimate pretty accurately how the case stood for the poor Roman in the first and second centuries A.D. The best preserved of these are the Baths of Caracalla, in which sixteen hundred bathers could be accommodated at once. The enclosed area was 360 yards square, or considerably larger than Lincoln's Inn Fields; but this included a course for foot-races, in which, I suppose, the younger bathers contended when fresh from the delights of hot and cold baths, while their elders looked on from the porticoes adjoining. The bathing establishment proper, however, was 240 yards in length, by 124 yards in width, in which the divisions of the "tepidaria," "calidaria," and "frigidaria," are still confidently pointed out in Baedeker, and attested by guides if you like to hire them. But the part which interested me most, apart from the huge masses of wall still standing, was the depression in the floor, which is said to have been the swimming-bath, and which is at least twice as large as those of the Holborn and Lambeth baths, the two largest in London in my time, put together.

The remains of the walls are just astounding, eight feet and ten feet thick, and (I should say) in several places fifty feet high; the thin Roman bricks, and the mortar in which they are built, as hard as they were in the second century. I wish I could feel any confidence that any of our London brickwork would show as well even a century hence. When the floors were all covered with mosaic pavement, of which small pieces now carefully preserved still remain, and the brickwork of the walls was faced with marble, and the statues which have been found here and removed to museums, still stood round the central fountain and in the courts, my imagination quite fails to picture what the baths must have looked like. But the Baths of Caracalla, though best preserved, are not by any means the largest. Those of Diocletian, on the Quirinal and partly facing the railway station, were almost twice as big, for the circumference of the bath buildings was about 2000 yards, or half as large again as the Baths of Caracalla, while they would accommodate (it is said) three thousand bathers at once. It is even more impossible, however, to reconstruct these baths in one's fancy than those of Caracalla, for the church of St. Bernardo occupies one domed corner of the area, and a prison another corner; while a convent, with the Church of St. Maria degli Angeli attached— built by Michael Angelo by order of Pius IV.—stands over what was the "tepidarium." There is still, however, space enough left for the large square, as big as Bedford Square, and surrounded by cloisters said to be also the work of Michael Angelo, in which stand a number of the most interesting statues and busts, and architectural fragments lately exhumed.

I have by no means exhausted the opportunities enjoyed by the Roman citizen under the Antonines for getting a satisfactory, not to say a luxurious, wash in the Roman summer, but must turn aside for a minute to tell you of an interesting little scene which I saw outside on leaving the Baths of Diocletian. Along the bottom of the old ruined wall still standing, and looking as firm as that of Caracalla, for about fifty yards, earth and rubbish has been allowed to accumulate to the height of twelve or fourteen feet. This dirt-heap covers some twenty feet of the open space between the old wall and the footway, and, the face of it having been trampled hard, forms a steep slope, of which the Roman urchin of to-day seems to have taken possession, and thereon thoroughly to enjoy himself after his own fashion. This is a very different way from that of our street-boys, if I may judge by what I saw in passing. A group of some dozen little ragged urchins—four with bare feet— were at high jinks as I came up; and this was their pastime. The biggest of them, a sturdy boy of (perhaps) eleven or twelve, stood at the bottom of the steep slope, facing the wall, with his feet firmly set, and his arms wide open. The rest, who were at the top of the slope, against the wall, ran down one after another and threw themselves into his arms, clasping him round the neck, and getting a good hug before he dropped them. The object seemed to be (so far as I could see) to throw him over backwards, but he stood his ground firmly, only staggering a little once or twice during the two rounds which I was able to watch. I was obliged then to leave, wondering, and debating in my mind what would be the result of such a game if tried by our street boys in a London suburb.

To go back to the Baths, there are remains of three more which must have been no unworthy rivals of Caracalla's and Diocletian's—viz. those of Constantine, Agrippa, and Titus. The first were also on the Quirinal, and are said to have occupied the greater part of the present Piazza del Quirinale, including the site of the Royal Palace. But as all that is left of them is a fragment of the old boundary-wall here and there, one can form no notion of their size or shape. One may, however, judge of their character by magnificent colossal marble statues of the "Horse-tamers," which are known to have stood one on each side of the principal entrance, and are believed to remain almost in the place where they stand to-day. The Baths of Agrippa lay behind the Pantheon, but a fluted column and ruined dome are all that remain of them in the neighbouring streets, "Pumbella" and "Cumbella." Lastly, there were the Baths of Titus, begun by him in A.D. 80, on the Esquiline, which included the sites of Mæcenas' Villa and the Golden Palace of Nero, which (I suppose) he must have demolished to make room for them; but the tradition as to these ruins seems even more vague than that of any of the other baths. I think you must allow that so far I have proved my case, that Rome is the city of surprises.

Ever since my "Roman baths' round," the contrast of Imperial Rome and our London has been popping up. Why have not we, at any rate, one or two public baths on something like the old Roman scale? Did they really let any Roman citizen bathe free of charge? Could we possibly do that? and how? Well, after all, it only wants a Cæsar to work the "panem et circenses" trick astutely. And have not we got at last our equivalent for Nero or Titus in our County Council? True, our many-headed Cæsar has not the tribute of a conquered world to draw on, or an unlimited supply of prisoners of war, slaves, and poor Christians to set to the work. But has not he the rates of London at his mercy—not a bad equivalent—and the Collectivist Trade-Unionist, who may possibly be relied on to do as fair a day's work at the scale-wages as the unpaid slave or Christian did for Titus? Well, I do not know that I should protest vigorously—only I am no longer a London ratepayer.

Rome—Easter Day

We get our London papers here as regularly as you do, only forty-eight hours later, and I see that readers at home have been able to follow the course of the services in St. Peter's and the Roman Churches during Passion Week about as well as we who are on the spot, and so to appreciate the thoroughness which the priesthood, from cardinals downwards, for I am sorry to say the Pope is still unable to take his usual part, throw into the attempt to reproduce the supreme drama of our race, so far as this can be done, day by day, almost hour by hour. I have not, however, noticed any mention of the "Tenebræ" at St. John Lateran, a service of rather more than an hour, from 4.30 to 5.30, on the afternoon of Good Friday, when the last words have fallen from the cross, and Joseph of Arimathæa, with the faithful women, has borne away the scarred and bleeding body of the Lord of Life to his own grave, in which no man has yet lain—

All the toil, the sorrow done,

All the battle fought and won,

as Arthur Stanley says, in one of the noblest hymns in the English language. We had the good fortune the day before to meet one of the Monsignori, an old friend, formerly a hard-working and successful London incumbent, who suggested that we should go, and to whom I shall always feel grateful for the advice. We accordingly were at the door of that splendid, but to my mind too sumptuously decorated church, punctually at 4.30. The procession had already reached the chancel, and were taking their allotted places. Most of your readers will probably be familiar with the church, but for those who are not, I may say that the chancel is wider, I think, than that in any of our cathedrals, and that the whole space from the high altar to the solid marble rails—about three and a half feet high, which divide the chancel from the rest of the church—is open, with the sole exception of the row of stalls which run along each sidewall, and which are reserved for, and were now filled by, priests. For this particular service, however (and for this only, as I was told), a row of chairs was placed just within the chancel-rails, for the Monsignori and other priests of the Pope's household, who were already seated, all in deep black, with their faces to the altar and their backs to the congregation. They remained seated during the whole service (though several of the priests from the side-stalls stepped down at intervals and took part in the service), thus, it seemed to me, emphasising the division between priests and people, and impressing on us beyond chancel-rails, the fact that we were there rather as sightseers, spectators of a solemn ceremony, than joint-sharers in an act of worship.

When we arrived the service had scarcely commenced, though the organ was pealing solemnly through the vast church; but the whole of the space in front of the chancel-rails was already filled by a dense crowd. Many of those who were in front, close to the chancel-rails, knelt, leaning on the rails, but by no means all, and the rest stood—a noteworthy assembly. For there were at least as many men as women, and of all classes. It is not easy nowadays to recognise rank by dress or bearing; but there were certainly a considerable minority of well-dressed, well-to-do people, mixed with soldiers in half a dozen different uniforms (as I was glad to see), artisans, peasants, men and women in force, the latter generally leading a child or two by the hand, with a sprinkling of young men, preparing, I suppose by their dress, for priests' orders, who for the most part had books in which they followed the service attentively,—no easy task under the surrounding conditions. For though the front ranks, two or three deep next the chancel-rails, were for the most part stationary, the great mass behind was constantly moving about and talking in low tones,—not irreverently, but rather as they would be in England at any large gathering where they could take no part themselves in the performance, but felt that it was the right thing to be there, and that they must not interfere with the minority, who seemed to understand and appreciate what was going on. I was not one of these latter, as I do not understand music, and had no book of the words; though I was quite sensible that the pathos, chequered with occasional bursts of triumph, and rendered by exquisite tenors and boys' voices, was equal to any music I had ever heard. Moreover, the sight of the splendidly dressed priests, moving frequently about before the altar, without any reason so far as I could see, and the swinging of censers, the clouds of incense, and gestures to which I could attach no meaning, inclined me to get out of the crowd. With this view I looked about for my companion, who, I found, had managed to reach the altar-rails. So in order that we might be sure to meet at the end of the service, I got quietly back to the door by which we had entered, where I could hear the music and voices perfectly, though out of sight of the chancel. Here I resolved to wait, and at once became much interested in the people who were constantly passing in or leaving the church. Soon I remarked that almost all of the former, especially the peasant men and women with children, turned to the right and disappeared for a minute or two before going on to join the crowd in front of the chancel. So I followed, and can scarcely say how much I was impressed by what I saw. In a small side-chapel, near the entrance, which was their destination, dimly lighted, a crucifix with a life-sized figure of our Lord upon it was lying on a stone couch raised some two feet from the floor. There was no priest in charge, only two bright little choristers (I suppose) in their white gowns; and perfect silence reigned in the chapel by the entrance of which I stood and saw several men and women kneeling. They got up one by one, and approaching the figure dropped again on their knees, and, stooping, kissed, some the nail-prints in the hands or feet, some the spear-wound in the side, but none the face. The most touching sight was the fathers or mothers when they rose from their knees lifting the children and teaching them to kiss the wounds. I stood there for at least twenty minutes, until the end of the service in fact, and must have seen at least a hundred men, women, and children enter. Of these, three only failed to kneel and kiss the cross, the first, a well-dressed, middle-aged woman, leading a restless small lap-dog, which pulled and whined whenever his mistress was not attending to him; the others, two young girls—but quite old enough to have known better—who marched in amongst the kneeling figures, open guide-book in hand, noticed something in the chapel to which it referred, and then marched out. They passed close enough for me to catch a word or two of their talk, which I am glad to say was not English.

As I stood there and watched and listened, the distant voices seemed to be chanting that grand old monk's-Latin hymn, the "Dies Iræ," and I fancied (I am afraid it was pure fancy) I could hear:—

Quærens me sedisti lassus,

Redeinisti crucem passas,

Tantus labor non sit cassus!

More than once I was haunted by the wish to enter and kneel and kiss the cross, by the side of some poor Italian woman and her child. I wish now that I had, but hope it was a genuine Protestant instinct which hindered me. At any rate I shall never have another chance. This crucifix is only brought out once a year—on Good Friday—and I shall never again be in St. John's Lateran on that day for the "Tenebræ" service.

JOHN TO JONATHAN

An Address delivered in the Music Hall, Boston, on the 11th of October 1870

This Address is printed precisely as it was spoken, at the request of friends who had read extracts in our newspapers. I am quite aware how superficial it must seem to English readers, and would only remind them that I had no Parliamentary debates, or other documents, to which to refer. I am thankful myself to find that, while there are startling gaps in it, there are no gross blunders as to facts or dates. The kindliness with which it was listened to by the audience, and discussed in the American press, allows me to hope that the time has come when any effort to put an end to the unhappy differences between the two countries will be looked upon favourably in the United States. The true men and women on both sides of the Atlantic feel, with Mr. Forster, that a war between America and England would be a civil war, and believe with him that we have seen the last of civil war between English-speaking men. Both nations are, I hope and believe, for a hearty reconciliation, and it only remains for the Governments to do their part.

Thomas Hughes.

It is with a heavy sense of responsibility, my friends, and no little anxiety, that I am here to-night to address you on this subject. I have been in this country now some two months, and from the day I crossed your frontier I have received, from one end of the land to the other, from men and women whom I had never seen in my life, and on whom I had no shadow of a claim that I could discover, nothing but the most generous, graceful, and unobtrusive hospitality. I am not referring to this city and its neighbourhood, in which all Englishmen are supposed to feel very like home, and in which most of us have some old and dear friend or two. I speak of your States from New York to Iowa and Missouri, from the Canadian border to Washington. Everywhere I have been carried about to places of interest in the neighbourhood, lodged, boarded, and cared for as if I had been a dear relative returning from long absence. However demoralised an Englishman may become in his own country, there is always one plank in his social morals which he clings to with the utmost tenacity, and that is paying his own postage stamps. My hold even on this last straw is sadly relaxed. I am obliged to keep vigilant watch on my letters to hinder their being stamped and posted for me by invisible hands. I never before have so fully realised the truth of those remarks of your learned and pious fellow-citizen, Rev. Homer Wilbur, whose lucubrations have been a source of much delight to me for many years, when he says somewhere, "I think I could go near to be a perfect Christian if I were always a visitor at the house of some hospitable friend. I can show a great deal of self-denial where the best of everything is urged upon me with friendly importunity. It is not so very hard to turn the other cheek for a kiss." I should be simply a brute if

I were not equally touched and abashed by the kindness I have received while amongst you. I can never hope to repay it, but the memory of it will always be amongst my most precious possessions, and I can, at least, publicly acknowledge it, as I do here this evening.

But, my friends, I must turn to the other side of the picture. There is nothing—at any rate, no kind of pleasure, I suppose—which is unmixed. From the deepest and purest fountains some bitter thing is sure to rise, and I have not been able, even in the New World, to escape the common lot of mankind in the Old. Everywhere I have found, when I have sounded the reason for all this kindness, that it was offered to me personally, because, to use the words of some whom I hope I may now look on as dear friends, "We feel that you are one of us." The moment the name of my country was mentioned a shade came over the kindest faces. I cannot conceal from myself that the feeling towards England in this country is one which must be deeply painful to every Englishman.

It was for this reason that I chose the subject of this lecture. I cannot bear to remain amongst you under any false pretences, or to leave you with any false impressions. I am not "one of you," in the sense of preferring your institutions to those of my own country. I am before all things an Englishman—a John Bull, if you will—loving old England and feeling proud of her. I am jealous of her fair fame, and pained more than I can say to find what I honestly believe to be a very serious misunderstanding here, as to the events which more than anything else have caused this alienation. You, who have proved your readiness as a people to pour out ease, wealth, life itself, as water, that no shame or harm should come to your country's flag or name, should be the last to wish the citizen of any other country to be false to his own. My respect and love for your nation and your institutions should be worth nothing to you, if I were not true to those of my own country, and did not love them better. For this reason, then, and in the hope of proving to you that you have misjudged the England of to-day—that she is no longer, at any rate, if she ever was, the haughty, imperious power her enemies have loved to paint her, interfering in every quarrel, subsidising and hectoring over friends, and holding down foes with a brutal and heavy hand, careless of all law except that of her own making, and bent above all things on heaping up wealth—I have consented to appear here tonight. I had hoped to be allowed to be amongst you simply as a listener and a learner. Since my destiny and your kindness have ordered it otherwise, I can only speak to you of that which is uppermost in my thoughts, of which my heart is full. If I say things which are hard for you to hear, I am sure you will pardon me as you would a spoilt child. You are responsible for having taught me to open my heart and to speak my mind to you, and will take it in good part if you do not find that heart and mind just what you had assumed them to be.

I propose then, to-night, to state the case of my country so far as regards her conduct while your great rebellion was raging. In a fight for life, and for principles dearer than life, no men can be fair to those who are outside. The time comes when they can weigh both sides of the case impartially. I trust that that time has now arrived, and that I can safely appeal to the calm judgment of a great people.

It is absolutely necessary, in order to appreciate what took place in England during your great struggle, to bear in mind, in the first place, that it agitated our social and political life almost as deeply as it did yours. I am scarcely old enough to remember the fierce collisions of party during the first Reform agitation, but I have taken a deep interest, and during the last twenty years an active part, in every great struggle since that time; and I say without hesitation, that not even in the crisis of the Free-trade movement were English people more deeply stirred than by that grapple between freedom and law on the one hand, and slavery and privilege on the other, which was so sternly battled through, and brought to so glorious and triumphant a decision, in your great rebellion. There can be, I repeat, no greater mistake than to suppose that there was anything like indifference on our side of the water, and no one can understand the question who makes it. There was plenty of ignorance, plenty of fierce partisanship, plenty of bewildered hesitation and vacillation amongst great masses of honest, well-meaning people, who could find no steady ground on the shifting sand of statement and counter-statement with which they were deluged by those who *did* know their own minds, and felt by instinct from the first that here was a battle for life or death; but there was, I repeat again, no indifference. Our political struggles do not, as a rule, affect our social life, but during your war the antagonism between your friends and the friends of the rebel States often grew into personal hostility. I know old friendships which were sorely tried by it, to put it no higher. I heard, over and over again, men refuse to meet those who were conspicuous on the other side. Any of you who had time to glance at our papers will not need to be told how fiercely the battle was fought in our press.

It is a mistake, also, to suppose that any section of our people were on one side or the other. Let me say a few words in explanation of this part of the subject. And first, of our aristocracy. I do not mean for a moment to deny that a great majority of them took sides with the Confederates, and desired to see them successful, and the great Republic broken up into two jealous and hostile nations. What else could you expect? Could you fairly look for sympathy in that quarter? Your whole history has been a determined protest against privilege, and in favour of equal rights for all men; and you have never been careful, in speech or conduct, to conciliate your adversaries. For years your papers and the speeches of your public men had rung with denunciations (many of them very unfair) of them and their caste. They are not much in the habit of allowing their sentiments to find public expression, but they know what is going on in the world, and have long memories. It would be well if many of us Liberals at home, as well as you on this side, would remember that in this matter they cannot help themselves. A man in England may be born a Howard, or a Cavendish, or a Cecil, without any fault of his own, and is apt to "rear up," as you say, when this accident is spoken of as though it were an act of voluntary malignity on his part, and to resent the doctrine that his class is a nuisance that should be summarily abated. So, as a rule, they sided with the rebellion; but that rule has notable exceptions.

There were no warmer or wiser friends of the Union than the Duke of Argyll, Lord Carlisle, and others; and it should be remembered that although the class made no secret of their leanings, and many of them, I believe, subscribed largely to the Confederate loan, no motion hostile to the Union was ever even discussed in the House of Lords. They have lost their money and seen the defeat of the cause which they favoured—a defeat so thorough, I trust, that that cause will never again be able to raise its head on this continent. I believe they have learnt much from the lesson, and that partly from the teaching of your war, partly from other causes to which I have no time to refer, they are far more in sympathy at this time with the nation than they have ever yet been.

Of course, those who hang round and depend upon the aristocracy went with them—far too large a class, I am sorry to say, in our country, and one whose voice is too apt to be heard in clubs and society. But Pall Mall and Mayfair, and the journals and periodicals which echo the voices of Pall Mall, do not mean much in England, though they are apt to talk as though they did, and are sometimes taken at their word.

The great mercantile world comes next in order, and here, too, there was a decided preponderance against you. The natural hatred of disturbances, which dominates those whose main object in life is making money, probably swayed the better men amongst them, who forgot altogether that for that disturbance you were not responsible. The worse were carried away by the hopes of gain, to be made out of the sore need of the States in rebellion, and in defiance of the laws of their own country. But amongst the most eminent, as well as in the rank and file of this class, you had many warm friends, such as T. Baring and Kirkman Hodgson; and the Union and Emancipation Societies, of which I shall speak presently, found a number of their staunch supporters in their ranks. The manufacturers of England were far more generous in their sympathies, as my friend Mr. Mundella, who is present here to-night and was himself a staunch friend, can witness. Cobden, Bright, and Forster were their representatives, as well as the representatives of the great bulk of our nation. I have no need to speak of them, for their names are honoured here as they are at home.

Now, before I speak of your friends, let me first remind you that it is precisely with that portion of the English nation of which I have been speaking that your people come in contact when they are in our country. An American generally has introductions which bring him into relations more or less intimate with some sections of that society to which our aristocracy gives its tone; or he is amongst us for business purposes, and comes chiefly across our mercantile classes. I cannot but believe that this fact goes far to explain the (to me) extraordinary prevalence of the belief here, that the English nation was on the side of the rebellion. That belief has, I hope and believe, changed considerably since the waves of your mighty storm have begun to calm down, and I am not without hopes that I may be able to change it yet somewhat more, with some at least of those who have the patience and kindness to listen to me this evening.

And now let me turn to those who were the staunch friends of the North from the very outset. They were gathered from all ranks and all parts of the kingdom. They were brought in by all sorts of motives. Some few had studied your history, and knew that these Southern men had been the only real enemies of their country on American soil since the War of Independence. Many followed their old anti-slavery traditions faithfully, and cast their lot at once against the slave-owners, careless of the reiterated assertions, both on your side of the Atlantic and ours, that the Union and not abolition was the issue. Many came because they had learned to look upon your land as the great home for the poor of all nations, and to love her institutions and rejoice in her greatness as though they in some sort belonged to themselves. All felt the tremendous significance of the struggle, and that the future of their own country was almost as deeply involved as the future of America. To all of them the noble words of one of your greatest poets and staunchest patriots, which rang out in the darkest moments of the first year of the war, struck a chord very deep in their hearts, and expressed in undying words that which they were trying to utter:—

O strange New World, thet yit wast never young,

Whose youth from thee by gripin' need was wrung,

Brown foundlin' o' the woods, whose baby-bed

Was prowled roun' by the Injun's cracklin' tread,

An' who grew'st strong thru shifts an' wants an' pains,

Nussed by stern men with empires in their brains,

Who saw in vision their young Ishmel strain

With each hard hand a vassal ocean's mane,

Thou, skilled by Freedom an' by gret events

To pitch new States ez Old-World men pitch tents,

Thou, taught by Fate to know Jehovah's plan

Thet man's devices can't unmake a man,

An' whose free latch-string never was drawed in

Against the poorest child of Adam's kin,—

The grave's not dug where traitor hands shall lay

In fearful haste thy murdered corse away!

It was in this faith that we took our stand, with a firm resolution that no effort of ours should be spared to help your people shake themselves clear of the dead weight of slavery, and to preserve that vast inheritance of which God has made you the guardians and trustees for all the nations of the earth, unbroken, and free from the standing armies, disputed boundaries, and wretched heart-burnings and dissensions of the Old World. It was little enough that we could do in any case, but that little was done with all our hearts, and on looking back I cannot but think was well done.

There was no need at first for any organisation. Until after the battle of Manassas Junction in 1861, there was scarcely any public expression of sympathy with the rebellion. The *Times* and that portion of the press which follows its lead, and is always ready to go in for the side they think will win, were lecturing on the wickedness of the war and the absurdity of the rebel States in supposing that they could resist for a month the strength of the North. The news of that first defeat arrived, and this portion of our press swung round, and the strong feeling in favour of the rebellion which leavened society and the commercial world began to manifest itself. The unlucky *Trent* business, and your continued want of success in the field, made matters worse. We were silenced for the moment; for though, putting ourselves in your places, we could feel how bitter the surrender of the two archrebels must have been, we could not but admit that our Government was bound to insist upon it, and that the demand had not been made in an arrogant or offensive manner. If you will re-read the official documents now, I think that you too will acknowledge that this was so. Then came Mr. Mason's residence in London, where his house became the familiar resort of all the leading sympathisers with the rebellion. The newspaper which he started, *The Index*, was full, week after week, of false and malignant attacks on your Government. The most bitter of them to us was the constant insistance, backed by quotations from Mr. Lincoln and Mr. Seward, that the war had nothing to do with slavery, that emancipation was far more likely to come from the rebels than from you.

"The lie that is half a truth is ever the blackest of lies," and we felt the truth of that wonderful saying. This had been our great difficulty from the first. Our generation had been reared on anti-slavery principles. We remembered as children how the great battle was won in England, how even in our nurseries we gave up sugar lest we might be tasting the accursed thing, and subscribed our pennies that the chains might be struck from all human limbs. Emancipation had been the crowning glory of England in our eyes. But we found that this great force was not with us, was even slipping away and drifting to the other side. It was not only Mr. Mason's paper, and the backing he got in our press, which was undermining it. The vehement protests of those who had been for years looked on by us as the foremost soldiers in the great cause on your side told in the same direction. I well remember the consternation and almost despair with which I read in Mr. Phillips' speech in this hall on 20th June 1861, "The Republicans, led by Seward, offer to surrender anything to save the Union. Their gospel is the constitution, and the slave clause their sermon on the mount. They think that at the judgment day the blacker the sins they have committed to save the Union the clearer will be their title to heaven."

Something must be done to counteract this, to put the case clearly before our people. Mr. Mason and his friends were already establishing a Confederate States Aid Association; it must be met by something similar on the right side. So in 1862 the Emancipation and the Union and Emancipation Societies were started in London and in Manchester, and in good time came Mr. Lincoln's proclamation of emancipation to strengthen our hands. The original manifesto of the Emancipation Society said—"To make it clear by the force of indisputable testimony that the South is fighting for slavery, while the North is fully committed to the destruction of slavery, is the principal object for which this society is organised. Its promoters do not believe that English anti-slavery sentiment is dead or enfeebled. They are confident that when the demands and designs of the South are made clear, there will be no danger of England being enticed into complicity with them." We pledged ourselves to test the opinion of the country everywhere by public meetings, and challenged the Confederate States Aid Association to accept that test. They did so; but I never could hear of any even quasi public meeting but one which they held in England. That meeting was at Mr. Mason's house, and was, I believe, attended by some fifty persons.

The first step of our societies was to hold meetings for passing an address of congratulation to your President on the publication of the Emancipation proclamation. It was New Year's Eve 1862. Our address said: "We have watched with the warmest interest the steady advance of your policy along the path of emancipation; and on this eve of the day on which your proclamation takes effect we pray God to strengthen your hands, to confirm your noble purpose, and to hasten the restoration of that lawful authority which engages, in peace or war, by compensation or by force of arms, to realise the glorious principle on which your constitution is founded—the brotherhood, freedom, and equality of all men." The address was enthusiastically adopted by a large meeting, chiefly composed of working men. It was clear at once that there was a grand force behind us, for we became objects of furious attack. The *Times* called us impostors, and said we got our funds for the agitation from American sources—the fact being that we always refused contributions from this side. The *Saturday Review* declared, in one of its bitterest articles, that if anything could be calculated upon as likely to defer indefinitely the gradual extinction of slavery, it would be Mr. Lincoln's fictitious abolition of it. We were meddlesome fanatics, insignificant nobodies, mischievous agitators. This was satisfactory and encouraging. We felt sure that we had taken the right course, and not a moment too soon. Then came the test of public meetings, which you at least are surely bound to accept as a fair gauge of what a people thinks and wills.

Our first was held on the 29th of January 1863. We took Exeter Hall, the largest and most central hall in London. We did nothing but simply advertise widely that such a meeting would be held, inviting all who cared to come, foes as well as friends. Prudent and timid people shook their heads and looked grave. The cotton famine was at its worst, and tens of thousands of our workpeople were "clemming" as they call it, starving as you might say. Your prospects looked as black as they had ever done; it was almost the darkest moment of the whole war. Even friends warned us that we should fail in our object, and only do harm by showing our weakness; that the Confederate States Aid Association would spare no pains or money to break up the meeting, and a hundred roughs sent there by them might turn it into a triumph for the rebellion. However, on we went,—we knew our own people too well to fear the result. The night came, and familiar as I am with this kind of thing, I have never seen in my time anything approaching this scene. Remember, there was nothing to attract people; no well-known orators, for we always thought it best to keep our Parliament men to their own ground; no great success to rejoice in, for you were just reeling under the recoil of your gallant army from the blood-stained heights of Fredericksburg; no attack on our own Government; no appeal to political or social hates or prejudices; only doors thrown wide open, with the invitation, "Now let Englishmen come forward and show on which side their sympathies really are in this war." Notwithstanding all these disadvantages the great hall was densely crowded, so that there was no standing room, and the Strand and the neighbouring streets blocked with a crowd of thousands who could find no place, long before the doors were open. We were obliged to organise a number of meetings on the spur of the moment in the lower halls, and even in the open streets. In the great hall—where two clergymen, the Hon. Baptist Noel and Mr. Newman Hall, and I myself, were the chief speakers—as well as in every one of the other meetings, we carried, not only without opposition, but, so far as I remember, without a single hand being held up on the other side, resolutions in favour of your Government, of the Union, and of emancipation. The success was so complete that in London our work was done.

Then followed similar meetings at Manchester, Sheffield, Bristol, Leeds, in all the great centres of population, with precisely the same result. I don't remember that the enemy ever even attempted to divide a meeting. The country was carried by acclamation. Our friends in Liverpool wrote with some anxiety as to the state of feeling there, and asked me to go down and deliver an address. I went, and the meeting carried the same resolutions by a very large majority; and those who, it was supposed, came to disturb the proceedings, thought better of it when they saw the temper of the audience, and were quiet. Without troubling you with any further details of our work, I may just add, as a proof of how those who profess to be the most astute worshippers of public opinion changed their minds in consequence of the answer of the country to our appeals, that in August 1863 the *Times* supported our demand on the Government for the stoppage of the steam-rams.

In addition to this political movement, we instituted also a number of freedmen's aid associations, in order that those abolitionists in England who were still unable to put faith in your Government might have an opportunity of helping in their own way. These associations entered into correspondence with those on your side, and sent over a good many thousand pounds' worth of clothing and other supplies, besides money. I forget the exact amount. It was a mere drop in the ocean of your magnificent war charities, but it came from thousands who had little enough to spare in those hard times, and I trust has had the effect of a peace-offering with those of your people who are conversant with the facts, and are ready to judge by their actual doings even those against whom they think they have fair cause of complaint.

So much for what I may call the unofficial, or extraparliamentary, struggle in England during your war. And now let me turn to the action of our Government and of Parliament. I might fairly have rested my case entirely upon this ground. In the case of nations blessed as America and England are with perfect freedom of speech and action within the limits of law—where men may say the thing they will freely, and without any check but the civil courts—no one in my judgment has a right to make the nation responsible for anything except what its Government says and does. But I know how deeply the conduct and speech of English society has outraged your people, and still rankles in their minds, and I wished by some rough analysis, and by the statement of facts within my own knowledge, and of doings in which I personally took an active part, to show you that you have done us very scant justice. The dress suit, and the stomach and digestive apparatus, of England were hostile to you, and you have taken them for the nation: the brain and heart and muscle of England were on your side, and these you have ignored and forgotten.

Now, for our Government and Parliament. I will admit at once, if you please, that Lord Palmerston and the principal members of his Cabinet were not friendly to you, and would have been glad to have seen your Republic broken up. I am by no means sure that it was so; but let that pass. I was not in their counsels, and have no more means of judging of them than are open to all of you. Your first accusation against us is, that the Queen's proclamation of neutrality, which was signed and published on the 13th of May 1861, was premature, and an act of discourtesy to your Government, inasmuch as your new Minister, Mr. Adams, only arrived in England on that very day. Well, looking back from this distance of time, I quite admit that it would have been far better to have delayed the publication of the proclamation till after he had arrived in London. But at the time the case was very different. You must remember that news of the President's proclamation of the blockade reached London on 3rd May. Of course, from that moment the danger of collision between our vessels and yours, and of the fitting out of privateers in our harbours, arose at once. In fact, your first capture of a British vessel, the *General Parkhill* of Liverpool, was made on 12th May. But if the publication of the proclamation of neutrality was a mistake, it was made by our Government at the earnest solicitation of Mr. Forster and other warm friends of yours, who pressed it forward entirely, as they supposed, in your interest. They wanted to stop letters of marque and to legitimise the captures made by your blockading squadron. The Government acted at their instance; so, whether a blunder or not, the proclamation was not an unfriendly act. Besides, remember what it amounted to. Simply and solely to a recognition of the fact that you had a serious war on hand. Mr. Seward had already admitted this in an official paper of the 4th of May, and your Supreme Court decided, in the case of the *Amy Warwick*, that the proclamation of blockade was in itself conclusive evidence that a state of war existed at the time. If we had ever gone a step further—if we had recognised the independence of the rebel States, as our Government was strongly urged to do by their envoys, by members of our Parliament, and lastly by the Emperor of the French—you would have had good ground of offence. But this was precisely what we never would do; and when they found this out, the Confederate Government cut off all intercourse with England, and expelled our consuls from their towns. So one side blamed us for doing too much, and the other for doing too little—the frequent fate of neutrals, as you yourselves are finding at this moment in the case of the war between Prussia and France.

Then came the first public effort of the sympathisers with the rebellion. After several preliminary skirmishes, which were defeated by Mr. Forster (who had what we lawyers should call the watching brief, with Cobden and Bright behind him as leading counsel, and who used to go round the lobbies in those anxious days with his pockets bulging out with documents to prove how effective the blockade was, and how many ships of our merchants you were capturing every day), Mr. Gregory put a motion on the paper. He was well chosen for the purpose, as a member of great experience and ability, sitting on our side of the House, so that weak-kneed Liberals would have an excuse for following him, and though not himself in office, supposed to be on intimate terms with the Premier and other members of the Cabinet. His motion was simply "to call the attention of the House to the expediency of prompt recognition of the Southern Confederacy."

It was set down for 7th June 1861, and I tell you we were all pretty nervous about the result. The *Spectator, Daily News, Star*, and other staunch papers opened fire, and we all did what we could in the way of canvassing; but until the Government had declared itself no Union man could feel safe. Well, Lord John Russell, as the Foreign Minister, got up, snubbed the motion altogether, said that the Government had no intention whatever of agreeing to it, and recommended its withdrawal. So Mr. Gregory and his friends took their motion off the paper without a debate, and did not venture to try any other during the session of 1861. In the late autumn came the unlucky *Trent* affair, to which I have already sufficiently alluded. Belying on the feeling which had been roused by it, and cheered on by the Mason club in Piccadilly and the *Index* newspaper fulminations, and by the severe checks of the Union armies, they took the field again in 1862. This time their tactics were bolder. They no longer confined themselves to asking the opinion of the House deferentially. Mr. Lindsay, the great shipowner, who it was said had a small fleet of blockade-runners, was chosen as the spokesman. He gave notice of motion, "That in the opinion of this House, the States which have seceded from the Union have so long maintained themselves, and given such proofs of determination and ability to support independence, that the propriety of offering mediation with a view to terminating hostilities is worthy of the serious and immediate attention of Her Majesty's Government." Again we trembled for the result, and again the Government came out with a square refusal on the 18th of July, and this motion shared the fate of its predecessor, and was withdrawn by its own promoters.

Then came the escape of the *Alabama*. Upon this I have no word to say. My private opinion has been expressed over and over again in Parliament (where in my first year, 1866, I think I was the first man to urge open arbitration on our Government) as well as on the platform and in the press. But I stand here to-night as an Englishman, and say that at this moment I have no cause to be ashamed of the attitude of my country. Two Governments in succession, Tory and Liberal, through Lords Stanley and Clarendon, have admitted (as Mr. Fish states himself in his last despatch on the subject) the principle of comprehensive arbitration on all questions between Governments. This is all that a nation can do. England is ready to have the case in all its bearings referred to impartial arbitration, and to pay whatever damages may be assessed against her without a murmur. She has also agreed (and again I use the language of Mr. Fish) "to discuss the important changes in the rules of public law, the desirableness of which has been demonstrated by the incidents of the last few years, and which, in view of the maritime prominence of Great Britain and the United States, it would befit them to mature and propose to the other states of Christendom." She has, in fact, surrendered her old position as untenable, and agreed to the terms proposed by your own Government. What more can you ask of a nation of your own blood, as proud and sensitive as yourselves on all points where national honour is in question?

But here I must remind you of one fact which you seem never to have realised. The *Alabama* was the only one of the rebel cruisers of whose character our Government had any notice, which escaped from our harbours. The *Shenandoah* was a merchant vessel, employed in the Indian trade as the *Sea King*. Her conversion into a rebel cruiser was never heard of till long after she had left England. The *Georgia* was actually reported by the surveyor of the Board of Trade as a merchant ship, and to be "rather crank." She was fitted out on the French coast, and left the port of Cherbourg for her first cruise. The *Florida* was fitted out in Mobile. She was actually detained at Nassau on suspicion, and only discharged by the Admiralty Court there on failure of evidence. On the other hand, our Government stopped the *Rappahannock*, the *Alexandra*, and the *Pampero*, and seized Mr. Laird's celebrated rams at Liverpool, and Captain Osborne's Chinese flotilla, for which last exercise of vigilance the nation had to pay £100,000.

Such is our case as to the cruisers which did you so much damage. I believe it to be true. If we are mistaken, however, you will get such damages for each and all of these vessels as the arbitrator may award. We reserve nothing. I as an Englishman am deeply grieved that any of my countrymen, for base love of gain or any other motive, should have dared to defy the proclamation of my Sovereign, speaking in the nation's name. I earnestly long for the time when by wise consultation between our nations, and the modification of the public law bearing on such cases, not only such acts as these, but all war at sea, shall be rendered impossible. The United States and England have only to agree in this matter, and there is an end of naval war through the whole world.

In 1863 the horizon was still dark. Splendid as your efforts had been, and magnificent as was the attitude of your nation, tried in the fire as few nations have been in all history, those efforts had not yet been crowned with any marked success. With us it was the darkest in the whole long agony, for in it came the crisis of that attempt of the Emperor of the French to inveigle us in a joint recognition of the Confederacy, on the success of which his Mexican adventure was supposed to hang. The details of those negotiations have never been made public. All we know is, that Mr. Lindsay and Mr. Roebuck went to Paris and had long conferences with Napoleon, the result of which was the effort of Mr. Roebuck (now in turn the representative of the rebels in our Parliament) to force or persuade our Government into this alliance. Then came the final crisis. On the 30th of June 1863, a day memorable in our history as in yours, at the very time that your army of the Potomac was hurrying through the streets of Gettysburg to meet the swoop of those terrible Southern legions, John Bright stood on the floor of our House of Commons, on fire with that righteous wrath which has so often lifted him above the heads of other English orators.

He dragged the whole plot to light, quoted the former attacks of Mr. Roebuck on his Imperial host, and then turning to the Speaker, went on, "And now, sir, the honourable and learned gentleman has been to Paris, introduced there by the honourable member for Sunderland, and he has sought to become, as it were, a co-conspirator with the French Emperor, to drag this country into a policy which I maintain is as hostile to its interests as it would be degrading to its honour." From that moment the cause of the rebellion was lost in England; for by the next mails came the news of the three days' fight, and the melting away of Longstreet's corps in the final and desperate efforts to break the Federal line on the slopes of little Round Top. A few weeks more and we heard of the surrender of Vicksburg, and no more was heard in our Parliament of recognition or mediation.

I have now, my friends, stated the case between our countries from an Englishman's point of view, of course, but I hope fairly and temperately. At any rate, I have only spoken of matters within my own personal knowledge, and have only quoted from public records which are as open to every one of you as they are to me. Search them, I beseech you, and see whether I am right or not. If wrong, it is from no insular prejudices or national conceit, and you will at any rate think kindly and bear with the errors of one who has always loved your nation well, through good report and evil report, and is now bound to it by a hundred new and precious ties. If right, all I beg of you is, to use your influences that old hatreds and prejudices may disappear, and America and England may march together, as nations redeemed by a common Saviour, toward the goal which is set for them in a brighter future.

Shall it be love, or hate, John?

It's you thet's to decide;

Ain't your bonds held by Fate, John,

Like all the world's beside?

So runs the end of the solemn appeal in "Jonathan to John," the poem which suggested the title of this lecture. It comes from one who never deals in wild words. I am proud to be able to call him a very dear and old friend. He is the American writer who did more than any other to teach such of us in the old country as ever learned them at all, the rights and wrongs of this great struggle of yours. Questions asked by such men can never be safely left on one side. Well, then, I say we *have* answered them. We know—no nation, I believe, knows better, or confesses daily with more of awe—that our bonds are held by fate; that a strict account of all the mighty talents which have been committed to us will be required of us English, though we do live in a sea fortress, in which the gleam of steel drawn in anger has not been seen for more than a century. We know that we are very far from being what we ought to be; we know that we have great social problems to work out, and, believe me, we have set manfully to work to solve them,—problems which go right down amongst the roots of things, and the wrong solution of which may shake the very foundations of society. We have to face them manfully, after the manner of our race, within the four corners of an island not bigger than one of your large States; while you have the vast elbow-room of this wonderful continent, with all its million outlets and opportunities for every human being who is ready to work. Yes, our bonds are indeed held by fate, but we are taking strict account of the number and amount of them, and mean, by God's help, to dishonour none of them when the time comes for taking them up. We reckon, too, some of us, that as years roll on, and you get to understand us better, we may yet hear the words "Well done, brother," from this side of the Atlantic; and if the strong old islander, who, after all, is your father, should happen some day to want a name on the back of one of his bills, I, for one, should not wonder to hear that at the time of presentation the name Jonathan is found scrawled across there in very decided characters. For we have answered that second question, too, so far as it lies in our power.

It will be love and not hate between the two freest of the great nations of the earth, if our decision can so settle it. There will never be anything but love again, if England has the casting vote. For remember that the force of the decision of your great struggle has not been spent on this continent. Your victory has strengthened the hands and hearts of those who are striving in the cause of government, for the people by the people, in every corner of the Old World. In England the dam that had for so many years held back the free waters burst in the same year that you sheathed your sword, and now your friends there are triumphant and honoured; and if those who were your foes ever return to power you will find that the lesson of your war has not been lost on them. In another six years you will have finished the first century of your national life. By that time you will have grown to fifty millions, and will have subdued and settled those vast western regions, which now in the richness of their solitudes, broken only by the panting of the engine as it passes once a day over some new prairie line, startles the traveller from the Old World. I am only echoing the thoughts and prayers of my nation in wishing you God-speed in your great mission. When that centenary comes round, I hope, if I live, to see the great family of English-speaking nations girdling the earth with a circle of free and happy communities, in which the angels' message of peace on earth and good-will amongst men may not be still a mockery and delusion. It rests with you to determine whether this shall be so or not. May the God of all the nations of the earth, who has so marvellously prospered you hitherto, and brought you through so great trials, guide you in your decision!

THE END

9 789362 092144